FOCUS 3

SECOND EDITION

B1/B1+

STUDENT'S BOOK

	VOCABULARY	GRAMMAR	LISTENING
1 A new look BBC p. 116 Distressing jeans	pp. 4–5 Clothes and accessories; fashion and style; personality Quiz: Style trial p. 15 Word list	p. 6 Dynamic and state verbs **GRAMMAR ANIMATION**	p. 7 Friendship Vocabulary: Relationship phrases Exam Focus: True/False Pronunciation Focus: Numbers
2 It's just a game BBC p. 118 The Brujas	pp. 18–19 Phrasal verbs; collocations; people in sport Reading: Sporting questions p. 29 Word list	p. 20 Narrative tenses **GRAMMAR ANIMATION**	p. 21 Role models Vocabulary: Phrasal verbs Exam Focus: Note completion Pronunciation Focus: Long vowel sounds
3 On the go BBC p. 120 A hotel in the clouds	pp. 32–33 Noun phrases; collocations; synonyms for *trip* Listening: Extreme journeys to school p. 43 Word list	p. 34 Present and past speculation **GRAMMAR ANIMATION**	p. 35 Different holiday experiences Vocabulary: Compound nouns Exam Focus: Multiple choice Pronunciation Focus: Word stress
4 Eat, drink and be healthy BBC p. 122 Umami	pp. 46–47 Fruit and vegetables; describing food; collocations Reading: Celebrity diets p. 57 Word list	p. 48 Future forms **GRAMMAR ANIMATION** p. 123 **FOCUS VLOG**	p. 49 Diets Vocabulary: Collocations Exam Focus: Matching Pronunciation Focus: Vowel sounds
5 Planet Earth BBC p. 124 Chameleons	pp. 60–61 Phrasal verbs; collocations; word families Quiz: Mysteries of the ocean p. 71 Word list	p. 62 Articles: no article, a/an or the **GRAMMAR ANIMATION** p. 125 **FOCUS VLOG**	p. 63 Eco school Vocabulary: Compound nouns; environment protection Exam Focus: Multiple choice Pronunciation Focus: Word stress
6 Good health BBC p. 126 Caffeine alternatives	pp. 74–75 Parts of the body; injuries; body idioms Reading: Excuses for missing school p. 85 Word list	p. 76 Second Conditional; *wish/if only* **GRAMMAR ANIMATION**	p. 77 Charity events Vocabulary: Charity fund-raising Exam Focus: Note completion Pronunciation Focus: Vowel sounds
7 Entertain me BBC p. 128 Shakespeare's avatars	pp. 88–89 Entertainment; people in entertainment; phrasal verbs Listening: An interview with a young performer p. 99 Word list	p. 90 Reported Speech – statements; reporting verbs **GRAMMAR ANIMATION**	p. 91 Viral videos Vocabulary: Collocations Exam Focus: Matching Pronunciation Focus: Word families and word stress
8 Modern society BBC p. 130 Coffee stalls	pp. 102–103 Crime and criminals; people involved in a crime case; the justice system Reading: UK crime trends p. 113 Word list	p. 104 The Passive **GRAMMAR ANIMATION**	p. 105 A young ex-offender Vocabulary: Prison Exam Focus: Multiple choice Pronunciation Focus: Word stress

pp. 116–131 Video worksheets   pp. 132–155 Grammar and Use of English reference and practice

WORD STORE BOOKLET   Word Stores 1–8, Word building, Use of English

READING	GRAMMAR	USE OF ENGLISH	WRITING	SPEAKING	FOCUS REVIEW
pp. 8–9 Icons of fashion **Vocabulary:** Clothing; compound adjectives **Exam Focus:** Note completion	p. 10 Present Perfect Continuous GRAMMAR ANIMATION p. 117 FOCUS VLOG	p. 11 Word formation – common suffixes Sentence transformation	pp. 12–13 **Writing Focus:** Describing a person **Language Focus:** Tentative language	p. 14 Describing a photo	pp. 16–17
pp. 22–23 Rafa: My story **Vocabulary:** Rituals and routines; word families **Exam Focus:** Gapped text	p. 24 Verb patterns GRAMMAR ANIMATION	p. 25 so, too, neither/nor, not either Multiple choice p. 119 FOCUS VLOG	pp. 26–27 **Writing Focus:** A story **Language Focus:** Linkers to describe events in a sequence	p. 28 Asking for and giving an opinion; agreeing and disagreeing ROLE-PLAY	pp. 30–31
pp. 36–37 Travel and the smartphone generation **Vocabulary:** Negative adjectives; verb phrases **Exam Focus:** Multiple choice	p. 38 Used to and would GRAMMAR ANIMATION p. 121 FOCUS VLOG	p. 39 Phrasal verbs Gapped sentences	pp. 40–41 **Writing Focus:** A personal email giving advice **Language Focus:** Ellipsis	p. 42 Asking for and giving advice ROLE-PLAY	pp. 44–45
pp. 50–51 The Real Junk Food Project **Vocabulary:** Collocations; cooking verbs **Exam Focus:** Open-ended questions	p. 52 Future Continuous and Future Perfect GRAMMAR ANIMATION	p. 53 Question tags Multiple choice	pp. 54–55 **Writing Focus:** A formal email asking for information and clarification **Language Focus:** Indirect questions	p. 56 In a restaurant; indirect questions ROLE-PLAY	pp. 58–59
pp. 64–65 Camping in the wild **Vocabulary:** In the woods; verb phrases **Exam Focus:** Multiple choice	p. 66 Non-defining relative clauses GRAMMAR ANIMATION	p. 67 Prepositions at the end of clauses Open cloze	pp. 68–69 **Writing Focus:** A 'for and against' essay **Language Focus:** Linkers	p. 70 Expressing and justifying an opinion; describing and contrasting pictures ROLE-PLAY	pp. 72–73
pp. 78–79 Medical professions **Vocabulary:** Health issues **Exam Focus:** Matching	p. 80 Third Conditional GRAMMAR ANIMATION	p. 81 Clauses of purpose Open cloze p. 127 FOCUS VLOG	pp. 82–83 **Writing Focus:** A factual article **Language Focus:** Comment and opinion adverbs	p. 84 At the doctor's surgery	pp. 86–87
pp. 92–93 Book soundtracks **Vocabulary:** Phrases related to reading; word building **Exam Focus:** Gapped text	p. 94 Reported Speech – questions and imperatives GRAMMAR ANIMATION	p. 95 Nouns Sentence transformation p. 129 FOCUS VLOG	pp. 96–97 **Writing Focus:** An article reviewing an event **Language Focus:** Modifiers with base and extreme adjectives	p. 98 Asking for permission; polite requests ROLE-PLAY	pp. 100–101
pp. 106–107 Random acts of kindness **Vocabulary:** Verb phrases; synonyms **Exam Focus:** Multiple choice	p. 108 Have something done GRAMMAR ANIMATION	p. 109 Reflexive pronouns Sentence transformation p. 131 FOCUS VLOG	pp. 110–111 **Writing Focus:** An opinion essay **Language Focus:** Giving your opinion and emphasising a point	p. 112 Opinions: talking about advantages and disadvantages ROLE-PLAY	pp. 114–115

p. 156 Prepositions   p. 157 Phrasal verbs   p. 158 Pronouns and numerals   p. 159 Irregular verbs

1

A new look

You never get a second chance to make a first impression.
Andrew Grant

BBC

BBC DISTRESSING JEANS

▶1 Watch the BBC video. For the worksheet, go to page 116.

VOCABULARY

1.1

Clothes and accessories • fashion and style • personality

I can describe people's personality, abilities and clothes.

SHOW WHAT YOU KNOW

1 Put the words in the box under an appropriate heading.

> ~~bald~~ cheerful cotton determined hoodie leather
> sensible sensitive slim suit wavy hair well-built

Personality	Appearance	Clothes/Materials
	bald	

2 **SPEAKING** Add more words under each heading. Use the words to describe somebody you know well.

Magda is slim with wavy hair. She's very determined. She usually wears …

STYLE TRIAL QUIZ

Read the statements below and put
A = I agree   **B** = it depends   **C** = I disagree

1 People say I'm trendy. ☐
2 I always use hair products (gel, hairspray, etc.) in the morning. ☐
3 I get bored with my clothes quickly. ☐
4 I love dressing up for parties. ☐
5 I don't mind where my clothes come from – I just want to look good. ☐
6 I'd never shave my head for charity. ☐
7 I believe that wearing make-up is not only for women. ☐
8 I'm interested in **what's in fashion** and **what's out of fashion**. ☐

YOUR RESULTS:

MOSTLY As
You're a fashionista! You're a party animal and you like to **be the centre of attention**. **You're trendy** and you **care about your appearance** but be careful you don't **come across as** shallow or vain.

MOSTLY Bs
You might have some trendy items in your wardrobe, but in general you **go for a casual look** rather than a formal one. You're down-to-earth and have a carefree attitude to clothes. That's why you like practical clothes like sportswear. You **feel comfortable in your own skin**, and people like you because you're easy-going and **you go with the flow**.

MOSTLY Cs
You're not interested in following trends and you tend to be a little rebellious. You're against 'fast-fashion'* and you believe in buying good-quality clothes that last a long time. You like to know where your clothes are made, and you don't mind paying a bit more for ethical brands.

*fast fashion – inexpensive fashionable clothes that are sold for a short time and then replaced by newer collections.

3 **SPEAKING** Do the quiz and compare your answers. How accurate is the description of you in Your results?

4 Tick the items in the list that you can see in the picture.

Clothes
a blouse ☐   a dark suit ☐   a denim jacket ☐
faded jeans ☐   a fleece ☐   leggings ☐
a sweatshirt ☐   a waistcoat ☐

Shoes and accessories
ankle boots ☐   bangles ☐   a beanie ☐
high heels ☐   a leather belt ☐   a necklace ☐
a silk tie ☐   vintage sunglasses ☐

Go to WORD STORE 1 page 3

WORD STORE 1A | Clothes and accessories

5 🔊 1.2 Complete WORD STORE 1A with the words from Exercise 4. Then listen, check and repeat.

6 **SPEAKING** Describe in detail the type of clothes you would wear in the following situations. Use the words in WORD STORE 1A and your own ideas.

at school   at home   on a night out   for a picnic
for an interview   for a date   at a wedding
at a house party   on a shopping trip

At home I usually wear comfortable clothes like jeans or leggings and a T-shirt or sweatshirt. Sometimes, I even wear my pyjamas!

WORD STORE 1B | Fashion and style

7 🔊 1.3 Complete WORD STORE 1B with the expressions in red from the quiz. Then listen, check and repeat.

8 **SPEAKING** Use the sentences in WORD STORE 1B to talk about the people you know. Choose the person most different from you and describe them in detail to a partner.

My friend Sasha cares a lot about his appearance. He spends a lot of money on clothes and rarely wears the same thing twice …

WORD STORE 1C | Personality

9 🔊 1.4 Complete WORD STORE 1C with the underlined words and expressions in the quiz. Then listen, check and repeat.

10 Complete the sentences with the most appropriate adjectives in WORD STORE 1C.
1 Tom never loses his temper or gets irritated. He's very _____ .
2 Ana is so _____ . She's only interested in how people look.
3 Will is _____ . He always knows how to solve practical problems.
4 Phil is extremely proud of his good looks. He's quite _____ .
5 Tammy never worries about anything. She's so _____ .
6 Joss is quite _____ . She doesn't like obeying rules.

11 **SPEAKING** Choose three people you have a photo of on your phone. Describe their personalities to a partner.

This is Maria. She's my cousin. She's a really easy-going person with a carefree attitude to life. She …

GRAMMAR

1.2

Dynamic and state verbs

I can use dynamic and state verbs correctly.

1 **SPEAKING** Imagine you are going to a weekend music festival in the summer. Discuss what you would wear.

2 🔊 1.5 Read and listen to Jo Mack and answer the questions.
   1 Who does she work for?   3 What is she doing there?
   2 Where is she now?

HOW TO DRESS: FESTIVAL FASHION

Welcome to our regular feature. This week we are looking at what people wear to music festivals.

Jo: Hi! I'm Jo Mack and I work as a fashion editor for *Hip* magazine. I think I must have the best job in the world because today I'm working at the Coachella music festival in California. The question I'm asking is 'What is the "Festival Look" this year?'. Ten thousand people are listening to music here and I believe the temperature is 32°. I know Radiohead are on later and I really want to watch them, but right now I'm speaking to people about what they're wearing and why.

3 Read the GRAMMAR FOCUS and look at the verbs in blue in Exercise 2. Which verbs describe an action and which describe a state?

GRAMMAR FOCUS

Dynamic and state verbs

- Most verbs have dynamic meanings. They describe actions: something 'happens'. You can use them with simple or continuous forms.
  I work as a fashion editor for Hip magazine.
  Today I'm working at the Coachella music festival.

- Some verbs have stative meanings. They describe states: nothing 'happens'. You cannot use them with continuous forms.
  I believe the temperature is 32°. (NOT *I'm believing*)

Note:
A few verbs (e.g. *think, have, look*) have both dynamic and stative meanings. The meanings are different:
I think I must have the best job in the world.
(think = believe → stative)
I'm thinking about going to see them.
(think = consider → dynamic)

4 🔊 1.6 Read and listen to Jo's interview with Anna. Decide which of the underlined verb phrases are state verbs and which are dynamic verbs.

Jo: Hi! I'm reporting on festival fashion for *Hip* magazine. I like your hat.
Anna: Thanks. I don't usually wear hats. But it's really hot, so I'm wearing this baseball cap. It belongs to my brother. He doesn't need it because he isn't here today. He's revising for his exams!
Jo: Oh, that's a shame.
Anna: No, it's OK. My brother hates festivals. He prefers listening to music at home. I really want to see Kings of Leon – I listen to their music all the time!

5 🔊 1.7 Complete Jo's interview with Tom with the correct Present Simple or Present Continuous form of the verbs in brackets. Then listen and check.

Jo: Hi! I'm reporting on festival fashion for *Hip* magazine. ¹Are you enjoying (you/enjoy) the festival?
Tom: Yes, I ² _____ (have) a really good time.
Jo: I ³ _____ (love) your T-shirt.
Tom: Oh, thanks! It's my festival T-shirt!
Jo: Oh, it ⁴ _____ (look) great. But why ⁵ _____ (you/wear) jeans? It's so hot!
Tom: My legs are very skinny and so I ⁶ _____ (never/wear) shorts, even in summer. In fact, I ⁷ _____ (not have) any shorts!
Jo: So which bands ⁸ _____ (you/want) to see today?
Tom: I ⁹ _____ (like) Foo Fighters, but I ¹⁰ _____ (not know) when they're on. I ¹¹ _____ (look) for a festival programme.
Jo: I have one here – oh, they ¹² _____ (play) now.
Tom: Oh right – thanks! See you.

6 Look at Jo's interview with Tom again. Find two verbs with both dynamic and stative meanings and explain the differences in meaning.

7 Write true sentences about yourself with the affirmative or negative form of the verbs in brackets in an appropriate present tense.
   1 I _____ (need) a new pair of trainers.
   2 I _____ (wear) my favourite T-shirt today.
   3 I _____ (buy) all my clothes online.
   4 I _____ (like) shopping.
   5 I _____ (think) most clothes are too expensive.
   6 I _____ (think) of going shopping later.

8 **SPEAKING** Ask each other questions based on the sentences in Exercise 7.
   Do you need a new pair of trainers?

Grammar page 132

1.3 LISTENING

True/False

I can understand the key points of a radio programme on a familiar topic.

A 'A friend is someone who knows everything about you and still likes you.'

B 'The best mirror you can have is an old friend.'

C 'There is nothing better than a friend, apart from a friend with chocolate.'

1 **SPEAKING** Read sayings A–C about friendship and discuss the questions.
  1 Which saying do you like best? Why?
  2 What qualities should a close friend have?
  3 How would you complete the sentence: 'A true friend …'?

2 🔊 1.8 Listen to a radio programme about friendship. What do the numbers in the box refer to?

  (2   16   17   5 or 6   313   3 or 4)

3 **SPEAKING** Discuss how many friends you have. Talk about online friends, close friends and friends of the opposite sex.

EXAM FOCUS True/False

4 🔊 1.8 Listen to the radio programme again. Are statements 1–6 true (T) or false (F)?
  1 Jenny **has a good relationship with** all her online friends. ☐
  2 Jenny thinks it takes time to **slowly find out about** somebody. ☐
  3 Jenny says friends sometimes **stop seeing each other** when they've **had an argument**. ☐
  4 Fraser has similar interests to his close friends. ☐
  5 Fraser doesn't think a good friend **is always reliable** in a crisis. ☐
  6 Fraser **socialises with** both boys and girls. ☐

WORD STORE 1D Relationship phrases

5 🔊 1.9 Complete WORD STORE 1D with the phrases in green in Exercise 4. Then listen, check and repeat.

6 🔊 1.10 Listen to dialogues 1–4 and match them with descriptions a–e. There is one extra description.
  1 ☐   2 ☐   3 ☐   4 ☐

  a They get along really well together.
  b They've lost touch.
  c They're always there for each other.
  d They've fallen out.
  e They're getting to know each other.

7 Complete the questions with an appropriate verb from WORD STORE 1D.
  1 How easy was it to get to _____ your best friend?
  2 Why do you _____ along so well together?
  3 Have you ever _____ out?
  4 What sort of places do you usually _____ out in?
  5 Will you always _____ there for your best friend?
  6 Do you think you'll ever _____ touch with each other?

8 **SPEAKING** Think about your best friend. Ask and answer the questions in Exercise 7 with a partner.

PRONUNCIATION FOCUS

9 🔊 1.11 Write the numbers in full. Then listen, check and repeat.
  1 515 – five hundred *and* fifteen
  2 214 – two hundred _____ fourteen
  3 3,330 – three thousand, _____ hundred _____ thirty
  4 901 – nine _____ _____ _____
  5 7,880 – _____ thousand, _____ _____ _____ eighty
  6 4,416 – four _____ , _____ _____ _____ _____

10 Write down three long numbers. Dictate the numbers to your partner. Check that your partner has written the same numbers as you.

1.4 READING

Note completion

I can identify key information in an extended article.

1 Choose a word from each box to describe the clothes you can see in the photos.

{ blue white / black } + { cotton leather / denim } + { jacket jeans / T-shirt }

2 **SPEAKING** Do you wear any of the clothes in the photos? Why?/Why not?

I wear jeans almost every day. They're comfortable and …
I never wear leather, because I'm a vegan.

3 Guess the answers to questions 1–5 below. Then read the article and check your ideas.
   1 Why is a T-shirt called a T-shirt?
   2 Which was the first profession to wear leather jackets?
   3 How is the phrase 'blue jeans' connected to France?
   4 When did young people start wearing jeans as fashion items?
   5 Why are these clothes still popular with young people?

EXAM FOCUS   Note completion

4 Read the article again. Complete the sentences with one or two words from the article.
   1 Over 100 years ago _____ was made of wool.
   2 The first leather jacket with a zip was created in _____ in the United States.
   3 _____ , such as James Dean, made T-shirts and leather jackets more popular.
   4 Up until the 1970s, T-shirts were mainly for _____ .
   5 Jeans are made of _____ , a type of cotton.
   6 Jeans used to be _____ in schools.

5 Look at the strategies which can help you guess the meaning of unknown words. Then discuss the meaning of the words in blue in the text.
   1 It looks like a word in my language.
   2 It looks like a member of a word family I know.
   3 It is made up of words I understand.
   4 The context can give me clues.

6 🔊 1.13 Match the words in blue in the text with the definitions. Then listen, check and repeat.
   1 a style worn by both men and women = _unisex_
   2 items of clothing = _____
   3 recognised by everyone = _____
   4 a person who makes clothes = _____
   5 clothing you wear next to your skin = _____
   6 material that clothes are made of = _____

WORD STORE 1E | Compound adjectives

7 🔊 1.14 Complete WORD STORE 1E with the underlined words in the article. Then listen, check and repeat.

8 Complete the message with the compound adjectives in WORD STORE 1E.

Hi Karen,
I'm going on a cycling weekend. As an experienced cyclist, what do you think I should wear?

Hi Sam,
Lucky you! Take at least two ¹_____ shirts or T-shirts and suntan lotion for your arms. You need a pair of ²_____ shorts – cycling damages shorts quickly, so invest in good ones. Lots of people wear black ones but I prefer ³_____ shorts and T-shirts so that car drivers can see you! A warm jacket – something that will keep you warm in the evening. A rain jacket that's made from ⁴_____ fabric. There's some amazing ⁵_____ technology out there in new fabrics for sports clothes. Oh, and don't forget your sunglasses! Have fun.

9 How do you say these compound adjectives in your language? How many of them can you use to describe clothes in your wardrobe?

10 **SPEAKING** Look at the photo and discuss the questions:
   1 Do you or anyone in your family own a hoodie?
   2 When and why do you wear it?
   3 What is the link between the hoodie and:
      American footballers?
      Break-dancers?
      Graffiti artists?
      Skate-boarders?
      A high-profile social media boss?

11 🔊 1.15 Listen to a podcast called *History of Streetwear: the Hoodie* and check your ideas to question 3 in Exercise 10. Do you think the hoodie is now an 'icon of fashion'?

12 **SPEAKING** What's the oldest item of clothing in your wardrobe? Tell your partner its 'history'.

I have a vintage coat. My grandmother used to wear it when she was younger …

ICONS *of fashion*

🔊 1.12

We think we look so cool, so modern and just a little rebellious in our jeans, white T-shirt and black leather jacket. But we're not as original as we think we are – this look goes back to the 1970s, right? Well, no, not exactly – as a matter of fact, you can trace most of it back to 100 years ago.

Take the white T-shirt and leather jacket. Both started life in the military. The T-shirt (so-called because of its shape like a T) was in fact underwear. In the American Navy, it was worn under a uniform. Until the early 20th century, underwear was woollen, but a revolution in textile production produced cotton jersey, a fast-drying fabric which fits tightly to the body and kept sailors warm. The short-sleeved T-shirt was born. Leather jackets were worn by fighter pilots in the First World War – they were hard-wearing, warm and fur-lined for maximum protection from the elements. Then, in 1928, an American raincoat company, Schott, designed the first leather motorcycle jacket with a zip.

By the 1950s both garments had reached iconic status when famous actors like Marlon Brando and James Dean wore them in films. Later, in the 1960s and 1970s, bands from the Beatles to the Ramones adopted the leather jacket, and it moved from motorcycle sports to teenage rebellion. In the 1970s T-shirts got a colourful update: brightly-coloured T-shirts were particularly popular as well as T-shirts with band logos and political slogans. Having started out as an undergarment for men, T-shirts became unisex in the 1970s and have been part of everyone's wardrobe since then.

You may think your fashionably distressed jeans are cutting-edge fashion items, but they can be traced even further back in history. In the 1800s denim, the material jeans are made of, was a kind of cotton made in Nîmes, France ('de Nîmes'). The first blue denim trousers were worn by sailors in Genoa – 'Gênes' in French. 'Bleu de Gênes' became 'blue jeans'.

Blue jeans as we know them originated during the 1849 Californian Gold Rush. They were developed by German storekeeper Levi Strauss and Latvian tailor Jacob Davis. Levi Strauss never wore a pair of jeans himself – he was a wealthy businessman, and jeans were only worn by manual workers and cowboys. But then their popularity spread after the Second World War. Young people started wearing jeans to imitate young Hollywood stars. However, they were associated with rebellious behaviour and were banned in schools.

So each time you wear your jeans, white T-shirt and black leather jacket, you're actually wearing 100 years of style history! The secret to their long life? They're comfortable, multi-purpose clothes made of natural materials that are easy to wear, keep you warm and give you a little attitude. What's not to love?

Marlon Brando

The Ramones

1.5 GRAMMAR

Present Perfect Continuous

I can use the Present Perfect Continuous and Present Perfect Simple.

1 **SPEAKING** Look at the different versions of the Mona Lisa and discuss the questions.
   1 Which version do you like best? Why?
   2 What do you know about the original painting?

A B  C

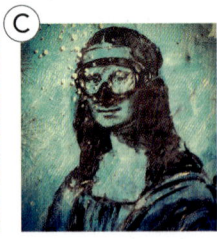

2 Read about the real Mona Lisa. Why does the curator think the Mona Lisa is smiling?

STOP ASKING SILLY QUESTIONS

My name is Henri Dubois. I've been working at the Louvre Museum in Paris for twenty-one years and I've been looking after the Mona Lisa for nearly ten. So, for the past ten years I've been
5 watching people's faces when they first see the Mona Lisa. There's something very special about that painting. I've also been answering the same questions over and over again. They ask me, 'How long has she been hanging in the Louvre?' I always say the Mona Lisa has been in the Louvre
10 since 1804. But it isn't quite true. The Mona Lisa hasn't been hanging in the Louvre since then because someone stole it in 1911. Fortunately the painting was returned two years later.

The other questions are impossible to answer. They ask me: 'Who was she? Why is she smiling?' Why? Because she's been
15 listening to people's silly questions for over two hundred years! Stop asking questions and look at the painting – it's beautiful!

3 Read the GRAMMAR FOCUS. Then underline six more examples of the Present Perfect Continuous in the text.

GRAMMAR FOCUS

Present Perfect Continuous

You use the **Present Perfect Continuous** to talk about unfinished actions that started in the past and continue in time 'up-to-now'. Use **for** or **since** to say how long.
I've been working here for twenty-one years.

Present Perfect Continuous: has/have + been + -ing form

+	I've been working.
−	He hasn't been working.
?	Have you been working? Yes, I have./No, I haven't.

Note: State verbs (*be, have, know,* etc.) do not take the continuous form.
The Mona Lisa has been in the Louvre since 1804.
(NOT *has been being* …)

4 Complete the dialogue between the Manager (M), a guest (G) and the guest's son Jack (J). Use the Present Perfect Continuous.

M: I'm sorry, the museum is really busy today. How long ¹_____ (wait)?
G: It's OK. We ²_____ (not wait) long. We ³_____ (stand) in this queue for about twenty minutes.
M: Right. Well, I'll introduce you to Henri, our curator. He ⁴_____ (work) here for over twenty years.
G: Thanks. My son, Jack, is very excited. He ⁵_____ (learn) about Leonardo da Vinci at school.
M: Well, I'm sure Henri can answer any questions. He ⁶_____ (look after) the Mona Lisa for ten years.
J: Er … How long ⁷_____ (the Mona Lisa/hang) in the Louvre?

5 Complete the sentences with the Present Perfect Simple or Continuous form of the verbs in brackets. Then add a time expression to make them true for you.
   1 I _'ve had_ (have) the same computer for _3 years_ .
   2 I _____ (study) English since _____ .
   3 I _____ (listen) to the same music since _____ .
   4 I _____ (go) to the same hairdresser's for _____ .
   5 I _____ (know) my oldest friend since _____ .
   6 I _____ (sit) in this chair since _____ .

6 **SPEAKING** Write questions for the sentences in Exercise 5 beginning with *How long have you …?* Then ask your partner.

How long have you had the same computer?

REMEMBER THIS

You use the **Present Perfect Simple** to talk about finished actions in time 'up-to-now'. You can say 'how many' but not 'when'.

Peter has visited the Louvre seven times. He has visited twenty-seven other museums.

7 Choose the most appropriate Present Perfect form. Which sentences are true for you?
   1 *I've seen / I've been seeing* the Mona Lisa twice.
   2 My mum *has bought / has been buying* a new car.
   3 *It's snowed / It's been snowing* since yesterday.
   4 *I've learnt / I've been learning* the piano for years.
   5 We *have never been going / have never been* abroad.
   6 I *haven't eaten / haven't been eating* lunch yet.

8 **SPEAKING** Write questions in the Present Perfect Simple or Continuous. Begin the questions with *How long …?* or *How many …?* Ask your partner.
   1 messages / receive / today?
   2 wear / the same watch?
   3 have / the same bag?
   4 foreign countries / visit?
   5 books / read / in the past three months?

FOCUS VLOG About clothes

▶4 Watch the Focus Vlog. For the worksheet, go to page 117.

Grammar page 133

1.6 USE OF ENGLISH

Word formation – common suffixes

I can form a range of nouns, verbs and adjectives using common suffixes.

1 **SPEAKING** Look at the photos and discuss which hairstyles you think are acceptable for school.

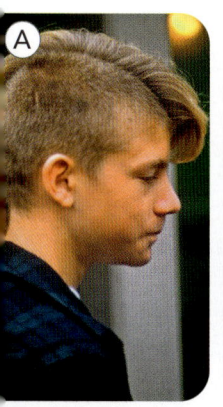

2 🔊 **1.16** Listen to a phone-in about Martha's situation at school and answer the questions.
   1 What's Martha's problem at school?
   2 Why did she change her hairstyle?
   3 How many callers thought the school was right?
   4 How many callers thought the school was wrong?

3 **SPEAKING** Discuss whether you think the school was right or wrong. How do you think your school would react?

4 🔊 **1.16** Listen again and choose the correct option.
   1 The *priority / obligation* of the school is to *educate / be respectful*.
   2 The reason it's so *successful / helpful* is that it has rules and *regulations / punishment*.
   3 Your rules are *pathetic / creative*.
   4 The school should focus on her *academic achievements / leadership*.
   5 Schoolchildren must *clarify / realise* that their school has rules.
   6 I *honestly / absolutely* think that it's absolutely *ridiculous / unacceptable* to make such a fuss about a shaved head.

5 Look at the words in all the options in Exercise 4 again and decide what part of speech they are.
   Nouns: _____
   Verbs: _____
   Adjectives: _____
   Adverbs: _____

6 Read the LANGUAGE FOCUS and complete the information with the words in the box.

   adjectives (x3)   adverbs   nouns   verbs

   ### LANGUAGE FOCUS

   Word formation – common suffixes
   - Many different words are formed by adding suffixes to nouns, verbs and adjectives.
     Forming ¹_____ : -ance/-ence, -ion, -ity, -ment, -ship
     Forming ²_____ : -ate, -en, -ify, -ise
     Forming ³_____ : -able, -al, -ed, -ful, -ic, -ing, -ive, -less, -ous
   - You can add prefixes **un-**, **in-**, **im-**, **il-**, **ir-**, **dis-** to some ⁴_____ to get the opposite meaning.
     acceptable – **un**acceptable, respectful – **dis**respectful

   Note: You form most ⁵_____ by adding **-ly**, **-y**, **-ily** to ⁶_____ .
   honest – hones**tly**, absolute – absolute**ly**, angry – ang**rily**

7 Complete the table with appropriate forms.

NOUN	VERB	ADJECTIVE	ADVERB
1 creation	create		
2		educational	
3		ridiculous	
4 achievement			
5	succeed		
6	accept		

8 **USE OF ENGLISH** Complete the sentences with the correct form of the word in brackets.
   1 The main duty of a school is to _____ its students. (education)
   2 It's _____ for schools to ban tattoos or piercings. (ridicule)
   3 You can't _____ a student for shaving his or her head. (punishment)
   4 Female students worry more about their _____ than male students. (appear)
   5 The fewer _____ about what students can and can't wear, the better. (regulate)
   6 It's _____ for students to deliberately ignore sensible school rules. (accept)
   7 _____ performance is not linked to how the students look. (academy)

9 **SPEAKING** Discuss whether you agree or disagree with the statements in Exercise 8. Give reasons for your answers.

Use of English page 134

1.7 WRITING

Describing a person

I can write a personal email to describe a person.

1 **SPEAKING** Look at your partner for ten seconds. Then close your eyes and describe their appearance and clothing in as much detail as you can.

2 Below, Maggie describes her friend Claire. Before you read, make a list of the things you think she might include.

age, hair (length and colour), interests …

3 Now read Maggie's message and see which things on your list in Exercise 2 she mentioned.

Hi Dominic,

Zara told me you are looking for a new singer for your band. Is that right? If so, I think my friend might be perfect.

Her name's Claire. The first thing you notice about her is that she looks a little older than she is. She's our age, but she looks like she's already in her early twenties. She's very easy-going and I think she has a great sense of humour – we get on really well. She's also a very creative person and a fantastic singer. She plays the piano and writes her own songs and has even made a video to go with one of them. She's into all sorts of music, from classical to rap and I think she's the kind of person who is open to new ideas. I think she'd make a great singer for the band.

She's also very pretty ;-). She's about medium height and slim, and she's got long, straight, dark hair. She dresses fashionably, though usually in black. I think she looks kind of punky but in a good way.

On the negative side, she isn't exactly punctual and she can be a little moody at times. She tends to get upset if you criticise her. But hey, she's a creative!

Watch her video (attached) and let me know what you think.

Love Maggie x

Dominic is not online at the moment. We'll deliver your message next time Dominic logs in.

4 **SPEAKING** Discuss whether you think you would get on well with Claire. Give reasons for your answers.

5 Complete the WRITING FOCUS with the words in purple in the message in Exercise 3.

WRITING FOCUS

Describing a person

- Give first impressions
  The first thing you notice about her is that she looks older than she is.
- Mention age
  He's (about) my/your/¹____our____ age.
  He's in his teens/²_____/mid-/late twenties.
- Describe personality and interests
  He's a very easy-going/interesting, etc. person.
  She has a great sense of humour.
  She's the sort/type/kind of person ³_____ always remembers your birthday/loves kids.
  She'd ⁴_____ a great teacher/doctor/friend.
  He's ⁵_____ music/fashion/skateboarding.
- Describe hair, eyes, skin and face
  He's got cool, short, ⁶_____ hair.
  She's got beautiful, long, ⁷_____ , blond hair.
  She's got a kind/friendly/unusual smile/face.
- Mention height/build
  She's short/⁸_____/tall.
  He's fairly well-built/⁹_____ .
- Mention clothes
  She ¹⁰_____ casually/smartly/well/in black.
  He always wears casual/smart/scruffy/fashionable/stylish clothes.

6 Complete the description with the words in the WRITING FOCUS. Do you know anybody like Martin? Tell your partner.

My friend Martin is the ¹_____ of person who can argue about anything. He always ²_____ smartly and he's a very interesting ³_____ . But he's not always serious. He's ⁴_____ music and dancing, and he has a great ⁵_____ of humour. He's ⁶_____ age, but he looks older. He's got short ⁷_____ and a friendly ⁸_____ . I think he'd ⁹_____ a good politician.

7 Complete the LANGUAGE FOCUS with the underlined examples in the message in Exercise 3.

LANGUAGE FOCUS

Tentative language: making language less negative or extreme

- **kind of/sort of**
  She looks kind of cool/unusual/mysterious/nervous/ ¹___punky___ .

- **tend to be/get + adjective**
  ~~She gets upset~~ = She tends ²_____ .

- **can be/could be + a little/a bit + adjective**
  ~~His hair's too long~~ = His hair could be a bit shorter.
  ~~She's moody.~~ = She can be ³_____ .

- Negative adjective to positive adjective with **always, exactly, particularly**
  ~~He's lazy.~~ = He isn't always hard-working.
  ~~He's mean.~~ = He's not particularly generous.
  ~~She's always late.~~ = She isn't ⁴_____ .

- **Quantifiers/softeners**
  ~~She's skinny.~~ = She's a bit too slim.
  ~~He's tiny.~~ = He's a little short.
  ~~She's old.~~ = She looks ⁵_____ .

8 Rewrite the sentences to make them less negative or extreme. Use the word in brackets.
1 Amanda's rude. Amanda _____ . (polite)
2 Bryan's mean. Bryan _____ . (exactly)
3 Caroline's lazy. Caroline _____ . (always)
4 David's loud. David _____ . (could)
5 Elena's insensitive. Elena _____ . (can)
6 Freddie's untidy. Freddie _____ . (tends)

9 Choose one of the photos. Imagine he or she is your friend. Write a description including physical appearance, style and personality. The description should be exactly 50 words. Compare with your partner.

A

B

C

SHOW WHAT YOU'VE LEARNT

10 Do the writing task. Use the ideas in the WRITING FOCUS and the LANGUAGE FOCUS to help you.

A friend is going to visit the city where your cousin lives. Your cousin has agreed to show your friend around the city. They have never met before. Write an email to your cousin and:

- describe your friend's appearance,
- describe your friend's personality,
- mention some of your friend's interests,
- thank your cousin for agreeing to show your friend around.

1.8 SPEAKING

Describing a photo

I can describe a photo and speculate about the people in it.

1 Look at the adjective order key and put the clothes descriptions 1–5 in the right order. Is anybody in the class wearing one of these items?

Adjective order

Opinion	Size/Age	Colour/Pattern	Material	Make/Type	Noun
a lovely	big old	brown	leather	flying	jacket

1 trainers / Nike / New
2 A / cotton / shirt / patterned
3 jeans / blue / Fashionable / skinny
4 leather / high-heeled / Black / boots
5 A / striped / jumper / big / woollen

2 **SPEAKING** Take it in turns to describe clothes in the class. Use at least two adjectives to describe each item. Guess who your partner is describing.

3 Look at photo A. Can you use any of the adjectives in Exercise 1 to describe the clothes?

4 🔊 1.17 How would you describe the situation in photo A? Think of two adjectives to describe how the woman is feeling. Then listen and check your ideas.

SPEAKING FOCUS

Beginning a description
The photo shows …
In this photo, I can see …/there is …/there are …

Saying where (in the photo)
in the background/in the middle/in the foreground
on the left/on the right
in front of/behind/next to

Showing uncertainty
It's hard to say/make out …, but …
I'm not sure …, but …

Speculating
He/She/It looks …
He/She/It looks as if/as though/like …
It seems to be …/Perhaps it's …/Maybe it's …
I imagine they're …/They're probably …

Giving your opinion
I (don't) think …/I prefer …/Personally, …/In my opinion …

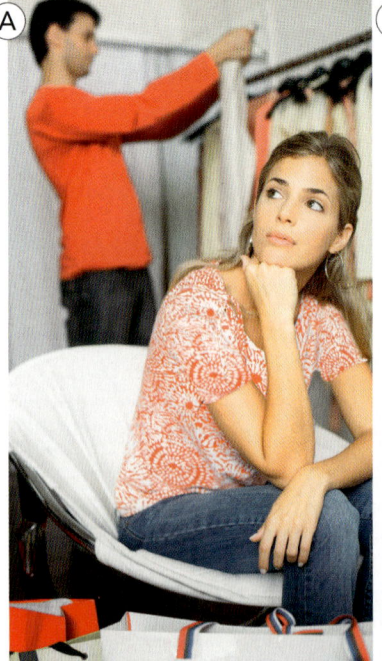

5 🔊 1.17 Read the SPEAKING FOCUS and complete the description of photo A with one word in each gap. Then listen again and check.

The photo ¹_____ a man and a woman shopping together. It's ²_____ to say exactly how old they are, but I ³_____ they're in their twenties, and they're ⁴_____ a couple. The man's wearing a red top and grey jeans. The woman is sitting on a white chair and she ⁵_____ bored. On the floor, ⁶_____ to her chair, there are several shopping bags. I'm not ⁷_____ what's in them, but I think they're probably clothes, and I ⁸_____ they've been shopping for a few hours already.
It's hard to ⁹_____ out exactly what kind of shop they are in, but it ¹⁰_____ to be a men's clothes shop. It looks as ¹¹_____ they're near the changing rooms because there's a white curtain in the ¹²_____ . The man is holding up a shirt or a pair of trousers. He looks ¹³_____ if he's thinking about trying it on. I ¹⁴_____ think the woman looks very interested. ¹⁵_____ , I think she wants to go to a women's clothes shop.

6 **SPEAKING** Look at photo B. Then follow the instructions below to talk about it. Use the phrases in the SPEAKING FOCUS to help you.

- Say what the photo shows.
- Speculate about the people and the situation.
- Take it in turns to describe the photo to your partner.

7 **SPEAKING** Ask and answer three more questions based on photos A and B.

1 How often do you go shopping?
2 Who do you usually go with? Why?
3 What are your favourite or least favourite shops? Why?

UNIT 1 — A new look — Word list

1.1 Vocabulary 🔊 4.1
ankle boots /ˈæŋkəl buːts/
attitude /ˈætətjuːd/
bald /bɔːld/
bangles /ˈbæŋgəlz/
be the centre of attention /bi ðə ˌsentər əv əˈtenʃən/
beanie /ˈbiːni/
blouse /blaʊz/
care a lot about /ˌkeər ə ˈlɒt əˌbaʊt/
carefree /ˈkeəfriː/
come across as /ˌkʌm əˈkrɒs əz/
cotton /ˈkɒtn/
dark suit /ˌdɑːk ˈsuːt/
denim jacket /ˌdenɪm ˈdʒækət/
disobedient /ˌdɪsəˈbiːdiənt/
down-to-earth /ˌdaʊn tu ˈɜːθ/
easy-going /ˌiːzi ˈgəʊɪŋ/
ethical brand /ˌeθɪkəl ˈbrænd/
faded jeans /ˌfeɪdɪd ˈdʒiːnz/
fashionable /ˈfæʃənəbəl/
fast fashion /ˌfɑːst ˈfæʃən/
feel comfortable in your own skin /ˌfiːl ˈkʌmftəbəl ɪn jɔːr əʊn ˈskɪn/
fleece /fliːs/
follow trends /ˌfɒləʊ ˈtrendz/
friendly /ˈfrendli/
go for /ˈgəʊ fɔː/
go with the flow /ˌgəʊ wɪð ðə ˈfləʊ/
high heels /ˌhaɪ ˈhiːəlz/
in/out of fashion /ˌɪn/ˌaʊt əv ˈfæʃən/
kind /kaɪnd/
leather belt /ˌleðə ˈbelt/
leggings /ˈlegɪŋz/
look /lʊk/
necklace /ˈnekləs/
practical clothes /ˌpræktɪkəl ˈkləʊðz/
rebellious /rɪˈbeljəs/
shallow /ˈʃæləʊ/
silk tie /ˌsɪlk ˈtaɪ/
slim /slɪm/
sweatshirt /ˈswetʃɜːt/
trendy /ˈtrendi/
vain /veɪn/
vintage sunglasses /ˌvɪntɪdʒ ˈsʌnˌglɑːsəz/
waistcoat /ˈweɪskəʊt/
wear /weə/
wear make-up /ˌweə ˈmeɪk ʌp/

1.2 Grammar 🔊 4.2
band /bænd/
baseball cap /ˈbeɪsbɔːl kæp/
report on /rɪˈpɔːt ɒn/
revise /rɪˈvaɪz/
shorts /ʃɔːts/
skinny /ˈskɪni/
trainers /ˈtreɪnəz/

1.3 Listening 🔊 4.3
be always there for /bi ˌɔːlweɪz ˈðeə fə/
close friend /ˌkləʊs ˈfrend/
fall out with /ˌfɔːl ˈaʊt wɪð/
find out about /ˌfaɪnd ˈaʊt əˌbaʊt/
get along (well) with /ˌget əˈlɒŋ (wel) wɪð/
get to know /ˌget tə ˈnəʊ/
hang out with /ˌhæŋ ˈaʊt wɪð/
have a good relationship with /ˌhæv ə ˌgʊd rɪˈleɪʃənʃɪp wɪð/
have a lot in common with /ˌhæv ə ˌlɒt ɪn ˈkɒmən wɪð/
have an argument /ˌhæv ən ˈɑːgjəmənt/
have similar interests /ˌhæv ˌsɪmələr ˈɪntrəsts/
lose touch with /ˌluːz ˈtʌtʃ wɪð/
online friend /ˌɒnlaɪn ˈfrend/
opposite sex /ˌɒpəzət ˈseks/
reliable /rɪˈlaɪəbəl/
socialise with /ˈsəʊʃəlaɪz wɪð/
stop seeing each other /ˌstɒp ˈsiːɪŋ iːtʃ ˌʌðə/
suit /suːt/

1.4 Reading 🔊 4.4
banned /bænd/
brightly-coloured /ˌbraɪtli ˈkʌləd/
cool /kuːl/
cutting-edge /ˈkʌtɪŋ edʒ/
distressed jeans /dɪˌstrest ˈdʒiːnz/
fabric /ˈfæbrɪk/
fast-drying /ˌfɑːst ˈdraɪɪŋ/
fur-lined /ˈfɜː laɪnd/
garment /ˈgɑːmənt/
hard-wearing /ˌhɑːd ˈweərɪŋ/
iconic /aɪˈkɒnɪk/
imitate /ˈɪmɪteɪt/
look like /ˈlʊk laɪk/
multi-purpose /ˌmʌlti ˈpɜːpəs/
originate /əˈrɪdʒɪneɪt/
popular /ˈpɒpjələ/
raincoat /ˈreɪnkəʊt/
rain jacket /ˈreɪn ˌdʒækɪt/
rebellion /rɪˈbeljən/
short-sleeved /ˌʃɔːt ˈsliːvd/
suntan lotion /ˈsʌntæn ˌləʊʃən/
tailor /ˈteɪlə/
the elements /ði ˈeləmənts/
trousers /ˈtraʊzəz/
underwear /ˈʌndəweə/
unisex /ˈjuːnɪseks/
wardrobe /ˈwɔːdrəʊb/
woollen /ˈwʊlən/
zip /zɪp/

1.5 Grammar 🔊 4.5
curator /kjʊˈreɪtə/
look after /ˌlʊk ˈɑːftə/
over and over again /ˈəʊvər ənd ˈəʊvər əˈgen/
queue /kjuː/

1.6 Use of English 🔊 4.6
accept /əkˈsept/
acceptable /əkˈseptəbəl/
acceptably /əkˈseptəbli/
acceptance /əkˈseptəns/
achievable /əˈtʃiːvəbəl/
achieve /əˈtʃiːv/
achievement /əˈtʃiːvmənt/
educate /ˈedjʊkeɪt/
education /ˌedjʊˈkeɪʃən/
educational /ˌedjʊˈkeɪʃənəl/
educationally /ˌedjʊˈkeɪʃənəli/
hope /həʊp/
hopeful /ˈhəʊpfəl/
hopefully /ˈhəʊpfəli/
hopeless /ˈhəʊpləs/
hopelessly /ˈhəʊpləsli/
succeed /səkˈsiːd/
success /səkˈses/
successful /səkˈsesfəl/
successfully /səkˈsesfəli/

1.7 Writing 🔊 4.7
blond /blɒnd/
casual /ˈkæʒuəl/
get on well with /ˌget ɒn ˈwel wɪð/
hard-working /ˌhɑːd ˈwɜːkɪŋ/
in his early/mid/late twenties /ɪn hɪz ˌɜːli/ˌmɪd/ˌleɪt ˈtwentiz/
in his teens /ɪn hɪz ˈtiːnz/
medium height /ˌmiːdiəm ˈhaɪt/
mysterious /mɪˈstɪəriəs/
nervous /ˈnɜːvəs/
open to /ˈəʊpən tə/
rude /ruːd/
scruffy /ˈskrʌfi/
sense of humour /ˌsens əv ˈhjuːmə/
she'd make a great … /ˌʃid ˌmeɪk ə ˈgreɪt…/
short /ʃɔːt/
smart /smɑːt/
straight/dark/short/long hair /ˌstreɪt/ˌdɑːk/ˌʃɔːt/ˌlɒŋ ˈheə/
stylish /ˈstaɪlɪʃ/

1.8 Speaking 🔊 4.8
jumper /ˈdʒʌmpə/
look as if/as though /ˌlʊk əz ɪf/əz ðəʊ/
patterned /ˈpætənd/
shirt /ʃɜːt/
striped /straɪpt/
top /tɒp/
try on /ˌtraɪ ˈɒn/

FOCUS REVIEW 1

VOCABULARY AND GRAMMAR

1 Complete the sentences with the words in the box. There are three extra words.

> carefree centre denim faded
> rebellious skin vain vintage

1 I like to wear a _____ jacket with jeans because they are both blue.
2 Kelly found some amazing _____ sunglasses at a charity shop – I think they were made in the 1960s.
3 Bob tends to be a little _____ – he can't stand current fashions and wears anything just to be different.
4 I feel comfortable in my own _____ and don't worry too much about my appearance.
5 Jill comes across as relaxed and _____ , but I know that she worries about things all the time.

2 Read the definitions in brackets and complete the words. The first letter of each word is given.

1 I didn't mean to f_____ (*have an argument with*) out with Kelly, but now she won't speak to me.
2 This g_____ (*item of clothing*) is so practical that you can wear it as a top, a dress or a skirt.
3 Some of the most c_____ (*latest and most advanced*) fashions come out of Japan, where they are not afraid to experiment with forms and materials.
4 When it comes to clothes, teenagers usually go with the f_____ (*follow what other people do*).
5 Jane twisted her ankle because she is not used to running in high h_____ (*women's shoes which are higher in the back than the front*).

3 Complete the sentences with the Present Simple or Present Continuous form of the verbs in brackets.

1 Why _____ (you/look) at me like that? Is there something wrong with my hair?
2 Pam always _____ (listen) carefully to her friends' advice, but she never does what they suggest.
3 I _____ (think) about having a talk with Jack about his rude behaviour.
4 Stuart _____ (look) very smart in his new woollen suit and black leather shoes.
5 Jane, _____ (believe) that people should always be kind to each other?

4 Complete the sentences with the Present Perfect Simple or Present Perfect Continuous form of the verbs in brackets.

1 Our uncle is on holiday and we _____ (look) after his dog since Monday.
2 Tim _____ (have) the same school uniform for two years and it's a bit small now.
3 My sister _____ (make) her own clothes since she was a teenager.
4 Gillian _____ (work) as a model once or twice, but she doesn't want to do it as a career.
5 Helen is very busy at university but she _____ (not lose) touch with her friends.

USE OF ENGLISH

5 Choose the correct answer, A, B or C.

1 X: _____ a new T-shirt in this photo?
   Y: It's not new. It's my dad's old T-shirt from the 80s.
   A Do you wear B Are you wearing C Have you worn
2 X: Did you make the jacket you're wearing?
   Y: I did! I'm usually _____ at making clothes but this project was pretty successful.
   A hope B hopeless C success
3 X: What have you been doing?
   Y: Nothing special. I _____ an email to Lucy to ask her about our project. I hope she replies soon.
   A 'm writing B 've written C 've been writing
4 X: Sarah looks ridiculous in those tight jeans!
   Y: You know, I don't think it's _____ to make rude comments about people's appearance.
   A achievable B accept C acceptable
5 X: Can you have a look at this picture? _____
   Y: Well, I'm not sure either.
   A I can't make out what it shows.
   B I don't think it is very interesting.
   C It looks as though you could help me.

6 Read the text and choose the correct answer, A, B or C.

Fashion and the Human Form

In every period throughout history there have been specific ideas of what the perfect human body should look like. Different body types have gone **1**_____ and out of fashion just like clothes and hairstyles, and these ideals led to the **2**_____ of fashions. The ancient Greeks, who admired slim, athletic bodies, went for a casual look, with soft **3**_____ and comfortable shapes. In Britain, the Elizabethans preferred women's clothes which forced their bodies into totally unnatural shapes, causing a lot of discomfort. During the early 19th century, Europeans believed that the Greek look was the best, and women's clothes became much more comfortable, but this did not last. The Victorians thought that a very small waist made women attractive, and women wore such tight garments they sometimes caused actual injuries. Nowadays, some of the most **4**_____ designers make clothes that fit all shapes and sizes. But judging by all the diet plans, exercise programmes and plastic surgery procedures that are available, it seems that things **5**_____ much up to now.

1 A on   B in   C at
2 A created   B creative   C creation
3 A fabrics   B skins   C suits
4 A success   B succeeded   C successful
5 A haven't changed   B didn't change
  C haven't been changing

READING

7 Read the text. Complete the sentences with one or two words from the article.

Stella McCartney

When designer Stella McCartney arrived on the fashion scene, many people claimed her success was due to her famous name. Her father is, after all, Beatles legend Paul McCartney. This, however, is not true. For Stella, her achievements took hard work, determination and, of course, talent.

In 1995, after graduating from Central St Martins College of Art and Design in London, she enjoyed almost immediate success. Two short years later, at the age of twenty-six, she became the head designer at Chloé – a famous Parisian fashion house. After four highly successful years at Chloé, Stella launched her own fashion label and showed her first collection of cutting-edge designs in 2001.

Since then her company has been growing steadily. In that time, it has gained acceptance as a fashion company with a difference. When Stella was growing up on a farm, her parents taught her to respect animals, to be aware of nature, and to understand that human beings must get along well with other creatures. This down-to-earth approach has had a huge impact on her and, as a result, she believes in ethical fashion now. Ethical fashion covers issues such as working conditions, child labour, fair trade and responsible production that does not harm the environment.

As a lifelong vegetarian, Stella does not use any natural leather or fur in her designs. The fabric she prefers is organic cotton and she has been experimenting with eco-friendly materials and production processes. She always tries to find the most responsible production methods. Recently, Stella decided not to work with a fabrics factory because the process it used to colour the fabrics was very harmful to the environment. An entire river near the factory became red, making the water unsuitable for drinking or for use in agriculture.

Stella's ethical fashion also aims to help poor workers. For this reason, she has created a range of cloth bags together with the United Nations' International Trade Centre. The programme provides work for poor communities in Kenya, where the bags are created by hand. So far, 160 people in disadvantaged areas have been involved in the production. They are earning money, which has improved their lives.

Stella McCartney has an interesting philosophy. She believes designers should ask themselves how they make their clothes and accessories, where they make them, and what materials they use. Thinking about these questions makes designing more challenging and more interesting, but still allows designers to create luxurious, beautiful items that people want to buy. Stella McCartney is proof of that.

1 Stella McCartney worked at Chloé as the _____ .
2 She _____ her own fashion company in 2001.
3 Stella cares about _____ issues in fashion, e.g. child labour or fair trade.
4 Her favourite material is _____ .
5 She did not want to cooperate with a _____ which did not use eco-friendly production methods.
6 People from _____ in Kenya are involved in making cloth bags for Stella.

SPEAKING

8 Look at the photos. They show people discussing what clothes to wear. In pairs, take turns to compare the photos and say why the people might have different opinions about the clothes.

A

B

9 Ask and answer the questions.
1 What do you think the woman in photo A is telling the girl? What are the couple discussing in the second photo?
2 Do your parents ever comment on your clothes? Why?/Why not?
3 Do you find it easy to choose what clothes to wear? Do you often ask for advice when you go shopping?

10 Can you wear informal clothes everywhere? Discuss.

WRITING

11 Read the writing task and write an email.

Your friend from the UK has got a summer job for a teen magazine. He/she has to interview young people who are interested in fashion. Suggest somebody you know as a person to interview. In your email describe:
- this person's fashion interests,
- what he/she usually wears,
- his/her personality

and confirm that he/she will agree to take part in the interview.

2

It's just a game

You can't score if you don't shoot.
A proverb

BBC

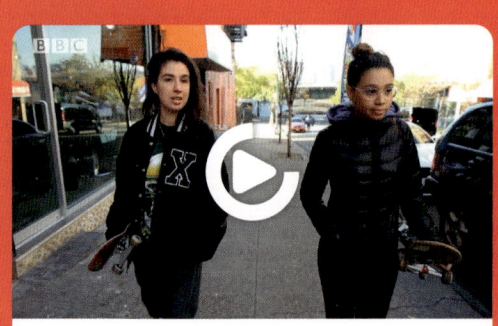

THE BRUJAS

▶ 5 Watch the BBC video.
For the worksheet, go to page 118.

2.1 VOCABULARY

Sport • phrasal verbs • collocations
• people in sport

I can talk about sports.

SHOW WHAT YOU KNOW

1 Add the verb *do*, *go* or *play* to each list of sports/forms of exercise.
   1 _____ badminton, basketball, ice hockey, table tennis, volleyball, American football
   2 _____ kayaking, cycling, rowing, sailing, skating, skiing
   3 _____ aerobics, athletics, boxing, judo, karate, yoga

2 **SPEAKING** Add any other sports you know to the lists. Then discuss the questions.
   1 What other sports do you do, go, play (or watch)?
   2 Which sports do you do on a court, a course, a pitch, a rink, a track or in a ring?
   3 Which are individual sports and which are team sports?
   4 What do you call the people who do these sports?

   basketball – basketball player   cycling – cyclist
   athletics – athlete

3 Read the blog post and comments. Then write your own comment and compare it with a partner.

4 **SPEAKING** Discuss these choices. Which do you prefer and why?
1 individual sports or team sports?
2 indoor sports or outdoor sports?
3 winter sports or summer sports?
4 doing sport or watching sport?
5 sport or no sport?

SPORTING QUESTIONS

Following news this week that the total number of teenagers taking up team sports has fallen, we're asking why so many people prefer individual sports. Sure, there are advantages: if you work out at the gym, you **burn off** calories and keep in shape and do it at a time that is convenient for you. But what about the friendship and the feeling of togetherness you get when you play for a team?

Are you a team player or do you prefer to do it alone? Here's what our readers said.

Jordan, 16
Not everyone has the confidence or the ability to participate in team sports. I'm 16 and I like **taking on** new challenges, but I'm not good enough to **get into** my school football team.

Jack, 17
When I play tennis, it's just me against my opponent – it's quite lonely without teammates. When I'm preparing for a competition I just see my coach. When I compete in a tournament and I beat an opponent, there's just my family **to cheer me on**. I love tennis, I love winning matches, but I miss the sense of belonging you get in a team.

Sherri, 16
I prefer team sports, but sometimes it's difficult when you **let your team down**. Last year, I had such a lot of school work that I had to **drop out of** my basketball team halfway through the season. I felt terrible.

Megan, 17
I do an individual sport, karate, but feel part of a team and I'm motivated to score points for my club. I **go in for** competitions, and when I came first recently, I felt it was for the club, not for myself. With the trainers, other club members and supporters, it's like a big family.

Go to **WORD STORE 2** page 5

WORD STORE 2A | Phrasal verbs

5 🔊 1.18 Complete WORD STORE 2A with the base forms of the phrasal verbs in red in the blog. Then listen, check and repeat.

6 **SPEAKING** Complete the questions with the verbs in WORD STORE 2A. Then ask and answer.
1 Are you somebody who likes to _____ on a challenge?
2 What do you shout when you _____ your team on?
3 Do you think a national team _____ the country down when it loses?
4 Have you ever had to _____ out of a team for any reason?
5 Which school team is it easiest to _____ into?
6 Does your school _____ in for many inter-school competitions?
7 What is the best type of exercise to _____ off calories?

WORD STORE 2B | Collocations

7 🔊 1.19 Complete WORD STORE 2B with the underlined words in the blog. Then listen, check and repeat.

8 🔊 1.20 Put the lines of one person's views about sport in the correct order. Then listen and check.
[1] I'm not into competitive sport. I'll never **break**
[ ] a goal! I like being healthy and **keeping**
[ ] first. I've seen men cry when the opposing team **scores**
[ ] a prize for sport. In fact, I usually **come**
[2] a world record, and I'm sure I'll never **win**
[ ] last in races and if I'm in a team we always **lose**
[ ] in shape. But I don't need to **beat**
[ ] the match. I don't understand people who need to **come**
[ ] my opponent – I'm happy just to take part.

9 **SPEAKING** Discuss which is more important: to win or to take part?

WORD STORE 2C | People in sport

10 🔊 1.21 Match the pictures in WORD STORE 2C with the words in the box. Then listen, check and repeat.

11 Complete the sentences with the words in WORD STORE 2C.
1 We play for the same team. He's my _____ .
2 I have a whistle, a red and a yellow card. I'm a _____ .
3 I organise training and help you improve. I'm your _____ .
4 I follow my team everywhere. I'm their biggest _____ .
5 I play against you. I want to beat you. You're my _____ .
6 I buy a ticket and watch the game. I'm a _____ .

12 **SPEAKING** Work in pairs. Student A: think of a sport. Student B: use the vocabulary from the lesson and ask twenty yes/no questions to find out the sport your partner is thinking of.
B: *Is it a team sport?* A: *Yes.*

19

GRAMMAR

2.2 Narrative tenses

I can describe a past event using the Past Simple, Perfect and Continuous.

1 Read *Running Wild*. Answer the questions.
  1 Had Chris Stewart run in Africa before?
  2 Why wasn't he running very fast?
  3 Why did a local runner overtake him at high speed?

RUNNING WILD

Chris Stewart and two other British **athletes were competing** in a 20-kilometre race in Kenya. **They hadn't competed** in Africa before, but **Chris believed** that it was important to save energy on a long-distance race so **he wasn't running** very fast. After three kilometres, **he was leading** when suddenly, **a local runner overtook** him at high speed. **He knew** his rival would get tired later in the race so **he didn't speed up** – but then **he looked round and saw** that **a large rhinoceros had crashed through** the trees next to the road and **it was chasing** after them …

2 Look at the verb phrases in blue in the text. Put them in the correct category below.
  • Past Simple: *Chris believed*
  • Past Continuous: *athletes were competing*
  • Past Perfect: *They hadn't competed*

3 Read the GRAMMAR FOCUS and complete it with the name of the appropriate tense.

GRAMMAR FOCUS

Narrative tenses

• You use the ¹*Past Continuous* to set the scene.
  … athletes **were competing** in a 20-kilometre race in Kenya.

• You use the ² _____ to describe the main events of a story.
  He **didn't speed up** – but then he **looked round** and **saw** …

• You often use the **Past Continuous** with the **Past Simple** – usually when a short action (Past Simple) interrupted a longer unfinished action (Past Continuous).
  He **was leading** when suddenly, a local runner **overtook** him.

• You use the ³ _____ to make it clear that one past action happened before another past action.
  He saw that a large rhinoceros **had crashed through** the trees.

4 Choose the best ending for each sentence. Compare with a partner.
  1 Tom couldn't play because
    a he had forgotten his trainers.
    b he forgot his trainers.
  2 Jeff broke his leg when
    a he skied.   b he was skiing.
  3 The referee blew his whistle and
    a the game started.   b the game was starting.
  4 Sue and Jenny were excited because
    a they hadn't been to a football match before.
    b they didn't go to a football match before.
  5 It was snowing when
    a the marathon had begun.   b the marathon began.
  6 Paula was leading the cycle race when
    a she fell off her bike.   b she had fallen off her bike.

5 🔊 1.22 Read *Lucky Break* and choose the correct verb form. Then listen and check.

LUCKY BREAK

In 1956, goalkeeper Bert Trautmann ¹(*was playing*) / *had played* for Manchester City in his first FA Cup final when he ²*dived* / *was diving* for the ball in the 75th minute. He ³*was knowing* / *knew* that he ⁴*hurt* / *had hurt* himself but he ⁵*was carrying on* / *carried on* playing. He ⁶*helped* / *had helped* his team to beat Birmingham City 3–1. He then ⁷*had gone* / *went* to hospital where the doctors couldn't believe he ⁸*had been* / *was* still alive. He ⁹*was breaking* / *had broken* his neck!

6 Write questions about *Lucky Break* using the correct tense.
  1 Who / win / the 1956 FA Cup final and what / be / the score?
    Who won the 1956 FA Cup final and what was the score?
  2 Trautmann / ever play / in an FA Cup final before?
  3 What position / Trautmann / play / when he got injured?
  4 How / Trautmann / hurt himself?
  5 Trautmann / stay / on the pitch for the whole game?
  6 Why / doctors / think / Trautmann was lucky?

7 **SPEAKING** Ask and answer the questions in Exercise 6.

8 **SPEAKING** You are going to tell your partner a story. Choose option A or option B. Think about what to say and how to say it. Then tell the story.

  Option A: Think of an exciting sports event you've seen or an exciting game you've played in.
  Option B: Choose one of the true stories in this lesson. Close your book.

  I'll never forget the time I scored the winning goal for our school team. We were playing in the final of …

Grammar page 135

2.3 LISTENING

Note completion

I can understand the key points of a radio interview on a familiar topic.

A — Serena Williams
B — Robert Kubica
C — Cristiano Ronaldo

1 **SPEAKING** Discuss what you know about the sports people in photos A–C.

2 🔊 1.23 Listen and match each speaker with their favourite sports star A–C. What human quality do all three sports stars have in common?

Speaker 1: ☐   Speaker 2: ☐   Speaker 3: ☐

3 🔊 1.23 Match sports stars A–C with three adjectives each according to the speaker's opinions. Then listen again and check.

caring ☐   courageous ☐   determined ☐
generous ☐   passionate ☐   positive ☐
powerful ☐   strong ☐   supportive ☐

4 **SPEAKING** Discuss which sports star you would choose as a good role model. Give reasons for your choice.

5 🔊 1.24 Listen to an interview with Jackie Smith, a windsurfing champion. Answer the questions.

1 Who were her role models when she started windsurfing?
2 What other water sports has she tried?
3 Who are her role models now?

EXAM FOCUS   Note completion

6 🔊 1.24 Listen again and complete the sentences with a word or short phrase.

1 Jackie was _____ when she won the international windsurfing championship.
2 When Jackie's mum was _____, she took part in windsurfing events herself.
3 Jackie learnt to swim when she was about _____.
4 Although Jackie is _____ younger, she has always admired Rachel.
5 Jackie and Rachel both became members of a _____ when they were young.
6 Jackie's mum encouraged her when she took up _____.
7 In Jackie's first windsurfing competition, she finished in _____ place.
8 Jackie thinks that she is very much like her _____.

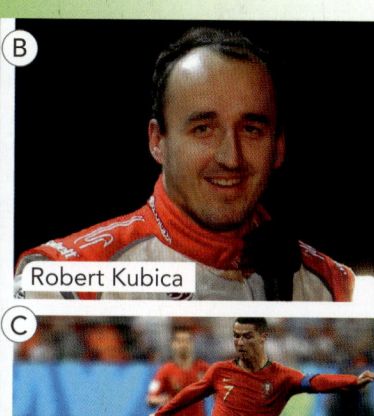

WORD STORE 2D   Phrasal verbs

7 🔊 1.25 Complete WORD STORE 2D with the phrasal verbs in the box. Then listen, check and repeat.

8 **SPEAKING** Complete the questions with the particles in WORD STORE 2D and then discuss them with a partner.

1 In terms of sporting ability, do you take _____ your mother or your father?
2 Has anybody ever talked you _____ taking up a sport or joining a team?
3 What new sport or leisure activity would you like to try _____?
4 Which sports person do you look _____ to?
5 Do you find it easy to pick _____ the rules to a new game or sport?
6 Have you ever given _____ in a race and just stopped?
7 Think of a sport you don't like. What puts you _____ it?

PRONUNCIATION FOCUS

9 🔊 1.26 Listen and repeat the words in the table.

Sound	Examples
1 /iː/	team _____ _____
2 /ɜː/	serve _____ _____
3 /ɔː/	sport _____ _____
4 /uː/	shoe _____ _____
5 /ɑː/	start arm _____

10 🔊 1.27 Add the words in the box to the table in Exercise 9. Then listen, check and repeat.

~~arm~~   court   draw   first   grew   heart   loose
ski   speed   world

2.4 READING

Gapped text

I can identify key information in an extended article.

1 **SPEAKING** Complete UK TODAY with the words in the box. Then discuss the questions.

> champions   district   grass   matches
> ~~tournament~~   white

1 What other tennis tournaments do you know?
2 How many tennis players can you name in 60 seconds?
3 What are the rules of tennis – how do you score?

2 Match the sportspeople with the rituals.
1 Sidney Crosby (Canada, ice hockey)
2 Stephanie Rice (Australia, swimming)
3 Cristiano Ronaldo (Portugal, football)
4 Laura Kenny (UK, cycling)
5 Rafael Nadal (Spain, tennis)

a always waits near the net to let the opponent reach his/her chair first.
b steps on a wet towel while wearing clean socks before a race.
c swings his/her arms eight times, splashes his/her body with water four times and then presses his/her goggles into his/her face four times.
d steps onto the pitch with his/her right foot first.
e has used the same stick for years.

3 Read the note about Rafael Nadal and then read an extract from his autobiography. Answer the questions.
1 What are the five steps in Nadal's final preparations for the match?
2 Which Wimbledon rule upsets Nadal's rituals?
3 How often does Nadal drink from his water bottle?
4 How important are his family to Nadal at a tournament like Wimbledon?
5 Why doesn't Nadal smile during the match?

EXAM FOCUS   Gapped text

4 Read the text again. Complete gaps 1–3 with sentences A–E. There are two extra sentences.

A We shook hands, exchanged the faintest of smiles, and then each pretended the other wasn't there.
B Some call it superstition, but it's not. If it were superstition, why would I keep doing the same thing over whether I win or lose?
C It's another manoeuvre that requires no thought, but I do it slowly, carefully, tying it tightly and very deliberately behind the back of my head.
D At one o'clock, with an hour to go before the start of play, we went back down to the locker room.
E It's part of Wimbledon protocol on Final Day. It doesn't happen anywhere else.

UK TODAY

- Wimbledon is the world's oldest tennis [1] tournament, established in 1877.
- Wimbledon is a [2] _____ in southwest London.
- It is the only Grand Slam played on [3] _____ .
- Players must wear mostly [4] _____ clothes.
- There are 674 [5] _____ over the two weeks.
- [6] _____ receive a ¾ size replica trophy.

5 🔊 1.29 Match the expressions in the box with the definitions. Use the phrases in blue in the text to help you. Then listen and repeat.

> the point of no return   repeat a sequence
> the first/last step   a decisive moment
> do the same thing over   give sb peace of mind
> ~~a break from your routine~~   the first/last phase

1 sth different from what you normally do = <u>a break from your routine</u>
2 an important point in time = _____
3 the first/last stage in a process = _____
4 the first/last action in a series of actions = _____
5 make sb feel calm = _____
6 the moment when you can no longer change anything = _____
7 repeat one action = _____
8 do a series of actions again = _____

6 **SPEAKING** Choose three expressions in Exercise 5 and write your own sentences. Discuss how important rituals and routines are in your life.

WORD STORE 2E   Word families

7 🔊 1.30 Complete WORD STORE 2E with the correct form of the underlined words in the text. Mark the stress in the new words. Then listen, check and repeat.

8 Complete the sentences with the correct form of the words in WORD STORE 2E. Which sentences are true for you? Compare with a partner.
1 I'm not a _____ person. (superstition)
2 I find it difficult to show _____ when people criticise me. (resilient)
3 I know swimming is good for me, but I find it boring and _____ . (repeat)
4 I'm sure that leaving school will be a _____ moment in my life. (decide)
5 I don't lead a very _____ life. I'm quite lazy and don't like sports. (action)

A: *I'm definitely not a superstitious person. What about you?*
B: *Oh, I'm very superstitious – everybody in my family is.*

From RAFA MY STORY

🔊 1.28

> **Rafael Nadal** was born in Spain in 1986. He began playing tennis at the age of three and turned professional at fifteen. Nadal has won seventeen Grand Slam titles including eleven French Opens and two Olympic gold medals. He beat Roger Federer in the longest final in Wimbledon history in 2008. He won Wimbledon again in 2010, and in 2011 he was named Laureus World Sportsman of the Year.

Chapter 1
The Silence of the Centre Court

Forty-five minutes before the game was scheduled to start I took a cold shower. Freezing cold water. I do this before every match. It's the point before the point of no return; the first step in the last phase of what I call my pre-game ritual.
⁵ Under the cold shower, I enter a new space in which I feel my power and resilience grow. I'm a different man when I emerge. I'm activated.

After Titin, my physical therapist, had bandaged my knee, I stood up, got dressed, went to a basin, and ran water
¹⁰ through my hair. Then I put on my bandanna. ¹_____ There's a practical point to it: keeping my hair from falling over my eyes. But it's also another moment in the ritual, another decisive moment, like the cold shower, when I am aware that very soon I'll be entering battle.

¹⁵ An official in a blazer walked in and told us it was time. Now I was supposed to hand over my bag to a court attendant for him to carry it to my chair. ²_____ I don't like it. It's a break from my routine. I handed over my bag but took out one racket. I led the way out of the locker room, along corridors
²⁰ with photographs of past champions and trophies behind glass frames, down some stairs and left and out into the cool English July air and the magical green of the Centre Court.

I sat down, took off my white tracksuit top, and took
²⁵ a sip from a bottle of water. Then from a second bottle. I repeat the sequence, every time, before a match begins, and at every break between games, until a match is over. A sip from one bottle, and then from another. And then I put the two bottles down at my feet, in front of my
³⁰ chair to my left, one neatly behind the other, diagonally aimed at the court. ³_____ It's a way of placing myself in a match, ordering my surroundings to match the order I seek in my head.

The last part of the ritual, as important as all the
³⁵ preparations that went before, was to look up and search for my family members among the blur of the Centre Court crowd. I don't let them intrude on my thoughts during a match – I don't ever let myself smile during a match – but knowing they are there, as they always have
⁴⁰ been, gives me the peace of mind on which my success as a player rests. I build a wall around myself when I play, but my family is the cement that holds the wall together.

23

GRAMMAR 2.5

Verb patterns

I can use a range of verb patterns.

1 What does a sports psychologist do? Read the text and find out.

THINK LIKE A WINNER

I'm a sports psychologist. I work with top athletes and I **help them to prepare** for important competitions. Of course, they **need to prepare** physically: they **should get** plenty of sleep, remember to drink lots of fluids and avoid drinking alcohol. That's the easy part! But after they've **spent time preparing** their body, I **make them relax** and prepare the mind. I focus on three areas: visualisation, positive thinking and relaxation.

2 Read the GRAMMAR FOCUS. Complete the examples with the phrases in blue in the text.

GRAMMAR FOCUS

Verb patterns

- **verb + to infinitive**
  Of course, they **need** ¹ _to prepare_ physically.
  Examples: aim, arrange, attempt, can't afford, decide, expect, hope, intend, manage, offer, plan, refuse, remember, seem, tend, try, want

- **verb + object + to infinitive**
  I **help them** ² _____ for important competitions.
  Examples: advise, allow, encourage, force, remind, teach, urge, warn (not)

- **verb + -ing**
  But after they've **spent time** ³ _____ their body, I …
  Examples: avoid, can't help, can't stand, don't mind, enjoy, fancy, finish, imagine, keep, miss, stop, waste time

- **modal verb + infinitive without *to***
  … they **should** ⁴ _____ plenty of sleep …
  Examples: can, could, might, should, would

- **verb + object + infinitive without *to***
  I **make them** ⁵ _____ and prepare the mind.
  Examples: make, let

3 🔊 1.31 Complete the text with the correct verb pattern using the words in brackets. Then listen and check.

Visualisation

Before an important event, I **advise** ¹ _athletes to visit_ (athletes/visit) the stadium. This **allows** ² _____ (them/visualise) the day of the competition. They **can** ³ _____ (imagine) the smells and the sounds in the stadium, and they **imagine** ⁴ _____ (win) the competition. Then, when the day of the competition arrives, they **try** ⁵ _____ (recreate) the success they imagined.

Positive thinking

I **encourage** ⁶ _____ (athletes/talk) to themselves before a big race. I **force** ⁷ _____ (them/concentrate) on the times when they won. They **need** ⁸ _____ (stay) in the present and tell the negative voice in their head to **stop** ⁹ _____ (talk). Good athletes **want** ¹⁰ _____ (win), but top athletes **expect** ¹¹ _____ (win). That's positive thinking!

Relaxation

Even top athletes **can't help** ¹² _____ (feel) nervous, especially when they find themselves standing next to last year's champion! I **let** ¹³ _____ (them/talk) to me about their worries, but on the day of the competition, negative thoughts are not allowed! It's a simple fact that if they **manage** ¹⁴ _____ (control) their nerves, they **tend** ¹⁵ _____ (do) better. Winning – it's all in the mind!

4 List some sports that you like watching or doing. In your opinion, which sports need more mental and which ones more physical preparation?

5 Write a second sentence so that it has a similar meaning to the first. Use the words in brackets. Which sentences are true for you?
  1 I'm happy to lend money to my friends. (don't mind)
    I don't mind lending money to my friends.
  2 I don't have enough money to buy new trainers. (can't afford)
  3 I would like to learn how to skate one day. (hope)
  4 My uncle showed me how to swim. (teach)
  5 I don't want to take up jogging. (not intend)
  6 My parents won't allow me to stay out all night with my friends. (let)

6 Complete the sentences to make them true for you. Write four true sentences and one false one.
  1 I can't stand …
    I can't stand watching sport on TV.
  2 I enjoyed …
  3 I wasted a lot of time …
  4 I spend a lot of time …
  5 I've refused …

7 **SPEAKING** Read your sentences. Guess which of your partner's sentences is false.

Grammar page 136

2.6 USE OF ENGLISH

so, too, neither/nor, not either

I can respond to news and opinion using so, too, not … either **and** neither … nor.

A Marathon
B Hockey
C Football
D Motor racing
E Tennis

1 🔊 1.32 Listen to dialogues 1–5 about sports and match them with photos A–E. Then answer the questions.
   1 What was the final score in the match?
   2 What are the players doing after the game?
   3 What do the man and woman find surprising about this sport?
   4 In which sports do women still get paid less than men?
   5 What do the two friends both decide to join?

2 🔊 1.32 Complete the exchanges with the correct auxiliary. Then listen again and check.
   1 We had so many chances. → So _____ they!
   2 I don't aim at your head. → Neither _____ I!
   3 I find this really boring. → Really? I _____ .
   4 I can't think of any women drivers. → I _____ either.
   5 I've never thought about it. → Nor _____ I.
   6 He's one of the best players in the country. → So _____ Steph Houghton.
   7 I couldn't do it. → No, neither _____ I.
   8 I'd love to be able to run properly. → I _____ too.

3 Read the LANGUAGE FOCUS. Then match statements 1–6 with replies a–f.

LANGUAGE FOCUS

so, too, neither/nor, not either

- To say that something is the same or agree with a positive statement, use the following:
  so + auxiliary/modal verb + subject or
  subject + auxiliary/modal verb + *too*.
  He is one of the best players in the country. → *So* is Steph Houghton./Steph Houghton is *too*.
  You serve so fast! → *So* do you./You do *too*.

- To say something is the same or agree with a negative statement, use the following:
  neither/nor + auxiliary/modal verb + subject or
  subject + auxiliary/modal verb + *either*.
  I can't think of any women drivers. → *Neither* can I./I can't *either*.
  We didn't score a single goal. → *Nor* did they./They didn't *either*.

- To say something is different, or disagree with a statement, use the following:
  I find this really boring. → *Really? I don't*.
  I never had the chance to do go-karting. → *Oh. I did*.

   1 Our neighbours do a lot of sport.   d
   2 My mum can't stand watching football on TV.   ☐
   3 I'd love to have a go in a Formula One car.   ☐
   4 I've played for the school team several times.   ☐
   5 My brother couldn't ride a bike until he was eight.   ☐
   6 My best friend is going to take up running.   ☐

   a So am I.   c So have I.   e Really? I wouldn't.
   b I couldn't either. d Ours do too.   f Nor can mine.

4 **SPEAKING** Take it in turns to read statements 1–6. Give your own replies.

5 **USE OF ENGLISH** Choose the correct response, A, B or C.
   1 X: I must do more exercise.   Y: _____
      A Yes, I must too.   B So do I.
      C Really? I don't.
   2 X: I've never been to a football match.
      Y: _____
      A Nor do I.   B Neither have I.
      C I didn't either.
   3 X: My parents are very sporty.   Y: _____
      A Really? Mine aren't.   B Mine aren't either.
      C Nor are mine.
   4 X: My local sports centre hasn't got a sauna.
      Y: _____
      A Mine hasn't either.   B Oh, mine hasn't.
      C Mine too.
   5 X: We went swimming yesterday.   Y: _____
      A Oh, we did.   B So we did.
      C So did we.

6 Complete the sentences to make them true for you.
   1 I'd like to …   4 I used to …
   2 I'm interested in …   5 I don't mind …
   3 I can't …   6 I should …

7 **SPEAKING** Take it in turns to listen to your partner's sentences and respond. How similar are you?

FOCUS VLOG About sport

▶ 8 Watch the Focus Vlog. For the worksheet, go to page 119.

Use of English page 137

25

2.7 WRITING

A story

I can write a story with a simple linear sequence.

1 SPEAKING Look at photos A–F and match them with the extreme sports in the box. Then discuss the questions.

bungee jumping ◯   mountain biking ◯   rafting ◯
rock climbing ◯   snowboarding ◯   water skiing ◯

1 What extreme sports have you tried?
2 What extreme sports would you like to try?
3 What extreme sports would you never like to try? Why?

2 Read the beginning of the story. What do you think went wrong?

There's a first time for everything!

I don't think many people have been in a situation like the one Lilly and I experienced last winter. We were learning to snowboard for the first time in the spectacular mountains of Austria. Of course, many things
5 can go wrong when you're new to an extreme sport, but what happened to us was very unusual. The old saying, 'there's a first time for everything' is definitely true based on our experience!

We**'d booked** lessons <u>before</u> we arrived, and **were both**
10 **feeling** quite nervous as we **took** the lift up the mountain with Max, our enthusiastic instructor. 'Don't worry' he said, 'you might fall over a bit, but you'll love it!' The first lesson was really challenging and we fell over A LOT! <u>By the end of</u> the first day, we were **completely**
15 **exhausted** but, as promised, we'd had a brilliant time and fallen totally in love with snowboarding.

The <u>following</u> day, Max was demonstrating how to turn. As our eyes followed him down the slope, he suddenly disappeared. **'Where did he go?'** I asked Lilly, as we
20 headed for where he'd disappeared. We discovered Max at the bottom of a big hole. 'I think it's broken' he said holding his left leg. We called for help on his radio and **twenty minutes later** the three of us were in a helicopter heading for the medical centre.

25 I'm pretty sure we enjoyed the helicopter ride more than poor Max! The doctor confirmed that he had broken his leg. She said it was the first time she'd ever seen learners bring their instructor in for treatment.

3 Read the story and put the events a–g in chronological order (1–7).

a They arrived in Austria ◯
b They rode in a helicopter ◯
c They radioed for help ◯
d They booked lessons ◯
e Max fell down a hole ◯
f They had their first lesson ◯
g They met Max ◯

4 SPEAKING Discuss your own experiences of trying out a sport for the first time.

5 Read the advice for writing a story and complete the examples in the WRITING FOCUS with the words in purple from the story.

WRITING FOCUS

A story

- **Beginning your story**
  - Use an opening sentence and interesting title that makes the reader want to read on.
  - Set the scene for the story so the reader can imagine what might happen next.
  - Finish the beginning section with a problem, or at a point which is exciting or interesting.

- **Telling your story**
  - Use a range of different narrative tenses to tell the story.
    Use the **Past Continuous** to set the scene.
    We ¹ <u>were both feeling</u> quite nervous.
    Use the **Past Simple** to describe the main events.
    We ² _____ the lift up the mountain.
    Use the **Past Perfect** to make it clear that one past action happened before another past action.
    We ³ _____ lessons before we arrived.
  - Use adverbs and strong adjectives to make the story exciting.
    By the end of the first day, we were
    ⁴ _____.
  - Use sequencers so the reader can follow the story.
    ⁵ _____ the three of us were in a helicopter …
  - Use one or two short sentences for dramatic effect.
    We discovered Max at the bottom of a big hole.
  - Use some direct speech to make the story come alive.
    ⁶ '_____', I asked Lilly.

- **Ending your story**
  - Think of an exciting, funny or unexpected ending to the story to help the reader remember it.

6 Find and underline more examples of the narrative tenses from the WRITING FOCUS in the story.

7 Complete the story with the correct narrative form of the verbs in brackets.

'3-2-1 bungee'!
I wanted to jump, but my legs wouldn't move.

I ¹_____ (visit) New Zealand when I ²_____ (decide) to try bungee jumping. I ³_____ (never do) it before, but felt quietly confident as I watched from the ground. An hour later though, as I stood on the edge of the bridge looking down, I ⁴_____ (realise) that all that confidence ⁵_____ (disappear). 'Come on Dan! You can do it!' shouted the other jumpers. 'Three-two-one bungee'! … Nothing. 'I … I … I'll have to get down' I said. And so I did, though not quite as planned.
As I turned to climb off the platform, I ⁶_____ (stand) on a rope and lost my balance. My cry of horror ⁷_____ (become) a scream of pure joy as I fell towards the ground. That ⁸_____ (be) the day I fell in love with bungee jumping.

8 Complete the LANGUAGE FOCUS with the underlined examples in the story in Exercise 2.

LANGUAGE FOCUS
Linkers to describe events in a sequence
- **Beginning:** ¹_before_ we arrived/left/got there, (at) first, on the first morning/day
- **Middle:** then, later, the ²_____ morning/evening, after that/three days, on the third/fourth day
- **End:** eventually (meaning after a long time), finally, in the end
- **Other:** ³_____ the first day/lesson/journey/holiday

9 Choose the correct option.

The longest weekend of my life
Some weekends are special for the wrong reasons. Last weekend was one of them. ¹*After / Then* very little training, my best friend and I attempted our first 100km walking race. ²*Finally / On the first morning* we fell out because he'd forgotten to pack the map. Luckily, we were able to borrow somebody's extra one. ³*After six hours / At first* we reached the first rest stop. We'd fought most of the way about which was the fastest way to go. ⁴*Finally / By the end of the first day* we'd walked forty-three kilometres and were not really speaking to each other anymore. ⁵*The following morning / The day before*, we started walking again at 5 a.m. and I can honestly say I've never heard so much complaining in all my life! ⁶*Eventually / Before*, we reached the finishing line after thirty-two hours of walking and an entire weekend of arguing. We haven't seen or spoken to each other since.

SHOW WHAT YOU'VE LEARNT

10 Do the writing task. Use the ideas in the WRITING FOCUS and the LANGUAGE FOCUS to help you.

Write a story about trying a new sport or activity for the first time and:
- use the first sentence and title to catch the reader's attention.
- set the scene and mention the characters involved in the story.
- use a range of narrative tenses to tell the story.
- finish the story with something exciting, funny or unexpected.

2.8 SPEAKING

Asking for and giving an opinion
• agreeing and disagreeing

I can ask for, give, agree with and disagree with an opinion.

SPEAKING FOCUS

Asking for someone's opinion
What do you think about …?

Giving an opinion
I think …/I (just) don't think …/If you ask me …/The thing is …/To be honest …

Agreeing with an opinion
I agree./That's true./Absolutely!

Half agreeing with an opinion
I'm not so sure about that./I'm not convinced.

Disagreeing
That's not true./I'm sorry, I don't agree with you.

Disagreeing strongly
No way! (informal)/Are you kidding? (informal)
I'm afraid I completely disagree.

Note:
If you have no strong opinions, you can say:
Personally, I don't feel strongly one way or the other.

---

1 Look at the jobs in the box and number them from most (5) to least (1) important for society.

an actor ☐   a farmer ☐   a football player ☐   a nurse ☐
a pilot ☐   a police officer ☐   a scientist ☐   a surgeon ☐

2 🔊 1.33 Read and listen to a conversation between a brother and sister and answer the questions.

1 What do they disagree about?
2 Who does their father agree with?
3 Who do you agree with?

3 🔊 1.33 Use the SPEAKING FOCUS to complete the phrases in the conversation. Then listen again and check.

Tom: Goal! Messi's just scored a fantastic goal! He's definitely the best footballer in the world!
Jan: Hm, I'm not ¹_____ about that.
Tom: What do you know about football?
Jan: I know that some football players get millions of euros a month! If ²_____ , they earn too much.
Tom: That's ³_____ . Only a few players earn that much and they deserve it.
Jan: No way! Football players don't save lives! Football's just a game!
Tom: Are ⁴_____ ? It's the most popular game in the world.
Jan: That's true but they don't do anything important. They just kick a ball!
Tom: The ⁵_____ , football players can only play when they're young so they have to earn a lot in a short time.
Jan: I'm ⁶_____ . I just don't think footballers are good role models.
Tom: I'm sorry, ⁷_____ – they're great role models. They train really hard …
Dad: Hey, what's going on in here? Calm down you two.
Jan: He thinks it's OK to pay Messi two million euros a month! What ⁸_____ that?
Dad: That's ridiculous.
Jan: You see!
Dad: To ⁹_____ , I think he should get at least ten million!

4 🔊 1.34 Read the opinions below and choose the appropriate responses in a and b. Then listen and check.

1 I think female athletes should earn the same salary as male athletes.
  a *I agree. / No way!* All athletes should be paid equally.
  b *Absolutely. / I'm not convinced.* Male athletes attract more spectators.
2 If you ask me, running is the best sport in the world.
  a *I'm afraid I completely disagree. / That's true.* You can do it anywhere and any time.
  b *Absolutely. / That's not true.* Playing team sports is much better.
3 In my opinion, golf is for old people.
  a *I agree. / I'm not convinced.* It's too slow for young people.
  b *Are you kidding? / I agree.* My brother is twenty and he loves playing golf.
4 I think boxing should be banned. It's too dangerous.
  a *Absolutely. / No way!* I think it's great.
  b *I'm sorry, I don't agree with you. / That's true.* It's too violent.

5 SPEAKING Practise the dialogues in Exercise 4. Choose answer a or b according to your own opinion.

6 SPEAKING Discuss the topics below. Use the SPEAKING FOCUS to help you.
  • We should do more sport at school.
  • Animals should not be used in sport.

ROLE-PLAY   Asking for and giving an opinion

📹 9 Watch the video and practise. Then role-play your dialogue.

UNIT 2 — It's just a game — Word list

2.1 Vocabulary 🔊 4.9

athlete /ˈæθliːt/
athletics /æθˈletɪks/
athletics track /ˌæθletɪks træk/
badminton/squash/tennis court /ˈbædmɪntən/ˈskwɒʃ/ˈtenəs kɔːt/
basketball/handball/netball/volleyball court /ˈbɑːskətbɔːl/ˈhændbɔːl/ˈnetbɔːl/ˈvɒlibɔːl kɔːt/
beat/defeat an opponent/the champion /ˌbiːt/dɪˌfiːt ən əˈpəʊnənt/ðə ˈtʃæmpɪən/
boxing /ˈbɒksɪŋ/
boxing/sumo/wrestling ring /ˈbɒksɪŋ/ˈsuːməʊ/ˈreslɪŋ rɪŋ/
break a world record /ˌbreɪk ə ˌwɜːld ˈrekɔːd/
burn sth off /ˈbɜːn ˌsʌmθɪŋ ˈɒf/
challenge /ˈtʃæləndʒ/
cheer sb on /ˌtʃɪə ˌsʌmbədi ˈɒn/
coach /kəʊtʃ/
come first/second/last /ˌkʌm ˈfɜːst/ˈsekənd/ˈlɑːst/
compete /kəmˈpiːt/
competitive sport /kəmˌpetətɪv ˈspɔːt/
competitor /kəmˈpetɪtə/
cricket/football/hockey/rugby pitch /ˈkrɪkət/ˈfʊtbɔːl/ˈhɒki/ˈrʌɡbi pɪtʃ/
drop out of /ˌdrɒp ˈaʊt əv/
fan/supporter /fæn/səˈpɔːtə/
get into /ˌɡet ˈɪntuː/
go in for /ˌɡəʊ ˈɪn fə/
golf course /ˈɡɒlf kɔːs/
hockey /ˈhɒki/
individual/team sport /ˌɪndəvɪdʒuəl/ˌtiːm ˈspɔːt/
indoor/outdoor sport /ˈɪndɔː/ˌaʊtˈdɔː spɔːt/
judo /ˈdʒuːdəʊ/
keep fit/in shape /ˌkiːp ˈfɪt/ɪn ˈʃeɪp/
let sb down /ˌlet ˌsʌmbɒdi ˈdaʊn/
lose a match/a game /ˌluːz ə ˈmætʃ/ə ˈɡeɪm/
lose a point /ˌluːz ə ˈpɔɪnt/
match /mætʃ/
miss a goal /ˌmɪs ə ˈɡəʊl/
motor racing track /ˈməʊtə ˌreɪsɪŋ træk/
opponent /əˈpəʊnənt/
opposing team /əˌpəʊzɪŋ ˈtiːm/
player /ˈpleɪə/
red/yellow card /ˌred/ˌjeləʊ ˈkɑːd/
referee /ˌrefəˈriː/
rink /rɪŋk/
sailing /ˈseɪlɪŋ/
score a goal/points /ˌskɔːr ə ˈɡəʊl/ˈpɔɪnts/
skating /ˈskeɪtɪŋ/
spectator /spekˈteɪtə/
squash /skwɒʃ/
(table) tennis /ˈ(teɪbəl) ˌtenəs/
take on (a challenge) /ˌteɪk ˈɒn ə (ˈtʃæləndʒ)/
teammate /ˈtiːmmeɪt/
tournament /ˈtʊənəmənt/
trainer /ˈtreɪnə/
training /ˈtreɪnɪŋ/
volleyball /ˈvɒlibɔːl/
win a point /ˌwɪn ə ˈpɔɪnt/
win a game/match/prize /ˌwɪn ə ˈɡeɪm/ˈmætʃ/ˈpraɪz/
work out /ˌwɜːk ˈaʊt/
wrestling /ˈreslɪŋ/

2.2 Grammar 🔊 4.10

blow a whistle /ˌbləʊ ə ˈwɪsəl/
break your neck /ˌbreɪk jə ˈnek/
chase after /ˈtʃeɪs ˌɑːftə/
crash through /ˈkræʃ ˌθruː/
cycle race /ˈsaɪkəl reɪs/
dive for the ball /ˌdaɪv fə ðə ˈbɔːl/
FA cup /ˌef eɪ ˈkʌp/
final /ˈfaɪnəl/
get injured /ˌɡet ˈɪndʒəd/
goalkeeper /ˈɡəʊlˌkiːpə/
hurt yourself /ˈhɜːt jɔːˌself/
lead /liːd/
(long-distance) race /ˌ(lɒŋ ˈdɪstənts) reɪs/
marathon /ˈmærəθən/
overtake /ˌəʊvəˈteɪk/
position /pəˈzɪʃən/
rival /ˈraɪvəl/
runner /ˈrʌnə/
speed /spiːd/
speed up /ˌspiːd ˈʌp/
sports event /ˈspɔːts ɪˌvent/

2.3 Listening 🔊 4.11

be passionate about /bi ˈpæʃənət əˌbaʊt/
caring /ˈkeərɪŋ/
courageous /kəˈreɪdʒəs/
determined /dɪˈtɜːmənd/
enter a competition /ˌentər ə ˌkɒmpəˈtɪʃən/
generous /ˈdʒenərəs/
give (sth) up /ˌɡɪv (ˌsʌmθɪŋ) ˈʌp/
inspiration /ˌɪnspəˈreɪʃən/
inspiring /ɪnˈspaɪərɪŋ/
join a club /ˌdʒɔɪn ə ˈklʌb/
look up to /ˌlʊk ˈʌp tə/
modest /ˈmɒdəst/
pick up /ˌpɪk ˈʌp/
positive /ˈpɒzətɪv/
put sb off /ˌpʊt ˌsʌmbɒdi ˈɒf/
role model /ˈrəʊl ˌmɒdl/
row /rəʊ/
sailing club /ˈseɪlɪŋ klʌb/
take after /ˌteɪk ˈɑːftə/
talk sb into /ˌtɔːk ˌsʌmbɒdi ˈɪntə/
try out /ˌtraɪ ˈaʊt/

2.4 Reading 🔊 4.12

action /ˈækʃən/
activate /ˈæktɪveɪt/
active /ˈæktɪv/
bandage a knee /ˈbændɪdʒ ə niː/
bandanna /bænˈdænə/
bounce the ball /ˌbaʊns ðə ˈbɔːl/
break from your routine /ˌbreɪk frəm jə ruːˈtiːn/
decide /dɪˈsaɪd/
decision /dɪˈsɪʒən/
decisive /dɪˈsaɪsɪv/
decisive moment /dɪˌsaɪsɪv ˈməʊmənt/
do the same thing over /ˌduː ðə ˌseɪm ˌθɪŋ ˈəʊvə/
emerge /ɪˈmɜːdʒ/
fall over sth /ˌfɔːl ˈəʊvə ˌsʌmθɪŋ/
give sb peace of mind /ˌɡɪv ˌsʌmbɒdi ˌpiːs əv ˈmaɪnd/
goggles /ˈɡɒɡəlz/
gold medal /ˌɡəʊld ˈmedl/
hand over /ˌhænd ˈəʊvə/
intrude on /ɪnˈtruːd ɒn/
locker room /ˈlɒkə ruːm/
physical therapist /ˌfɪzɪkəl ˈθerəpəst/
power /ˈpaʊə/
powerful /ˈpaʊəfəl/
racket /ˈrækət/
repeat a sequence /rɪˌpiːt ə ˈsiːkwəns/
repetition /ˌrepɪˈtɪʃən/
repetitive /rɪˈpetɪtɪv/
resilience /rɪˈzɪliəns/
resilient /rɪˈzɪliənt/
splash your body with water /ˌsplæʃ jə ˌbɒdi wɪð ˈwɔːtə/
superstition /ˌsuːpəˈstɪʃən/
superstitious /ˌsuːpəˈstɪʃəs/
swimming /ˈswɪmɪŋ/
swing your arms /ˌswɪŋ jə(r) ˈɑːmz/
take a sip /ˌteɪk ə ˈsɪp/
the first/last phase /ðə ˌfɜːst/ˌlɑːst ˈfeɪz/
the first/last step /ðə ˌfɜːst/ˌlɑːst ˈstep/
the point of no return /ðə ˌpɔɪnt əv ˌnəʊ rɪˈtɜːn/
trophy /ˈtrəʊfi/
turn professional /ˌtɜːn prəˈfeʃənəl/

2.5 Grammar 🔊 4.13

jogging /ˈdʒɒɡɪŋ/
refuse /rɪˈfjuːz/
stadium /ˈsteɪdiəm/
urge /ɜːdʒ/

2.6 Use of English 🔊 4.14

(hockey) stick /ˈ(hɒki) stɪk/
motor racing /ˈməʊtə ˌreɪsɪŋ/
sauna /ˈsɔːnə/

2.7 Writing 🔊 4.15

cry of horror /ˌkraɪ əv ˈhɒrə/
extreme sport /ɪkˌstriːm ˈspɔːt/
mountain biking /ˈmaʊntən ˌbaɪkɪŋ/
rafting /ˈrɑːftɪŋ/
rock climbing /ˈrɒk ˌklaɪmɪŋ/
slope /sləʊp/
take the lift up the mountain /ˌteɪk ðə ˌlɪft ʌp ðə ˈmaʊntən/
walking race /ˈwɔːkɪŋ reɪs/
water skiing /ˈwɔːtə ˌskiːɪŋ/

2.8 Speaking 🔊 4.16

deserve sth /dɪˈzɜːv ˌsʌmθɪŋ/
do sport /ˌduː ˈspɔːt/
kick a ball /ˌkɪk ə ˈbɔːl/
ridiculous /rɪˈdɪkjələs/
violent /ˈvaɪələnt/

FOCUS REVIEW 2

VOCABULARY AND GRAMMAR

1 Choose the correct option.
1 The *opponent / referee* showed two red cards during the first half of the match.
2 I'm confident England can *win / beat* almost any team they play against this season.
3 Steven was sorry for *letting / dropping* the other players down when he missed the goal.
4 Julie was so fast that she *hit / broke* the world record by five seconds.
5 Giles is a popular *trainer / spectator* because he shows players how they can improve.
6 I've decided not to *come / go* in for the basketball team this year, but I'll still play for fun.

2 Complete the sentences with the correct form of the words in capitals.
1 In figure skating, constant _____ is the best way to learn difficult tricks. **REPEAT**
2 You can _____ your device by touching the screen and entering the password. **ACTIVE**
3 That runner has such a _____ start that he seems to take off like a racing car. **POWER**
4 You have to be _____ in a game like basketball because there is no time to stop and think. **DECIDE**
5 Athletes need to show _____ when they are recovering from injuries and defeat. **RESILIENT**
6 That player is so _____ that he won't go on the field without wearing his 'lucky' ring. **SUPERSTITION**

3 Write sentences from the prompts. Use the Past Simple, Past Continuous or Past Perfect.
1 The match / not / start / at 7 o'clock / because / it / snow.
2 Ann / get / lots of / money / when / she / win / the tennis competition?
3 John / buy / squash racket / even though / he / not / play / squash / before.
4 you / play / golf / when / you / hurt / yourself?
5 I / swim / calmly / when / suddenly / someone / jump / into the pool.
6 When / Juliet / get home / Henry / already / go to / the match.

4 Choose the correct option.
1 I don't think my parents will let me *go / to go* to the rugby match on my own.
2 The doctor has advised me *give up / to give up* professional sport if I don't want to get injured seriously.
3 Tim tends *getting tired / to get tired* easily, so he has to be very active to keep in shape.
4 You really should stop *wasting / to waste* your time at table tennis practice.
5 Everyone at the stadium expected their team *winning / to win* the match.
6 I can't help *laughing / to laugh* when I see that video of me trying to learn to ski.

USE OF ENGLISH

5 Choose the correct answer, A, B or C, to complete both sentences in each pair.
1 Sarah and Lena _____ after their mother – they look the same and have similar personalities too.
James is always ready to _____ on a challenge. Now he is training to climb Mt Everest.
A go B take C come
2 Marcus was thrilled to get _____ the school swimming team after doing the trials three times.
We tried to talk my dad _____ coaching the rugby team, but he just didn't have time.
A about B out of C into
3 If you're tired of karate, maybe you should try _____ kickboxing. It's a lot of fun!
After hurting his knee, Brad dropped _____ of the long jump competition.
A out B off C on
4 I look _____ to famous athletes who help young people.
Darren picked _____ basketball while playing with his older brothers.
A around B out C up
5 Maria was excited to score the final _____ of the match.
It looked like a perfect shot, but he missed the _____ by centimetres.
A goal B mark C point
6 Learning about the risk of head injuries put Todd _____ American football completely.
Going to the gym is good, but you can burn _____ even more calories in a dance class.
A out B off C up

6 Choose the word or phrase, A, B or C, that has a similar meaning to the underlined words in each sentence.
1 In the end, <u>Joanna didn't join the team, and Kim didn't either</u>.
A either Joanna or Kim joined the team
B neither Joanna nor Kim joined the team
C Joanna joined the team but Kim didn't
2 <u>If you ask me</u>, golf is a very boring sport.
A I agree that B I'm sorry but C I think that
3 <u>The athletes completed the 20-kilometre run and then</u> they got ready for the swimming race.
A After the athletes had completed the 20-kilometre run,
B Before completing the 20-kilometre run,
C While the athletes were completing the 20-kilometre run,
4 I enjoy playing baseball and <u>my sister enjoys it as well</u>.
A so does my sister B nor does my sister
C so my sister does
5 The local football team coach <u>tries not to talk</u> to the press after his team loses a match.
A stops talking B refuses to talk C avoids talking

LISTENING

7 🔊 **1.35** Listen to Jim and Beth's conversation and complete the sentences with a word or short phrase.
1 Beth is going _____ for running shoes.
2 She needs them for a competition _____ .
3 Jim trains _____ times a week.
4 Jim is sure Beth will start winning _____ soon.
5 Beth is taking part in the _____-metre race on Sunday.
6 Jim has a match in the morning, but he's free after _____ .
7 Beth's event starts at _____ o'clock.

READING

8 Read the article and choose from the sentences (A–E) the one which fits each gap. There are two extra sentences.

Olympic Opening Ceremonies

The Olympic Opening Ceremony is always a highlight of the games. Read on to find out how different countries have used the ceremony to promote their cultures.

The opening ceremony of the Sydney games in 2000 explored Australia's history from the earliest days of Aboriginal culture. **1**_____ The show celebrated the great Australian landscape, the cities and the diversity of the people.

In 2004 the Olympics returned to their birthplace, and Greece presented a stunning picture of its history and achievements. **2**_____ This vision symbolised Greece as a tiny country with far-reaching ideas that changed the world.

China's ceremony in 2008 definitely scored a goal. An awe-inspiring display by 15,000 performers was almost military in its exactness. **3**_____ For sheer size and precision, the Beijing ceremony seems impossible to beat.

Not surprisingly, the 2012 London ceremony was a total contrast. It replaced Chinese precision with British eccentricity and humour. Perhaps Queen Elizabeth II parachuting from a plane in the arms of James Bond seemed unrelated to the Olympic spirit, but it certainly made a statement about Britain!

A While there were several mistakes during the show, on the whole it was an amazing display.
B It is hard to imagine the training that had gone into keeping so many people in order.
C It painted a picture of the energetic, multicultural country Australia has become.
D Some Greek people thought hosting the Olympics was too expensive, but others saw big advantages.
E As the centrepiece of the ceremony, the stadium floor filled with water and a young boy in a small boat sailed across it.

SPEAKING

9 Do the task in pairs.

Student A

Your school wants to organise a Family Sport Day. Your class is responsible for preparing a competition in any sport you choose. Start the conversation with Student B to discuss what you have to do. Topics you should mention:
- Awards
- Age groups
- Judges
- Type of sport

Student B

You're Student A's classmate. Your school wants to organise a Family Sport Day. Your class is responsible for preparing a competition in any sport you choose. Student A starts the conversation to discuss what you have to do. Use some or all of the following sentences:
- So, tell me, what kind of sports competition should we organise?
- I'm not sure it's a good idea.
- I think we need to organise the competition for different age groups.
- What exactly do you mean by (a small prize)?

WRITING

10 Read this announcement in an international magazine for schools and write a short story in reply.

Holiday surprises

We are looking for stories about surprises that you've had on holiday. Write a story that begins with this sentence:

I woke up feeling sad because it was the last day of my holiday.

Mention in your story:
- the beach
- a competition.

3

On the go

The world is a book and those who do not travel read only one page.

St Augustine

BBC

A HOTEL IN THE CLOUDS

▶ 10 Watch the BBC video.
For the worksheet, go to page 120.

VOCABULARY

3.1

Means of transport • noun phrases
• collocations • synonyms for *trip*

I can talk about travelling and means of transport.

SHOW WHAT YOU KNOW

1 List as many different means of transport as you can think of.

on land	on water	in the air
train		

2 **SPEAKING** Talk about the last time you travelled by these means of transport.

   A: *When was the last time you travelled by train?*
   B: *About three months ago. I went to …*

EXTREME JOURNEYS TO SCHOOL
TRAVEL PODCAST

For some students, the journey to school is just a stroll around the corner or a short drive and the biggest problems they face are <u>getting stuck</u> in <u>traffic jams</u> during <u>rush hour</u> or <u>public transport</u> delays. For others, getting to school involves crossing deserts, rivers or dangerous urban neighbourhoods. They have to travel long distances on foot, or by boat, bicycle, rickshaw or sledge.

Next time you <u>miss the school bus</u> and feel like complaining about your journey to school, think about these schoolchildren who don't have access to buses or even roads.

Click here to listen to this report by our travel journalist Brian Walker.

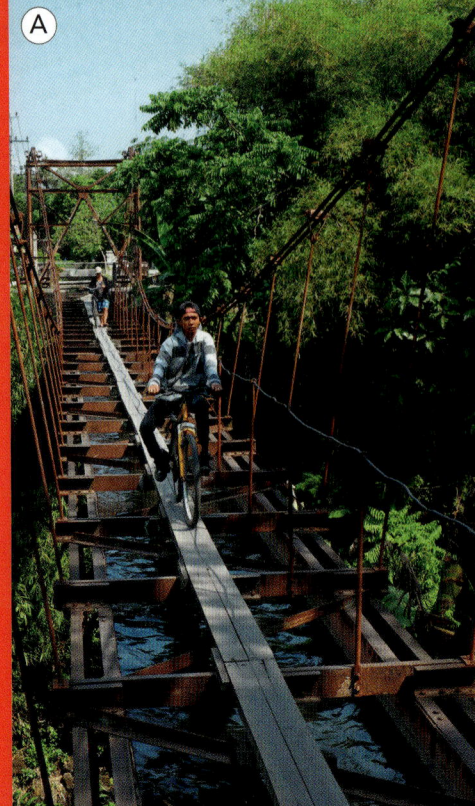

A

B

C

3 Read the introduction to *Extreme journeys to school* and match students' comments 1–6 with photos A–F.
1 'I cross a fast-flowing river on a wire …'
2 'I take a short cut by cycling across a valley …'
3 'I cross a valley on a homemade cable car …'
4 'I walk or run barefoot to school along a dirt track …'
5 'I ride a donkey along narrow winding paths …'
6 'I barely have time to fasten my seatbelt …'

4 🔊 1.36 Listen to the report. Then complete comments 1–6 in Exercise 3 with reasons a–f.
a '… because my school is so remote.'
b '… because the suspension bridge collapsed.'
c '… because it's such a short flight.'
d '… because I don't want to cycle uphill.'
e '… because I can't catch a bus as there aren't any.'
f '… because it's so deep.'

5 **SPEAKING** Compare your own journey to school with the ones in the report. How do you get to school and what route do you usually take?

Go to WORD STORE 3 page 7

WORD STORE 3A Noun phrases

6 🔊 1.37 Complete WORD STORE 3A with the words in red in the text and Exercises 3 and 4. Then listen, check and repeat.

7 Complete the sentences to make them true for your city or country. Use the phrases in WORD STORE 3A and your own ideas.
1 Morning _____ hour in my city is from … to …
2 There is a _____ bridge in my country in …
3 The cheapest form of _____ transport is …
4 The worst road or street for _____ jams is …
5 A _____ cut from my house to the school is …
6 The nearest _____ car to here is …

WORD STORE 3B Collocations

8 🔊 1.38 Complete WORD STORE 3B with the underlined words in the text and Exercises 3 and 4. Then listen, check and repeat.

9 Write true sentences with *I've/I've never* + an appropriate verb from WORD STORE 3B.
1 _____ a river in a small boat.
2 _____ stuck in a traffic jam.
3 _____ the wrong train.
4 _____ the bus.
5 _____ barefoot in a park.
6 _____ downhill at over fifty kilometres per hour.

10 **SPEAKING** Choose one of the experiences you have had and tell your partner about it.

I've missed the school bus. It was a couple of months ago. I was …

WORD STORE 3C Synonyms for *trip*

11 🔊 1.39 Complete WORD STORE 3C with the words in the box. Then listen, check and repeat.

12 Complete the blog entry with the words in WORD STORE 3C.

Travels in America blog

We arrived in Seattle on an overnight ¹f_____ from London and picked up a car at the airport. The car hire was just a short bus ²r_____ from the terminal, and we were on the road just one hour after landing. We were excited about the ³d_____ along the West Coast to San Francisco. The ⁴j_____ took around twelve hours. Once we got to San Francisco, we went on a ⁵t_____ of the city by cable car. That was my favourite thing about this trip, although the ⁶c_____ around San Francisco Bay was amazing too – we sailed around the Bay for three hours and visited Fisherman's Wharf and its sea lion colony. On another day we went to Alcatraz island. It's just a short ⁷c_____ by boat from the mainland.

13 **SPEAKING** Choose five words from WORD STORE 3C and write a question with each word. Then ask your partner.

What's the longest flight you've ever taken?
When did you last go on a bike ride?

GRAMMAR

3.2
Present and past speculation

I can use modal verbs to speculate about the present and the past.

1 Look at the pictures and complete the sentences.
1 Picture ___ **must be** a lion because of the long hair around the head and neck.
2 Picture ___ **might be** a puma or it **could be** a cheetah.
3 Picture ___ **can't be** a tiger because the head is too small.

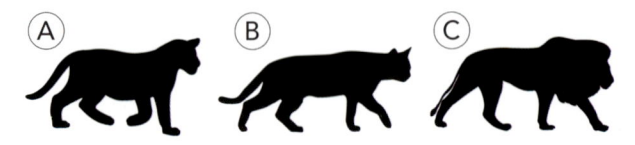

A B C

2 Look at the sentences you have completed in Exercise 1. Which sentence means:
a I'm sure it is … ☐
b I'm sure it isn't … ☐
c I think it's possible that it is … ☐

3 Read the short newspaper article. Are statements 1–3 true (T) or false (F)?
1 The man is sure he saw a lion. ☐
2 The woman is sure she heard a lion. ☐
3 The police are sure a lion escaped from a zoo. ☐

LION ON THE LOOSE IN ESSEX?

On Sunday evening at 8 p.m. a holidaymaker was walking to his caravan with his eleven-year-old son when he believed he saw a lion. He told reporters, 'It was dark, but I could see a large animal. It **can't have been** a domestic animal – it was too big. I thought it **might have been** a lion. So we ran, very quickly!' The seaside resort was full of holidaymakers and at least ten people saw the animal. One woman said 'I heard a loud roar at 10 p.m. It **must have been** a lion. No other animal can roar like that.' Police have told everybody to stay inside as they believe a lion may have escaped from a nearby zoo.

4 Read the GRAMMAR FOCUS and complete the examples with the verb forms in blue in the article.

GRAMMAR FOCUS
Present and past speculation

You can use modal verb structures to speculate about things.
- You use **must** when you are sure something is or was true.
  Present: It **must be** a lion. Past: It ¹_____ a lion.
- You use **might**, **may** or **could** when you think it's possible something is or was true.
  Present: It **might be** a lion. Past: It ²_____ a lion.
- You use **can't** (or **couldn't**) when you are sure something isn't or wasn't true.
  Present: It **can't be** a domestic animal.
  Past: It ³_____ a domestic animal.

Modal verb forms for speculation
Present: **must/might/may/could/can't** + infinitive
Past: **must/might/may/could/can't** + **have** + past participle

5 🔊 1.40 Rewrite the sentences using the words in brackets. Then listen to the interviews about the incident and check your sentences.
1 I'm sure it's a lion. (must)
  It must be a lion.
2 It's possible it escaped from the zoo. (might)
3 Perhaps it is very hungry by now. (could)
4 It's possible it was somebody's pet. (could)
5 Perhaps it grew too big. (may)
6 I'm sure it isn't a lion. (can't)

6 🔊 1.41 What do you think really happened? Listen to the news report and check your ideas. What did the police conclude?

7 Complete the sentences with an appropriate modal structure and the verb in brackets.
1 Dave <u>can't have left yet</u>, his coat is still here. (not yet leave)
2 The traffic's really bad, I'm worried we _____ our train. (miss)
3 They're not at home. They _____ away for the weekend. (go)
4 I can't find Jo. She _____ home. (go)
5 The plane landed over an hour ago. Bill _____ in baggage reclaim. (still be)
6 Buy a laptop? With my pocket money?! You _____ serious. (not be)

8 Choose a sentence below and write a dialogue including the sentence. Then act out your dialogue to the class.
1 I must have left it in the shop.
2 You might have hurt yourself!
3 You must be joking!
4 I can't have left it/them at home.
5 There must be some mistake.

A: *Oh no!*
B: *What's wrong?*
A: *I can't find my wallet. I must have left it in the shop.*
B: *Oh dear. Never mind. Let's go back and look for it.*

Grammar page 138

3.3 LISTENING

Multiple choice

I can identify key details in an informal conversation on a familiar topic.

1 **SPEAKING** Look at the photos and discuss which type of holiday you would like best or least. Give reasons for your answers.

I think I would like a skiing holiday best. I love winter sports but I haven't been skiing for two years.

2 🔊 1.42 Listen to six recordings about holidays and match them with the photos in Exercise 1. Which recording does not have a photo?

A ☐ B ☐ C ☐ D ☐ E ☐

EXAM FOCUS Multiple choice

3 🔊 1.42 Listen to the recordings again. For questions 1–6, choose the correct answer, A, B or C.
  1 The speaker thinks her sister is
    A selfish. B stupid. C boring.
  2 The man wants to spend the night
    A in a youth hostel. B in a three-star hotel. C in a tent.
  3 Mr Baker
    A has to pay for one breakfast.
    B has to pay for two breakfasts.
    C has already paid for two breakfasts.
  4 Skiers in Megève
    A couldn't ski last week because of the rain.
    B have nothing to do in Megève when they can't ski.
    C have good skiing conditions in Megève now.
  5 The advert is for
    A a beach holiday. B a travel company.
    C a job of tour leader.
  6 The mother
    A doesn't want her daughter to go away.
    B is worried about the dangers of travelling alone.
    C wants her daughter to go to Canada only.

WORD STORE 3D Compound nouns

4 🔊 1.43 Complete WORD STORE 3D with the nouns in the box. Then listen, check and repeat.

5 Complete the questions with appropriate compound nouns in WORD STORE 3D. Sometimes more than one answer is possible.

Have you ever …
  1 been snowboarding at a well-known _____ ?
  2 stayed in a _____ in a foreign country?
  3 been on a _____ with your friends?
  4 booked a _____ in a hotel?
  5 dreamt of going on a _____ ?
  6 thought about working for a _____ ?

6 **SPEAKING** Ask and answer the questions in Exercise 5. Give as much detail as possible.
  A: *Have you ever been snowboarding at a well-known ski resort?*
  B: *Yes, I have. My parents and I went to the French Alps.*
  A: *When was that?*
  B: *About …*

PRONUNCIATION FOCUS

7 🔊 1.44 Listen and repeat the names of places in the box. Mark the stress.

> ~~the Andes~~ the Canaries ~~Cyprus~~ the Danube
> Hawaii the Himalayas Naples the Nile
> the Pyrenees ~~the Thames~~ Vienna ~~Warsaw~~

8 🔊 1.45 List the places in the correct column. Then listen, check and repeat.

Cities	Islands	Rivers	Mountain ranges
Warsaw	_____	_____	_____
_____	Cyprus	_____	the Andes
_____	_____	the Thames	_____

9 Where in the world are the places in Exercise 8? Compare your answers with a partner.

READING

3.4 Multiple choice

I can identify the key information in an extended article.

1 **SPEAKING** Imagine you are going on a journey alone to a distant location. Discuss whether the following are advantages or disadvantages of travelling with a smartphone.
   - You don't need to carry flight/train/bus tickets.
   - You can text your parents as soon as you land at your destination.
   - You'll never get lost – you've got a map on your phone and GPS.
   - You can post selfies on social media and make everyone jealous.
   - You can show photos of your family and home to new friends.
   - You can stay in touch with new friends on social media.
   - You can keep up-to-date with everything that's going on at home.

2 Below are some reasons for travelling. Can you think of any more? Add them to the list.
   - For a holiday
   - For a life-changing experience
   - To do voluntary work

3 Read the article. Which of the reasons for travelling in Exercise 2 are mentioned? Are any other reasons given?

EXAM FOCUS   Multiple choice

4 Read the article again. For questions 1–5, choose the correct answer, A, B, C or D.
   1 William Sutcliffe believes that
      A backpackers had worse travel experiences twenty years ago.
      B young people worry about their hostel being comfortable.
      C young people find it hard to leave their daily lives behind.
      D travel was much easier in a pre-digital world.
   2 Charlotte Johnstone
      A went on the same journey as William Sutcliffe.
      B found it hard to live in a foreign culture.
      C learnt new things about the world thanks to her smartphone.
      D experienced a different culture in spite of her smartphone.
   3 Charlotte Johnstone believes that
      A William Sutcliffe is wrong about the benefits of travel.
      B the way we travel has changed the world.
      C smartphones are an advantage in travel situations.
      D teenagers in remote places don't use social media.
   4 Charlotte Johnstone thinks that Millennials
      A are less independent than their parents' generation.
      B can be in touch with home and still enjoy experiences.
      C want to have different experiences from those of their parents.
      D have a hard time saving up for and planning a gap year trip.
   5 In the article
      A both writers disagree about the importance of travel.
      B William Sutcliffe is critical of Millennials.
      C Charlotte Johnson argues that smartphones haven't changed the way we travel.
      D both writers think that if you have Wi-Fi, you can't have a life-changing experience.

5 **SPEAKING** Think about the holidays and trips you go on. Discuss how they would be different without Wi-Fi. Would that be a problem for you?

WORD STORE 3E Negative adjectives

6 🔊 1.47 Complete WORD STORE 3E with the negative prefixes *dis-* or *un-*. Use the words in blue in the article to help you. Then listen, check and repeat.

7 Choose the correct option. Use WORD STORE 3E to help you. Where would you expect to hear or see these announcements?
   1 Passengers should make themselves *familiar / unfamiliar* with emergency procedures.
   2 Due to poor weather conditions, delays may be *avoidable / unavoidable*.
   3 The hotel would like to wish guests a *pleasant / unpleasant* stay.
   4 Guests' digital devices should be *connected / disconnected* during a thunderstorm.
   5 When driving abroad, you need to be *informed / uninformed* about the country's road laws.

8 🔊 1.48 Complete the verbs phrases with the words in the box. Use the underlined phrases in the article to help you. Then listen, check and repeat.

   challenge   cut yourself off from
   ~~immerse yourself in~~
   withdraw money from   take

   1 *immerse yourself in* a foreign culture
   2 _____ your beliefs
   3 _____ your family/home
   4 _____ a gap year
   5 _____ a cash point

9 **SPEAKING** Replace the underlined phrases with words or phrases with a similar meaning in Exercise 8. Which do you agree with? Discuss with a partner.
   1 If you never go abroad, you never think critically about our own opinions.
   2 It's impossible to stop communicating completely with home when you have unlimited access to the Internet.
   3 I don't like being a tourist. It's better if you live with local people and experience their lifestyle.
   4 Nobody gets money from a machine outside a bank or a shop these days. You just use your phone to pay for things.
   5 Travelling abroad for a year before going to university is a waste of time and money.

Can travel still broaden the minds of the smartphone generation?

No

Travel writer William Sutcliffe believes that smartphones have changed backpacking in a bad way.

I believe that travel ought to be a profound experience. By cutting us off from everything that has previously been **familiar** to us, travel challenges our beliefs and makes us see the world
5 in new ways. But when so many relationships and social support networks are carried out digitally, and with every backpacker hostel from Machu Picchu to Dharamsala offering Wi-Fi, it's actually impossible for Millennials* to cut themselves off
10 from home. What has this done to the nature of travel?

A modern traveller will probably be more concerned about whether their room has Wi-Fi than whether it has a bathroom. To be
15 **disconnected** is **unthinkable**. But this means that they have one foot firmly planted at home at all times. I don't think you can consider this way of travelling as a journey of self-discovery.

Yes

Charlotte Johnstone, a Millennial, argues that her smartphone did not get in the way of life-altering travel experiences.

I took my gap year a couple of years ago, and
20 I'm really glad I did, because it changed my life. The time I spent in India and Zambia were the hardest and most **rewarding** of my life. Despite the fact that I had my smartphone in my pocket, I really felt that I had immersed myself in a foreign
25 culture, and I learned a lot about myself and the world around me.

So I think Mr Sutcliffe is **uninformed** when he belittles the experience of today's travellers. Of course, the way we travel has changed; the
30 world around us has changed. It's **unavoidable**. There are lots of pluses: you can call home when something happens, book plane tickets on your phone, withdraw money from a cash point, even find hidden temples on Google Maps. And don't
35 think that teenagers in remote Sub-Saharan African villages don't have Facebook accounts – they do, and you can stay in touch long after you have left.

Staying connected doesn't detract from travelling
40 – independence doesn't necessarily have to be solitary and young people don't need to be cut off from home to explore the wider world and appreciate their place in it. Just as much as our parents' generation did, we Millennials want to
45 watch the sun rise, make friends with like-minded strangers as we dip our feet into the waters of a deserted beach after an **unpleasant** overnight journey on two different buses. The values and aspirations are the same.

50 We also have to address the same challenges. Saving up for, planning and executing a gap year trip is hard work. During the trip – even if you are only a text away from your friends at home – you still have to learn how to budget, problem-solve
55 and develop people skills in order to survive.

I've made a promise to myself: if I have children, I shall never tell them 'it's not like it was in my day'.

*Millennial – someone born between 1980 and 2000

GRAMMAR

3.5

Used to and *would*

I can talk about past states and repeated actions using used to *and* would.

1960s

Now

1 Are the statements about road travel in the 1960s true (T) or false (F)? Compare with a partner.

1 Roads **used to be** quieter.
2 People **used to talk** about traffic pollution.
3 Cars **didn't use to have** seat belts.
4 Children **would play** video games on long journeys.
5 GPS didn't exist so people **would follow** maps.

2 🔊 **1.49** Listen to Zoe's grandfather talking about road travel when he was young. Check your ideas in Exercise 1.

3 Read the GRAMMAR FOCUS and answer the questions.
   1 Which sentences in Exercise 1 describe past actions?
   2 Which sentences in Exercise 1 describe past states?

GRAMMAR FOCUS

Used to and would

- You can use **used to** + verb or **would** + verb to talk about regular past actions that don't happen any more.
  Harry **used to** *go to school by bus. He'd leave the house at 8 a.m.*

- You can use **used to** + verb (NOT ~~would + verb~~) to talk about past states that are no longer true. (Usually with stative verbs: *be, have, love,* etc.)
  Harry **used to** *be a good student.*

Note:
Don't use **used to** or **would** for single past actions.
In 1963 my granddad **bought** *his first car.* (NOT ~~used to buy~~ … or ~~would buy~~ …)

4 Rewrite the statements using *would*. If *would* is not possible, use *used to*.

1 Air travel <u>was</u> cheaper than now.
   Air travel used to be cheaper than now.
2 Air travel <u>was</u> more comfortable.
3 The flight from London to New York <u>took</u> longer.
4 People <u>smoked</u> on the plane.
5 People <u>wore</u> their best clothes to travel by air.
6 Airports <u>didn't have</u> so many security checks.

5 🔊 **1.50** Which of the sentences in Exercise 4 do you think are true? Compare with a partner. Then listen and check.

6 🔊 **1.51** Complete the text with the verbs in brackets.
- Use *would* + verb (where possible)
- Use *used to* + verb (where *would* is not possible)
- Use the Past Simple (where *would* or *used to* are not possible)

Then listen and check. Is the UK the only country where people drive on the left?

Left or right?

Today, 75% of cars drive on the right, but it ¹*didn't always use to be* (not always be) like that. In fact, everybody used to travel on the left! In Roman times, roads ² _____ (be) dangerous and travellers ³ _____ (carry) swords in their right hands. Travellers on horses ⁴ _____ (ride) on the left side of the road so that the right hand was free to use the sword. Then Napoleon ⁵ _____ (change) the rule. Why? Because he was a revolutionary! Before the French Revolution, the aristocracy ⁶ _____ (travel) on the left and poor people ⁷ _____ (stay) on the right. After the Revolution, the aristocracy joined the poor people on the right and driving on the right ⁸ _____ (become) the new law. What about the rest of the world? China, Portugal, Sweden and parts of Canada used to drive on the left and only changed the law during the mid-twentieth century. More than fifty countries including the UK, Australia, Japan and India still drive on the left today.

7 Write six sentences about your life when you were ten. Use *used to* or *would*. Use the suggestions in the box or your own ideas.

clothes you wore	sports you did
food you liked/didn't like	things you read
music you listened to	your bedroom

I didn't use to like mushrooms or green beans.

8 Compare your sentences in Exercise 7. Did you use to be similar or different?

FOCUS VLOG About holidays

▶ 13 Watch the Focus Vlog. For the worksheet, go to page 121.

Grammar page 139

3.6 USE OF ENGLISH

Phrasal verbs

I can understand and use separable and inseparable phrasal verbs.

1 🔊 1.52 Look at a photo of the Zapp family and listen to Jenny James talking about them. What do the numbers in the box refer to?

(2000 100 3 → 6 80 65)

2 🔊 1.52 **SPEAKING** Discuss the questions. Then listen again and check your ideas.
1 What did the couple **walk away from** to go travelling?
2 Where did they **set off** from?
3 Why did they decide to **carry on** travelling?
4 What do they do when they **run out of** money?
5 Who sometimes **put** them **up**?
6 Why did they **put** a tent **up** on the car roof?
7 What did the car seats **turn into**?
8 What happened when the car **broke down**?

3 **SPEAKING** Can you imagine your own family travelling around the world for seventeen years? Would it be a good experience for you and your siblings? Why?/Why not?

4 Read the LANGUAGE FOCUS and complete the examples using the phrasal verbs in bold in Exercise 2.

LANGUAGE FOCUS

Phrasal verbs – verb + particle(s)

When you are learning phrasal verbs you need to understand both the meaning and the grammar.

- Meaning
  Sometimes the meaning is literal –
  they ¹ __put__ a tent up (= construct or erect)
  Sometimes the meaning is idiomatic –
  local people ² _____ them up (= let sb stay)

- Grammar
  Some phrasal verbs are separable –
  they bring children up (= raise)
  Some phrasal verbs are inseparable – *the car seats*
  ³ _____ *into a bed* (= change)

- Separable phrasal verbs
  If the object is a noun, it can come before or after the particle:
  bring children *up* or *bring up* children
  If the object is a pronoun it can only come before the particle:
  bring them *up* but NOT ~~bring up them~~

The Zapp family

5 Match the phrasal verb dictionary entries in the box with definitions 1–7. How do dictionaries show whether phrasal verbs are separable or inseparable or don't take an object?

(drop sb off   hold sb up   keep up with sb
  head for sth   pick sb up   ~~pull over~~   turn up)

1 __pull over__ = stop in a car by the side of the road
2 _____ = take somebody in a car and leave them somewhere
3 _____ = go in the direction of somewhere
4 _____ = delay somebody
5 _____ = arrive at a place
6 _____ = collect somebody, usually in a car
7 _____ = go at the same speed as somebody

6 **USE OF ENGLISH** Choose one word, A, B or C to complete both sentences.
1 I'll drop you _____ at the next bus stop.
  Tell the driver where you want to get _____ .
  A over   **B** off   **C** in
2 This car has never broken _____ before.
  She walked _____ the steps into the sunshine.
  A up   **B** along   **C** down
3 When do you think they'll turn _____ ?
  Mum's picking me _____ at midday.
  A up   **B** into   **C** off
4 Can I try _____ your new motorbike?
  Oh, no! We've run _____ of petrol.
  A for   **B** on   **C** out
5 It's kind of them to put us _____ .
  I don't want to hold you _____ – I know you're in a hurry.
  A away   **B** up   **C** over

7 Write one false and two true sentences about yourself. Use a different phrasal verb in each sentence. Then read out your three sentences. Your partner guesses which one is false.

▶ Use of English page 140

3.7 WRITING

A personal email

I can write a personal email giving advice.

1 Match problems 1–3 to advice a–c.
   1 Should I go to university in my hometown, or in another city?
   2 I want to ask Katie on a date, but I'm too shy.
   3 Mum's worried about me camping overnight at the music festival.

   a If I were you I wouldn't ask her. She might say no.
   b Tell her there are six of us. We'll look after each other.
   c You should study at your local university and live with your parents.

2 **SPEAKING** Discuss how good the advice in Exercise 1 is. Think of an alternative solution for each problem.

3 Read Tim's message to his older brother Ben and answer the questions.
   1 Which problem from Exercise 1 does Tim describe?
   2 What advice would you give him?

4 Read Ben's reply. Did he mention any of the advice you thought of?

To: Tim
Subject: Re: How are you?

Hey little brother,

Having a great time back at uni. You should come and visit soon.

Congratulations on the offers – I'm really proud of you. ¹I understand what a difficult decision it is, but it's better than having no options! Can't believe you're going to uni already! Seems like five minutes ago we were playing Lego together!

²Have you thought about making a list of the pluses and minuses? E.g. if you study at home and live with Mum and Dad (plus or minus? ;-)), you won't have to do your own washing, cooking, etc. On the other hand, if you go to Edinburgh, you'll have to look after yourself, but you'll have your freedom. ³If I were you, I'd find out more about the courses as well.

⁴By the way, thanks for the mix – I played it at Scotty's party on Friday and everyone loved it. Great to have a DJ for a little brother :-)

I'm sure ⁵everything will be OK.

Hope to see you soon,

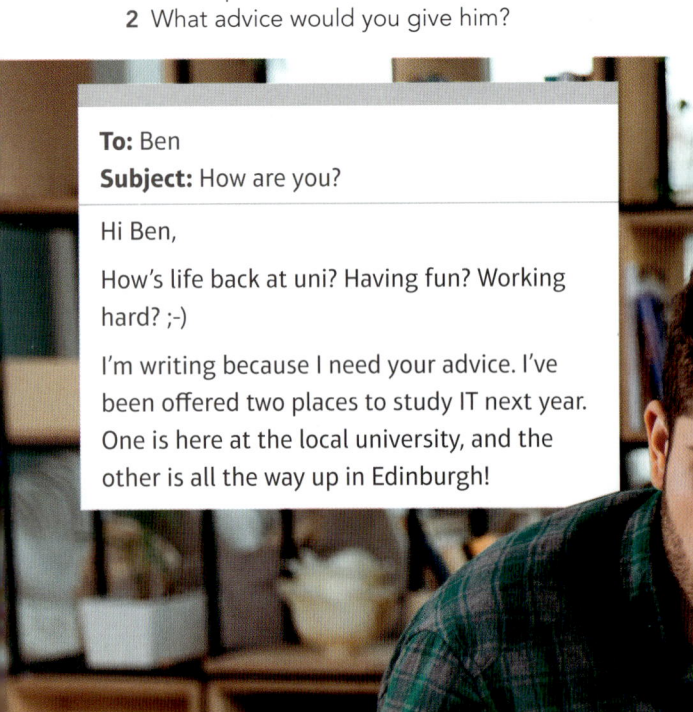

B.

To: Ben
Subject: How are you?

Hi Ben,

How's life back at uni? Having fun? Working hard? ;-)

I'm writing because I need your advice. I've been offered two places to study IT next year. One is here at the local university, and the other is all the way up in Edinburgh!

5 Match the phrases in purple in the email (1–5) with phrases that have a similar meaning (a–e).

   a Incidentally,
   b I can see why you are confused
   c things will work out fine
   d Why don't you make …
   e It's a good idea to …

6 Read the WRITING FOCUS and check your answers in Exercise 5.

WRITING FOCUS

A personal email giving advice

- Start with general news and/or a reference to what your friend wrote in their last email.
- Express sympathy for your friend's situation
  I understand what a difficult decision it is.
  I can see why you're worried/unhappy.
- Offer advice by asking a question
  Have you thought about … (making a list)?
  Why don't you … (talk to your friend)?
- Offer advice by making a statement
  If I were you, I'd … (find out more).
  It's a good idea to … (read about it online/ask a teacher you get on well with).
  (See also *Giving advice* SPEAKING FOCUS p. 42)
- Change the subject and say something positive or give more news
  By the way, thanks for …
  Incidentally, did you hear that …?
- Reassure your friend at the end of the email
  I'm sure everything will be OK.
  I'm sure things will work out fine.

7 Look at the underlined phrases in the email. What do you notice about them? Complete the LANGUAGE FOCUS with *It*, *It's*, *I* (x2) or *I'm*.

LANGUAGE FOCUS

Ellipsis

- In informal English, you can leave words out. This is called ellipsis. You usually leave out subject pronouns and auxiliary verbs at the beginning of a clause when the meaning is obvious:
  Having a great time … = ¹_____ having a great time …
  Can't believe you're going to uni … = ²_____ can't believe you're going to uni …
  Seems like five minutes ago … = ³_____ seems like five minutes ago …
  Great to have a DJ for a little brother. = ⁴_____ great to have a DJ for a little brother.
  Hope to see you soon. = ⁵_____ hope to see you soon.
- You can also leave out repeated words:
  Feeling a bit tired but I always am. = I'm feeling a bit tired but I'm always tired.

8 Make this email more informal by removing seven words or phrases.

To: Carla
Subject: How are you?

Hi Carla,

Thanks for your email! I felt really sick last week but I'm getting better now thanks. Mum was worried, but she always is worried. I finally finished my essay, so that's good. My tutor was pleased! I can't believe it's nearly summer. I'm looking forward to being on holiday.

I'll see you next weekend,

L xx

9 Read the message from a friend and mark the advice ✗ = bad idea, ✓ = it might work, ✓✓ = good idea. Compare your ideas with a partner.

> How r u? I'm :-(((Mum doesn't want me to go to the festival next weekend. Says she's worried about us camping overnight there. She said she could come with us to make sure we are safe!!!! LOL! What can I say or do to stop her worrying?

1 Forget about the festival. Your mum is right.
2 Just go for the day and come home in the evening.
3 Promise her you'll call before you go to bed and first thing in the morning.
4 Remind her that my big brother is coming. He'll look after us.
5 Ask your mum to come with us. It'll be fun.
6 Tell her you're staying at my house.

SHOW WHAT YOU'VE LEARNT

10 Do the writing task. Use the ideas in Exercise 9, the WRITING FOCUS and the LANGUAGE FOCUS to help you.

Reply to the message in Exercise 9. Write a personal email and:
- express sympathy for your friend's situation,
- offer some advice,
- change the subject and give some positive news,
- reassure your friend at the end of the email.

Just a quick email to answer your message.
_____
_____
_____
_____

3.8 SPEAKING

Asking for and giving advice

I can ask for, give and accept advice.

1. Imagine you are going to England to do an English course and you are going to stay with an English family for a month. Write a list of things you need to take with you. Compare your list with a partner.

   DON'T FORGET
   - tickets
   - passport
   - phone
   - phone charger
   - money …

2. 🔊 2.1 Listen to Markus asking Sophie for advice about what to take to England and answer the questions.
   1. Which of the things on your list do they mention?
   2. Why does Sophie want Markus to remember his phone charger?

3. 🔊 2.1 Listen again and tick the expressions in the SPEAKING FOCUS that you hear. Which three expressions on the list are not used in the dialogue?

SPEAKING FOCUS

Asking for advice
Can you do me a (big) favour? ✓
Can you give me some advice? ☐
Do you think I need …? ☐
What do you think I should …? ☐

Giving advice
The first thing you should do is … ☐
If I were you, I'd/I wouldn't … ☐
I think/don't think you should … ☐
You need/don't need to … ☐
You (really) ought to … ☐
You must/mustn't … ☐
The best thing would be to … ☐
It's a good idea to … ☐
Why don't you …? ☐

Accepting advice
Good idea! ☐
Good thinking! ☐
That's really helpful. ☐
Oh, I didn't think of that! ☐

4. Imagine a friend from England wants to visit your country during the winter. Complete the advice with one or two words from the SPEAKING FOCUS.
   1. The _____ you should do is book your flights.
   2. If I _____ , I'd pack lots of warm clothes.
   3. You _____ to bring a lot of formal clothes.
   4. I _____ you should bring lots of cash.
   5. You _____ remember to get some travel insurance.
   6. You _____ to make sure you have a warm winter coat.

5. **SPEAKING** Look at the photo and discuss the questions.
   1. Which form of transport do you prefer for long journeys?
   2. What's the longest journey you've ever made by car, train or bus?
   3. When did you last travel by bus?

6. **SPEAKING** Discuss which ideas below are good and which are bad for a very long bus journey. Give reasons. Then complete the table.

   a big coat   water   earphones for smartphone or iPod
   fizzy drinks   a good book   light, comfortable clothes
   a pillow   snacks   snow boots   sunglasses   tissues
   chocolate   very warm clothes

	Good idea	Bad idea
Things to wear		
Things to take		

7. **SPEAKING** Follow the instructions below to prepare a dialogue. Use the SPEAKING FOCUS to help you. Then act it out to the class.

   Student A: You're from England. You're going to travel to Student B's country by bus. You've never been on a long bus journey before. Ask Student B for advice about what to wear, what to take for the journey and what kind of presents to take for the family.

   Student B: Student A is visiting you from England. He/She is going to travel to your country by bus. Give him/her some advice about what to wear, what to take for the journey and what kind of presents to bring for your family.

   A: *Hi Marcel. Can you do me a big favour? I need your help.*
   B: *Yes, sure. What's the problem?*
   A: *Well, you know I'm travelling to your country by bus. I've never been on a long bus journey before and I'm not sure what to take. Can you …*

   ### ROLE-PLAY   Asking for and giving advice

   ▶ 14 Watch the video and practise. Then role-play your dialogue.

UNIT 3 — On the go — Word list

3.1 Vocabulary 🔊 4.17
airport /ˈeəpɔːt/
arrive /əˈraɪv/
bay /beɪ/
boat /bəʊt/
cable car /ˈkeɪbəl kɑː/
car hire /ˈkɑː haɪə/
catch a bus/a train /ˌkætʃ ə ˈbʌs/ə ˈtreɪn/
collapse /kəˈlæps/
cross a continent /ˌkrɒs ə ˈkɒntɪnənt/
cross a river/valley /ˌkrɒs ə ˈrɪvə/ˈvæli/
crossing /ˈkrɒsɪŋ/
cruise /kruːz/
cycle downhill/uphill /ˌsaɪkəl ˌdaʊnˈhɪl/ ˌʌpˈhɪl/
dirt track /ˈdɜːt træk/
donkey /ˈdɒŋki/
drive /draɪv/
fasten a seatbelt /ˌfɑːsən ə ˈsiːtbelt/
ferry /ˈferi/
flight /flaɪt/
for pleasure /ˌfə ˈpleʒə/
get a lift /ˌget ə ˈlɪft/
get stuck in traffic /ˌget ˌstʌk ɪn ˈtræfɪk/
have access to /ˌhæv ˈækses tə/
helicopter /ˈhelɪkɒptə/
journey /ˈdʒɜːni/
land /lænd/
miss a bus/a train /ˌmɪs ə ˈbʌs/ə ˈtreɪn/
neighbourhood /ˈneɪbəhʊd/
on foot /ˌɒn ˈfʊt/
plane /pleɪn/
public transport /ˌpʌblɪk ˈtrænspɔːt/
remote /rɪˈməʊt/
rickshaw /ˈrɪkʃɔː/
ride /raɪd/
route /ruːt/
rush hour /ˈrʌʃ aʊə/
sea lion /ˈsiː ˌlaɪən/
sail /seɪl/
school bus /ˈskuːl bʌs/
short cut /ˈʃɔːt kʌt/
sledge /sledʒ/
stroll /strəʊl/
suspension bridge /səˈspenʃən brɪdʒ/
terminal /ˈtɜːmənəl/
tour /tʊə/
traffic jam /ˈtræfɪk dʒæm/
train /treɪn/
travel by train /ˌtrævəl baɪ ˈtraɪn/
travel journalist /ˈtrævəl ˌdʒɜːnəlɪst/
urban /ˈɜːbən/
valley /ˈvæli/
voyage /ˈvɔɪɪdʒ/
walk barefoot /ˌwɔːk ˈbeəfʊt/
winding path /ˌwaɪndɪŋ ˈpɑːθ/

3.2 Grammar 🔊 4.18
baggage reclaim /ˈbæɡɪdʒ ˌrɪkleɪm/
cheetah /ˈtʃiːtə/
domestic animal /dəˌmestɪk ˈænəməl/
holidaymaker /ˈhɒlədeɪˌmeɪkə/
lion /ˈlaɪən/
on the loose /ˌɒn ðə ˈluːs/
pet /pet/
puma /ˈpjuːmə/
roar /rɔː/
tiger /ˈtaɪɡə/
zoo /zuː/

3.3 Listening 🔊 4.19
adventure /ədˈventʃə/
beach holiday /ˈbiːtʃ ˌhɒlədi/
budget/three-star hotel /ˌbʌdʒɪt/ˌθriː stɑː həʊˈtel/
bus journey /ˈbʌs ˌdʒɜːni/
business trip /ˈbɪznəs trɪp/
campsite /ˈkæmpsaɪt/
get off /ˌget ˈɒf/
go away /ˌɡəʊ əˈweɪ/
mountain /ˈmaʊntən/
overland tour /ˌəʊvəlænd ˈtʊə/
package holiday /ˈpækɪdʒ ˌhɒlɪdeɪ/
put up a tent /ˌpʊt ˌʌp ə ˈtent/
return journey /rɪˈtɜːn ˌdʒɜːni/
round-the-world trip /ˌraʊnd ðə ˌwɜːld ˈtrɪp/
seaside resort /ˌsiːsaɪd rɪˈzɔːt/
single/double/twin room /ˌsɪŋɡəl/ ˌdʌbəl/ˌtwɪn ˈruːm/
ski resort /ˈskiː rɪˌzɔːt/
skiing holiday /ˈskiːɪŋ ˌhɒlədi/
tour guide /ˈtʊə ɡaɪd/
tour leader /ˈtʊə ˌliːdə/
travel agent /ˈtrævəl ˌeɪdʒənt/
travel company /ˈtrævəl ˌkʌmpəni/
trekking /ˈtrekɪŋ/
youth hostel /ˈjuːθ ˌhɒstl/

3.4 Reading 🔊 4.20
appreciate /əˈpriːʃieɪt/
avoidable /əˈvɔɪdəbl/
backpacker /ˈbækˌpækə/
belittle /bɪˈlɪtl/
book plane tickets /ˌbʊk ˈpleɪn ˌtɪkɪts/
budget /ˈbʌdʒɪt/
challenge beliefs /ˌtʃæləndʒ bəˈliːfs/
connected /kəˈnektɪd/
cut yourself off from your family/home /ˌkʌt jɔːˌself ɒf frəm jə ˈfæməli/ˈhəʊm/
destination /ˌdestəˈneɪʃən/
detract from /dɪˈtrækt frəm/
dip /dɪp/
disconnected /ˌdɪskəˈnektɪd/
execute /ˈeksɪkjuːt/
familiar /fəˈmɪliə/
go backpacking /ˌɡəʊ ˈbækˌpækɪŋ/
GPS /ˌdʒiːˌpiː ˈes/
have one foot firmly planted at home /ˌhæv wʌn fʊt ˌfɜːmli ˌplɑːntɪd ət ˈhəʊm/
keep up-to-date with /ˌkiːp ˌʌp tə ˈdeɪt wɪð/
immerse yourself in a foreign culture /ɪˌmɜːs jɔːˌself ɪn ə ˌfɒrən ˈkʌltʃə/
informed /ɪnˈfɔːmd/
Millennial /mɪˈleniəl/
overnight journey /ˌəʊvənaɪt ˈdʒɜːni/
passenger /ˈpæsɪndʒə/
pleasant /ˈplezənt/
problem-solve /ˈprɒbləm sɒlv/
profound /prəˈfaʊnd/
rewarding /rɪˈwɔːdɪŋ/
save up for /ˌseɪv ˈʌp fə/
solitary /ˈsɒlɪtəri/
survive /səˈvaɪv/
take a gap year /ˌteɪk ə ˈɡæp jɪə/
temple /ˈtempəl/
thinkable /ˈθɪŋkəbəl/
ticket /ˈtɪkət/
travel abroad /ˌtrævəl əˈbrɔːd/
traveller /ˈtrævələ/
unavoidable /ˌʌnəˈvɔɪdəbəl/
unfamiliar /ˌʌnfəˈmɪliə/
uninformed /ˌʌnɪnˈfɔːmd/
unpleasant /ʌnˈplezənt/
unrewarding /ˌʌnrɪˈwɔːdɪŋ/
unthinkable /ʌnˈθɪŋkəbəl/
withdraw money from a cash point /wɪðˌdrɔː ˈmʌni frəm ə ˈkæʃ pɔɪnt/

3.5 Grammar 🔊 4.21
go through security /ˌɡəʊ θruː sɪˈkjʊərəti/
security check /sɪˈkjʊərəti tʃek/
sword /sɔːd/
traffic pollution /ˈtræfɪk pəˌluːʃən/
travel on the left/right /ˌtrævəl ɒn ðə ˈleft/ˈraɪt/

3.6 Use of English 🔊 4.22
break down /ˌbreɪk ˈdaʊn/
head for /ˈhed fə/
hold sb up /ˌhəʊld ˌsʌmbɒdi ˈʌp/
keep on /ˌkiːp ˈɒn/
keep up with /ˌkiːp ˈʌp wɪð/
pick sb up /ˌpɪk ˌsʌmbɒdi ˈʌp/
pull over /ˌpʊl ˈəʊvə/
put sb up /ˌpʊt ˌsʌmbɒdi ˈʌp/
run out of /ˌrʌn ˈaʊt əv/
set off (on a journey) /ˌset ˈɒf (ɒn ə ˈdʒɜːni)/
turn into /ˌtɜːn ˈɪntə/
walk away from /ˌwɔːk əˈweɪ frəm/

3.7 Writing 🔊 4.23
express sympathy /ɪkˌspres ˈsɪmpəθi/
hometown /ˌhəʊmˈtaʊn/
incidentally /ˌɪnsɪˈdentəli/
reassure your friend /ˌriːəˌʃʊə jə ˈfrend/
uni /ˈjuːni/

3.8 Speaking 🔊 4.24
pillow /ˈpɪləʊ/
snow boots /ˈsnəʊ buːts/
tissue /ˈtɪʃuː/
travel by bus /ˌtrævəl baɪ ˈbʌs/
travel insurance /ˈtrævəl ɪnˌʃʊərəns/

FOCUS REVIEW 3

VOCABULARY AND GRAMMAR

1 **Complete the sentences with the correct form of the verbs in the box. There are two extra verbs.**

board   catch   cross   cycle   fasten   get   miss

1 We need to leave right away or we're going to _____ our train!
2 We had to _____ the river by boat because the bridge was damaged.
3 The first thing to do after you take your seat on a plane is _____ your seatbelt.
4 I can _____ the bus just outside my house, which is really convenient.
5 I hope we don't _____ stuck in traffic because we are already late.

2 **Complete the sentences with words from the unit. The first letter of each word is given.**

1 Our t_____ g_____ told us some fascinating stories as he showed us around Oxford.
2 There were no s_____ rooms available, so they put me in a room with two large beds.
3 In Mexico, we stayed in a seaside r_____ which had three pools, a club and several restaurants.
4 It's cheaper to pay for a r_____ journey instead of buying two single tickets.

3 **Complete the second sentence using the word in capitals so that it has a similar meaning to the first. Do not change the word in capitals.**

1 I'm sure that snake isn't dangerous. There aren't any poisonous snakes in this area. **CAN'T**
That snake _____ dangerous. There aren't any poisonous snakes in this area.
2 I don't know how they got to London, but it's possible that they travelled by train. **MAY**
They _____ to London by train.
3 I'm certain that animal is a jaguar – look how fast it can run! **MUST**
That animal _____ – look how fast it can run!
4 Let's print out our itinerary. It's possible that we'll need it. **MIGHT**
Let's print out our itinerary. We _____.
5 I'm sure Jack lived in China as a child. **MUST**
Jack _____ as a child.

4 **Complete the sentences with the correct form of the verbs in brackets and *used to* or *would*. Sometimes both are possible.**

1 We _____ (take) at least two guidebooks on holiday, but these days I only need my smartphone.
2 I _____ (not like) travelling by train as a child – I was afraid of the noise they made.
3 Public transport _____ (be) really slow when I was younger, but it's improved a lot since then.
4 _____ (you/cycle) to work or take the train before you bought your car?

USE OF ENGLISH

5 **Choose the correct answer, A, B or C.**

1 It was hard for me to _____ with the others on the cycling tour.
   A turn up   B drop off   C keep up
2 Allan's grandparents _____ travel agents, so his family always got an extra discount for their holiday.
   A was   B would be   C used to be
3 X: Why don't you go by train?
   Y: You're right. _____ . I'll avoid the overcrowded bus again.
   A I don't think I should do it.
   B I didn't think of that.
   C I'm not sure about that.
4 You can just _____ at the airport. Don't wait around for my flight to leave.
   A drop me off   B pick me up   C hold me up
5 _____ stay in France for a few months. You won't learn much in a week.
   A In my opinion, you mustn't   B If I were you, I would
   C I don't think I would

6 **Read the text. Choose the correct answer, A, B or C.**

A Holiday to Help Others

Last summer, my friend Kara and I had a unique opportunity. Instead of going on a package holiday as we ¹_____ normally do, we decided to volunteer in Puerto Rico.

Our friends and parents said it could be dangerous as we had to ²_____ the continent and we knew little about the place. However, we were determined to go. We went to a travel ³_____ who arranges holidays for volunteers and she organised everything.

We ended up in a mountain village in Puerto Rico which had been seriously damaged in a terrible storm. We stayed in a small hotel in the valley, so we had to cycle ⁴_____ to the village every morning. The ride was hard and the work was even harder, but it was very satisfying.

A couple of evenings a week we ⁵_____ a lift into the nearest town where we could have a delicious meal or go dancing with other volunteers. I have to say that Puerto Rican food might be the best I have ever tasted! We weren't ready to leave after two weeks, and our ⁶_____ home was a sad one. After this experience, I will never go on an ordinary holiday again.

1 A must   B would   C had
2 A cross   B miss   C fly
3 A guide   B leader   C agent
4 A forward   B uphill   C back
5 A used to get B were getting C might have got
6 A tour   B travel   C journey

LISTENING

7 🔊 **2.2** Listen to three conversations and choose the correct answer, A, B or C.

1 How did the woman get to the village?

A B C

2 How did the man <u>not</u> travel on his holiday?

A B C

3 What is the woman's problem?

A B C

WRITING

8 Read the writing task and match parts 1–4 with sentences a–e. There is one extra sentence.

a If I were you, I'd find out if there are any organised trips for students.
b India must be a great place to visit in the summer.
c Congratulations on getting into university.
d Last summer, I convinced my parents to let me go to a concert in Paris alone.
e I can see why your parents don't want you to go to India on your own.

Your friend in Australia has been offered a place at university. Before she starts studying, she'd like to travel alone around an exotic country. Her parents do not want her to go.

Write an email to you friend and
1 congratulate her on her place at university and say you hope she will enjoy it
2 express your opinion on her parents' worries
3 offer advice on her problem
4 describe a problem you recently had and how you solved it.

9 Write the email in Exercise 8.

SPEAKING

10 In pairs, roleplay a conversation.

Student A

Each year you go kayaking in the lake district in your country. You're talking to a friend from the UK and you would like to invite him/her to join you. Start the conversation and mention:

- Transport
- Other attractions
- Training before the trip
- Accomodation

Student B

You're a friend of Student A who each year goes kayaking in the lake district in his country, and has invited you to join him/her. Use some or all of the following sentences after Student A starts the conversation:

- Which part of the country will it be in? How can I get there from (the airport)?
- What interesting places are we going to visit?
- Do you have to be fit to take part?
- But I've never slept in a tent! Will you help me put it up?

11 Look at the photos. They show different holidays people like to go on. In pairs, follow these steps.

- Talk to each other about why people like to go on these holidays.
- Decide on the type of holiday the right weather is most important for.

A B C D E

12 Ask and answer the questions.

1 Some people say it's better to learn a lot about places in your own country before travelling abroad. What do you think? Why?
2 Do you think it's a good idea to plan a holiday in advance or decide what to do at the last moment? Why?
3 Where would your ideal holiday be? Why?

4

Eat, drink and be healthy

One man's meat is another man's poison.

A proverb

BBC

UMAMI

▶ 15 Watch the BBC video. For the worksheet, go to page 122.

4.1 VOCABULARY
Fruit and vegetables • describing food • collocations

I can talk about food that I like and don't like.

SHOW WHAT YOU KNOW

1 Choose the odd one out in each group. Add other items to each list.
   1 You can boil … potatoes, eggs, cheese, pasta.
   2 You can chop … onions, carrots, fruit, salt.
   3 You can fry … an omelette, soup, salmon, bacon.
   4 You can mix … a sauce, ingredients, spices, meat.
   5 You can slice … honey, bread, ham, cake.

2 **SPEAKING** Discuss the questions.
   1 Who is the best cook in your family?
   2 What dishes can you cook?

STRANGE CELEBRITY DIETS

When I read about the weird and wacky diets of famous celebrities, I think that being in the public eye can make people a bit crazy. And it's nothing new – more than two centuries ago, the romantic poet Lord Byron wanted to be
5 pale and thin, so he only ate **stale**, dry biscuits, soda water and potatoes covered in vinegar – yuck! So **sour**! No wonder he died at the age of thirty-six!

Here's my list of today's top five strangest celebrity diets.

10 **#5** Once, when **Beyoncé** was preparing for a video shoot, she went on a detox. This involved living on lemon juice, sweetened with maple syrup and made a little less **bland** with cayenne pepper. Give that woman some chocolate cake!

#4 Gwyneth Paltrow, Jennifer Aniston and Reese Witherspoon
15 choose the baby food diet which involves eating fourteen jars of baby food a day, and one low-calorie meal of **lean** meat or fish and green salad.

3 Read the blog post and discuss which celebrity diet you think is:
- the most appealing
- the easiest to do
- the least appealing.

4 Imagine you are doing the colour diet. Add the correct colour heading to each list of foods. Check meanings in your dictionary if necessary.

1 _red_	2 _____	3 _____
cherries	apricots	avocados
chilli peppers	carrots	cabbage
radishes	pumpkin	spinach
4 _____	5 _____	6 _____
grapefruit	cauliflower	aubergines
pineapple	coconut	beetroot
sweetcorn	garlic	figs

#3 **American singer Jennifer Hudson** thinks the Cookie Diet™ is more fun – instead of breakfast, lunch and snacks, you have six biscuits. But these are not delicious, crunchy biscuits with milk chocolate on top. Dr Siegal, the inventor of the Cookie Diet, was careful to make his cookies taste good, but not too good.

#2 **Katy Perry** keeps in shape with the mushroom diet, but instead of enjoying a bowl of delicious mushroom soup, she swaps one meal a day with raw mushrooms for fourteen days at a time.

#1 – **MY FAVOURITE! Christina Aguilera** does the seven-day colour diet, eating food of a different colour every day for a week. Day one is white, but that means white fruit and vegetables, not white bread or white rice! This is followed by red, green, orange, purple, yellow and on the seventh day, all of the colours. This diet might encourage you to try new things, like deep-red cherries, ripe avocados or fresh figs, and you'd get plenty of vitamins. I think this is the only one I would actually try.

Go to WORD STORE 4 page 9

WORD STORE 4A Fruit and vegetables

5 🔊 2.3 Match the photos in WORD STORE 4A with the words in Exercise 4. Then listen, check and repeat.

6 **SPEAKING** Mark the items in WORD STORE 4A as follows:
✓ = 'I like this'
✗ = 'I don't like this'
? = 'I've never tried this'.
Compare with your partner. What other items can you add to each list?
A: *I don't like radishes, what about you?*
B: *I don't think I've ever tried them. What do they taste like?*

WORD STORE 4B Describing food

7 🔊 2.4 Complete WORD STORE 4B with the adjectives in red in the blog post. Then listen, check and repeat.

8 Complete the sentences with an appropriate adjective from WORD STORE 4B. Which sentences are true for you?
1 Thai and Indian curries are too spicy for me. I know it's boring but I prefer _____ food.
2 My friend likes anything _____ : she particularly loves ice cream and chocolate.
3 The taste of dark chocolate or strong coffee is too _____ for me.
4 If we have any old, _____ bread, we feed the birds.
5 I've never tried sushi. I don't like the idea of eating _____ fish.
6 I can't eat salad if the dressing has a lot of vinegar. It's too _____ for me.
7 I don't like bananas that are too _____ . I prefer them to be white and firm.
8 I only like _____ meat so I cut off the fat and leave it on the side of my plate.

WORD STORE 4C Collocations

9 🔊 2.5 Complete WORD STORE 4C with the underlined examples in the blog post. Then ask and answer.

10 **SPEAKING** Complete the questions with appropriate collocations from WORD STORE 4C. Then ask your partner.
1 Have you ever eaten _____ ?
2 When was the last time you had _____ ?
3 Which do you prefer: _____ or _____ ?
4 In what kind of recipes do you use _____ ?
5 Where would I find _____ in your kitchen?

11 **SPEAKING** You are going to write a menu for either the most delicious or the most disgusting meal you can imagine. Use the words in WORD STORE 4A, 4B, 4C and your own ideas.
- Think about some delicious or disgusting food.
- Use words from the lesson and your own ideas.
- Write a menu with a starter, a main course and a dessert.
- Who has the best or worst menu in the class?

4.2 GRAMMAR

Future forms

I can talk about the future using a range of future forms.

1 SPEAKING Read about the best restaurant experiences in London. Which one would you most like to visit and why?

BEST RESTAURANT EXPERIENCES IN LONDON

- **Circus restaurant**
As you dine, performers entertain you.

- **Inamo**
You place your order via a 3D menu and you choose a virtual tablecloth. You can even order a taxi home from your table.

- **Pitch black**
You eat in the dark and the waiters are blind. They don't tell you what you're eating.

- **Oblix in The Shard**
You get the best view in London from the thirty-second floor of The Shard.

2 🔊 2.6 Listen to Charlie and Lianne. Which restaurant is Charlie going to, and which one is Lianne going to?

3 🔊 2.6 Listen again and choose the correct future form.

1 Are you doing anything special? *Will / Shall* I organise something?
2 *I'll go / I'm going* there with my mum and dad next week.
3 *I'm eating / I'm going to eat* as much as possible because my parents are paying.
4 Soon you *can't / won't be able to* go to a restaurant without having an experience!
5 It *opens / will open* at 6:30.
6 It's a Saturday night so *it is / it's going to be* crowded.
7 *I'll message / I'm messaging* you as soon as *I leave / I'll leave* the theatre.

4 Read the GRAMMAR FOCUS. Match the rules with the examples in Exercise 3. Use one of the examples twice.

GRAMMAR FOCUS

Future forms

- You use the **Present Simple** to talk about a fixed future event on a timetable, a schedule or a programme. ¹ _5_
- You use the **Present Continuous** to talk about a future arrangement. You often mention a time, a date or a place. ² ___
- You use **be going to** to talk about a future intention – something you have already decided to do ³ ___ or a future prediction based on what you can see or what you know. ⁴ ___
- You use **will/won't** to talk about a spontaneous decision when you react to circumstances ⁵ ___ or a future prediction based on your opinion. ⁶ ___
- You use **shall** (NOT ~~will~~) for offers and suggestions. ⁷ ___

Note: When you talk about the future, you use the present tense after the conjunctions *if, when, as soon as, unless, before* and *after*. ⁸ ___

5 Complete the messages with appropriate future forms of the verbs in brackets.

Hi. I'm out of the theatre.

How was it?

Brilliant. You must see it and it's selling out fast.

I know. I've already decided I ¹_____ (get) tickets tomorrow.

You can go with Max and Jenny – they ²_____ (go) next Thursday.

Oh right. I ³_____ (call) Max. Anyway, let's do something now. ⁴_____ (I/come) and meet you?

Yes, okay. I ⁵_____ (go) and wait for you in the café next to the theatre. Hurry up – I think it ⁶_____ (close) at 11 o'clock.

Right. I ⁷_____ (be) there in twenty minutes.

6 Complete the sentences with appropriate future forms of the verbs in brackets. Then rewrite them to make them true for you.

1 My local shop _____ (open) at 6 a.m. tomorrow.
2 I've decided that I _____ (stop) eating meat.
3 I'm really hungry so when I _____ (get) home from school, I _____ (have) a snack.
4 It's my birthday on Saturday and I _____ (meet up) with my friends for a pizza.
5 I think supermarkets _____ (disappear) as more people shop online.
6 I don't feel very well. I think I _____ (be) sick!

7 SPEAKING Talk about the things below.

1 Your plans or intentions for this evening.
2 An arrangement you've made for the weekend.
3 Ideas or plans you have for your next holiday.

FOCUS VLOG | About food

▶ 16 Watch the Focus Vlog. For the worksheet, go to page 123.

Grammar page 141

4.3 LISTENING

Matching

I can understand the main points of a narrative about a familiar topic.

1 **SPEAKING** Look at the photos in the leaflet and decide whether they show healthy or unhealthy diets.

2 Take *The Healthy Diet Test* and compare your results with a partner.

The Healthy Diet Test
Remember, the more ticks you get, the healthier you are.

1. I don't eat too much salt (e.g. in crisps and fast food).
2. I don't eat too much sugar (e.g. in sweets and fizzy drinks).
3. I am not difficult or fussy – I like most things.
4. I have a balanced diet – I eat a variety of different kinds of fresh food.
5. I eat fish at least once a week.
6. I don't eat red meat more than three times a week.
7. I feel well – I have plenty of energy.
8. I look well – my skin and my hair look healthy.

3 🔊 2.7 Listen to a nutritionist giving advice. Which statement in *The Healthy Diet Test* does she not mention at all?

EXAM FOCUS Matching

4 🔊 2.8 Listen to four people talking about their diets. Match statements A–E with speakers 1–4. There is one extra statement.

Speaker 1: ☐ Speaker 2: ☐ Speaker 3: ☐ Speaker 4: ☐

The speaker's diet …
A is based on fresh local produce.
B doesn't involve any cooking.
C used to include lots of sweet things.
D is based on Mediterranean produce.
E changed when he/she became a teenager.

5 🔊 2.8 Answer the questions. Is it speaker 1, 2, 3 or 4? Listen again and check.
1 Who couldn't become a vegetarian? ☐
2 Who has a lot of energy? ☐
3 Who supports animal rights? ☐
4 Who rarely eats the same thing as his/her family? ☐
5 Who doesn't use animal products? ☐
6 Who has realised that his/her favourite food is unhealthy? ☐

6 **SPEAKING** Discuss the questions in Exercise 5 about your family and friends.

My sister is a vegan and supports animal rights. She never eats the same things as the rest of my family, because they all love meat.

WORD STORE 4D Collocations

7 🔊 2.9 Complete the collocations in WORD STORE 4D with *diet*, *food*, *meal* and *snack*. Then listen, check and repeat.

8 You are going to find out how well you know your partner's attitude to food.
 • Write three true sentences and one false one to describe your attitude to food.
 • Begin your sentences with *I …* or *My …* and include the collocations in Exercise 7.
 • Swap your sentences with a partner.
 • Guess which sentence is false.

*I think I have a very balanced diet.
I often have a quick snack between meals.
I have a hot meal every lunchtime.*

PRONUNCIATION FOCUS

9 🔊 2.10 Listen and repeat the words. Notice that the vowels in green have the same sound in each group.
1 c**o**ffee **o**range c**au**liflower
2 b**ee**f b**ea**ns _____
3 gr**a**pes c**a**kes _____
4 ban**a**na av**o**cado _____
5 cabb**a**ge spin**a**ch _____

10 🔊 2.11 Add the words in the box to the correct group in Exercise 9. Then listen, check and repeat.

~~cauliflower~~   lettuce   potato
sardines   tomato

READING 4.4

Open-ended questions

I can identify the key information in an extended article.

1 SPEAKING Read UK TODAY and discuss the questions.
1 Which facts do you find most shocking?
2 Do you think the situation is similar or different in your country?

UK TODAY

- £13bn of food is thrown away each year.
- 71 percent of food waste comes from households.
- More than 50 percent of household food waste could have been eaten.
- Average UK household loses £470 per year due to avoidable food waste.
- 32 percent of children regularly skip breakfast before school.

2 SPEAKING Read the title of the article, look at the photos and discuss what you think it's about. Then read the article and check your ideas.

3 Match headings a–f with paragraphs 1–4 in the article. There are two extra headings.
a Everyone is welcome in The Real Junk Food cafés.
b Food past its sell-by date is consumed by animals.
c Children are taught how to make positive changes at home.
d One man's mission is to end food waste by feeding people, not bins.
e Food served in The Real Junk Food cafés is checked by officials.
f A healthy Australian diet and lifestyle is the best solution.

EXAM FOCUS Open-ended questions

4 Read the article again and answer questions 1–5.
1 How did Adam Smith get the idea to set up The Real Junk Food Project?
2 What is the point of selling meals on a pay-as-you-feel basis?
3 What kind of work can volunteers do for The Real Junk Food Project?
4 How can customers be sure that it's safe to eat at The Real Junk Food cafés?
5 What does the Fuel for School initiative teach children about food?

5 SPEAKING Discuss whether you would consider eating or working in one of The Real Junk Food cafés. Give reasons for your answer.

WORD STORE 4E Collocations

6 🔊 2.13 Complete WORD STORE 4E with the examples in blue in the article. Then listen, check and repeat.

7 SPEAKING Complete the questions with an appropriate noun from WORD STORE 4E. Then discuss them with a partner.
1 Have you ever thought about working in the voluntary _____?
2 Would you eat anything that was past its sell-by _____?
3 Do you do anything at home to recycle household _____?
4 Would you like a job in the catering _____?
5 Could you do anything at school to reduce energy _____?
6 Are you worried that food waste has reached record _____?

8 🔊 2.14 The article talks about reducing leftovers. Listen to three people talking about their favourite leftovers recipes. Answer the questions:
1 What is the main ingredient in all three?
2 Have you ever made any of these dishes?
3 Which recipe do you like best?

9 🔊 2.14 Use the words in the box to complete the instructions for the first recipe in Exercise 8. Then put the instructions in the correct order. Listen again and check.

(~~boil~~   chop   mix   pour   put   slice)

Bread and butter pudding
a Heat some milk in a small pan. Don't _boil_ it. ☐
b _____ the slices of bread and butter in a dish with some dried fruit. ☐
c _____ up some ripe bananas and put them in the dish. ☐
d _____ the stale bread and put butter on it. [1]
e _____ three eggs and three large spoons of sugar with the warm milk. ☐
f _____ the mixture over the bread and fruit and cook in the oven for forty-five minutes. ☐

10 SPEAKING Discuss the questions.
1 What happens to leftovers in your home?
2 What could your family, your school or your country do to cut down on food waste?

We don't have a lot of leftovers in my home. If there are any, my brother and his friends eat them.

The Real Junk Food Project

🔊 2.12

1 _____

Adam Smith is the founder of **THE REAL JUNK FOOD PROJECT**. He is passionate about collecting food that has been discarded by supermarkets, and transforming this wasted food into healthy nutritious meals.

Smith worked as a head chef for ten years and thought of the idea for The Real Junk Food Project when he was travelling in Australia and witnessed the scale of **food waste** in the **agricultural sector** and **catering industry**. The **global statistics** are shocking: roughly one third of food produced in the world for human consumption every year gets lost or wasted. Over 800 million people in the world (that's one in every nine people on Earth) do not have enough food to lead a healthy, active life. Smith founded The Real Junk Project to fill the gap between hunger and excess food, and to raise awareness about how much food goes to waste.

> " Over 800 million people in the world (that's one in every nine people on Earth) do not have enough food... "

2 _____

Smith started the project and opened the first Real Junk Food café in his hometown Leeds in 2013. Since then, the concept has been exported as far away as Los Angeles and Brazil, Warsaw and Zurich. The idea is simple: volunteers go out and collect food from various sources: farms, restaurants, factories and supermarkets. Meals are produced and sold in cafés on a 'pay-as-you-feel' (PAYF) basis so that nobody is excluded. The cafés are for the community in general, not only for the poor. Those who can afford it pay what they think the meal is worth, while those who can't afford to buy meals from the café can earn their meals by volunteering – for instance, they can help with the washing up.

3 _____

There is some controversy around the fact that some of the food served in The Real Junk Food cafés is past its **sell-by date**. Smith explains that chefs inspect the food and use their judgement to decide whether it is safe to eat. The food is cooked in accordance with official **government standards**, and cafés are inspected regularly by the environmental health department. They've fed over 10,000 people and nobody's been ill yet! Anything that isn't fit for **human consumption** goes to feed animals or as compost on vegetable gardens.

4 _____

Smith believes that change needs to happen immediately and on a **local level**. Too many people are completely uneducated about food, and this was the incentive for setting up an educational branch of The Real Junk Food Project called Fuel for School. The initiative has two aims – to get breakfast to every hungry schoolchild in the country and secondly, to teach children the value of food so that they can reduce the amount of leftovers in their own homes. The idea is that if children know what they're eating, where it's come from and how it's prepared, they develop an engagement with food and life skills for the future.

GRAMMAR

4.5 Future Continuous and Future Perfect

I can use the Future Perfect and Continuous to talk about future actions.

1 SPEAKING Look at the photo and read the advert. Then discuss the questions.
1. Would you like to go to Cook Camp? Why?/Why not?
2. How many things listed in the advert can you make?
3. Which dishes would you like to learn how to make?

teenage cook camp

In a few years, you will have graduated from school and will be living in a student house with other people your age.

▶ **WILL YOU KNOW HOW TO FEED YOURSELF?**

At Cook Camp we believe that basic cooking skills are an important life skill but many young people will be leaving school and home without them.

▶ **JOIN OUR WEEKEND COOK CAMP NOW**

By the end of the weekend, you'll have learnt how to make:

*a pasta sauce   vegetable soup   pizza   cakes and biscuits
three chicken dishes   an apple pie   and much, much more!*

2 Read the GRAMMAR FOCUS and underline examples of the Future Continuous and Future Perfect in Exercise 1.

GRAMMAR FOCUS

Future Continuous and Future Perfect

- You use the **Future Continuous** to talk about longer unfinished actions in progress at a time in the future.
  In a few years, you will be living in a student house.
  Future Continuous: will + be + -ing

+	I'll be working.
−	She won't be working.
?	Will they be working? Yes, they will./No, they won't.

- You use the **Future Perfect** to talk about an action that will be completed before a certain time in the future.
  By 9 a.m. they'll have had their breakfast.
  Future Perfect: will + have + past participle

+	You'll have finished.
−	He won't have finished.
?	Will they have finished? Yes, they will./No, they won't.

3 Look at tomorrow's schedule at Cook Camp. Choose the correct option.
1. At 6 a.m. they'll *be getting up* / have got up.
2. By 9 a.m. they'll *be having / have had* their breakfast.
3. In the morning they won't *be working / have worked* in the kitchen.
4. By 3 p.m. they'll *be finishing / have finished* lunch.
5. In the afternoon they'll *be cooking / have cooked* in the kitchen.
6. By 11 p.m. they'll be ready for bed. They will *be having / have had* a busy day!

Cook Camp   day 1

6 a.m.	get up, breakfast
9 a.m.	field work: planting, gardening
12 p.m.	lunch
3 p.m.	kitchen basics: chopping, peeling, cleaning; talk by a guest speaker
6 p.m.	dinner
9 p.m.	film or games
11 p.m.	bed

4 Write your schedule for tomorrow. Use the Future Continuous.

At 7 a.m. I'll be having breakfast.

5 SPEAKING Ask each other about your schedules for tomorrow. How similar or different are they?

A: *Will you be having breakfast at 7 a.m.?*
B: *No, I won't. I'll be …*

6 Use the prompts to write about things you *will* or *won't have done* by the end of today.

By the end of today …
1. eat/pieces of fruit
   By the end of today, I'll have eaten three or four pieces of fruit.
2. drink/water
3. cook/meals
4. receive/text messages
5. speak to/people
6. go into/shops
7. spend/money
8. do/homework

7 Use the prompts in Exercise 6 to make questions with *you*.
1. *How many pieces of fruit will you have eaten by the end of the day?*

8 SPEAKING Ask and answer the questions in Exercise 7.

Grammar page 142

4.6 USE OF ENGLISH

Question tags
I can use a range of question tags.

1 **SPEAKING** Imagine you and your friends want to order a pizza delivery. Discuss the questions.
   1 How do you order?
   2 Who do you order from?
   3 What type of pizzas do you order?

2 🔊 2.15 Listen to a conversation between three friends in *Pizza Delivery* Part 1. How do they answer the questions in Exercise 1?

3 🔊 2.15 Complete the example sentences in LANGUAGE FOCUS I with the correct auxiliary verb. Then listen again and check.

LANGUAGE FOCUS I

Question tags
- You use question tags to change affirmative or negative statements into questions.
- You form question tags with an **auxiliary/modal verb + pronoun**.

Positive statement + negative tag
You've got the Food Delivery App,[1] _haven't_ you?
We can use Regal Pizzas, [2]_____ we?

Negative statement + positive tag
I'm not the only one, [3]_____ I?
We haven't had pizza for ages, [4]_____ we?

Special cases
That's unusual, [5]_____ it?
Let's order some pizzas, [6]_____ we?

4 🔊 2.16 Listen to *Pizza Delivery* Part 2. What is the problem?

5 🔊 2.16 Read LANGUAGE FOCUS II and complete the exchanges from *Pizza Delivery* Part 2. Does the intonation rise or fall? Listen again and check.

LANGUAGE FOCUS II

Intonation and meaning in question tags
- Tags which have rising intonation ↑ mean 'Please answer my question – I don't know if my statement is true'.
- Tags which have falling intonation ↓ mean 'Please agree with my statement – I think my statement is true'.

1 Hi, you ordered food, _didn't you_ ?
2 That's everything, _____ ?
3 You are Mr and Mrs Whitecross, _____ ?
4 We don't look like Mr and Mrs anybody, _____ ?
5 And this isn't 102 Corn Street, _____ ?

6 Work with a partner.
   - Add an appropriate tag to statements 1–5.
   - Think about your partner and decide whether you think the statement is true or you have no idea.
   - Use appropriate intonation to practise the questions tags.

1 You don't have any special dietary needs, _____ ?
2 There's a restaurant near your house, _____ ?
3 You didn't go out for a meal last Saturday, _____ ?
4 Your mum can cook really well, _____ ?
5 You'd like to have a snack right now, _____ ?

7 **USE OF ENGLISH** Choose the correct question tag, A, B or C to complete *Pizza Delivery* Part 3.

Jess: Listen, I'm so hungry. We could just take the curries, [1]_____
Delivery 1: Mr and Mrs Whitecross wouldn't be too happy, [2]_____
Olly: They won't know, [3]_____
Maggie: No, that's just wrong. We can wait a bit longer, [4]_____. Listen, number 102 is across the road. You won't get lost again now, [5]_____
Delivery 1: I'll try not to. Thanks!
Delivery 2: Hello. This is 120 Corn street, [6]_____
All: Yes, it is.
Olly: Have you got our pizzas?

1 A shall we?   B could we?   C couldn't we?
2 A are they?   B would they? C would he?
3 A will they?   B would they? C won't they?
4 A shall we?   B can we?   C can't we?
5 A do you?   B won't you?   C will you?
6 A isn't it?   B is this?   C is it?

8 🔊 2.17 Listen and check your answers in Exercise 7.

9 Work in groups of three. Write a conversation between three friends deciding on a food delivery order. Your conversation must include the question tags in the box.

| did she?   hasn't he?   isn't it?   shall we?   will you? |

▶ Use of English page 143

4.7 WRITING

A formal email asking for information and clarification

I can write a formal email to request information.

Manchester School of Cookery

Dear Miss Read,

We are delighted to inform you that you have won first prize in our 'Ideal School Meals Competition'. The menu you suggested represents an ideal combination of healthy and exciting food. Your prize is a place on one of our 'Teen Cuisine' weekend cookery courses for teenagers at the Manchester School of Cookery. For more information, please contact Diane Walsh at d_walsh@cookeryschool.com and include details of any cookery experience you may have so that we can place you in the correct group.

Yours sincerely,

Diane Walsh

---

1 Read the letter. Is it formal or informal? Think of three questions you would ask about the prize mentioned in the letter.

2 Read Mia's reply. Does she ask any of your questions in Exercise 1?

---

¹Hi Diane,

Thanks for your letter **telling** me that I have won the competition. ²**I'm** very **happy** and I ³**can't wait for** the 'Teen Cuisine' experience. I am ⁴**getting in touch** to ask for more information about the course. I have **lots of** questions that I **want** to ask.

First, what are the dates and times of the next course? Also, do I need to bring anything with me? I do not have my own special clothing or kitchen **stuff**.

You asked about cookery experience and in fact, I have never done a cookery course before. However, we did have some cookery lessons at school and I do quite a lot of cooking at home. You mentioned placing me in the correct group, but ⁵you didn't say which levels are available.

Thank you once again for choosing my menu as the winner. ⁶Write back and answer my questions soon.

Yours sincerely,

Mia Read

---

3 Parts of Mia's email are too informal. Match the words in purple in the email with the more suitable formal alternatives below.

1 equipment – _____
2 informing – _____
3 would like – _____
4 a number of – _____
5 Thank you – _____
6 pleased – _____

4 Replace the underlined phrases in the email with the more formal alternatives below.

a I hope to hear from you …
b I am …
c could you clarify …?
d Dear Ms Walsh,
e contacting you …
f I am looking forward to

5 Read the WRITING FOCUS and complete it with the phrases in Exercise 4.

WRITING FOCUS

A formal email asking for information and clarification

- Start the email politely.
  Dear Sir or *Dear Madam*
  Dear Sir/Madam (if gender is unknown)
  Dear Mr, Dear Mrs or *Dear Miss* (to a young woman) + surname
  Dear Ms + surname (to an unmarried woman, or if you are not sure) ¹*Dear Ms Walsh*

- Don't use:
  - **abbreviations**: ~~Thanks~~ = Thank you
  - **informal phrases**: ~~lots of~~ = several, a number of
    ~~I can't wait for~~ = ² _____
  - **contractions**: ~~I'm~~ = ³ _____

- In the first paragraph, refer to the letter/email/advert you are responding to and say why you are writing.
  Thank you for your letter/email informing me that …/ regarding …
  I am ⁴ _____ *to enquire about/ask for …*

- If something is unclear, ask for clarification.
  ⁵ _____ *which levels are available?*
  Could you confirm/explain when/where/what/how/whether/ if …?

- In the final paragraph, mention that you would like a reply.
  I look forward to receiving your reply soon.
  ⁶ _____ *soon.*

- Close the email politely.
  Yours sincerely (if you know the name of the person you are writing to)
  Yours faithfully (if you started the letter with *Dear Sir/Madam* or *Dear Sir or Madam*)

6 Choose the more formal alternative.

1. a Hello there   b Dear Mr Stein
2. a Thank you for contacting me …
   b Thanks for your email …
3. a I want to know about …
   b I would like to enquire about …
4. a I look forward to hearing from you soon
   b Please write back soon
5. a All the best,   b Yours sincerely,

7 Complete the LANGUAGE FOCUS with direct questions from Mia's email.

LANGUAGE FOCUS

Indirect questions

You can use indirect questions to be more polite:
Direct: ¹ _____
Indirect: *Could you tell me what the dates and the times of the next course are?*
Direct: ² _____
Indirect: *I would also like to know whether I need to bring anything else.*

Note: The word order in indirect questions is the same as in affirmative statements.
You use **if/whether** for yes/no questions. You don't use *do, does* or *did*.

8 Write indirect questions using the question beginnings in brackets.

1. What time do I have to arrive?
   (Could you tell me …)
2. Is the school near the station?
   (Can you tell me …)
3. How many students are there on the course?
   (I would like to know …)
4. Do you offer accommodation on campus?
   (Could you tell me …)
5. Do students get a certificate at the end?
   (I would like to know …)

9 Rewrite Mia's email request for further information using indirect questions where possible.

Dear Ms Walsh,

Thank you for your email and for sending details of the different kinds of accommodation on offer. I've thought about all the possibilities, and I've decided that I would like to stay with a host family, please. I've got a few questions about meals. Will I have breakfast and dinner with the host family or only breakfast? I am vegetarian so can the host family provide vegetarian meals?

As for the payment to the host family, do I have to pay in advance? And if so, can I do a bank transfer, or would they prefer cash?

I'd like to cycle to school from the host family, but that depends on the distance. How far is the host family from the school? Alternatively, is there is a bus?

I hope to hear from you soon.

Yours sincerely,

Mia Read

SHOW WHAT YOU'VE LEARNT

10 Do the writing task. Use the ideas in the WRITING FOCUS and the LANGUAGE FOCUS to help you.

A famous chocolate company have chosen you as the winner of their online competition to suggest an interesting new flavour for their chocolate. The prize is a visit for you and a friend to their chocolate factory in Switzerland. Write an email and:

- thank the company for choosing your suggestion as the winner,
- say how you feel about the prize,
- ask about dates, travel arrangements and accommodation,
- ask for confirmation that your friend will also travel and stay for free.

4.8 SPEAKING

In a restaurant

I can use indirect questions in a simple conversation on a familiar topic.

1 SPEAKING Imagine you are in Mario's restaurant. Look at the lunch menu. What would you choose? What questions would you ask?

Mario's lunch menu
2 courses €10

Main course
- Pizza Margherita
- Cheeseburger and chips
- Mario Special Salad
- Mario Special Pasta
- Soup of the day

Dessert
- Chocolate mousse
- Fruit salad and ice cream
- Cheese and biscuits

2 🔊 **2.18** Listen to a conversation between Alex and a waiter. What are the problems? What solution do they find?

3 🔊 **2.18** Complete the conversation with phrases in the SPEAKING FOCUS. Listen again and check.

Alex: Excuse me – ¹_____?
Waiter: Certainly. What can I get you?
Alex: ²_____
Waiter: Sure. It's a salad with lettuce, red peppers and chicken.
Alex: Oh. ³_____
Waiter: Vegetarian? What about pasta?
Alex: ⁴_____
Waiter: Yes, it's a delicious salmon sauce.
Alex: Oh, I don't eat fish.
Waiter: You don't eat fish? Can I suggest a very good vegetarian restaurant, just five minutes from here?
Alex: No, it's OK. ⁵_____
Waiter: Ah, it's vegetable soup today! Would you like the soup?
Alex: Er maybe. But first ⁶_____
Waiter: Yes, it's a vegetable soup. There are onions in it. Is that a problem?
Alex: Yes, I'm sorry, but I'm allergic to onions.
Waiter: Right. How about the salad without chicken?
Alex: Yes, salad sounds good. ⁷_____
Waiter: Yes, of course. Is that everything?
Alex: Yes, thanks.
...
Waiter: Would you like to see the dessert menu?
Alex: No thanks. ⁸_____

SPEAKING FOCUS

Ordering food
a Can I order, please?
b Do you have any vegetarian dishes?
c Can I have chips with that?
d Could I have the bill, please?

Asking for information with indirect questions
e Can you tell me what the soup is?
f Can you tell me what the Mario Special Salad is?
g Do you know what the pasta sauce is?
h I'd like to know if there are onions in it.

4 🔊 **2.19** Listen to the end of the conversation. Why does the waiter change his attitude to Alex?

5 SPEAKING Write indirect questions using the question beginnings in brackets. Then ask and answer the questions.
1 What's your favourite fruit? (Can you tell me …)
2 Where's an Italian restaurant near your house? (Do you know …)
3 Is there anything you don't eat? (I'd like to know …)
4 Are you a good cook? (I'd like to know …)
5 Where can I get the best ice cream? (Can you tell me …)
6 Who's the fussiest eater you know? (Could you tell me …)

6 Follow the instructions below to prepare a restaurant dialogue. Use the SPEAKING FOCUS and phrases in the dialogue in Exercise 3 to help you.

Student A: You are a customer in a restaurant. You're a vegetarian and you're allergic to eggs and mushrooms. You don't like peppers very much. Ask the waiter for information about: pizza, pasta, soup and salad. Explain why you can't eat some dishes.

Student B: You are a waiter. Take Student A's order. Answer Student A's questions about the dishes and make suggestions.
- pizza: ham, eggs, tomatoes, cheese
- pasta: prawn sauce
- soup: mushroom
- salad: chicken, green beans, lettuce, peppers

7 SPEAKING Practise the dialogue and act it out. Take it in turns to be A and B.

ROLE-PLAY In a restaurant

▶ 18 Watch the video and practise. Then role-play your dialogue.

UNIT 4 — Eat, drink and be healthy — Word list

4.1 Vocabulary 🔊 4.25

apricot /ˈeɪprɪkɒt/
aubergine /ˈəʊbəʒiːn/
avocado /ˌævəˈkɑːdəʊ/
bacon /ˈbeɪkən/
beetroot /ˈbiːtruːt/
bitter /ˈbɪtə/
black/cayenne/ground pepper /ˌblæk/ˌkeɪen/ˌɡraʊnd ˈpepə/
bland /blænd/
boil /bɔɪl/
brown/long-grain/white rice /ˌbraʊn/ˌlɒŋ ɡreɪn/ˌwaɪt ˈraɪs/
cabbage /ˈkæbɪdʒ/
cake /keɪk/
carrot /ˈkærət/
cauliflower /ˈkɒliˌflaʊə/
cherry /ˈtʃeri/
chilli pepper /ˌtʃɪli ˈpepə/
chocolate/maple/sugar syrup /ˈtʃɒklət/ˌmeɪpəl/ˌʃʊɡə ˈsɪrəp/
chop (up) /ˌtʃɒp (ˈʌp)/
coconut /ˈkəʊkənʌt/
coffee /ˈkɒfi/
cook /kʊk/
cooked /kʊkt/
crunchy/dry/stale biscuits /ˌkrʌntʃi/ˌdraɪ/ˌsteɪl ˈbɪskəts/
cut off /ˌkʌt ˈɒf/
(dark/milk) chocolate /(ˌdɑːk/ˌmɪlk) ˈtʃɒklət/
delicious /dɪˈlɪʃəs/
disgusting /dɪsˈɡʌstɪŋ/
fatty /ˈfæti/
feed /fiːd/
fig /fɪɡ/
firm /fɜːm/
fresh /freʃ/
fry /fraɪ/
garlic /ˈɡɑːlɪk/
grapefruit /ˈɡreɪpfruːt/
green salad /ˌɡriːn ˈsæləd/
homemade pizza /ˌhəʊmmeɪd ˈpiːtsə/
homemade/tinned soup /ˌhəʊmˈmeɪd/ˌtɪnd ˈsuːp/
hot/spicy /ˌhɒt/ˈspaɪsi/
ice cream /ˌaɪs ˈkriːm/
ingredient /ɪnˈɡriːdiənt/
jar /dʒɑː/
juice /dʒuːs/
lean /liːn/
low-calorie meal /ˌləʊ ˌkæləri ˈmiːl/
main course /ˌmeɪn ˈkɔːs/
menu /ˈmenjuː/
mild /maɪld/
milk /mɪlk/
mix /mɪks/
mixed salad /ˌmɪkst ˈsæləd/
mushroom /ˈmʌʃruːm/
mushroom soup /ˈmʌʃruːm suːp/
omelette /ˈɒmlət/
onion /ˈʌnjən/
orange /ˈɒrəndʒ/
pineapple /ˈpaɪnæpəl/
plate /pleɪt/
potato /pəˈteɪtəʊ/
pumpkin /ˈpʌmpkɪn/
radish /ˈrædɪʃ/
raw /rɔː/
ripe /raɪp/
roast /rəʊst/
rotten /ˈrɒtn/
salmon /ˈsæmən/
salt /sɔːlt/
side salad /ˌsaɪd ˈsæləd/
slice /slaɪs/
sliced/white/wholemeal bread /ˌslaɪst/ˌwaɪt/ˌhəʊlmiːl ˈbred/
soda/sparkling/still water /ˌsəʊdə/ˈspɑːklɪŋ/ˌstɪl ˌwɔːtə/
sour /saʊə/
sour milk /ˌsaʊə ˈmɪlk/
spinach /ˈspɪnɪdʒ/
starter /ˈstɑːtə/
strong /strɒŋ/
sushi /ˈsuːʃi/
sweet /swiːt/
sweetcorn /ˈswiːtkɔːn/
unripe /ˌʌnˈraɪp/
vitamin /ˈvɪtəmən/

4.2 Grammar 🔊 4.26

animal products /ˈænəməl ˌprɒdʌkts/
olive /ˈɒlɪv/
olive oil /ˈɒlɪv ɔɪl/
order /ˈɔːdə/
protein /ˈprəʊtiːn/

4.3 Listening 🔊 4.27

add /æd/
balanced/fattening/healthy diet /ˌbælənst/ˌfætn-ɪŋ/ˌhelθi ˈdaɪət/
beef /biːf/
butter /ˈbʌtə/
cold/healthy/light/quick snack /ˌkəʊld/ˌhelθi/ˌlaɪt/ˌkwɪk ˈsnæk/
crisps /krɪsps/
crispy /ˈkrɪspi/
dried /draɪd/
fast food /ˌfɑːst ˈfuːd/
fattening/healthy food /ˌfætn-ɪŋ/ˌhelθi ˈfuːd/
fizzy drink /ˌfɪzi ˈdrɪŋk/
fussy /ˈfʌsi/
grape /ɡreɪp/
healthy meal /ˌhelθi ˈmiːl/
heat /hiːt/
heavy meal /ˌhevi ˈmiːl/
hot meal /ˌhɒt ˈmiːl/
lettuce /ˈletəs/
local produce /ˌləʊkəl ˈprɒdjuːs/
nutritionist /njuːˈtrɪʃənəst/
organic food /ɔːˌɡænɪk ˈfuːd/
pour /pɔː/
pudding /ˈpʊdɪŋ/
red meat /ˌred ˈmiːt/
sardines /ˌsɑːˈdiːnz/
three-course meal /ˌθriː kɔːs ˈmiːl/
vegan /ˈviːɡən/
vegetarian diet /ˌvedʒəˈteəriən ˈdaɪət/
warm /wɔːm/

4.4 Reading 🔊 4.28

agricultural sector /ˌæɡrɪkʌltʃərəl ˈsektə/
alarming/official statistics /əˌlɑːmɪŋ/əˌfɪʃəl stəˈtɪstɪks/
assist /əˈsɪst/
catering/tourist industry /ˈkeɪtərɪŋ/ˈtʊərəst ˌɪndəstri/
chef /ʃef/
curry /ˈkʌri/
discarded /dɪsˈkɑːdɪd/
due date /ˌdjuː ˈdeɪt/
energy consumption /ˈenədʒi kənˌsʌmpʃən/
expiry date /ɪkˈspaɪəri deɪt/
financial/voluntary sector /faɪˈnænʃəl/ˈvɒləntəri ˌsektə/
food/household waste /ˈfuːd/ˈhaʊshəʊld weɪst/
frying pan /ˈfraɪɪŋ pæn/
global statistics /ˌɡləʊbəl stəˈtɪstɪks/
government/international standards /ˌɡʌvənmən/ˌɪntəˈnæʃənəl ˈstændədz/
healthy lifestyle /ˌhelθi ˈlaɪfstaɪl/
human consumption /ˌhjuːmən kənˈsʌmpʃən/
incentive /ɪnˈsentɪv/
industrial waste /ɪnˌdʌstriəl ˈweɪst/
leftovers /ˈleftˌəʊvəz/
local level /ˌləʊkəl ˈlevəl/
manufacturing industry /ˌmænjʊˈfæktʃərɪŋ ˌɪndəstri/
meat consumption /ˈmiːt kənˌsʌmpʃən/
minimum/record level /ˈmɪnɪməm/ˈrekɔːd ˌlevəl/
mixture /ˈmɪkstʃə/
nutritious /njuːˈtrɪʃəs/
oven /ˈʌvən/
pan /pæn/
recipe /ˈresəpi/
safety standards /ˈseɪfti ˌstændədz/
sell-by date /ˈsel baɪ deɪt/
serve /sɜːv/
spoon /spuːn/
throw away /ˌθrəʊ əˈweɪ/
waste /weɪst/

4.5 Grammar 🔊 4.29

apple pie /ˌæpəl paɪ/
chicken /ˈtʃɪkən/
dinner /ˈdɪnə/
pasta sauce /ˈpæstə sɔːs/
peel /piːl/
vegetable soup /ˈvedʒtəbəl suːp/

4.6 Use of English 🔊 4.30

dietary needs /ˈdaɪətəri niːdz/

4.7 Writing 🔊 4.31

cookery course/lessons /ˈkʊkəri kɔːs/ˌlesənz/
cuisine /kwɪˈziːn/

4.8 Speaking 🔊 4.32

be allergic to /bi əˈlɜːdʒɪk tə/
bill /bɪl/
cheeseburger /ˈtʃiːzbɜːɡə/
chips /tʃɪps/
chocolate mousse /ˌtʃɒklət ˈmuːs/
fruit salad /ˈfruːt ˌsæləd/
green beans /ˌɡriːn ˈbiːnz/
prawn sauce /ˌprɔːn ˈsɔːs/
red pepper /ˌred ˈpepə/

FOCUS REVIEW 4

VOCABULARY AND GRAMMAR

1 **Complete the adjectives in the sentences. The first letter of each adjective is given.**

1 Eating r_____ meat is not safe. Always make sure that it is cooked all the way through.
2 I find s_____ water more refreshing than normal water in hot weather.
3 We always use w_____ bread for sandwiches because it is tastier than white bread.
4 I hate the b_____ taste of coffee. I always drink it with milk.
5 You don't have to use fresh tomatoes to prepare this dish. It's OK to use t_____ ones.
6 The apples on our tree are still u_____ so we have to wait a couple of weeks before we can eat them.

2 **Complete the sentences with the phrases in the box.**

fattening food   ground pepper   human consumption
tourist industry   vegetarian diet

1 I believe that if food is not safe for _____ , animals shouldn't eat it either.
2 Because the _____ is growing in our town, many new restaurants are opening.
3 I really enjoy _____ like chips and cakes, but I'm trying to make healthier choices.
4 Following a _____ can have a positive impact on your health.
5 Freshly _____ has a lot of flavour and I love it in soups.

3 **Complete the sentences with will/won't, going to, the Present Continuous or Present Simple form of the verbs in brackets.**

1 I don't think I _____ (bake) a cake for Kate's birthday after all – it's better to buy one.
2 The local shops _____ (close) at five, so if you need anything you should go now.
3 We _____ (eat) dinner at that new restaurant tomorrow evening. I've just made the reservation.
4 It's too heavy for you! I _____ (help) you carry it!
5 We _____ (have) some friends over for dinner next weekend. Would you like to come?
6 I am glad we are going to the cooking class together next week. _____ (I/pick you up) at ten?

4 **Complete the sentences with the Future Continuous or Future Perfect form of the verbs in brackets.**

1 Let's make a simple chocolate cake. I promise we _____ (finish) baking by 12 o'clock.
2 _____ (you/use) this knife? If not, please wash it and put it in the drawer.
3 Tomorrow at 8 o'clock we _____ (watch) a cooking competition. It's the final episode.
4 _____ (John/open) his own nutrition clinic by the end of the year?
5 The cakes in this bakery are very popular. I'm sure they _____ (sell out) by lunchtime.

USE OF ENGLISH

5 **Choose the correct answer, A, B or C.**

1 X: Tom is going to come to our dinner party, ___ ?
   Y: He's hoping to, but it's possible he'll have to work instead.
   A won't he   B isn't he   C will he
2 X: Have you got any vegetarian dishes?
   Y: ___
   A Is that everything, Madam?
   B Could you tell me what vegetarian is?
   C How about pasta with vegetable sauce?
3 X: Ugh! These biscuits are not soft and they taste old!
   Y: There's nothing worse than ___ biscuits, is there?
   A stale   B crunchy   C sliced
4 X: What time is it?
   Y: 7 o'clock. Tomorrow at 7 o'clock we ___ sushi in a Japanese restaurant. I can't wait.
   A will have   B will be having   C will have had
5 X: You haven't told Sam about the party, ___ ? I want it to be a surprise.
   Y: I promise to keep quiet about it.
   A will you   B do you   C have you
6 X: ___
   Y: Sure. What can I get for you?
   A Can I order please?
   B Can I have fries with that?
   C Could I have the bill please?

6 **Choose the word or phrase, A, B or C, that has a similar meaning to the underlined words and completes the second sentence.**

1 I have made a promise to myself <u>not to eat</u> any sweets.
   I have promised myself that I ___ any sweets.
   A don't eat   B am not going to eat   C shall not eat
2 This yogurt has been in the fridge for days, so could you check <u>if we can still eat it</u>?
   This yogurt has been in the fridge for days, so could you check its ___ date?
   A sell-by   B used   C best
3 To have a <u>healthy</u> diet with all the nutritious elements, you must include all of the food groups.
   To have a ___ diet, you must include all of the food groups.
   A regular   B lean   C balanced
4 Excuse me. <u>I'd like to know</u> what today's special is, please.
   Excuse me. ___ what today's special is, please?
   A Could you tell me   B Can you know
   C Do you tell me
5 Next month <u>will mark</u> five years that Pam has worked at our restaurant.
   Next month Pam ___ at our restaurant for five years.
   A will work   B has been working
   C will have worked

READING

7 Read the article and answer the questions.

NO MORE SHOPPING?

How to decide which service is best for you?

One of the hottest trends in the food industry is delivering boxes of fresh food to people's homes. The problem right now is the large number of new companies offering this type of service. In fact, there are so many new delivery services that it is increasingly hard to know which to choose.

Best for the enthusiastic cook who can't get to the shops.

One growing trend is delivering all the fresh ingredients you need to make a three-course meal. You'll receive the correct amount of ingredients and step-by-step instructions. For those who have little time for shopping but like to cook, this can be an ideal solution.

A positive move in several ways but with a risk.

Another option is to get a week's supply of local, organic vegetables, eggs and even meat delivered to your door. This is great for the environment, since no chemicals are used, little transport is needed and the food is good for you. The downside is that what they deliver sometimes depends on what is available, so you don't always get what you want. Even the freshest spinach leaves are no use if your family refuse to eat them.

A less frequent and longer-lasting option.

One other approach, which has been around longer, is having specific goods such as frozen food, dairy products or meat brought to your home. A company which delivers frozen vegetables and meat has been operating in the US for decades, and many households rely on the service. It is certainly convenient, and deliveries do not happen so often which is also a bonus.

1 What is the main problem with food box delivery services?
2 What is included in the three-course meal boxes?
3 What are the benefits of local vegetable boxes?
4 Why is frozen food delivery popular?
5 Which service would you choose for yourself and why?

SPEAKING

8 Look at the photos of some people eating out. In pairs, take turns to compare the photos and discuss where you would prefer to eat with your friends.

A

B

9 Ask and answer the questions.
1 Why do you think the people in the first photo are buying food in the street instead of going to a restaurant?
2 How do you feel about throwing away food?
3 Would you like to work as a cook or a waiter? Why?/Why not?

WRITING

10 Read part of an email you have received from the people running a TV cookery competition and write your reply.

We are really glad that you are interested in entering the competition. Please email us and tell us about your cooking experience and any queries you might have about dates, what to bring with you, clothes to wear, etc.
We look forward to hearing from you.
Yours sincerely,
Ruth Martin

5 Planet Earth

Let nature be your teacher.
William Wordsworth

BBC

CHAMELEONS

▶19 Watch the BBC video. For the worksheet, go to page 124.

5.1 VOCABULARY
Phrasal verbs • collocations • word families

I can talk about geographical features and oceans.

SHOW WHAT YOU KNOW

1 Choose the odd one out in each group and explain why.
 1 Cyprus   Munich   Naples
 2 the Himalayas   the Nile   the Pyrenees
 3 Africa   China   Europe
 4 the Atlantic   the Pacific   the Sahara
 5 the Mediterranean   Niagara   the Baltic

 1 Cyprus is the odd one out because it is an island. Munich and Naples are cities.

2 List the ten geographical categories you used in Exercise 1. Choose five of the categories and add one more example to each one.
 islands, cities …

MYSTERIES OF THE OCEAN

Around 70 percent of the Earth's surface is covered by oceans. But how much do you know about the mysteries hidden under the surface?

TRUE or FALSE?

1 The sea is blue because it reflects the colour of the sky.
2 Winding rivers with strong currents exist deep under the ocean.
3 The blue whale is the largest animal known to have ever existed.
4 Most volcanic eruptions are underwater.
5 The Pacific Ocean was named after the person who discovered it.
6 Humpback whales live all year round in the calm seas around Hawaii.
7 It's impossible to surf huge waves of over twenty metres high.
8 The longest mountain range in the world is found underwater.
9 The Great Barrier Reef is composed of 900 tropical islands and can be seen from the moon.
10 The difference in the depth of water between low tide and high tide can be up to sixteen metres.

3 🔊 2.20 Do the quiz with a partner. Then listen and check your answers.

4 Compare how many answers you guessed correctly. Which fact were you most surprised by?

5 🔊 2.20 Answer the questions. Then listen again and check.
1 When the seabed is **disturbed** by stormy weather, what happens to the colour of the sea?
2 What caused the blue whale to almost **become extinct**?
3 What sometimes **increases the temperature** of seawater to 400 degrees Celsius?
4 What did Ferdinand Magellan **find by chance** and then name in 1520?
5 How many individual reefs and how many islands **is** the Great Barrier Reef **formed from**?
6 Where does the water depth only change by ten centimetres when the tide **rises** and **falls**?

Go to WORD STORE 5 page 11

WORD STORE 5A | Phrasal verbs

6 🔊 2.21 Complete WORD STORE 5A with the words and phrases in red in Exercise 5. Then listen, check and repeat.

7 **SPEAKING** Complete the questions with an appropriate particle. Then discuss the questions with a partner.

Can you name a place or region in your country where …
1 … you can come _____ empty beaches with no tourists?
2 … the landscape is made _____ of rivers, lakes and forests?
3 … the tide goes _____ (and comes _____) a long way?
4 … a tradition or custom is dying _____?
5 … storms often stir _____ the sea and cause huge waves?

WORD STORE 5B | Collocations

8 🔊 2.22 Complete WORD STORE 5B with the underlined words in the quiz. Then listen, check and repeat.

9 Choose a collocation from WORD STORE 5B and write an example sentence that is either a well-known fact or true for you.

There is a strong current in our local river as it flows under the main bridge.
or
When I swim in the sea I worry about the dangerous currents.

WORD STORE 5C | Word families

10 🔊 2.23 Complete WORD STORE 5C with some of the words used in the quiz and your own ideas. Use your dictionary if necessary. Then listen, check and repeat.

11 Complete the sentences with an appropriate form of the words in brackets.
1 I can't swim very well so I stay out of the _____ (depth) end of the swimming pool.
2 I could never do kite surfing. I don't have enough _____ (strong) in my arms.
3 I'm shorter than my dad but about the same _____ (high) as my mum.
4 I completely agree with the saying: 'Travel _____ (breadth) the mind'.
5 I think the _____ (long) of your education is less important than the _____ (broad).
6 I believe the gap between generations has _____ (width) recently.

12 **SPEAKING** Ask questions and find out whether the sentences in Exercise 11 are true or false for your partner. How similar or different are you?

61

GRAMMAR

5.2 Articles: no article, *a/an* or *the*

I can use the definite, indefinite and zero article.

1 SPEAKING Discuss questions 1–3. Then read the text and check your ideas.

1 What was the world population in 1900? What is it now? What will it be in 2050?
2 What is the biggest change in *where* people live?
3 What are 'megacities'?

The world's growing problem

A famous scientist said recently that there's a growing problem in the world, and the problem is people – there are just too many of us! Because of economic growth, food has improved, healthcare has improved and people are living longer. During the twentieth century, the population of the world grew from 1.65 billion to 6 billion. Today it is 7.6 billion and by 2050 it is predicted to reach 9.7 billion. For the first time in history, more people live in cities than in the countryside. Across the globe there are thirty-one megacities – cities with more than 10 million inhabitants – and by 2030 the United Nations predicts the total will be forty-one. Megacities are more common in Asia, particularly in India and China. The biggest megacity is still Tokyo with a population of 38,140,000.

2 Read the GRAMMAR FOCUS. Complete the examples in the table using the phrases in blue in the text.

GRAMMAR FOCUS

Articles

No article
- You don't use articles to talk about things in general.
  Ø healthcare has improved and ¹Ø people are living longer.
- You don't use articles with continents, countries or cities.
  Ø Asia, Ø India, ²_____
  Exceptions: *The United States, The United Kingdom, The Netherlands*

Indefinite article *a/an*
- You use ***a/an*** to talk about something for the first time when it means 'one of many'.
  There is ³_____ … (there are many problems)
- You use ***a/an*** with jobs. ⁴_____ said recently …

Definite article *the*
- You use ***the*** when the thing you are talking about has already been mentioned.
  There's a growing problem in the world, and ⁵_____ is people …
- You use ***the*** when the thing you are talking about is known or is 'the only one'.
  the population of ⁶_____ … in the countryside
- You use ***the*** with historical periods, superlative adjectives and ordinal numbers.
  During the twentieth century … ⁷_____ megacity is still Tokyo …

3 🔊 **2.24** Read and complete the text with *a*, *the* or Ø (no article). Then listen and check. What has Jack Ng invented and why?

Vertical farms in Singapore

¹ *The* biggest problem that megacities have is how to provide ²____ food and ³____ water for their inhabitants but one small country may have found ⁴____ solution. Singapore is ⁵____ tiny country which is famous for ⁶____ innovation but has very little space to grow ⁷____ food. Fortunately, ⁸____ vertical farm invented by Jack Ng, ⁹____ farmer, does not need much space at all. At the moment, ¹⁰____ farm only produces a few different kinds of vegetable but there are ¹¹____ plans to expand production to include more. Perhaps in the future Jack Ng's invention will help feed ¹²____ world!

4 Cross out *the* if it is incorrect in these general statements about a country.

1 ~~The~~ poverty doesn't exist.
2 The cheapest form of public transport is the bus.
3 The food is mainly sold in big supermarkets.
4 The education and the healthcare are free.
5 The capital city is located in the centre of the country.

5 SPEAKING Discuss whether the statements in Exercise 4 are true for your country. Rewrite them to make them all true.

6 SPEAKING Complete the questions with *a*, *an* or *the*. Then ask each other the questions.

1 Do you live in __the__ countryside?
2 Have you ever been to _____ UK?
3 Did you have _____ snack this morning?
4 Would you like to be _____ farmer?
5 Are you _____ oldest student in _____ class?

7 Complete the sentences to make them true for you.

1 My father is _____ (a job).
2 I've never been to _____ (a continent).
3 I'd like to visit _____ (a country).
4 _____ (a city) is _____ (a superlative adjective) city in the world.
5 _____ (a problem) is/are a big problem in my country.

FOCUS VLOG | About the environment

▶ **21** Watch the Focus Vlog. For the worksheet, go to page 125.

Grammar page 144

5.3 LISTENING

Multiple choice

I can understand the key points of a radio interview on a familiar topic.

1 **SPEAKING** Read UK TODAY and discuss the questions.
  1 What are your top three environmental worries?
  2 What do you recycle, turn off and do less to protect the environment?

UK TODAY

Did you know that two-thirds of British teenagers admit they can do more to protect the environment?

What are British teenagers' top three environmental worries?
- poor air quality
- global warming
- not enough recycling

What do British teenagers say they can do?
- recycle more
- turn off unnecessary lights
- spend less time in the shower

2 **SPEAKING** Look at the features in the box. Which would you expect an eco-school to have? Use your dictionary if necessary.

> solar panels ☐   no textbooks, only tablets ☐
> Technology lessons on renewable energy ☐
> low-energy light bulbs ☐   bicycle rack ☐
> Science lessons on global warming ☐
> a large car park ☐   recycling bins ☐
> an organic vegetable garden ☐

3 🔊 **2.25** Listen to the programme and check your ideas in Exercise 2.

EXAM FOCUS   Multiple choice

4 🔊 **2.25** Listen to the interview again. For questions 1–5, choose the correct answer, A, B, C or D.
  1 Friends of the Planet is an after-school club with members from
    A one school.   C seven schools.
    B twelve schools.   D six schools.
  2 The interview with Michael is taking place
    A in the school garden.   C with a group of architects.
    B in a radio studio.   D on the roof of the school.
  3 School dinners will include vegetables from
    A the kitchen.
    B a local farm.
    C the local supermarket.
    D the school garden.
  4 Science and Technology lessons will
    A be the same as in other secondary schools.
    B not focus on **climate change**.
    C sometimes take place in the school grounds.
    D concentrate more on **environmental issues**.
  5 During the interview, the interviewer comes to the conclusion that
    A Michael is probably not a typical teenager.
    B Michael is like every other person of his age.
    C Michael likes games and gadgets.
    D Michael cares about the environment as much as his friends.

WORD STORE 5D | Compound nouns

5 🔊 **2.26** Complete WORD STORE 5D with the words in green in Exercises 2 and 4. Then listen, check and repeat.

6 Complete the sentences with the words in WORD STORE 5D.
  1 Solar ___panels___ make buildings look ugly.
  2 There aren't enough recycling _____ in my area.
  3 Climate _____ doesn't affect my country.
  4 More renewable _____ is the only way to stop global _____.
  5 Everybody should use low-energy light _____ to save electricity.
  6 People in my country are not interested in environmental _____.

7 **SPEAKING** Discuss the statements in Exercise 6. Decide whether you agree or disagree. Explain your opinion.

PRONUNCIATION FOCUS

8 🔊 **2.27** Listen and put the words in the box into groups A, B, or C depending on the stress.

> ~~environment~~   interesting   located   organic   recycling
> renewable   responsible   secondary   vegetable

A ■ ▪ ▪	B ▪ ■ ▪	C ▪ ■ ▪ ▪
		environment

9 🔊 **2.28** Listen, check and repeat the words.

5.4 READING

Multiple choice

I can understand an extract from a travel book and some survival advice.

1 **SPEAKING** Imagine you are camping in a mountainous or forested region in your country.
  1 Which of the following might be a problem?

  ants   bears   bees   bulls   mosquitoes
  snakes   wolves

  2 Which of the following might be useful?

  a backpack   a flashlight   insect repellent
  a sharp knife   nail clippers   pepper spray
  a sleeping bag   sunscreen

  3 What other potential problems or useful items can you think of?

2 Read both texts. According to Text 2, what did the campers in Text 1 do wrong?

EXAM FOCUS Multiple choice

3 Read Texts 1 and 2 again. For questions 1–5, choose the correct answer, A, B, C or D.

Text 1
1 Bill and Stephen went into their tents because
  A they'd finished all their food.
  B tiny insects were annoying them.
  C the weather made them sleepy.
  D they wanted to get in their sleeping bags.
2 Bill woke up because
  A his friend was snoring loudly.
  B he found a nest of ants in his tent.
  C he heard something moving in the bushes.
  D he'd left his backpack outside the tent.
3 Bill and Stephen
  A were equally alarmed about the noise.
  B had heard a skunk in their camp.
  C both saw the animal's eyes in the dark.
  D were armed against animal attacks.

Text 2
4 If you meet a bear in the wild
  A turn around and walk away.
  B shout and scream loudly.
  C aim a gun at the bear's head.
  D be ready to use pepper spray.
5 The text focuses on
  A useful ways of avoiding bears in the wild.
  B the different weapons you can use against bears.
  C avoiding and defending yourself against bears.
  D territories where bear encounters are frequent.

4 🔊 2.30 Listen to the last part of the book extract (Text 1). What animal caused the disturbance?

5 **SPEAKING** Describe a time when you had an unexpected encounter with an animal. What happened?

6 🔊 2.31 Complete the lists using the words in blue in the texts. Then listen, check and repeat.
  Places:
  1 a clearing   2 a path   3 a pond   4 a sp____
  5 a tr____
  Trees:
  1 br____   2 leaves   3 roots   4 a trunk
  Animals:
  1 a b____   2 a fox   3 a hedgehog   4 a sk____
  5 a squirrel
  Hunting:
  1 a predator   2 pr____

7 Complete the email with words in Exercise 6.

> We had a great weekend. We went camping in the forest. During the day we hiked a ¹_____ through the forest. We found a lovely ²_____ in the trees for a picnic. We were close to a ³_____ so we refilled our water bottles. It was very peaceful but suddenly there was a loud noise of breaking ⁴_____ . I imagined a big hungry bear hunting its ⁵_____ , but then I remembered we weren't in bear territory! Maybe it was another hiker.

8 **SPEAKING** Describe one of the following activities to your partner. Use words from Exercise 6.

  The last time I went …   a) camping …   b) for a picnic …
  c) for a walk in the woods …

WORD STORE 5E Verb phrases

9 🔊 2.32 Complete WORD STORE 5E with the underlined verbs in the texts. Then listen, check and repeat.

10 Replace the underlined words and phrases with an appropriate verb phrase in WORD STORE 5E.
  1 I continue sleeping in spite of my alarm going off in the morning.
  2 The first thing I pick up when I wake up is my phone.
  3 I don't like strong cheese that smells as if it's too old to eat.
  4 In our city we have urban foxes that look for food in bins at night.
  5 I once encountered a cow when I was walking in the countryside.
  6 I'm frightened of thunderstorms. I'm afraid of being killed by a lightning strike.
  7 I like nothing better than relaxing and doing nothing with friends on a campsite.

11 **SPEAKING** Find out whether the sentences in Exercise 10 are true or false for your partner.

  A: *I think you always sleep through your alarm going off in the morning.*
  B: *Sometimes, but not always! I think you …*

Adapted extract from A Walk in the Woods by Bill Bryson

Text 1 🔊 2.29

We hiked till five and camped beside a spring in a small, grassy clearing in the trees just off the trail. Because it was our first day back on the trail, we had plenty of food, including cheese and bread that had to be eaten before they went off or were shaken to bits in our backpacks, so we rather gorged ourselves, then sat around chatting lazily until numerous little flying insects drove us into our tents. It was perfect sleeping weather, cool enough to need a sleeping bag but warm enough that you could sleep in your underwear, and I was looking forward to a long night's sleep – indeed was enjoying a long night's sleep – when, at some dark hour, there was a sound nearby that woke me up suddenly. Normally, I slept through everything – through thunderstorms, through Katz's snoring – so something big enough to wake me was unusual. There was a sound of breaking branches, something heavy pushing through the trees, and then a kind of loud breathing noise.

I sat straight up. Every neuron in my brain was awake. I reached for my knife, then realized I had left it in my backpack, just outside the tent. After many quiet nights, I was no longer worried about having to defend myself in the night. There was another noise, quite near.

'Stephen, you awake?' I whispered.

'Yup,' he replied in a tired but normal voice.

'What was that?'

'How should I know.'

'It sounded big.'

'Everything sounds big in the woods.'

This was true. Once a skunk had come through our camp and it had sounded like a stegosaurus. There was another noise and then the sound of drinking at the spring. It was having a drink, whatever it was.

I moved on my knees to the foot of the tent, carefully opened the entrance and looked out, but it was pitch black. As quietly as I could, I brought in my backpack and with the light of a small flashlight searched through it for my knife. When I found it and opened it I was shocked at how small it looked. It was perfectly suitable for, say, putting butter on pancakes, but useless for defending oneself against 400 pounds of hungry bear.

Carefully, very carefully, I climbed from the tent and put on the flashlight, which shone a disappointingly feeble light. Something about fifteen or twenty feet away looked up at me. I couldn't see anything at all of its shape or size – only two shining eyes. It went silent, whatever it was, and stared back at me.

'Stephen,' I whispered at his tent, 'did you pack a knife?'

'No.'

'Have you got anything sharp at all?'

He thought for a moment. 'Nail clippers.'

Text 2

HOW TO SURVIVE A BEAR ATTACK

You're more likely to die from a bee sting than you are to be killed by a bear, but in the unlikely event of meeting a bear in the wild, here are a few tips.

The best way to survive a bear encounter is to never have one. This is not too difficult because most bears just want to be left alone.

Bears often want your food, so if you're camping in bear territory, make sure you store your food carefully, at least 100 metres from your tent.

To avoid surprising a bear in the wild, make a noise as you walk, sing loudly, clap your hands.

Never get between a female bear and her cubs.

If you do come face to face with a bear, don't turn your back and run - you're acting like prey. Stay calm and walk backwards and slowly take out your pepper spray - it's better than a gun. If the bear runs towards you, aim the spray just above the bear's head. It almost always works!

If the bear keeps coming towards you, lie down on your front with your hands over the back of your neck to protect it, and pretend to be dead. Don't move for at least twenty minutes.

GRAMMAR

5.5 Non-defining relative clauses

I can use non-defining relative clauses to add information.

1 **SPEAKING** Discuss the questions.
   1 What are your favourite/least favourite animals? Why?
   2 What good or bad experiences have you had with animals?

2 Read Story 1. How did the elephant save the rancher's life?

Story 1

The elephant and the rancher

A rancher, who was working in the bush, came across a small herd of about twenty elephants. The leader of the herd, which is usually the largest, oldest and most aggressive female elephant,
5 attacked him and he fell off his horse. Later, rescuers found the rancher, whose leg was broken. The same elephant was standing over him. The rancher told his rescuers that the elephant had lifted him with her trunk and placed him under
10 a tree, where he was protected from the sun. For the rest of the day she watched over him, brushing him gently with her trunk every so often.

3 Read the GRAMMAR FOCUS. Cross out the four non-defining relative clauses in blue in the text. Does the story make sense without them?

GRAMMAR FOCUS

Non-defining relative clauses

You use non-defining relative clauses to give extra information about the person or thing you are talking about. The sentence makes sense without it.

A rancher, who was working in the bush, came across a small herd …

Note: Start and end a non-defining relative clause with a comma. Use relative pronouns *who*, *which*, *where* and *whose* but don't use *that*.

4 🔊 2.33 Complete Story 2 with relative clauses a–f. Then listen and check. How did the gorilla save the boy's life?
   a whose baby was still in her arms
   b which was called Binti Jua
   c who is now twenty-one years old
   d where he made a complete recovery
   e who was unconscious
   f where a female gorilla was feeding her baby

Story 2

The gorilla and the toddler

An American boy, ¹_____ , owes his life to a gorilla at Brookfield Zoo. When he was three years old his family took him to the zoo. He wanted a better view of the gorillas so he climbed a wall and fell six metres into the gorilla cage, ²_____ . The gorilla, ³_____ , went over to the boy, ⁴_____ . Then, the gorilla, ⁵_____ , lifted the boy up gently and carried him to the door. The boy spent four days in hospital, ⁶_____ . Binti Jua is still at Brookfield Zoo near Chicago.

5 Read the extra information 1–6 from Story 3. What do you think happened? Read the story and check your ideas.
   1 Todd Endris lived next to the beach.
   2 The shark was five metres long.
   3 Todd's friend was surfing close by.
   4 Todd's right leg was now in the shark's mouth.
   5 Dolphins had been playing in the waves nearby.
   6 Surgeons from the hospital managed to save his leg.

Story 3

The surfer, the shark and the dolphins

It was a perfect day for surfing off the coast of California. Todd Endris, *who lived next to the beach*, was out on his surfboard. Without warning,
5 something hit him from under the water. Todd knew immediately that it was a shark. He got back on his board but the shark bit him on the back. Todd's friend saw the huge shark and at first thought it was a whale. Todd was kicking the shark with his free leg, and didn't see the dolphins. Suddenly, the shark let go
10 of his leg. The dolphins had surrounded the injured surfer and were protecting him from the shark. Three friends helped Todd get back on his board and reach the beach. A helicopter transported him to hospital. Six weeks later Todd was back in the water.

6 🔊 2.34 In pairs, rewrite the story including the extra information in Exercise 5.
   • Find appropriate places in the text to add extra information 1–6.
   • Rewrite the extra information as a suitable relative clause.
   • Listen to the completed story and check your answers.

7 **SPEAKING** Discuss the questions.
   1 Which of the stories do you like best?
   2 Which wild animals are you most afraid of?

Grammar page 145

5.6 USE OF ENGLISH

Prepositions at the end of clauses

I can use prepositions at the end of clauses.

1 SPEAKING Look at the photos and discuss the questions.
1. What natural disasters do the photos illustrate?
2. What other natural disasters can you name?
3. Which natural disasters are common in your country?
4. Have you ever experienced a natural disaster? What happened?

2 🔊 2.35 Listen to a radio programme called *Violent Earth*. Where are the two reporters and what natural disasters are they reporting on?

3 🔊 2.35 Put the words in the sentences and questions from the programme in the correct order. Then listen again and check. What type of word comes at the end of each sentence or question?
1. the crops / A tropical storm / which / on / flattened / rely / people
2. are / being criticised / What / for / the public services / ?
3. with / These situations / very difficult / to deal / are
4. The firefighters / which / don't know / on / ones / to focus
5. for / Which island / heading / it / is / ?
6. people / anybody / with / don't / Some / can / stay / they / have
7. those people / getting / Who / from / are / help / ?

4 Read the LANGUAGE FOCUS and add two more examples from Exercise 3.

LANGUAGE FOCUS

Prepositions at the end of clauses

- In relative clauses
  Not everybody has somebody (who) they can stay **with**.
  ¹_____.

- In wh- questions
  Who are those people getting help **from**? ²_____

- In infinitive structures
  These situations are very difficult to deal **with**.

5 Complete the sentences with your own ideas and the phrases in the box to make them true for you. Then compare them with a partner.

agree with   believe in   ~~care about~~   focus on
happen to   wait for

1. *Animal welfare* is something which I really *care about*.
2. … is somebody who I nearly always _____.
3. … is something which I've never _____.
4. … is somebody who I always have to _____.
5. … is something which I find difficult to _____.
6. … is somebody who strange things always _____!

6 SPEAKING Write questions for these answers using the verb in brackets and an appropriate preposition. Then ask each other the questions and give your own answers.

1. A: _____ (worry)?   B: Global warming.
   What sort of things do you worry about?
2. A: _____ (listen)?   B: Heavy metal.
3. A: _____ (spend money)?   B: Clothes.
4. A: _____ (want to work)?   B: A technology company.
5. A: _____ (borrow money)?   B: My sister.
6. A: _____ (have lunch)?   B: My classmates.

7 USE OF ENGLISH Complete the text with one word in each gap.

The natural world is something I care ¹_____ and one of the things I'm most worried about is the increase in the number of forest fires near where I live. It's not something you can ever get used ²_____ and it takes a long time for nature to recover ³_____ the effects. I think the government needs to ⁴_____ on the causes of the fires. That's the first thing they should spend money ⁵_____.

▶ Use of English page 146

5.7 WRITING

A 'for and against' essay

I can present and support arguments in a simple discursive essay.

1 **SPEAKING** Discuss which of these things it would be most difficult to live without.

> electricity   medicine   school   shops   running water

2 Read the essay on contacting rainforest tribes and answer the questions.
   1 How many arguments for and against the topic does the writer give?
   2 What is your personal opinion on the topic in the essay?

---

1 Nowadays, many of us live in a world of high technology and instant communication. For most people, it is hard to believe that, in places like the Amazonian rainforest, there are still tribes who have never had contact with the outside world. Some people think that we should make contact with such groups, but others believe they should be left alone.

2 **On the one hand**, there are several arguments for making contact. **First of all**, the people in these tribes could enjoy a better standard of living. For example, they could get access to electricity and running water. **Furthermore**, their young people could go to school and benefit from a modern education. They would probably be amazed to learn about modern technology and life in other parts of the world.

3 On the other hand, there are also many arguments against making contact. Firstly, after contact, many tribal people suffer and die from diseases that do not exist in the forests where they live. Next, history shows that they often join larger society at the lowest level. **For instance**, many become beggars or tourist 'attractions'.

4 **To sum up**, there are clearly strong arguments for and against making contact with rainforest tribes. **Personally, I think** they should be left alone to continue their traditional way of life until they choose to make contact with the outside world.

---

3 Look at the essay again. In which paragraphs does the writer:
   a give a personal opinion?
   b present arguments against the topic?
   c introduce both sides of the issue?
   d present arguments for the topic?
   e make some general, historical or factual comments about the topic?
   f make a statement summarising the main arguments?
   g support arguments with examples

4 Read the WRITING FOCUS and check your answers in Exercise 3.

WRITING FOCUS

A 'for and against' essay

- Paragraph 1 – Introduction
  Begin with general comments or facts about the topic.
  End with a statement that mentions both sides of the issue.
- Paragraph 2 – Arguments for
  Present two or three arguments for the topic.
  Include some examples to support arguments.
- Paragraph 3 – Arguments against
  Write a similar paragraph presenting and supporting arguments against the topic.
- Paragraph 4 – Conclusion
  Make a summarising statement.
  Add your personal opinion.

5 Read the LANGUAGE FOCUS and complete the examples with the linkers in purple in the essay.

LANGUAGE FOCUS

Linkers

- List arguments: ¹ _First of all_ , Firstly, Secondly, ² _____ , In addition, Finally
- Give examples: *For example,* ³_____
- Show contrast: *However,* ⁴_____ , *On the other hand*
- Give a personal opinion: *In my opinion,* ⁵_____
- Introduce a conclusion: *In conclusion,* ⁶_____

6 Read this short essay discussing tourism. Choose the correct linkers.

Tourist trap

As travel to remote and exotic locations becomes more affordable, there is a growing demand for trips to developing countries that haven't been considered as holiday destinations until now. This can have both positive and negative effects on the countries.

[1]*For example / First of all*, let's look at some positive effects. Tourism can bring wealth to developing countries. [2]*In my opinion / For instance*, jobs are created and tourists use local shops and businesses. [3]*However / Secondly*, tourism encourages traditional customs, festivals and local handicrafts. [4]*On the other hand / Furthermore*, communication between local people and tourists promotes better cultural understanding.

[5]*In conclusion / On the other hand*, the jobs created by tourism are often seasonal and badly paid. [6]*For instance / Furthermore*, tourism drives up the cost of basic products and local people cannot afford to do their shopping in supermarkets and local shops. [7]*In addition / To sum up*, it can damage the natural environment and increase pollution.

[8]*In conclusion / For instance*, tourism must be managed carefully in developing countries. [9]*Personally, I think / Furthermore*, tourists need to be more respectful of the local culture and environment.

7 Add appropriate linkers to the social media post below.

My parents booked a holiday to a Caribbean island which has been badly damaged by a tropical storm. [1]_____ , they should have cancelled their holiday. [2]_____ , I think it's wrong to relax on a beach while local people are rebuilding their homes. [3]_____ , there may be a shortage of water and food, and tourists will make matters worse.

Some people disagree. [4]_____ , they say that those destinations may rely on tourism income. [5]_____ hotels, restaurants and taxi drivers will struggle to survive. [6]_____ , people want to go back to normal as soon as possible.

Some tourists may want to help. [7]_____ , it's important that they do it through an organisation.

[8]_____ , my parents should do some research before they go and find out what the local people think.

COMMENTS

I agree with you! Your parents should cancel their holiday and send the money to the people who have lost everything.

8 You are going to write an essay on the topic of keeping animals in zoos. Mark the arguments F (for) or A (against).
  1 There are opportunities for research.
  2 The animals suffer from stress and depression.
  3 It is very difficult to recreate the animals' natural environments.
  4 Endangered species can be protected.

9 Match the arguments in Exercise 8 with supporting examples below.
  a For instance, birds kept in zoos can never fly freely like wild birds.
  b For example, we have learned more about genetics from studying zoo animals.
  c For instance, some species which used to be wild are now only found in zoos.
  d For example, some animals become stressed because of contact with zoo visitors.

10 Write two more arguments for or against keeping animals in zoos. Write supporting examples.

> **SHOW WHAT YOU'VE LEARNT**
>
> **11** Do the writing task. Use the ideas in Exercises 8 and 9, and the WRITING FOCUS and the LANGUAGE FOCUS to help you.
>
> Write an essay in which you present arguments for and against keeping animals in zoos.

5.8 SPEAKING

Expressing and justifying an opinion

I can describe a picture and express and justify my opinion about it.

SPEAKING FOCUS

Describing, comparing and contrasting pictures
The three pictures show/focus on/illustrate …
Picture X is/looks interesting/attractive, but …
Picture X is more … than the other pictures.
Picture X isn't as … as the other pictures.

Choosing one of the options and justifying the choice
I think the best option would be X because …
I prefer/I'd go for/I'd (definitely) choose picture X because …
I like the (first/second) picture best for two reasons. Firstly, because … and secondly, because …
Out of these three pictures, I'd choose picture X because …

Explaining reasons for rejecting other options
The problem with picture X is that …
Personally, I wouldn't go for X because …
I wouldn't choose the picture showing … because …
The reason I don't like X is because …

---

1 SPEAKING Look at the logos and discuss which one you would choose and why.

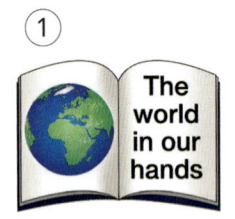

2 🔊 **2.36** Listen to the head teacher and two students discussing the three logos. Which logo do they choose and why?

3 🔊 **2.36** Read the SPEAKING FOCUS and complete the dialogue with one word in each gap. Then listen again and check.

HT: So, what do you think of these three designs?

S1: Personally, I think they're all great. The three logos focus ¹_____ the environment. Logos 2 and 3 are attractive and amusing. But I think the best option would be logo number 1 ²_____ it has a serious message about learning.

S2: I agree, but the ³_____ with logo number 1 is that it doesn't mention 'Eco School'. Logo number 2 looks attractive, but it doesn't ⁴_____ school or learning. So ⁵_____ choose number 3 because it's clever and simple.

S1: Personally, I wouldn't ⁶_____ for number 3. I'd definitely ⁷_____ logo number 1 because it's ⁸_____ effective ⁹_____ the other two, and the message is clear. The words suggest that we are responsible for the future of the planet.

HT: ¹⁰_____ of these three logos, I'd choose logo number 3. I ¹¹_____ choose the logo showing vegetables because it doesn't look serious. I like logo number 3 for two reasons. ¹²_____, because the glasses suggest learning and ¹³_____ , because I think we need the words 'Eco School' in the logo. So let's go for number 3. I'll call the designer …

4 Rewrite the sentences about the posters below using the words in brackets. Which sentences do you agree with?

1 Posters 1, 2 and 3 illustrate the effects of global warming. (show)
2 Poster 2 is more shocking than Posters 1 and 3. (not as … as)
3 Poster 2 is effective but I like Poster 1 better. (prefer)
4 The meaning of Poster 2 is not clear. (problem)
5 I don't like Poster 2 because it's frightening. (reason)

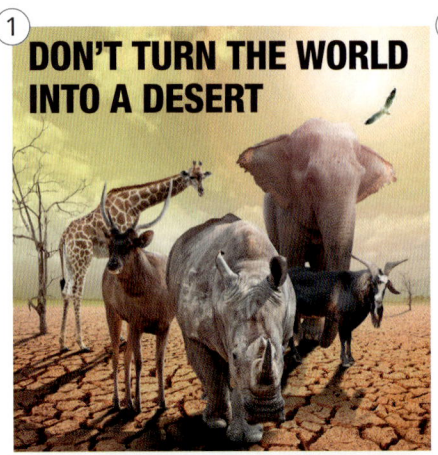

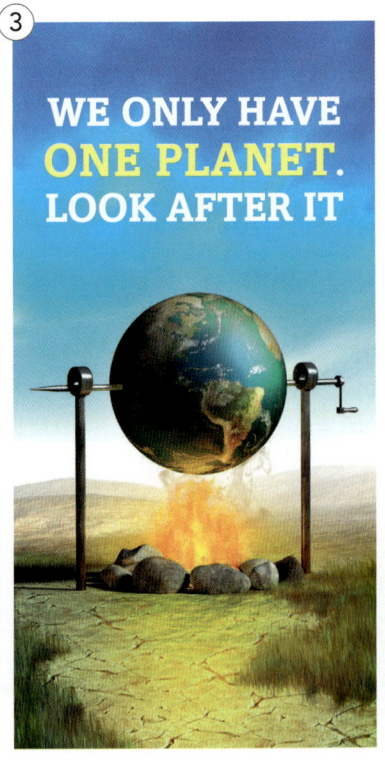

5 SPEAKING You are organising a Stop global warming! campaign at school and need to choose a poster to advertise it. Use the SPEAKING FOCUS to help you.

- Choose the poster in Exercise 4 which, in your opinion, is most appropriate and support your choice with some reasons.
- Explain why you have rejected other options.

ROLE-PLAY Expressing and justifying an opinion

▶ **23** Watch the video and practise. Then role-play your dialogue.

UNIT 5 — Planet Earth — Word list

5.1 Vocabulary 🔊 4.33
be made up of /bi ˌmeɪd ˈʌp əv/
breadth /bredθ/
broad /brɔːd/
broaden /ˈbrɔːdn/
calm sea /ˌkɑːm ˈsiː/
come across /ˌkʌm əˈkrɒs/
come in /ˌkʌm ˈɪn/
dangerous current /ˌdeɪndʒərəs ˈkʌrənt/
deep /diːp/
deepen /ˈdiːpən/
depth /depθ/
desert/remote island /ˌdezət/rɪˌməʊt ˈaɪlənd/
die out /ˌdaɪ ˈaʊt/
fast-flowing/slow-moving river /ˌfɑːst ˌfləʊɪŋ/ˌsləʊ ˌmuːvɪŋ ˈrɪvə/
flow /fləʊ/
giant/huge wave /ˌdʒaɪənt/ˌhjuːdʒ ˈweɪv/
go out /ˌɡəʊ ˈaʊt/
heat up /ˌhiːt ˈʌp/
heavy/rough sea /ˌhevi/ˌrʌf ˈsiː/
height /haɪt/
heighten /ˈhaɪtn/
high/rising tide /ˌhaɪ/ˌraɪzɪŋ ˈtaɪd/
length /leŋθ/
lengthen /ˈleŋθən/
long /lɒŋ/
low tide /ˌləʊ ˈtaɪd/
mountain peak /ˈmaʊntən piːk/
mountain range /ˈmaʊntən reɪndʒ/
mountain ridge /ˈmaʊntən rɪdʒ/
ocean current /ˈəʊʃən ˌkʌrənt/
river bank /ˈrɪvə bæŋk/
seabed /ˈsiːbed/
stir up /ˌstɜːr ˈʌp/
strength /streŋθ/
strengthen /ˈstreŋθən/
strong /strɒŋ/
strong current /ˌstrɒŋ ˈkʌrənt/
tidal wave /ˈtaɪdl weɪv/
tropical island /ˌtrɒpɪkəl ˈaɪlənd/
volcanic eruption /vɒlˌkænɪk ɪˈrʌpʃən/
whale /weɪl/
wide /waɪd/
widen /ˈwaɪdn/
width /wɪdθ/
winding river /ˌwaɪndɪŋ ˈrɪvə/

5.2 Grammar 🔊 4.34
capital city /ˌkæpɪtl ˈsɪti/
continent /ˈkɒntənənt/
country /ˈkʌntri/
economic growth /ˌekənɒmɪk ˈɡrəʊθ/
expand /ɪkˈspænd/
inhabitant /ɪnˈhæbətənt/
innovation /ˌɪnəˈveɪʃən/
locate /ləʊˈkeɪt/
megacity /ˈmeɡəsɪti/
population /ˌpɒpjəˈleɪʃən/
poverty /ˈpɒvəti/
predict /prɪˈdɪkt/
production /prəˈdʌkʃən/
provide /prəˈvaɪd/
vertical /ˈvɜːtɪkəl/

5.3 Listening 🔊 4.35
affect /əˈfekt/
air quality /ˈeə ˌkwɒləti/
bicycle rack /ˈbaɪsɪkəl ræk/
climate /ˈklaɪmət/
climate change /ˈklaɪmət tʃeɪndʒ/
electricity /eˌlekˈtrɪsəti/
environment /ɪnˈvaɪrənmənt/
environmental issues /ɪnˌvaɪrənˈmentl ˈɪʃuːz/
gadget /ˈɡædʒət/
global warming /ˌɡləʊbəl ˈwɔːmɪŋ/
in the school grounds /ɪn ðə ˈskuːl ˌɡraʊndz/
low-energy light bulb /ˌləʊ ˌenədʒi ˈlaɪt bʌlb/
organic /ɔːˈɡænɪk/
recycle /ˌriːˈsaɪkəl/
recycling bin /ˌriːˈsaɪklɪŋ bɪn/
renewable energy /rɪˌnjuːəbəl ˈenədʒi/
save electricity /ˌseɪv eˌlekˈtrɪsəti/
solar panels /ˌsəʊlə ˈpænlz/

5.4 Reading 🔊 4.36
backpack /ˈbækpæk/
bear /beə/
bear encounter /ˈbeər ɪnˌkaʊntə/
bee /biː/
branch /ˈbrɑːntʃ/
clearing /ˈklɪərɪŋ/
come face to face with /ˌkʌm ˌfeɪs tə ˈfeɪs wɪð/
cub /kʌb/
defend /dɪˈfend/
die from /ˈdaɪ frəm/
flashlight /ˈflæʃlaɪt/
fox /fɒks/
go off /ˌɡəʊ ˈɒf/
gorge yourself /ˈɡɔːdʒ jɔːˌself/
hedgehog /ˈhedʒhɒɡ/
in the bushes /ɪn ðə ˈbʊʃɪz/
insect repellent /ˈɪnsekt rɪˌpelənt/
leaf/leaves /liːf/liːvz/
nail clippers /ˈneɪl ˌklɪpəz/
pancake /ˈpænkeɪk/
path /pɑːθ/
pepper spray /ˈpepə spreɪ/
pitch black /ˌpɪtʃ ˈblæk/
pond /pɒnd/
predator /ˈpredətə/
prey /preɪ/
reach for /ˈriːtʃ fə/
root /ruːt/
search through /ˌsɜːtʃ ˈθruː/
sharp knife /ˌʃɑːp ˈnaɪf/
sit around /ˌsɪt əˈraʊnd/
skunk /skʌŋk/
sleep through /ˌsliːp ˈθruː/
sleeping bag /ˈsliːpɪŋ bæɡ/
snore /snɔː/
spring /sprɪŋ/
squirrel /ˈskwɪrəl/
store food /ˌstɔː ˈfuːd/
sunscreen /ˈsʌnskriːn/
trail /treɪl/
trunk /trʌŋk/

5.5 Grammar 🔊 4.37
bite /baɪt/
cage /keɪdʒ/
coast /kəʊst/
dolphin /ˈdɒlfən/
female elephant/gorilla/bear /ˈfiːmeɪl ˈeləfənt/ɡəˈrɪlə/ˈbeə/
herd /hɜːd/
leader /ˈliːdə/
make a complete recovery /ˌmeɪk ə kəmˌpliːt rɪˈkʌvəri/
owe /əʊ/
rescuer /ˈreskjuːə/
shark /ʃɑːk/
surgeon /ˈsɜːdʒən/
surround /səˈraʊnd/
unconscious /ʌnˈkɒnʃəs/

5.6 Use of English 🔊 4.38
agree with /əˈɡriː wɪð/
believe in /bəˈliːv ɪn/
care about /ˈkeər əˌbaʊt/
criticised for /ˈkrɪtɪsaɪzd fə/
crops /ˈkrɒps/
deal with /ˈdiːl wɪð/
earthquake /ˈɜːθkweɪk/
erupt /ɪˈrʌpt/
evacuate /ɪˈvækjueɪt/
evacuation /ɪˌvækjuˈeɪʃən/
focus on /ˈfəʊkəs ɒn/
get help from /ˌɡet ˈhelp frəm/
happen to /ˈhæpən tə/
hurricane /ˈhʌrəkeɪn/
rely on /rɪˈlaɪ ɒn/
tsunami /tsʊˈnɑːmi/
volcano /vɒlˈkeɪnəʊ/
wait for /ˈweɪt fə/
wind /ˈwɪnd/

5.7 Writing 🔊 4.39
affordable /əˈfɔːdəbəl/
beggar /ˈbeɡə/
benefit from /ˈbenəfɪt frəm/
developing countries /dɪˌveləpɪŋ ˈkʌntriz/
endangered species /ɪnˌdeɪndʒəd ˈspiːʃiːz/
get access to /ˌɡet ˈækses tə/
instant communication /ˌɪnstənt kəˌmjuːnəˈkeɪʃən/
local handicrafts /ˌləʊkəl ˈhændɪkrɑːfts/
location /ləʊˈkeɪʃən/
make contact with /ˌmeɪk ˈkɒntækt wɪð/
outside world /ˌaʊtsaɪd ˈwɜːld/
pollution /pəˈluːʃən/
rainforest /ˈreɪnfɒrɪst/
recreate /ˌriːkriˈeɪt/
running water /ˌrʌnɪŋ ˈwɔːtə/
shortage of water and food /ˈʃɔːtɪdʒ əv ˌwɔːtə ənd ˈfuːd/
tourism income /ˈtʊərɪzəm ˌɪŋkʌm/
tribal people /ˌtraɪbəl ˈpiːpəl/
tribe /traɪb/
way of life /ˌweɪ əv ˈlaɪf/

5.8 Speaking 🔊 4.40
desert /ˈdezət/
effective /ɪˈfektɪv/
frightening /ˈfraɪtnɪŋ/
reject /rɪˈdʒekt/
shocking /ˈʃɒkɪŋ/

FOCUS REVIEW 5

VOCABULARY AND GRAMMAR

1 Complete the sentences with the words in the box. There are two extra words.

calm   fast   heavy   long   low   remote   strong

1 It is dangerous to swim here because of the _____ current which could pull you out to sea.
2 Going kayaking on such a _____-flowing river is exciting but it needs a lot of skill.
3 North Keeling is such a _____ island that few people have ever been there.
4 The beach is so much bigger at _____ tide that it takes ages to walk down to the water.
5 It was such a _____ sea that our boat hardly moved up and down at all.

2 Choose the correct option.

1 I can't believe you slept *away / through / along* the storm. The wind was really loud!
2 It is important to develop *returnable / renewable / reusable* energy instead of depending on oil, gas and coal.
3 It is obvious that climate *turn / exchange / change* is happening, but not everyone agrees on the cause.
4 We were really scared when we *went / came / turned* face to face with a bear in the forest.
5 Because of global *heating / changing / warming*, storms are becoming more frequent and dangerous.

3 Complete the sentences with *a*, *an*, *the* or Ø (no article).

1 We were about to start our hike when we saw that ___ tree had fallen across ___ trail.
2 In ___ 20th century, almost fifty percent of the global population lived in ___ cities.
3 In fact, ___ scientists expect ___ major earthquake to hit ___ Los Angeles soon.
4 There was no ___ running water in ___ village where my granddad lived as ___ child.
5 ___ Europe isn't ___ largest continent in ___ world.

4 Add the information in brackets to the sentences using non-defining relative clauses.

1 Tokyo is the capital of Japan. (It is a megacity.)
_____
2 My friend Jenny knows a lot about environmental issues. (Her mother is a scientist.)
_____
3 The company builds houses all over the country. (It has been accused of cutting down too many trees.)
_____
4 The tribal leader wants to teach his people about the outside world. (He studied in Paris.)
_____
5 People in Liverpool are working to improve the environment. (Janet opened her shop there.)
_____

USE OF ENGLISH

5 Complete the sentences with the correct form of the words in brackets. Use up to six words in each gap and make any changes necessary.

1 Some people claim that water shortage is _____ (which/we/should/worry), and I think they are right.
2 The bald eagle, _____ (be/national/bird) the United States of America, is no longer on the list of endangered species.
3 That environmental protester, _____ (now/sit) in the biggest tree in the park, says he will come down when they promise not to cut it down.
4 Instead of just complaining about damage to the environment, the issues _____ (we/need/focus) are preserving nature and using renewable energy.
5 Several members of this group, _____ (purpose/be) to stop cutting down trees in the area, have been arrested by the police.

6 Complete the text with the correct form of the words in brackets.

ECOLOGICAL TOUR

It may be true that travel can ¹_____ (BROAD) the mind, but going on an ecological tour can ²_____ (DEEP) your knowledge in ways that simple tourism can't do. For example, I went on a tour of the Amazon River which taught me a lot about the damage we are doing to the planet. I also realised why some people have such ³_____ (STRENGTH) arguments for environmental protection. It was an amazing holiday and although we didn't travel the entire ⁴_____ (LONG) of the Amazon, we saw trees of an amazing ⁵_____ (HIGH) that may one day disappear from our planet. Because of the ⁶_____ (WIDE) of the river it is sometimes called a sea and it is home to hundreds of plants, animals and fish. I can't imagine one day waking up and finding that all of this life is gone.

LISTENING

7 🔊 **2.37** Listen to a radio interview about monarch butterflies and choose the correct answer, A, B, C or D.

1 What is true about monarch butterflies?
 A Most of them live in the United States.
 B Many of them stay in Mexico after the winter.
 C The species no longer exists in North America.
 D They migrate from the US to Mexico in winter.
2 How are the monarch butterfly and the milkweed plant connected?
 A The monarch causes damage to the milkweed.
 B The milkweed needs the monarch to survive.
 C The milkweed is necessary for young monarch butterflies.
 D The monarch eats milkweed when there is nothing else.
3 Dr Clarke says that people in Mexico
 A can't help the monarch in any way.
 B should stop destroying the forests.
 C shouldn't use chemicals in agriculture.
 D must plant milkweed in their gardens.
4 Dr Clarke mainly talks about
 A why monarch butterflies migrate over long distances.
 B the effects of farming on the life of monarch butterflies.
 C why monarch butterflies fly to warmer climates.
 D the problems monarch butterflies are facing.

WRITING

8 Ask and answer the questions.

1 What are the advantages of having a pet?
2 What are the disadvantages of having a pet?

9 Read the exam task and plan your essay. In pairs, discuss your ideas.

> People who want to adopt a pet from an animal shelter often have to prove they have the space and time to look after a new pet. Write an essay in which you present arguments for and against this rule.

10 Write the essay in Exercise 9.

SPEAKING

11 Ask and answer the questions.

1 What can people do to protect animal rights better in your country?
2 Some people say that animals should have the same rights as humans because they have emotions. Do you agree? Why?/Why not?
3 What animals are the most popular pets and why?
4 Why do you think some people keep exotic, and often dangerous, animals as pets?

12 Describe the posters and discuss which one is most effective.

A HELP THE BIRD SANCTUARY. MAKE A DONATION TODAY!

B SAVE A LIFE! ADOPT, DON'T BUY!

C HELP US LOOK AFTER WILD ANIMALS. BECOME A FRIEND OF THE ZOO.

13 Look at the diagram. It shows different ways to help animals. In pairs, follow these steps.
- Talk to each other about the advantages and disadvantages of these ways of helping animals.
- Decide which is the best way to help animals.

- report people who are cruel to animals
- donate to animal charities
- adopt pets from rescue centres
- join online campaigns
- help out at animal sanctuaries

What are the advantages and disadvantages of these ways of helping animals?

6

Good health

The only way to keep your health is to eat what you don't want, drink what you don't like, and do what you'd rather not.

Mark Twain

BBC

CAFFEINE ALTERNATIVES

▶ 24 Watch the BBC video. For the worksheet, go to page 126.

6.1 VOCABULARY

Parts of the body • injuries • body idioms

I can talk about parts of the body and injuries.

SHOW WHAT YOU KNOW

1 Draw a man or a woman's body and label it with the words in the box. Compare your drawing with a partner.

> bottom   chest   eyebrow   fingernail   forehead   hip   knee
> lips   neck   shoulder   big toe   tongue

2 Label as many other parts of the body on your drawing as you can in sixty seconds. Compare again. How many words do you know?

3 **SPEAKING** Look at the cartoon and read the excuses for missing school on page 75. Discuss the questions.
   1 Which excuses does the picture illustrate?
   2 Which excuse is the most believable?
   3 Which excuse is the least believable?

These are all genuine excuses that students have given for missing school.

Dear Sir …

1 I slipped on a coin and **sprained my ankle**.
2 My parrot has flu and I need to take care of it.
3 I fell out of bed and **dislocated my shoulder**.
4 My toe got stuck in the bath tap and it's broken (the toe, not the tap).
5 My nose is blocked and I can't breathe.
6 I **burnt my hand** on the toaster.
7 I poked myself in the eye while combing my hair and I've got bruises and a black eye.
8 I **broke my arm** trying to catch a falling sandwich.
9 I got dizzy from reading too much.
10 I've got **a sore finger**.
11 I've been **bitten by an insect**.
12 I was there all the time – you just didn't notice me.

C

D

Go to WORD STORE 6 page 13

WORD STORE 6A Parts of the body

4 🔊 2.38 Label the picture in WORD STORE 6A with the words in the box. Use a dictionary if necessary. Then listen, check and repeat.

5 SPEAKING Test your partner's physical abilities! Use the words in WORD STORE 6A and find out what your partner can do.

Can you touch your left ankle with your chin?
Can you touch your right cheek with your left shoulder?

WORD STORE 6B Injuries

6 🔊 2.39 Complete WORD STORE 6B with the words in red in Exercise 3. Then listen, check and repeat.

7 Choose the correct option. Then ask and answer the questions.

Have you ever …
1 … been bitten by *a dog / a plant*?
2 … broken your *hair / thumb*?
3 … burnt your *tongue / spine*?
4 … dislocated your *shoulder / forehead*?
5 … had a black *eye / neck*?
6 … sprained your *fingernail / ankle*?

8 SPEAKING Choose one of the minor injuries you identified in Exercise 7 or think of another one and tell your partner about the circumstances.

I'll tell you about the time I broke my thumb.
I was playing with my friends in the woods behind my house.
I was about nine or ten. We were …

WORD STORE 6C Body idioms

9 🔊 2.40 Listen to six dialogues. Complete the typical English idioms with the correct body part.

1 I'm pulling your _____ .
2 She broke his _____ .
3 I laughed my _____ off.
4 Can you give me a _____ ?
5 I couldn't believe my _____ .
6 It's on the tip of my _____ .

10 🔊 2.41 Complete WORD STORE 6C with the idioms in Exercise 9. Then listen, check and repeat.

11 SPEAKING Write a short dialogue including an idiom. Act out your dialogue to the class and decide which one is the best.

A: *I heard this fantastic joke yesterday.*
B: *Really?*
A: *Yes, it's so funny I just laughed my head off. It's about a man who …*

75

6.2 GRAMMAR

Second Conditional • wish/if only

I can talk about imaginary situations using the Second Conditional and I wish/If only.

1 What do you know about first aid? Do the quiz and compare your answers with a partner.

DR MAXWELL'S FIRST AID QUIZ

1 If I had a nosebleed, I'd …
 a hold my nose and look up.
 b hold my nose and look down.

2 If I burnt my hand, I'd …
 a hold it under the cold water tap.
 b put oil on it.

3 If I twisted my ankle, I'd …
 a put it in a bowl of hot water.
 b put ice on it.

4 If I got a black eye, I'd …
 a put ice on it.
 b put some eye drops in.

5 If a bee stung me, I'd …
 a take some antihistamine tablets.
 b put a plaster on the sting.

6 If I cut my finger and it was bleeding, I'd …
 a wash and dry it and then put a plaster on.
 b tie something around my wrist to stop the blood flowing.

2 ◉ 2.42 Listen to Dr Maxwell's podcast and check your answers in Exercise 1.

3 Read GRAMMAR FOCUS I and answer the questions.
 1 Are the example sentences about real or imaginary situations?
 2 Are they about the present/future or the past?
 3 Do you have to begin a conditional sentence with 'if'?

GRAMMAR FOCUS I

Second Conditional

You use the **Second Conditional** to talk about the present or future result of an imaginary situation.

imaginary situation → result
 if + Past Simple, would('d)/wouldn't + verb

If I **burnt** my hand, I'**d hold** it under the cold water tap.
I'**d put** ice on the sting if I **didn't have** any tablets.

4 Complete the Second Conditional sentences with the correct form of the verbs in brackets. Which sentences are true for you?
 1 If I *didn't feel* (not feel) well at school, I _____ (go) home.
 2 If I _____ (have) hay fever, I _____ (get) some antihistamine tablets.
 3 I _____ (take) a cold shower if I _____ (have) sunburn.
 4 If I _____ (have) flu, I _____ (not come) to school.
 5 I _____ (have) a cat if I _____ (not be) allergic to them.
 6 If I _____ (hear) a mosquito in my room, I _____ (not be able) to sleep.

5 ◉ 2.43 Listen to Ron talking to a friend. What problems does he have with the following?

 the cat   the window   the neighbours
 his foot   the doctor's phone number

6 ◉ 2.43 Match the sentence halves to show what Ron says about his problems. Then listen again and check.
 1 I wish the cat wouldn't ☐
 2 If only it wasn't ☐
 3 I wish they wouldn't ☐
 4 I wish I wasn't ☐
 5 If only I had ☐

 a so hot.
 b so clumsy.
 c the doctor's phone number.
 d come into the house.
 e play loud music at night.

7 Read GRAMMAR FOCUS II and find another example of each use of *wish/if only* in Exercise 6.

GRAMMAR FOCUS II

wish/if only

- You can use **wish/If only + Past Simple** to say that you really want a present situation to be different.
 I wish I wasn't so clumsy.

- You use **wish/if only + would + verb** to say that you want somebody's present behaviour to change.
 If only the neighbours would be quiet.

Note:
If only is stronger than *wish*.

8 Write a second sentence to show that you would like the situation or behaviour to be different. Which wishes are true for you?
 1 I'm allergic to nuts.
  I wish I wasn't allergic to nuts.
 2 I don't live near the beach.
 3 Our teacher gives us a test every week.
 4 I don't have a motorbike.
 5 I can't play the guitar.
 6 My friend won't let me copy his homework.

9 Complete the sentences. Then write a Second Conditional sentence to explain your wishes.
 1 I wish my parents/sister/brother would/wouldn't …
  I wish my sister would get her own laptop. If she had her own laptop, she wouldn't use mine.
 2 I wish I had/didn't have …
 3 If only I was/wasn't …
 4 I wish I knew …
 5 If only I could …

Grammar page 147

6.3 LISTENING

Note completion

I can understand a news report and an informal conversation on a common topic.

1 **Read UK TODAY and answer the questions.**
   1 How much do UK charities raise every year?
   2 How many people donate money?
   3 What do people do to raise money?

2 **SPEAKING** Discuss which of the charities listed you would give money to.

UK TODAY

Did you know that people donate almost £10 billion to UK charities every year?

Who donates money?
- Over half the adult population.
- The average amount is £18.
- Over 25 percent of people donate online.

What sort of events raise the most money?

London Marathon
- 40,000 participants run a marathon around London.
- Over £890 million has been raised for various charities.

London to Brighton Cycle
- 25,000 participants ride about eighty-seven kilometres.
- The event has raised over £65 million for the British Heart Foundation.

Red Nose Day
- 7.5 million viewers watch a TV 'telethon' organised by British comedians.
- Over £1 billion has been raised so far.
- Money goes to help vulnerable people in the UK and Africa.

3 🔊 **2.44** Listen to two dialogues and a news report. Answer the questions.
   1 Which event is Rob taking part in?
   2 What did Rob's grandfather die of?
   3 How is Rob training for the cycle?
   4 What does Rob's mother want to buy him?
   5 How old is the London to Brighton Cycle?
   6 How old do you have to be to do the London to Brighton Cycle?

EXAM FOCUS Note completion

4 🔊 **2.44** **Listen again to the three recordings. Complete the summary with up to three words in each gap.**

Rob is preparing for the London to Brighton cycle ride. Last year his friend Anna raised ¹_____ pounds for cancer research. Rob wants to raise money for the British Heart Foundation. Anna suggests setting up ²_____. She says it's a good idea to ask adults for sponsorship because they have ³_____ than people Rob and Anna's age. Rob's mother doesn't think his old ⁴_____ enough. She wants to buy him a new one.
The cycle ride starts just after ⁵_____ in the morning. It will take approximately ⁶_____ for most people to reach the coast.

5 🔊 **2.45** Put the sentences in an appropriate order to describe how Rob is going to raise money for charity. Then listen and check.

   [1] Rob is taking part
   [ ] and asks his friends to sponsor
   [ ] the page with people who will donate money
   [ ] money for charity. He sets up a webpage
   [ ] online. The money goes straight to the charity.
   [2] in a cycle race and he wants to raise
   [ ] memory of his grandfather who died from a heart
   [ ] attack. He's going to share
   [ ] him. He explains that he's doing it in

WORD STORE 6D Charity fund-raising

6 🔊 **2.46** Complete WORD STORE 6D with the prepositions or particles in the box. Then listen, check and repeat.

7 **SPEAKING** Complete the questions with an appropriate verb phrase in WORD STORE 6D. Then ask and answer the questions.

   Have you ever …
   1 _____ in a fund-raising event?
   2 _____ for your school?
   3 _____ a friend or a family member?
   4 _____ a webpage to support a charity?
   5 _____ to a local charity?
   6 _____ for a charity sporting event?

8 **SPEAKING** Think of charity events that take place in your country or local area. How do they raise money and what do they use it for?

PRONUNCIATION FOCUS

9 Say the words and cross out the ones with a different vowel sound. In one group more than one answer is possible.
   1 hear heel knee heart
   2 waist hay calf sprain
   3 ice rib wrist sting
   4 burn thumb work hurt
   5 view blood bruise flu

10 🔊 **2.47** Listen, check and repeat.

6.4 READING

Matching

I can scan several short, simple texts on the same topic to find specific information.

1 **SPEAKING** Discuss the questions.
   1 How many different jobs in the medical profession can you think of?
   2 What kind of daily tasks do you think each job involves?
   3 Do you know someone who works in medicine? Tell your partner about them.

2 Read about three medical practitioners. What examples do they give of things that give them job satisfaction?

> **EXAM FOCUS** Matching
>
> 3 Read again and match texts A–C with sentences 1–4. One text has two matching sentences.
>
> This medical practitioner …
> 1 was anxious that he/she would be unable to save his/her patient's life.
> 2 would like to have more say in choosing who he/she treats.
> 3 feels that it is his/her duty to deal with all sorts of different situations.
> 4 knows that if he/she overreacts, it doesn't help anybody.

Life in Medicine – Three Snapshots

🔊 3.1

If you like surprises, and can face dealing with accidents, injuries, births and deaths, medicine is for you. For those of you considering a career in medicine, three people give a snapshot of their medical life.

A **Dr Richard Young told us about the more unusual and unexpected locations where he's used his medical skills.**

'I'm a doctor, and I work in a doctor's surgery where I treat patients, write prescriptions, and generally help people recover from illnesses and injuries. But that's only part of the story!

5 I've given people first aid in public places several times – once I helped a man who collapsed in a park. Another time, a teenager was suffering from a nut allergy.

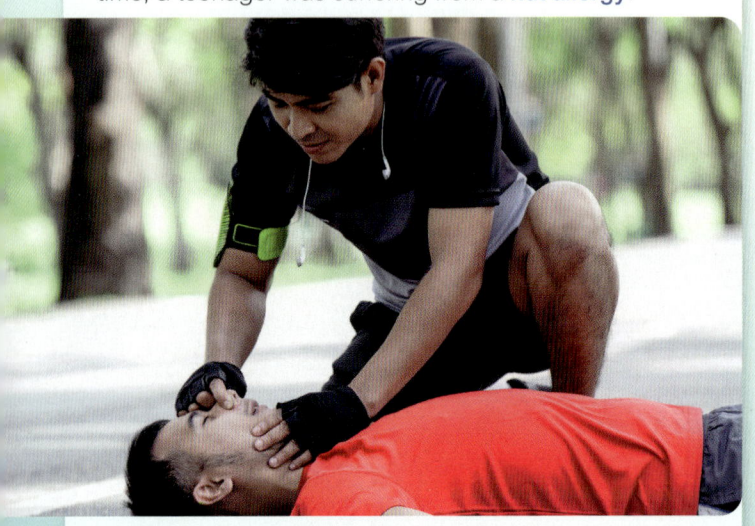

On flights, nervous passengers often have panic attacks and doctors are asked to calm them down. When I hear
10 "Is there a doctor on board?" I always offer my help. Once, on a flight from London to Los Angeles I helped a woman who was seriously ill. I spent the twelve-hour flight caring for her. I stayed with her after we landed until the ambulance arrived, which meant that I missed
15 my connecting flight, but I was happy to help. In my job, saving lives must come first, even when I'm off duty.'

B **Some nurses choose to work in extreme conditions, like war zones. Senior nurse Sonia Costa spent two months in Yemen as part of a Doctors without Borders* emergency team.**

'I decided to work in Yemen because, as a result of war, there was a cholera epidemic and over 620,000 people were suffering from the disease. In places where there's no clean food or water, people catch diseases easily.
5 I worked on the children's ward and one of my patients was a six-month-old baby boy who was so ill that he looked like a two-week-old. Each morning, I arrived at the hospital, afraid that I may not see the child in his bed. But finally, he started gaining weight and when he was well enough to go
10 home, I was the happiest nurse in the hospital.'

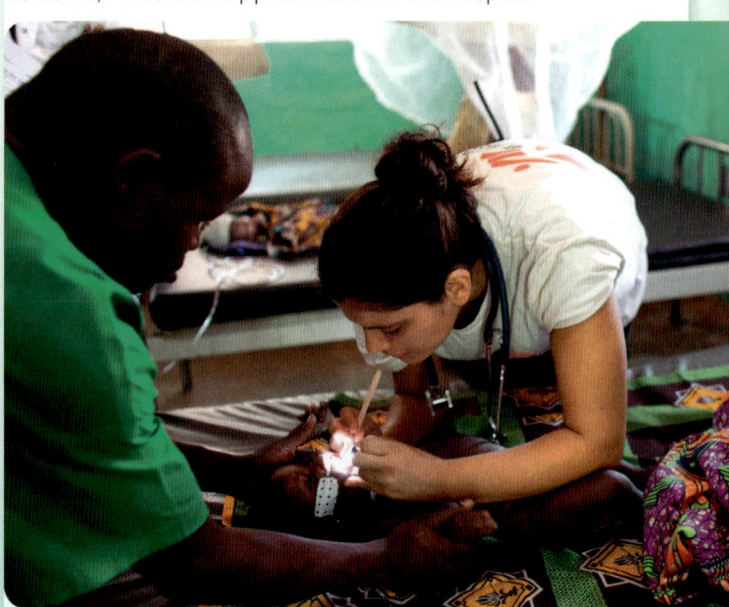

**Doctors without Borders, also known as Médecins Sans Frontières, is an international organisation helping people in war zones and developing countries.*

78

4 🔊 **3.2** Complete the collocations with a noun or adjective from the words in blue in the text. Then listen, check and repeat.

1. a food/a _nut_ allergy
2. a stable/a _____ condition
3. a deep/a _____ cut
4. a flu/a _____ epidemic
5. a muscle/a _____ pain
6. a local/a _____ surgery
7. a rescue/an _____ team
8. a maternity/a _____ ward

5 Use appropriate collocations in Exercise 4 to answer the comprehension questions. Then check your answers in the text.

1. Where does Dr Young usually treat patients?
2. What did he once treat a teenager in a restaurant for?
3. Why did Sonia Costa decide to work in Yemen?
4. Which ward did she work on in the hospital?
5. What is the most common call that Sally James deals with?
6. What sort of situations is she trained to deal with?

6 SPEAKING Think of three questions to ask your partner using different collocations in Exercise 4. Ask and answer the questions.

Have you got any food allergies?
Have you ever visited a maternity ward?

7 SPEAKING Discuss the pros and cons of working as one of the medical professionals described in the text. What would be the best or worst thing? Think about the following:

- qualifications
- hours
- job satisfaction
- training
- salary

8 SPEAKING Would you consider a career in medicine? Why?/Why not?

WORD STORE 6E Health issues

9 🔊 **3.3** Complete WORD STORE 6E with the underlined phrases in the text. Then listen, check and repeat.

10 🔊 **3.4** Put the sentences in an appropriate order to describe two funny experiences that Doctor Roberts has had. Then listen and check.

- [1] I'm Doctor Roberts and I'm proud to say I've saved
- [ ] attack. She recovered quickly when I gave her
- [ ] had some funny experiences. Once, I was on
- [ ] first aid. Then she told me I looked like her third husband.
- [ ] 'Two' she replied! Last week, I was treating
- [2] lives and helped many people. I've even delivered
- [ ] better, but the medicine tasted awful. I'd written
- [ ] a baby on a flight to New York. But I've also
- [ ] a bus when an elderly lady had a panic
- [ ] I asked her how many husbands she'd had.
- [ ] a patient for earache. Today she told me she felt much
- [ ] a prescription for eardrops!

11 SPEAKING Discuss what personality and what qualities a doctor needs. Do you think a sense of humour is one of them?

I think a doctor needs to be patient and hard-working. Everybody should have a sense of humour, not only doctors!

C Unpredictability is a daily reality for paramedics. Sally James says there is no such thing as a typical day.

'I work a twelve-hour shift. I never know when I might have to try and save someone's life, but I stay calm, because if I panic, everybody else gets anxious too.

Some days, nothing dramatic happens. The most
5 common call is **stomach pain**, and we get a lot of non-emergency calls like toothaches or **shaving cuts** or people who say they've burned themselves on their hair straighteners, which is annoying, but we have to take them seriously. While we're dealing with these time
10 wasters, we may get a call from someone who really needs us, but there's nothing we can do about it.

We're not doctors, but we're highly trained to deal with **serious conditions** like heart attacks. But my favourite thing is **delivering a baby**. If I can start my day by
15 getting someone's heart beating again, and end it with childbirth, I'm happy.'

6.5 GRAMMAR

Third Conditional

I can talk about hypothetical past results of a past action using the Third Conditional.

1 🔊 3.5 Read and listen to an incredible survival story. What two decisions did Simon Yates have to make? Do you think he made the right decisions?

DECISION TIME

In 1985, two young climbers, Joe Simpson and Simon Yates, were the first climbers to climb the west face of the Siula Grande mountain in the Andes. But as they were coming down the mountain, Simpson fell and broke his leg badly. Yates had to make a terrible decision – should he leave his friend or should he try to get him down the mountain. He chose the second option. If he had left his friend, Simpson would have died. Yates tied himself to Simpson with a rope and they slowly came down the mountain together. Then disaster struck again. Simpson fell and was hanging over a cliff. Yates couldn't hold him. He found his penknife and decided to cut the rope. Simpson fell twenty-five metres. Yates returned to base camp alone. He was sure Simpson was dead. But he also knew that if he hadn't cut the rope, he would have fallen and died too. Miraculously, Simpson didn't die. He pulled himself slowly along the ground with a broken leg for three days and nights. He arrived back at base camp just in time. Yates would have already left if Simpson had arrived a few hours later.

2 Answer the questions about the story.
  1 Why didn't Yates leave Simpson when he broke his leg?
  2 Why did Yates cut the rope?
  3 Why did Simpson arrive at base camp 'just in time'?

3 Read the GRAMMAR FOCUS and underline the three Third Conditional sentences in the story. Do you always begin a Third Conditional sentence with If?

GRAMMAR FOCUS

Third Conditional

You use the **Third Conditional** to talk about the imaginary past result of an imaginary past event.

imaginary past event → imaginary past result
if + Past Perfect, **would/wouldn't have** + Past Participle

… if he **hadn't cut** the rope, he **would have fallen** and **died** too.
(real past event: he cut the rope →
real past result: he didn't fall and die)

4 Complete more Third Conditional sentences about the story.
  1 If Simpson _hadn't fallen_ (not fall), he _____ (not break) his leg.
  2 If Simpson _____ (not break) his leg, the climbers _____ (come down) the mountain without a problem.
  3 If Yates _____ (be able) to hold Simpson, he _____ (not have to) cut the rope.
  4 Yates _____ (not be able) to cut the rope if he _____ (not find) a penknife.
  5 Yates _____ (not leave) Simpson on the mountain if he _____ (know) he was still alive.

5 Read about three more incredible survival stories. Use your imagination and write Third Conditional sentences to describe alternative outcomes for each story.

(A) In 2003, Aron Ralston went hiking alone in a canyon in Utah. He trapped his arm under a rock and couldn't move. He had a penknife. He cut off his own arm. Ralston survived.

(B) In 1996, Pete Goss was leading a round the world yacht race. During a terrible storm, he got an emergency call. Another competitor – Raphaël Dinelli – was in trouble and Goss's boat was the only one in the area. Goss turned back. He saved Dinelli's life but lost the race.

(C) In 1972, the pilot of a plane carrying a Uruguayan rugby team miscalculated his position and crashed 3,600 metres up in the Andes. The plane was white and the rescue teams couldn't see it. There was no food and the survivors had to eat their dead teammates. Only sixteen people survived.

A If Ralston had been hiking with a friend, his friend would have helped him.

6 **SPEAKING** Compare your sentences in Exercise 5 with a partner. Which story do you like best and why?

7 Use your imagination and write three Third Conditional sentences using three of the endings provided.
  1 … I would've been much happier.
  2 … I would've had a great weekend.
  3 … I wouldn't have felt so tired this morning.
  4 … I wouldn't have enjoyed it.
  5 … I wouldn't have bought one.

If I had got a bike for my last birthday, I would've been much happier.

Grammar page 148

6.6 USE OF ENGLISH

Clauses of purpose

I can use a range of clauses of purpose.

1 **SPEAKING** Discuss the questions.
   1 What's your ideal time for going to bed?
   2 How quickly do you fall asleep?
   3 What things prevent you from falling asleep?
   4 What do you do if you can't sleep?

2 🔊 3.6 Listen to a lecture on sleep. Which of the professor's tips do you think are the most useful?

3 🔊 3.6 Match the sentence halves from the lecture. Then listen again and check.
   1 Professor Turner carries out research
   2 You need to be relaxed in body and mind
   3 What can you do
   4 Your body temperature needs to drop by one degree Centigrade
   5 Make sure you have good curtains or blinds
   6 You can use an app
   7 You should go to bed at the same time every night

   a to track the number of hours and quality of sleep.
   b in order to understand insomnia.
   c in order not to wake up when the sun rises.
   d so as not to upset your body clock.
   e in order to fall asleep.
   f so that your metabolism can start slowing down.
   g to fall asleep within ten minutes?

4 Read the LANGUAGE FOCUS and complete the example sentences. How do you say the sentences in your language?

LANGUAGE FOCUS

Clauses of purpose

- You can use a **to infinitive** to say why somebody does something. You can also use **in order (not) to** or **so as (not) to** in a more formal style.
  You can use an app **to track** [1]_____ .
  Professor Turner carries out research **in order to understand** [2]_____ .
  You should go to bed at the same time every night **so as not to upset** [3]_____ .

- You can also use **so that** + subject + verb.
  Your body temperature needs to drop by one degree Centigrade **so that** [4]_____ .

5 **USE OF ENGLISH** Use one word in each gap to complete the clauses of purpose in this extract from an article by Professor Turner.

We need to sleep eight hours every night in [1]_____ to feel alert and well during the day, right? Well no, not necessarily. Different people need different amounts of sleep so [2]_____ to be at their best during the day. Everyone is different. Some people can drink coffee before going to bed and sleep like a baby, while others avoid drinking coffee in the afternoon so [3]_____ the caffeine won't keep them awake. But there are certain facts about sleep that are true for everyone: in order [4]_____ get to sleep you need a relaxed body and a quiet mind. The way you get there depends on what works for you. Some people listen to music [5]_____ mask other noises such as traffic and other city sounds, others read until they fall asleep, and you can always count sheep so [6]_____ not to allow your brain to worry about the stresses of the day.

6 Complete the sentences about you and the things you do. Then compare with a partner.
   1 I *set the alarm on my phone* in order not to oversleep.
   2 I _____ to keep warm.
   3 I _____ so as not to be late.
   4 I _____ in order to make friends.
   5 I _____ so that I can get fit.

7 **SPEAKING** Discuss why people do these things and complete the sentences. Use all the words in the box at least once.

   as   in   not   order   so   that   to

   1 People go on diets …
   2 Governments collect taxes …
   3 People climb mountains …
   4 People get tattoos …
   5 Teenagers use social media …
   6 People learn languages …

FOCUS VLOG | About health and sleep

▶ 27 Watch the Focus Vlog. For the worksheet, go to page 127.

Use of English page 149

6.7 WRITING

A factual article

I can write a simple article summarising key facts and using linking words.

1 **SPEAKING** Read the announcement below and discuss the questions.
   1 What facilities and classes should a good youth centre offer?
   2 How do young people benefit from such facilities and training?

LOCAL NEWS

HOME | NEWS | WORLD | FINANCE | CULTURE

Are you aged sixteen-eighteen and from the local area? If so, the city council would like to hear from you. Using government funding, we plan to invest in improving the lives of fourteen-eighteen year olds in our local community. What facilities should young people have access to in the place where they live and how would they benefit as a result? Write an article and send it to us at **b_y_c_@citycouncil.com**. All ideas will be considered for investment and your article could be published on our website.

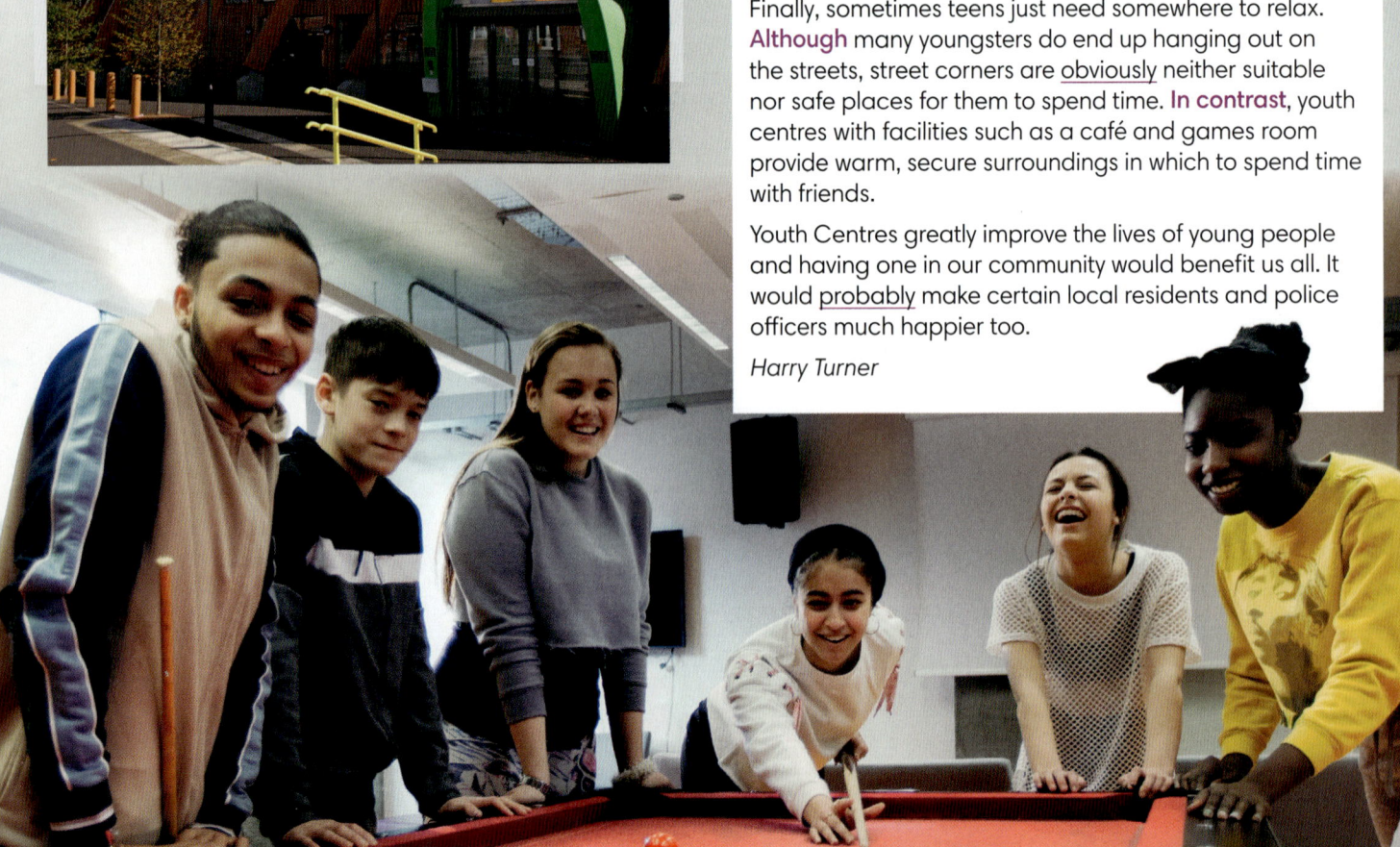

2 Read Harry's article. Which of your suggestions from Exercise 1 does he mention?

No more **street corners**!
The value of youth centres

"Go and make noise somewhere else!" Sadly, this is the type of complaint that many **young people** have to face far too frequently. Unhappy local residents are quick to complain about groups of **teens** hanging around the streets, **but what alternatives do they have**? "Go play outside your own house!" Unfortunately, that doesn't solve the real problem; there is often nowhere suitable for **youngsters** to go in their free time. What is needed are youth centres **so** teens can keep fit, learn new skills and socialise in a safe environment.

According to research, access to youth centres plays an important role in helping young people stay healthy. National statistics show that weight problems are increasingly common in the UK, and this is certainly visible in our community. Clearly, the opportunity to use a gym, or do yoga or dance classes at a youth centre could help solve this problem and improve lives. **Additionally**, according to experts, offering classes in things like fitness or martial arts is an effective way to encourage both health and self-discipline.

As well as this, centres for young people can provide training in a variety of practical skills. Most young people are very busy at school and **as a result**, they don't have time to learn things like first aid, cookery, or bike mechanics. Offering classes of this sort at a youth centre would certainly be a practical use of government money.

Finally, sometimes teens just need somewhere to relax. **Although** many youngsters do end up hanging out on the streets, street corners are obviously neither suitable nor safe places for them to spend time. **In contrast**, youth centres with facilities such as a café and games room provide warm, secure surroundings in which to spend time with friends.

Youth Centres greatly improve the lives of young people and having one in our community would benefit us all. It would probably make certain local residents and police officers much happier too.

Harry Turner

3 Complete the WRITING FOCUS with the words in purple from Harry's article.

WRITING FOCUS

A factual article

Title
- Give your article a catchy title:
  ¹*No more* street corners *!*

Body
- Engage the reader by addressing them directly at times (e.g. ask a question):
  ² *... but what _____ ?*
- Show a range of vocabulary and avoid repeating words:
  ... ³_____ have to face far too often ...
  ... groups of ⁴_____ hanging around the streets ...
  ... there is often nowhere for ⁵_____ to go ...
- Refer to statistics/official data:
  ... According to research ...
- Use a range of linkers.
- to add something: ⁶_____ ⁷_____
- to show a contrast: ⁸_____ ⁹_____
- to show a result: ¹⁰_____ ¹¹_____

Ending
- Write an ending that summarises the article, or is funny or interesting.

4 Link the pairs of sentences using the expression in brackets.

1. A youth centre is a place to make friends. It is a place to exercise. (as well as this)
   A youth centre _____.
2. Watching TV isn't an active pastime. Walking outdoors helps keep you fit. (in contrast)
   Watching TV _____.
3. We live in a large city. It can be difficult to access green areas. (so)
   We live _____.
4. Climbing is good exercise. You have to work with others to stay safe. (additionally)
   Climbing _____.
5. Cycling twenty-five kilometres off-road takes effort. At the end of the day, you feel you've achieved something. (As a result)
   Cycling _____.

5 Read and complete the LANGUAGE FOCUS with the underlined adverbs from the article.

LANGUAGE FOCUS

Comment and opinion adverbs

You can use adverbs to show your opinion of the subject you are writing about. You usually start the sentence with the opinion adverb followed by a comma.
¹clearly, ²c_____, fortunately, hopefully, interestingly, naturally, ³o_____, ⁴p_____, surprisingly, ⁵s_____, understandably, ⁶u_____

6 Read another article and choose the correct option.

Are you well?
Wellness in our schools

What do you think of when you hear the word wellness? Well (ha ha!), like a lot of people you're ¹*probably / certainly* picturing herbal tea, vegan food, yoga classes and meditation groups. However, encouraging wellness in our schools ²*hopefully / sadly* means promoting physical activity and thinking carefully about food consumption.

It is ³*certainly / naturally* easy to live an inactive life as a teenager these days. Lifts to school, endless hours of homework, and hobbies such as gaming mean we end up sitting more than we move. ⁴*Fortunately / Understandably*, there are simple ways to introduce more activity into our school days. These include building in regular outdoor breaks, with a strong focus on sports and encouraging movement in the classroom during lessons.

All machines need fuel, including the human ones! An important part of wellness in schools is attention to diet. ⁵*Unfortunately / Interestingly*, meal times at school are often rushed and offer limited healthy options. ⁶*Clearly / Understandably*, providing a healthy menu and allowing enough time to eat properly is important in ensuring pupils are refuelled and ready to learn. ⁷*Interestingly / Naturally*, research has shown that when students have more time for eating, they make healthier choices and throw away less food. Similarly, let's not forget the liquids! Schools must encourage water consumption and, with the environment in mind, every student should be required to have a reusable water bottle.

Wellness in schools means looking after ourselves as we learn. As the old saying goes, "Healthy body, healthy mind".

7 Rewrite the underlined parts of the sentences with appropriate adverbs and add commas where necessary. Sometimes more than one answer is possible.

1. We are very lucky that the countryside is easily accessible.
2. It's a shame that we don't do more outdoor activities at school.
3. Of course, there are also emotional benefits to being outside in the fresh air.
4. We're hoping that teens from urban areas will enjoy time away from the city.
5. We're surprised that trying risky activities can actually help us feel calmer in everyday life.

8 **SPEAKING** In what ways is spending time outdoors good for the body and mind?

SHOW WHAT YOU'VE LEARNT

9 Do the writing task. Use the ideas in the WRITING FOCUS and the LANGUAGE FOCUS to help you.

A young person's website has asked for articles on the importance of spending time outdoors doing physical activities and how this benefits young people's health, social skills and general well-being. Write a factual article and:

- discuss the range of outdoor activities available to teens living in your area
- describe some of the physical, social and personal benefits of taking part in these activities.

SPEAKING

6.8 At the doctor's surgery

I can describe basic symptoms to a doctor and talk about treatment.

1 **SPEAKING** Look at the pictures and discuss the ways in which you might get these injuries.

 1 A burn on your hand
 2 A cut on your chin
 3 A pain in your forehead
 4 A sprained ankle

2 🔊 3.7 Listen to four patients in a doctor's surgery describing how they got the injuries in Exercise 1. What happened? Did they mention any of your ideas?

3 🔊 3.7 Choose the correct option to complete the extracts from the dialogues. Then listen again and check.

Dialogue 1
A: Do you ¹*have / feel* a temperature?
B: Yes, it's thirty-nine degrees.
A: Well, I'm afraid your hand is infected. I'm going to give you a prescription. You need to take ²*stitches / antibiotics*. You also need to put a fresh ³*ice / bandage* on it every day.

Dialogue 2
A: Okay, let me see. Hm, it's a nasty cut. I think you need a few ⁴*bruises / stitches*.
B: Stitches?! Oh no, I think I'm going to ⁵*faint / bleed*.
A: Okay, calm down. Take some deep breaths. It's not going to ⁶*hurt / twist*.

Dialogue 3
A: Okay, I need to check your pulse and your ⁷*blood pressure / injection*. Can you roll up your sleeve, please?
B: Do you think I'm going to be okay? Do I need an ⁸*infection / X-ray*?
A: No, your blood pressure is fine and your ⁹*pulse / pain* is normal.

Dialogue 4
A: Now, are you allergic to anything?
B: Yes, I'm allergic to needles. Please get that needle away from me!
A: I'm not going to give you an ¹⁰*injection / operation*. But we do need to bring the ¹¹*bleeding / swelling* down. You need to take ¹²*painkillers / antibiotics* to ease the pain and then you'll need to put some ¹³*ice / plaster* on your ankle when you get home.

4 Complete the SPEAKING FOCUS with the verbs in the box.

[bring   check   give   put   put   take   ~~take~~]

SPEAKING FOCUS

Treatment
You need to ¹ _take_ antibiotics.
You need to ² _____ a fresh bandage/a plaster on it.
You need a few stitches.
I need to ³ _____ your blood pressure/pulse, etc.
I don't think you need an X-ray/operation, etc.
I'm not going to ⁴ _____ you an injection.
We need to ⁵ _____ the swelling down.
You need to ⁶ _____ painkillers to ease the pain.
You need to ⁷ _____ ice/ointment, etc. on your ankle.

5 Follow the instructions below to prepare a dialogue. Use the SPEAKING FOCUS to help you.

Student A: You're a student. You're doing a language course in the UK. You had a minor accident and hurt yourself, and have to go and see a doctor. Tell the doctor what happened, what your symptoms are and answer any questions.

Student B: You're a doctor. Your patient is a foreign student. Find out about their injury and ask questions. Give advice.

6 **SPEAKING** Practise the dialogue and act it out. Take it in turns to be A and B.

UNIT 6   Good health   Word list

6.1 Vocabulary 🔊 4.41
ankle /ˈæŋkəl/
arm /ɑːm/
bitten by a dog/rat /ˌbɪtn baɪ ə ˈdɒg/ ˈræt/
bitten by an insect/a snake /ˌbɪtn baɪ ən ˈɪnsekt/ə ˈsneɪk/
blocked nose /ˌblɒkt ˈnəʊz/
bottom /ˈbɒtəm/
break /breɪk/
break sb's heart /ˌbreɪk ˌsʌmbɒdɪz ˈhɑːt/
break your arm/leg/thumb/toe /ˌbreɪk jə ˈɑːm/ˈleg/ˈθʌm/ˈtəʊ/
burn /bɜːn/
burn your fingers/hand/tongue /ˌbɜːn jə ˈfɪŋɡəz/ˈhænd/ˈtʌŋ/
burn your hair /ˌbɜːn jə ˈheə/
cheek /tʃiːk/
chest /tʃest/
chin /tʃɪn/
comb your hair /ˌkəʊm jə ˈheə/
cut your finger /ˌkʌt jə ˈfɪŋɡə/
dislocate your hip/knee/shoulder/thumb /ˌdɪsləkeɪt jə ˈhɪp/ˈniː/ˈʃəʊldə/ ˈθʌm/
elbow /ˈelbəʊ/
eyebrow /ˈaɪbraʊ/
finger /ˈfɪŋɡə/
fingernail /ˈfɪŋɡəneɪl/
foot/feet /fʊt/fiːt/
forehead /ˈfɒrəd/
get dizzy /ˌget ˈdɪzi/
give sb a hand /ˌɡɪv ˌsʌmbɒdi ə ˈhænd/
have a black eye /ˌhæv ə ˌblæk ˈaɪ/
have a bruise /ˌhæv ə ˈbruːz/
have a cut /ˌhæv ə ˈkʌt/
have a sore finger /ˌhæv ə ˌsɔː ˈfɪŋɡə/
I couldn't believe my eyes /aɪ ˌkʊdənt bəˌliːv maɪ ˈaɪz/
knee /niː/
laugh your head off /ˌlɑːf jə ˌhed ˈɒf/
lips /lɪps/
neck /nek/
on the tip of your tongue /ɒn ðə ˌtɪp əv jə ˈtʌŋ/
poke /pəʊk/
pull sb's leg /ˌpʊl ˌsʌmbɒdɪz ˈleg/
rib /rɪb/
shoulder /ˈʃəʊldə/
spine /spaɪn/
sprain your ankle/foot/knee/wrist /ˌspreɪn jə ˈæŋkəl/ˈfʊt/ˈniː/ˈrɪst/
thigh /θaɪ/
thumb /θʌm/
toe /təʊ/
waist /weɪst/
wrist /rɪst/

6.2 Grammar 🔊 4.42
bleed /bliːd/
eye drops /ˈaɪ drɒps/
feel well /ˌfiːl ˈwel/
fever /ˈfiːvə/
flu /fluː/
hay fever /ˈheɪ ˌfiːvə/
look up/down /ˈlʊk ʌp/daʊn/

nosebleed /ˈnəʊzbliːd/
put a plaster on /ˌpʊt ə ˈplɑːstər ɒn/
put ice on /ˌpʊt ˈaɪs ɒn/
sting /stɪŋ/
stop the blood flowing /ˌstɒp ðə ˈblʌd ˌfləʊɪŋ/
sunburn /ˈsʌnbɜːn/
take (antihistamine) tablets /ˌteɪk (ˌæntɪˈhɪstəmiːn) ˌtæbləts/

6.3 Listening 🔊 4.43
cycle /ˈsaɪkəl/
die /daɪ/
die of (a disease) /ˌdaɪ əv (ə dɪˈziːz)/
donate money to /dəʊˈneɪt ˌmʌni tə/
foundation /faʊnˈdeɪʃən/
get on (your bike) /ˌget ˈɒn (jə ˈbaɪk)/
heel /hiːl/
in memory of /ɪn ˈmeməri əv/
participant /pɑːˈtɪsəpənt/
raise money for /ˌreɪz ˈmʌni fə/
safety /ˈseɪfti/
set up a webpage /ˌset ʌp ə ˈwebpeɪdʒ/
share a webpage /ˌʃeər ə ˈwebpeɪdʒ/
sponsor /ˈspɒnsə/
take part in /ˌteɪk ˈpɑːt ɪn/
train for /ˈtreɪn fə/
vulnerable people /ˌvʌlnərəbəl ˈpiːpəl/

6.4 Reading 🔊 4.44
catch (a disease) /ˌkætʃ (ə dɪˈziːz)/
consider /kənˈsɪdə/
deep cut /ˌdiːp ˈkʌt/
deliver a baby /dɪˌlɪvər əˈbeɪbi/
doctor's surgery /ˌdɒktəz ˈsɜːdʒəri/
emergency team /ɪˈmɜːdʒənsi tiːm/
flu/cholera epidemic /ˈfluː/ˈkɒlərə ˌepɪˌdemɪk/
food/nut allergy /ˈfuːd/ˈnʌt ˌælədʒi/
gain weight /ˌɡeɪn ˈweɪt/
give a snapshot of /ˌɡɪv ə ˈsnæpʃɒt əv/
give sb first aid /ˌɡɪv ˌsʌmbədi ˌfɜːst ˈeɪd/
hair straightener /ˈheə ˌstreɪtnə/
have a panic attack /ˌhæv ə ˈpænɪk əˈtæk/
heart attack /ˈhɑːt əˌtæk/
hospital /ˈhɒspɪtl/
illness /ˈɪlnɪs/
injury /ˈɪndʒəri/
local surgery /ˌləʊkəl ˈsɜːdʒəri/
maternity/children's ward /məˈtɜːnəti/ ˈtʃɪldrənz wɔːd/
medicine /ˈmedsən/
muscle/stomach pain /ˈmʌsəl/ˈstʌmək peɪn/
off-duty /ˌɒf ˈdjuːti/
paramedic /ˌpærəˈmedɪk/
patient /ˈpeɪʃənt/
recover from /rɪˈkʌvə frəm/
rescue team /ˈreskjuː tiːm/
save lives /ˌseɪv ˈlaɪvz/
seriously ill /ˌsɪəriəsli ˈɪl/
shaving cut /ˈʃeɪvɪŋ kʌt/
stable/serious condition /ˌsteɪbəl/ ˌsɪəriəs kənˈdɪʃən/
stomach /ˈstʌmək/

tooth/teeth /tuːθ/tiːθ/
treat patients /ˌtriːt ˈpeɪʃənts/
write a prescription /ˌraɪt ə prɪˈskrɪpʃən/

6.5 Grammar 🔊 4.45
get out of /ˌget ˈaʊt əv/
miscalculate /mɪsˈkælkjəleɪt/
penknife /ˈpen-naɪf/
rope /rəʊp/
survivor /səˈvaɪvə/
trap /træp/

6.6 Use of English 🔊 4.46
feel alert /ˌfiːl əˈlɜːt/
blinds /blaɪndz/
body clock /ˈbɒdi klɒk/
caffeine /ˈkæfiːn/
collect taxes /kəˌlekt ˈtæksɪz/
count sheep /ˌkaʊnt ˈʃiːp/
curtains /ˈkɜːtənz/
fall asleep /ˌfɔːl əˈsliːp/
insomnia /ɪnˈsɒmniə/
prevent sb from /prɪˈvent ˌsʌmbədi frəm/
set the alarm on your phone /ˌset ðə əˌlɑːm ɒn jə ˈfəʊn/

6.7 Writing 🔊 4.47
city council /ˌsɪti ˈkaʊnsəl/
clearly /ˈklɪəli/
facilities /fəˈsɪlətiz/
fortunately /ˈfɔːtʃənətli/
hopefully /ˈhəʊpfəli/
interestingly /ˈɪntrəstɪŋli/
meditation groups /ˌmedəˈteɪʃən gruːps/
naturally /ˈnætʃərəli/
refuelled /ˌriːˈfjuːəld/
reusable /ˌriːˈjuːzəbəl/
self-discipline /ˌself ˈdɪsəplɪn/
surprisingly /səˈpraɪzɪŋli/
sadly /ˈsædli/
understandably /ˌʌndəˈstændəbli/
weight problems /ˈweɪt ˌprɒbləmz/
wellness /ˈwelnəs/

6.8 Speaking 🔊 4.48
bandage /ˈbændɪdʒ/
feel dizzy/sick /ˌfiːl ˈdɪzi/ˈsɪk/
give an injection /ˌɡɪv ən ɪnˈdʒekʃən/
have a pain in your forehead /hæv ə ˌpeɪn ɪn jə ˈfɒrəd/
have a temperature /ˌhæv ə ˈtemprətʃə/
hurt /hɜːt/
infection /ɪnˈfekʃən/
operation /ˌɒpəˈreɪʃən/
see a doctor /ˌsiː ə ˈdɒktə/
stitch /stɪtʃ/
symptoms /ˈsɪmptəmz/
swollen /ˈswəʊlən/

FOCUS REVIEW 6

VOCABULARY AND GRAMMAR

1 Choose the correct option.

1 It is quite common for a sportsperson to *dislocate / burn* their shoulder during a game, but it's quite easy to put it back into place.
2 It was so funny that we laughed our *hearts / heads* off.
3 After the accident, Kelly had a *broken / black* eye from hitting her face on the steering wheel.
4 Luckily, Henry only *sprained / broke* his ankle, so none of the bones were damaged.
5 When Jim told me who was going to visit us, I knew he was pulling my *hand / leg*. It couldn't be true.

2 Complete the sentences with words from the unit. The first letter of each word is given.

1 The first time Julie went on the underground she had a p_____ a_____ because she is so afraid of closed spaces.
2 The r_____ team arrived three minutes after the accident.
3 Susan has an annoying food a_____ . She can't eat cucumbers or melons, among other things.
4 I've been feeling really tired, so I've made an appointment for a check-up at the local s_____ .
5 Would you like to take p_____ in our effort to save the l_____ of giant pandas?

3 Complete the sentences with the correct form of the verbs in the box.

can   have   not call   sponsor   not let

1 If I tried to text during the lesson, I'm sure my teacher _____ me keep my phone with me.
2 My mum always wants to know what I'm doing. If only she _____ me so often.
3 I want to go to New York to run the marathon. I wish someone _____ me.
4 My school is very small and old. I wish it _____ a sports centre with a swimming pool.
5 I hate cycling to school. If only I _____ get a driving licence at the age of sixteen.

4 Match the sentence halves. Then complete the Third Conditional sentences with the correct form of the verbs in brackets.

1 We _____ (not help) so many families ☐
2 If you _____ (not go) on such a strict diet, ☐
3 You _____ (help) the person with a cut ☐
4 If Andy _____ (put) some ice on his head, ☐
5 Sally _____ (win) the singing competition ☐

a if you _____ (do) a first aid course.
b he _____ (stop) the bleeding.
c if she _____ (not lose) her voice last week.
d if we _____ (not raise) so much money for the charity.
e you _____ (not feel) dizzy yesterday.

USE OF ENGLISH

5 Complete the second sentence so that it has a similar meaning to the first. Use up to five words in each gap.

1 It's a pity you can't take part in the first aid training.
If only _____ part in the first aid training.
2 Mark reached the hospital on time only because he had left home very early.
If Mark hadn't left home very early, he _____ the hospital on time.
3 You should shorten your run so that you don't get so tired.
You should shorten your run so as _____ tired.
4 My brother never tells me when he's angry with me.
I wish _____ when he's angry with me.

6 Read the text and choose the correct answer, A, B, C or D.

VEGETABLES AND VITAMINS

I don't think I was a particularly fussy eater as a child. Like many children, I simply didn't like vegetables. After eating my meat and potatoes quickly, I would stare bitterly at the vegetables left on my plate. If they had simply disappeared, I ¹___ very happy. Instead, I had to sit at the table until my plate was clean.

At that time I didn't know that my mum wanted me to eat vegetables to make sure that I was getting all the vitamins I needed. She was so afraid that I would develop a serious ²___ that, every now and then, she made an appointment at the doctor's and asked him to do a blood test on me. Blood tests were even worse than broccoli, as I've been afraid of needles all my life. Even today I wish my mum ³___ so concerned about me. After all, I'm a perfectly healthy adult.

A few days ago, I found a book about the history of science. I couldn't ⁴___ when I found a chapter explaining that some 100 years ago people didn't know anything about vitamins!

It was a Polish-born scientist, Kazimerz Funk, who formulated the concept of vitamins in 1912. It was a great discovery, but I keep thinking that if Funk ⁵___ vitamins, my mum wouldn't have made me eat all those vegetables.

1 A will be   B would be
  C had been   D would have been
2 A condition   B situation
  C injury   D epidemic
3 A couldn't be   B hasn't been
  C hadn't been   D wouldn't be
4 A pull my leg   B believe my eyes
  C give me a hand D laugh my head off
5 A didn't discover B would discover
  C hadn't discovered D haven't discovered

SPEAKING

7 Ask and answer the questions.
1 What do you do to get better when you have a cold?
2 What do you do to relax after a stressful day?
3 Do you ever worry about your health? Why?/Why not?

WRITING

8 Answer the questions.
1 Why is it important to know something about first aid?
2 What do you remember from the first aid quiz in lesson 6.2?

9 You have seen this announcement in an international students' magazine. Read the task and write an article.

> **Have you ever heard or read about a situation when first aid saved someone's life?**
>
> We're looking for articles about times when first aid really helped people.
>
> Write an article about the experience, saying what happened and why knowledge of first aid was important. Your article could be in the magazine!

READING

10 Read the texts. Match the descriptions of people who want to get fit with the places that are most suitable for them. There are two extra places.

1 ☐ **Adam** isn't very fit, but he'd like to find somewhere to do some gentle exercise. He prefers cheap or even free places. He can only go in the evenings and wants to get there on public transport.

2 ☐ **Margo** broke her ankle and wants to do some easy exercises once or twice a week with someone who can give her expert advice. She's worried she might injure it again if she isn't careful.

3 ☐ **Ben** was bitten by a dog while jogging in the park and is worried that it could happen again. He wants to find somewhere where he can run in safety at weekends, both day and night.

4 ☐ **Sandra** doesn't have a weight problem, but she has some bad eating habits. She also finds it difficult to sleep because she's stressed. She would like to have a fitness holiday and combine exercise with improvements in her eating habits and general lifestyle.

A MANHATTAN fitness centre
We offer an amazing experience. You can stay with us from one week to one month. With our well-equipped gym, full-sized swimming pool and beautiful gardens, you won't be bored. As well as supervised fitness training and physiotherapy help after injuries, we have relaxation therapy sessions to reduce stress and can give you expert dietary advice. You'll go home feeling like a new person. There are cheaper places, but none which offer such great value for money.

B Xanadu Fitness
Xanadu Fitness is open twenty-four hours a day, seven days a week. We have a large gym with modern machines for everyone, an indoor pool and our own, newly opened, private running track. We are situated outside the town centre but it is easy to reach us by car and we have our own, free car park for members.

C Babylon Health Centre
Babylon Health Centre is a great place to lose weight and get in shape. Our enthusiastic instructors use dance routines to really get you moving. It may look easy but you will come home after each class knowing that you have had a very good workout. Afterwards, why not treat yourself to a healthy snack in our cafeteria?

D Fit-4-all
We offer a great, well-equipped gym with something for everyone for an incredibly low price. Open 11 a.m.–midnight, seven days a week, you can find us in the town centre next to the bus station. We have running machines, weights, climbing walls and much more for fitness enthusiasts and total beginners. Go at your own pace or join one of our popular, and more demanding, classes.

E Fitness trail
Do you want to get fit and have fun free of charge? We have now completed our jogging and cycling tracks through the local park with exercise machines along the way. The fitness trail is open when the park is open, 8 a.m.–5 p.m. every day. There's a bus stop right outside the park entrance and it's only a short walk to the town centre.

F GO 4 IT
Go 4 it is a new gym with a difference. When you first join, we will create a personalised training plan just for you. No more worries about overdoing it on the first day! You can use the machines on your own or have your own, personal, medically-trained trainer to supervise you. We are situated in beautiful countryside and we are open Mon–Fri 9 a.m.–5 p.m.

7

Entertain me

Most people buy the highest quality television sets, only to watch the lowest quality TV shows.

Jarod Kintz

BBC

SHAKESPEARE'S AVATARS

▶ 28 Watch the BBC video.
For the worksheet, go to page 128.

7.1 VOCABULARY

Entertainment • people in entertainment • phrasal verbs

I can talk about people in music and television.

SHOW WHAT YOU KNOW

1 Put the words in the box under an appropriate heading. Then add at least one more word to each category and compare with a partner.

> box office   costume   episode   gig   ~~landscape~~
> news bulletin   orchestra   plot   portrait   post   sculpture
> soap opera   social media   video games   vocalist

art	film/theatre	music	digital	TV
landscape				

2 **SPEAKING** How much time do you devote to each area of entertainment? Discuss with a partner.

3 Guess which numbers in the box complete the facts about the stars.

> 1   2   4   Eleven   12   16   8 million   half a billion

DID YOU KNOW?

1 Ed Sheeran's hit single *Thinking Out Loud* **was streamed** _____ times on Spotify.
2 Ed started **doing live gigs** when he was _____ .
3 Ed **had a hit single** which reached number _____ before he even **signed a recording contract**.
4 Millie Bobby Brown **plays the part of** _____ in *Stranger Things*.
5 *Stranger Things* had over _____ viewers _____ weeks after it **came out**.
6 The cast of *School of Rock* are only _____ years old.
7 They **put on** a show _____ times a week.

4 🔊 3.8 Listen to an interview with Laura Martinez and check your answers.

5 🔊 3.8 Answer the questions. Then listen again and check.
1 Who has already appeared in a TV series?
2 Who has had great reviews for an album he/she released last month?
3 Whose albums are always in the charts?
4 Who started out by playing small venues in London?
5 Who has a kind of talent some actors only dream of?
6 Who wants the lead guitarist and lead singer of *School of Rock* to play on his/her next album?

6 Read *Top Tips for young performers* below. What do you think are the best three pieces of advice?

Top Tips for Young Performers

- If you can, take up a musical instrument when you're really young and sign up for lessons.
- Practise every day, and when you think you're ready, go for it.
- If you mess up on stage, don't worry. Just carry on.
- When you make a mistake, don't beat yourself up – we learn from our mistakes.
- When you feel you are stuck, keep practising and eventually the feeling will wear off.
- Be nice, be reliable, don't be moody and always turn up on time!

Go to WORD STORE 7 page 15

WORD STORE 7A Entertainment

7 🔊 3.9 Complete WORD STORE 7A with the base forms of the verbs in red in Exercises 3 and 5. Then listen, check and repeat.

8 **SPEAKING** Complete the questions with an appropriate word in WORD STORE 7A. Then ask and answer.
1 What is the worst single in the _____ at the moment?
2 When did your favourite band last release an _____ ?
3 Does your favourite band do many _____ gigs?
4 Does your favourite band usually play large or small _____ ?
5 If you could play the _____ of any fictional character, who would it be?
6 What is your favourite _____ single of all time?
7 Think of the music you listen to from the Internet. Is it downloaded or _____ ?

WORD STORE 7B People in entertainment

9 🔊 3.10 Match the pictures in WORD STORE 7B with the words in the box. Then listen, check and repeat.

10 Complete the definitions with the words in WORD STORE 7B.
1 all the performers in a play, film, musical, etc. = _____
2 a person who writes songs and sings them = _____
3 a person who plays drums in a band = _____
4 a person who plays a musical instrument, usually for a living = _____
5 the people who watch or listen to people performing in public = _____
6 a person who plays the main guitar part = _____
7 a person who watches TV = _____
8 a person who is the main singer = _____

11 Complete the sentences to make them true for you. Then compare with a partner.
1 If I were in a band, I'd be a …
2 The biggest audience I've ever been part of was …
3 My favourite singer-songwriter is …
4 I think the cast in … are very good.
5 A musician I admire is …

WORD STORE 7C Phrasal verbs

12 🔊 3.11 Complete WORD STORE 7C with the base forms of the underlined phrasal verbs in Exercises 3, 5 and 6. Then listen, check and repeat.

13 Complete the sentences with the correct form of the verbs in WORD STORE 7C. Then decide whether the sentences are true or false for you.
1 Our school always _____ on a show at the end of term.
2 I usually _____ up late when I meet my friends.
3 A new episode of my favourite TV series _____ out this week.
4 My parents want me to _____ up for singing lessons.
5 I _____ up piano when I was younger but I didn't _____ on.
6 I never want to act. I'm afraid of _____ up in front of an audience.

GRAMMAR

7.2

Reported Speech – statements

I can talk about what other people have said using Reported Speech.

1 **SPEAKING** Discuss whether you like the painting. Is it possible for a three-year-old child to paint something like this? Read the text and find out.

They said she was a genius

When Marla Olmstead was three years old, a woman saw one of her paintings in a coffee shop and asked how much it cost. Marla's mother wanted to keep the painting so she **told** her that it cost $250. The woman bought it! After that a gallery owner started showing Marla's paintings. He told her parents that their daughter was a genius. Her paintings began to sell for thousands of dollars. But not all of the attention was positive. Art critics **pointed out** that a child could not produce those paintings. One critic **suggested** that her father had painted them.

A TV channel contacted Marla's parents and told them that they wanted to film their daughter the following week. They **explained** that they wanted to prove that Marla was not a fake. Marla's parents **said** that their daughter would be uncomfortable in front of the cameras, but the TV director told them not to worry. He **added** that he was going to use a hidden camera. Over the next few days, Marla did a painting, but it was not as good as her other paintings. Her critics **claimed** that this proved someone else finished her paintings. The customers **replied** that they didn't care who had done them – they liked them anyway.

2 Match the people from the text with direct speech 1–7.

> some art critics   the TV director   one critic
> Marla's parents   the customers   a TV channel
> ~~a gallery owner~~

1 'Your daughter is a genius,' said <u>a gallery owner</u>.
2 'A child can't produce these paintings,' said _____ .
3 'Her father painted them,' said _____ .
4 'We want to film your daughter next week,' said _____ .
5 'Our daughter will be uncomfortable,' said _____ .
6 'I'm going to use a hidden camera,' said _____ .
7 'We don't care who has done them,' said _____ .

3 Underline the Reported Speech in the text that matches the direct speech in Exercise 2. Then complete the GRAMMAR FOCUS.

GRAMMAR FOCUS

Reported Speech – statements

In reported statements, verb forms change depending on the context.

Direct Speech		Reported Speech
Present Simple	→	Past Simple
Present Continuous	→	Past Continuous
Present Perfect	→	1 _____
Past Simple	→	2 _____
Past Perfect	→	Past Perfect
can/can't	→	3 _____
will/won't	→	4 _____
am/is/are going to	→	5 _____

Note:
tell sb sth – She **told me (that)** I was wrong.
say sth – She **said (that)** I was wrong. (NOT ~~She said me~~ I was wrong.)
Other reporting verbs like *say*:
add, claim, explain, point out, reply, suggest

4 Look at the reporting verbs in blue in the text and read the note in the GRAMMAR FOCUS. Then choose the correct reporting verb below.

1 'I've bought a painting,' Jim (told) / explained me.
2 'It's worth hundreds of dollars,' he claimed / told.
3 'A three-year-old girl painted it,' he told / added.
4 'A child can't paint like that!' I pointed out / told him.
5 'It's probably a fake,' I told / suggested.
6 'I don't care, I'm keeping it!' he replied / told me.
7 'It'll look great in my office,' he added / told.

5 Rewrite the sentences in Exercise 4 as Reported Speech.

1 *Jim told me that he had bought a painting.*

6 Read REMEMBER THIS. Then complete Reported Speech sentences 1–6. Use time expressions from the box and make other changes as necessary.

REMEMBER THIS

In reported statements there may be other changes depending on the context. For example:

time: **yesterday** → **the day before**
place: **here** → **there**
pronouns: **I/me** → **he** or **she/him** or **her**
possessive adjectives: **my** → **his** or **her**

> the month before   the day before   that day
> then   the following day   the following week

1 'I met her here last month.'
  He claimed *he had met her there the month before*.
2 'She gave us this painting yesterday.' They replied …
3 'We can't speak to you now.' They told us …
4 'I'm meeting my friends later today.' She explained …
5 'I'll see you here tomorrow.' He told her …
6 'We're going to fly to Paris next week.' They pointed out …

7 **SPEAKING** Discuss your own attitudes towards art. What do you like/dislike? What pictures do you have in your bedroom/home?

Grammar page 150

7.3 LISTENING

Matching

I can follow an informal interview on a common topic.

1 **SPEAKING** Read UK TODAY. Discuss how similar or different you think the situation is in your country.

UK TODAY

In the UK
- over 77 percent of the population shop online.
- clothes or sports goods are the most popular online purchase.
- over 40 percent of all advertising is online.

Most UK homes have
- super-fast broadband connections.
- at least three different devices connected to the Internet (TV, laptop, tablet, smartphone, etc.).
- at least six different types of screen.

One in three UK teenagers
- spends at least six hours a day online.
- has experienced cyberbullying.
- uses their smartphone everywhere (including in the toilet!).

2 🔊 3.12 **SPEAKING** Discuss the questions. Then listen and check your ideas.
   1 What is a 'viral video'?
   2 Where can you watch it?
   3 What kind of videos 'go viral'?

EXAM FOCUS Matching

3 🔊 3.13 Listen to four people talking about viral videos. Match statements A–E with speakers 1–4. There is one extra statement.

Speaker 1: ☐   Speaker 3: ☐
Speaker 2: ☐   Speaker 4: ☐

The speaker …
A gives an example of how an online video can help your career.
B talks about his/her own experience of producing a viral video.
C suggests a few reasons why some videos go viral.
D has to watch online videos as part of his/her job.
E enjoys watching videos of people doing silly things.

4 **SPEAKING** Discuss the questions and compare your ideas with a partner.
   1 What is the ideal length of a viral video? Why?
   2 What happened after the teenager's mother posted a video of him singing *Paparrazi*?
   3 Why do people laugh at videos where people have stupid accidents?
   4 Why does Nigel Brown spend so much time watching videos?
   5 How easy is it to produce a video that gets more than one million views?

5 🔊 3.13 Listen to the four speakers again and check your answers.

WORD STORE 7D Collocations

6 🔊 3.14 Complete WORD STORE 7D with the words in the box. Then listen, check and repeat.

7 🔊 3.15 Complete the text with the correct forms of the verbs in WORD STORE 7D. Then listen and check.

An early viral video

Nobody knows exactly why online videos ¹___go___ viral, and which ones will be ²_____ to social networking sites and shared millions of times. Often, not much happens in these clips, but they're short enough to appeal to the digital generation who ³_____ short attention spans, and they ⁴_____ our emotions. One of the first and most famous viral videos was the sneezing panda. It shows a mother panda eating bamboo with her baby asleep at her feet. Suddenly, the baby sneezes and ⁵_____ the mother by surprise. It's the mother's reaction which ⁶_____ you laugh. The video has been ⁷_____ over 221 million times. Why is it so popular? Probably because the baby panda is cute and the simple story ⁸_____ an element of surprise.

8 **SPEAKING** Think about an online video you have uploaded, shared or viewed recently. Discuss the questions.
   1 When, where and how did you see it?
   2 What was it about? What happened?
   3 How would you describe it? (funny? amazing? inspiring? …)

Yesterday I watched a funny dog video on my phone. My friend sent me a link. It shows a dog …

PRONUNCIATION FOCUS

9 Complete the groups with nouns formed from the verbs. Then practise saying the words and mark the stress.
   1 adapt/*adaptation*   connect/_____   compete/_____
   2 explain/_____   inform/_____   produce/_____
   3 suggest/_____   inspire/_____   present/_____

10 🔊 3.16 Which noun in each group has fewer syllables? Listen, repeat and check your answers.

7.4 READING

Gapped text

I can identify key information in an extended newspaper article.

1 **SPEAKING** Discuss the questions with a partner.
   1 How much time do you spend reading for pleasure?
   2 What kind of books do you prefer when reading for pleasure and which when studying: comic books, print books, e-books or audio books?
   3 Do you prefer listening to music while reading or reading in silence?

2 Read the online article and the comments. Decide what *you* think about the new app and write your own comment. Compare it with a partner.

EXAM FOCUS Gapped text

3 Read the text again. Complete gaps 1–4 with fragments A–E. There is one extra fragment.

   A There's no information about their backgrounds, ages, reading experience, etc., but it seems reasonable to assume that they were people who don't spend a great deal of time in libraries.
   B But reading is a different way of consuming content. I'm not sure a soundtrack can do anything but distract from the reading experience.
   C In comparison with this traditional way of reading, one that engages all the senses, the digitally downloaded text can seem dull.
   D In other words, can an audio soundtrack help people to understand a book and memorise it? The results were interesting.
   E Some people were critical: they felt distracted by things that they would prefer to leave to the imagination.

4 ◀) 3.18 Complete the phrases with an appropriate two-letter word. Then listen, check and repeat. How do you say the phrases in your language?

   1 be based *on*
   2 be critical _____
   3 be deeply engaging
   4 enhance the reading experience
   5 feel distracted _____
   6 find sth easy _____ follow
   7 improve literacy rates
   8 leave sth _____ your imagination
   9 read _____ the old-fashioned way
   10 review something positively

5 Use appropriate phrases in Exercise 4 to answer the comprehension questions.
   1 What is the aim of the new app?
   2 What does the writer describe as 'sensuous'?
   3 What is the connection between the American launch of the app and Sherlock Holmes?
   4 Why were some people critical of the app?
   5 How did the press react to the new app?
   6 How does the writer describe the technology behind the app?
   7 How are books with a soundtrack better than silent books, according to research?
   8 How might the new technology help in schools?

WORD STORE 7E Word building

6 ◀) 3.19 Complete WORD STORE 7E with nouns made from the infinitive form of the verbs in blue in the article and in Exercise 3. Add the suffixes *-ment* or *-ion* to verbs. Use a dictionary if necessary. Then listen, check and repeat.

7 Think of other parts of speech and note down any other words that form word families with the words in WORD STORE 7E. You have sixty seconds.

   creator, creative, creatively, …

8 Complete these further comments about the Booktrack app with the correct form of the word in brackets. Which ones do you agree with?
   1 'Music and sound effects would be a _____ . I don't like the idea.' (distract)
   2 'Adding sound effects is a great _____ on the traditional way of reading a printed book.' (improve)
   3 'Today's _____ doesn't make you use your imagination.' (entertain)
   4 'Anything is good if it motivates schoolchildren to read – they need a lot of _____ .' (encourage)
   5 'I can't see how an audio soundtrack can help you in the _____ of things.' (memorise)

9 **SPEAKING** Most studies suggest that teenagers are reading less fiction than they used to. Discuss the questions and give reasons for your answers.
   1 Is this a problem and, if so, what can be done about it?
   2 Are there any advantages of reading more fiction?
   3 Do you read more or less fiction than your partner?

   I'm not sure it's a problem that teenagers are reading less fiction. They don't have time because they are doing so many other things like messaging, watching videos, listening to podcasts, etc.

Can a new app enhance the reading experience?

🔊 3.17

Reading a book in the old-fashioned way (holding an object made of paper) is a sensuous experience. Books speak. Pages rustle. They smell – sometimes delicious, sometimes of previous owners. Spines
5 creak. And so on. ¹_____ . It's convenient but does not engage all the senses.

Not until now. In America last year, a group of investors launched an app called Booktrack, a 'revolutionary new technology' that dramatically improves the e-reading
10 experience. How? By creating a soundtrack for e-books including music and sound effects. A character knocks on the door: bang, bang, bang. Another puts a slice of bacon in the frying pan: sssssss. Someone kisses someone: well, no, perhaps not. And in between all
15 these bursts of activity: sympathetic music, or weather noises, or (if it's a scene outdoors) a bird singing at the end of the garden.

The American launch was based on *Sherlock Holmes: The Adventure of the Speckled Band.* ²_____ . But
20 it had a lot of fans too. In its first ten weeks on sale, *The Speckled Band* was downloaded more than 100,000 times. Since then, it has been downloaded in ninety-nine different countries and has been reviewed positively in the press: 'Phenomenal', 'Revolutionary',
25 'books without soundtracks could some day seem as old-fashioned as silent movies'.

The technology is entertaining and very impressive. How on earth does the page know which line of text our eyes are reading, and therefore when to do the
30 knocking on the door, etc.? Reading in this way is a deeply engaging experience. And I believe that for every reader who prefers to use their imagination, there will be a reader who is grateful for the extra fun.

But it's not just about having fun. Booktrack hired the
35 services of Liel Leibovitz, a professor of communications at New York University, to look into 'the cognitive advantages, if any, to reading accompanied by audio elements'. ³_____ . The research found that when readers read books with a soundtrack, they not only
40 found them easier to follow than 'silent' books, but also found them easier to remember.

People who took part in the research all came from New York and represented various levels of income and education. ⁴_____ . This could suggest that the greatest
45 benefit of the new technology will be to help improve literacy rates and encourage schoolchildren to read.

Our culture is becoming increasingly visual, but the success so far of Booktrack also shows that we're keen to live in an acoustic world. While it is common to
50 complain that computers cut us off from reality, you could also argue that in some ways computers remind us how much we rely on our senses.

COMMENTS

Personally, I prefer reading in silence or with some background music.

I don't mind trying this. Why not?

I like listening to books on the radio and when I'm driving, so I think I'll enjoy this new experience.

I don't think sound effects can add anything to a book … I'd hate it.

7.5 GRAMMAR

Reported Speech – questions and imperatives

I can talk about someone's orders and questions using Reported Speech.

1 **SPEAKING** Name some popular magazines in your country. Discuss which magazines you read and what topics you like reading about.

2 Darina Parfitt did an interview for a lifestyle magazine. Read the interview questions and guess what she does for a living.
   a a fashion designer   c a model
   b a film director   d a singer

Questions
- What are you going to wear to the Oscars?
- Who are you dating?
- Why did you split up with your fiancé?
- Have you put on weight?
- Are you on a diet?

Photo instructions
- Don't look too serious.
- Blow a kiss at the camera.

3 🔊 3.20 Listen to Darina talking to a friend about her interview. Check your answer in Exercise 2. Why is she so upset?

4 Read the GRAMMAR FOCUS. Then write Darina's reported questions and reported imperatives from the conversation.

They asked me …
1 what / wear / going to / to the Oscars / was / I
   what I was going to wear to the Oscars.
2 I / dating / who / was
3 had / why / split up with / I / my fiancé
4 if / put on / I / weight / had
5 was / I / whether / on a diet
6 serious / to look / too / not
7 a kiss / at / to blow / the camera

GRAMMAR FOCUS

Reported questions and imperatives

- When you report questions, the subject comes before the verb. You use **ask** as the reporting verb. You don't use **do/does/did**. You use **if** or **whether** for yes/no questions.
- When you report imperatives, you use **ask** or **tell sb (not) to do sth**.

Direct Speech	→	Reported Speech
yes/no questions		
'Do you live near here?'	→	He asked me *if I lived* near there.
'Are you happy?'	→	He asked me *whether I was* happy.
wh- questions		
'What is your name?'	→	I asked him *what his name was*.
'Who wrote these?'	→	I asked him *who had written* those questions.
Imperatives		
'Say "cheese".'	→	They *asked me to say* 'cheese'.
'Please don't move.'	→	She *told me not to move*.

5 🔊 3.20 Listen to the conversation again and check your answers in Exercise 4.

6 Report more questions and imperatives from Darina's interview. Begin with *They asked her …*
1 'Did your fiancé end your relationship?'
   They asked her if her fiancé had ended their relationship.
2 'Have you seen your ex recently?'
3 'Where did you buy your dress?'
4 'Help yourself to tea or coffee.'
5 'Who is going with you to the Oscars next week?'
6 'Why are you leaving so early?'
7 'Can we interview you again next month?'
8 'Don't leave before we've taken a photo.'

7 Read the report of another interview Darina gave. Which question did she refuse to answer?

Meet Darina Parfitt

We had the pleasure of meeting Darina Parfitt today and talked to her about her work. We asked her if she was excited about being nominated for an Oscar, and whether she thought
5 she could win. She told us that she was proud of her film and thought she had a good chance of winning. But she added that she hadn't seen the other films yet. We asked her when she had started making films and she told us it had only
10 been the year before but that she had been in the movie business for ten years. We asked her what her next project was going to be and she told us she was writing a screenplay but she hoped she would get the chance to direct another film. We
15 asked her who she was dating, but she asked us not to ask her about her private life.

8 Rewrite the report in Exercise 7 as a dialogue.

Interviewer: *Thanks for agreeing to do the interview.*
Darina: *You're welcome.*
Interviewer: *So, are you excited about being nominated for an Oscar?*
Darina: *Yes, it's wonderful …*

9 **SPEAKING** Act out your dialogue. Vote for the best dialogue in the class.

Grammar page 151

7.6 USE OF ENGLISH

Nouns

I can use various types of nouns with the correct articles.

1 **SPEAKING** Rate the TV series genres in the box from 1 = 'I can't stand them' to 5 = 'I love them'. What other series genres can you think of? Discuss the series you like most.

> cookery programmes   fantasy   science fiction
> silly humour   cool vampires

2 🔊 3.21 Listen to a conversation between a media industry expert and a TV journalist. Why are more and more young people watching cookery programmes?

3 🔊 3.21 Choose the correct option. Which one of the sentences is false? Listen again and check.
   1 The latest **news** *is / are* that **food** *has / have* become the most popular subject for reality TV programmes.
   2 **Research** *tells / tell* us that we spend more time watching food on TV than cooking it.
   3 **Series** such as *The Great British Bake-Off* and *Masterchef* *is / are* very popular with young people.
   4 Survey **information** *suggest / suggests* that people bake cakes to share on social media, not to eat.
   5 The **interests** of young people *isn't / aren't* very difficult to predict.
   6 **Life** *is / are* too short to stuff a mushroom!

4 Read the LANGUAGE FOCUS. What type of noun are the nouns in bold in Exercise 3?

LANGUAGE FOCUS

Nouns

- **Countable nouns** have a singular and a plural form and you choose an appropriate verb form. Add **-s** (or sometimes **-es**, **-ies** or **-ves**) to form plurals: *programme – programmes*.
  Exceptions:
  Nouns with the same singular and plural forms: e.g. *fish, series, sheep, species*
  Nouns with irregular plural forms: e.g. *child/children, foot/feet, woman/women, person/people*

- **Uncountable nouns** only have a singular form. You can't put *a/an* or a number in front of them and you only use a singular verb form.
  Progress is slow. (NOT *Progress are slow.*)
  I need (some) advice. (NOT *I need an advice.*)
  I bought (two pieces of) furniture. (NOT *I bought two furnitures.*)
  Common uncountable nouns: *advice, furniture, hair, information, knowledge, luggage, news, politics, research, traffic, weather*

- **Plural nouns** only have a plural form. You can't put *a/an* or a number in front of them and you only use a plural verb form.
  These jeans are nice. (NOT *This jean is nice.*)
  I have two pairs of black trousers. (NOT *I have two black trousers.*)
  Common plural nouns: *clothes, glasses, headquarters, interests, jeans, manners, scissors, trousers*

5 Complete the sentences with the phrases in the box to reflect your opinions. Then compare with a partner.

> is too much   are too many   isn't enough
> aren't enough

   1 There _____ news on the TV.
   2 There _____ politics in the news.
   3 There _____ TV series about crime.
   4 There _____ women directors.
   5 There _____ advice for young people about Internet safety.
   6 There _____ furniture in my bedroom.

6 **USE OF ENGLISH** Complete the sentences with the correct form of the words in brackets.
   1 One of the must-haves in your wardrobe _____ (be/pair/classic jeans).
   2 Today is a bad day. There _____ (be/no good news).
   3 It was raining and all _____ (child/be) bored.
   4 There _____ (be/a lot of/information) about *Masterchef* in the news yesterday.
   5 I don't think this _____ (be/good advice).
   6 My mum and her sister _____ (be/first/woman) in our family to go to university.

7 **SPEAKING** Complete these common sayings with the correct verb form. Then discuss whether you agree with the sayings and whether you have similar ones in your language.
   1 Laughter __is__ (be) the best medicine.
   2 Beauty _____ (be) only skin deep.
   3 Money _____ (not grow) on trees.
   4 Truth _____ (be) stranger than fiction.
   5 There _____ (be) plenty of fish in the sea.
   6 Knowledge _____ (be) power.
   7 Manners _____ (make) the man.
   8 No news _____ (be) good news.

FOCUS VLOG   About television

▶ 30 Watch the Focus Vlog. For the worksheet, go to page 129.

Use of English page 152

7.7 WRITING

An article reviewing an event

I can write an appealing description of a past event.

1 Read the announcement below and answer the questions.
1 What are you invited to do?
2 What could you win?

| HOME | FESTIVAL | FAQ'S | CONTACT |

Have you been to a fabulous festival this summer? *festivalwatch.org* would love to hear all about it! Send us an article reviewing a festival that you attended this season and suggesting improvements for next year. The best article will be published on our website and the winner will receive two free tickets to next year's Glastonbury Festival.

2 Read the winning article and choose the most interesting and appropriate title.
1 Brilliant bands + fabulous food = unforgettable experience
2 Queuing, not singing, in the rain!
3 Smells, Smiles, and Sounds at Sunny Silverfest
4 What I did and didn't enjoy about Silverfest
5 What a load of rubbish!

Winner of this year's festival review competition

My friends and I, and the other lucky festivalgoers at this year's Silverfest festival, drank 25,000 bottles of water, created nearly two tonnes of rubbish and raised £20,000 for charity. We did this while listening to some of the most talented bands around and enjoying delicious food from all over the world. What an amazing experience!

We arrived early, but as we queued to get in, we could already hear the music and smell the food. The sun was shining on the colourful tents and a DJ had already begun to entertain the crowd. This year, the music was excellent; from the beats of The Chemical Brothers to the punk rock of Vampire Weekend. I'll never forget the sight and sound of 10,000 happy people with their arms in the air.

As all festivalgoers know, dancing makes you extremely hungry, especially when the air is filled with the fabulous smells of Thai, Indian, Mexican and many other world cuisines. To be honest, I was expecting terrible festival food, but I was wrong – it was absolutely delicious.

The only thing I'd suggest changing next year is the number of rubbish bins. There should be twice as many – by the end of the day there was litter everywhere.

If you are looking for a really friendly festival with fantastic bands and tasty food (and if you don't mind a bit of rubbish!), then try Silverfest next year. You won't be disappointed.

3 Look at the article in Exercise 2 again. Tick the things that are included.
   1 an introduction which holds the reader's attention ☐
   2 a reason for writing ☐
   3 language which describes what the writer saw, heard, smelled and tasted ☐
   4 a variety of adjectives and modifiers ☐
   5 personal opinions ☐
   6 suggestions and recommendations ☐

4 Read the WRITING FOCUS box and check your answers to Exercise 3.

WRITING FOCUS

An article reviewing an event
- Begin with an interesting, funny or unusual title to attract the reader's attention.
- Hold the reader's attention with an introduction which asks a question or gives interesting facts.
- Describe the event using a variety of adjectives and modifiers.
- Make your descriptions interesting by describing what you saw, heard, smelled and tasted.
- Include personal opinions and suggestions.
- Finish with a recommendation for the reader.

5 Underline all the adjectives in the article and decide whether they can complete sentence A or B.
   A It was/They were very …
   B It was/They were absolutely …

6 Complete the table in the LANGUAGE FOCUS with some of the adjectives you found in the article.

LANGUAGE FOCUS

Modifiers with base and extreme adjectives
- You use different adverbs to modify base or extreme adjectives. Base adjectives are gradable e.g. *very bad* is worse than *quite bad*. Extreme adjectives are non-gradable e.g. *impossible* means impossible – you can't be 'more' *impossible* or 'less' *impossible*.

BASE ADJECTIVES	EXTREME ADJECTIVES
1 bad	terrible
2 difficult	impossible
3 _____	devastated
4 funny	hilarious
5 good	_____ , _____ , _____ , _____
6 _____	ecstatic
7 _____	starving
8 interesting	fascinating
9 _____	brilliant
10 _____	delicious
Modifiers: *very, rather, really, quite, extremely*	**Modifiers:** *absolutely* **Note:** *really* can also be used

7 Replace the underlined phrases with phrases in the LANGUAGE FOCUS to make the descriptions more interesting.
   1 This year's Charity Fun Day was <u>very good</u>/_____ and we raised lots of money.
   2 The birds were singing and the weather was <u>really good</u>/_____ .
   3 There were some <u>extremely bad</u>/_____ singers in the competition – that was the best bit!
   4 The exhibition of old photographs was <u>rather interesting</u>/_____ .
   5 I'd recommend the <u>rather tasty</u>/_____ homemade ice cream.
   6 If you're looking for a <u>very good</u>/_____ day out, come to next year's Charity Fun Day.

8 **SPEAKING** Think about a time when you had either an absolutely fantastic or an absolutely terrible 'day out'. Use at least six extreme adjectives. Consider the questions below and then tell your partner.
   - What kind of day out was it? (i.e. a music festival? a sports day? a school trip? a charity event? a family picnic? a day at the beach? etc.)
   - When did you have this day out?
   - Who did you go with?
   - What happened during the day?
   - What sort of things did you do?
   - What were the high/low points?
   - What is your best/worst memory?

SHOW WHAT YOU'VE LEARNT

9 Do the writing task. Use the ideas in the WRITING FOCUS and the LANGUAGE FOCUS to help you.

Your school recently organised a 'Charity Fun Day'. Local people were invited and a talent competition was held. Several student bands played and a variety of food was available. Write an article of to review the event and:
- describe and give your opinion on the various events of the day,
- make some suggestions for next year's event.

7.8 SPEAKING

Asking for permission • polite requests

I can give and refuse permission and make polite requests.

1 SPEAKING Look at the list of things you may want to do at school. Which things would you need permission for? Who would you ask?

```
not do PE
go home early
open a window
use your phone
eat or drink in the classroom
change your seat during a lesson
use a dictionary in an English test
leave the classroom during a lesson
```

2 Read the email and answer the questions.
1 What has Patty got permission to use?
2 What is she going to use it for?
3 What does she have to do next?

To: Patty Class 9
Subject: School Facebook page

Dear Patty,
You can use the school video camera on Thursday 4th April to film your class for the school Facebook page. You must ask your teachers POLITELY for permission to film their classes during the day. All students must sign a copy of the document attached.

3 🔊 **3.22** Listen to three conversations. Which teacher doesn't give Patty permission to film the class and why?

4 🔊 **3.22** Complete the conversations with words and phrases in the SPEAKING FOCUS. Then listen again and check.

1 **Patty:** Excuse me Miss Roberts. Is ¹_____ if we film your class today? It's for the school Facebook page.
   Miss R: Er, well, I'm ²_____ I'm going to give you a test today, and that won't be very interesting on film. How about tomorrow?
   Patty: We only have the camera today. ³_____ we do the test tomorrow?
   Miss R: Well OK, I ⁴_____ .
   Patty: Thanks, Miss Roberts – that's great.

2 **Patty:** Mrs Baker, Mrs Baker!
   Mrs B: Yes, hello, Patty. What can I do for you?
   Patty: Do ⁵_____ we film our Art class today, please?
   Mrs B: No, ⁶_____ all, go ahead. Is this for a project?
   Patty: No, it's for the school Facebook page.
   Mrs B: Oh right, I'll go and tidy up the classroom then.

3 **Mr O:** Come in.
   Patty: Excuse me, Mr Osborne.
   Mr O: Yes, what is it?
   Patty: Um, we ⁷_____ we could film your class today. We're making a film for the school Facebook page.
   Mr O: Oh, I see. Well, I'd like ⁸_____ , but I'm afraid I've got meetings all day and Ms Marks is taking my classes.
   Patty: Oh, OK, sorry to bother you, sir.

SPEAKING FOCUS

Asking for permission	Giving permission	Refusing permission
Can/Could I/we …?	Well, OK, I suppose so.	I'm sorry but …
Is it OK if I/we …?	Yes, that's fine. No problem.	I'd like to help but I'm afraid …
We were wondering if I/we could …?	Sure, I don't see why not.	I'm afraid …
Do you mind if I/we …?	No, not at all, go ahead.	Yes, I do actually.

5 Rewrite the following exchanges using the language in the SPEAKING FOCUS. Begin with the words in italics.

1 **A:** Lend me your calculator.   **B:** Right.
   A: *Could* …   **B:** *Well* …
2 **A:** Let me use your phone.   **B:** No, the battery is flat.
   A: *Is* …   **B:** *I'm* …
3 **A:** I want to open the window.   **B:** OK.
   A: *Do* …   **B:** *No* …
4 **A:** We want to leave early.   **B:** Fine.
   A: *We* …   **B:** *Sure*, …

6 🔊 **3.23** Listen and check your ideas in Exercise 5. Practise the exchanges with your partner.

7 SPEAKING You are going to write a dialogue asking permission for something. Use the SPEAKING FOCUS to help you.
- Decide on the situation, why you need permission and who from.
- Use the information in the box in Exercise 1 or your own ideas.
- Practise your dialogue. Then act out your dialogue to the class.

ROLE-PLAY Asking for permission

▶ 31 ▶ 32 ▶ 33 Watch the videos and practise. Then role-play your dialogue.

UNIT 7 — Entertain me — Word list

7.1 Vocabulary 🔊 4.49
admire /əd'maɪə/
appear in a TV series /ə'pɪər ɪn ə ˌtiː'viː ˌsɪəriːz/
audience /'ɔːdiəns/
be in the charts /bi ˌɪn ðə 'tʃɑːts/
beat yourself up /ˌbiːt jɔːˌself 'ʌp/
blame yourself /'bleɪm jɔːˌself/
box office /'bɒks ˌɒfəs/
carry on /ˌkæri 'ɒn/
cast /kɑːst/
come out /ˌkʌm 'aʊt/
do a live gig /ˌduː ə ˌlaɪv 'gɪg/
drummer /'drʌmə/
fictional character /ˌfɪkʃənəl 'kærəktə/
gradually disappear /ˌgrædʒuəli ˌdɪsə'pɪə/
have a hit single /ˌhæv ə ˌhɪt 'sɪŋgəl/
have great reviews /ˌhæv ˌgreɪt rɪ'vjuːz/
lead guitarist /ˌliːd gɪ'tɑːrəst/
learn from mistakes /ˌlɜːn frəm mə'steɪks/
mess up /ˌmes 'ʌp/
musician /mjuː'zɪʃən/
perform /pə'fɔːm/
performer /pə'fɔːmə/
play a venue /ˌpleɪ ə 'venjuː/
play the part of /ˌpleɪ ðə 'pɑːt əv/
put on /ˌpʊt 'ɒn/
release an album /rɪˌliːs ən 'ælbəm/
sign a recording contract /ˌsaɪn ə rɪˌkɔːdɪŋ 'kɒntrækt/
sign up for /ˌsaɪn 'ʌp fə/
singer-songwriter /ˌsɪŋə 'sɒŋˌraɪtə/
start out /ˌstɑːt 'aʊt/
streamed /striːmd/
take up /ˌteɪk 'ʌp/
turn up /ˌtɜːn 'ʌp/
viewer /'vjuːə/
vocalist /'vəʊkəlɪst/
wear off /ˌweər 'ɒf/

7.2 Grammar 🔊 4.50
art critic /'ɑːt ˌkrɪtɪk/
claim /kleɪm/
fake /feɪk/
film /fɪlm/
gallery owner /'gæləri ˌəʊnə/
genius /'dʒiːniəs/
hidden camera /ˌhɪdn 'kæmərə/
point out /ˌpɔɪnt 'aʊt/
reply /rɪ'plaɪ/
suggest /sə'dʒest/
TV channel /ˌtiː 'viː ˌtʃænl/
TV director /ˌtiː 'viː dəˌrektə/

7.3 Listening 🔊 4.51
adapt /ə'dæpt/
adaptation /ˌædæp'teɪʃən/
advertising /'ædvətaɪzɪŋ/
broadband connection /ˌbrɔːdbænd kə'nekʃən/
compete /kəm'piːt/
connect /kə'nekt/
connected to /kə'nektəd tə/
connection /kə'nekʃən/
contain an element of surprise /kənˌteɪn ən ˌeləmənt əv sə'praɪz/
cyberbullying /'saɪbəˌbʊliɪŋ/
engage emotions /ɪnˌgeɪdʒ ɪ'məʊʃənz/
explanation /ˌeksplə'neɪʃən/
go viral /ˌgəʊ 'vaɪərəl/
have a short attention span /ˌhæv ə ˌʃɔːt ə'tenʃən spæn/
hit /hɪt/
inform /ɪn'fɔːm/
information /ˌɪnfə'meɪʃən/
inspiration /ˌɪnspɪ'reɪʃən/
inspire /ɪn'spaɪə/
link /lɪŋk/
make sb laugh /ˌmeɪk ˌsʌmbədi 'lɑːf/
online purchase /ˌɒnlaɪn 'pɜːtʃɪs/
post /pəʊst/
present /prɪ'zent/
presentation /ˌprezən'teɪʃən/
produce /prə'djuːs/
production /prə'dʌkʃən/
sneeze /sniːz/
social networking site /ˌsəʊʃəl 'netwɜːkɪŋ saɪt/
stir up emotions /ˌstɜːr ˌʌp ɪ'məʊʃənz/
suggestion /sə'dʒestʃən/
take by surprise /ˌteɪk baɪ sə'praɪz/
tell a story /ˌtel ə 'stɔːri/
upload a video /ˌʌpˌləʊd ə 'vɪdiəʊ/
view /vjuː/
view a video /ˌvjuː ə 'vɪdiəʊ/
viral /'vaɪərəl/
viral video /ˌvaɪərəl 'vɪdiəʊ/

7.4 Reading 🔊 4.52
accompaniment /ə'kʌmpənimənt/
accompany /ə'kʌmpəni/
based on /'beɪsd ɒn/
cognitive /'kɒgnɪtɪv/
creak /kriːk/
create /kri'eɪt/
creation /kri'eɪʃən/
critical of /'krɪtɪkəl əv/
cut sb off from reality /ˌkʌt ˌsʌmbədi ˌɒf frəm ri'æləti/
deeply engaging /'diːpli ɪnˌgeɪdʒɪŋ/
distract /dɪ'strækt/
distraction /dɪ'strækʃən/
encourage /ɪn'kʌrɪdʒ/
encouragement /ɪn'kʌrɪdʒmənt/
engage /ɪn'geɪdʒ/
engagement /ɪn'geɪdʒmənt/
enhance /ɪn'hɑːns/
enhance the reading experience /ɪnˌhɑːns ðə ˌriːdɪŋ ɪk'spɪəriəns/
enhancement /ɪn'hɑːnsmənt/
entertain /ˌentə'teɪn/
entertainment /ˌentə'teɪnmənt/
feel distracted by /ˌfiːl dɪ'stræktəd baɪ/
find sth easy to follow /ˌfaɪnd ˌsʌmθɪŋ ˌiːzi tə 'fɒləʊ/
improve literacy rates /ɪm'pruːv 'lɪtərəsi reɪts/
improvement /ɪm'pruːvmənt/
in silence /ɪn 'saɪləns/
leave sth to your imagination /ˌliːv ˌsʌmθɪŋ tə jər ɪˌmædʒə'neɪʃən/
memorisation /ˌmeməraɪ'zeɪʃən/
memorise /'meməraɪz/
read in the old-fashioned way /ˌriːd ɪn ði ˌəʊld 'fæʃənd weɪ/
review positively /rɪˌvjuː 'pɒzətɪvli/
rustle /'rʌsəl/
scene /siːn/
sense /sens/
sensuous /'senʃuəs/
spine /spaɪn/
sympathetic /ˌsɪmpə'θetɪk/

7.5 Grammar 🔊 4.53
agree to do sth /əˌgriː tə 'duː ˌsʌmθɪŋ/
be nominated for an Oscar /bi ˌnɒmɪneɪtɪd fər ən 'ɒskə/
blow a kiss /ˌbləʊ ə 'kɪs/
date /'deɪt/
direct /də'rekt/
end a relationship /ˌend ə rɪ'leɪʃənʃɪp/
ex /eks/
fashion designer /'fæʃən dɪˌzaɪnə/
fiancé /fi'ɒnseɪ/
have a good chance of winning /ˌhæv ə ˌgʊd ˌtʃɑːns əv 'wɪnɪŋ/
interview /'ɪntəvjuː/
model /'mɒdl/
movie business /'muːvi ˌbɪznəs/
on a diet /ˌɒn ə 'daɪət/
put on weight /ˌpʊt ɒn 'weɪt/
screenplay /'skriːnpleɪ/
split up with /ˌsplɪt 'ʌp wɪð/

7.6 Use of English 🔊 4.54
headquarters /'hedˌkwɔːtəz/
manners /'mænəz/
popular with /'pɒpjələ wɪð/
presenter /prɪ'zentə/
reality TV /riˌæləti ˌtiː 'viː/

7.7 Writing 🔊 4.55
attend /ə'tend/
brilliant /'brɪljənt/
devastated /'devəsteɪtɪd/
ecstatic /ɪk'stætɪk/
fabulous /'fæbjʊləs/
fascinating /'fæsəneɪtɪŋ/
festivalgoer /'festəvəlˌgəʊə/
hilarious /hɪ'leəriəs/
impossible /ɪm'pɒsəbəl/
publish /'pʌblɪʃ/
starving /'stɑːvɪŋ/
suggest improvements /sə'dʒest ɪm'pruːvmənts/
talent competition /'tælənt ˌkɒmpəˌtɪʃən/
winner /'wɪnə/

7.8 Speaking 🔊 4.56
ask for permission /ˌɑːsk fə pə'mɪʃən/
video camera /'vɪdiəʊ ˌkæmərə/

FOCUS REVIEW 7

VOCABULARY AND GRAMMAR

1 Complete the sentences with the words and phrases in the box. There are two extra words.

carry on   cast   charts   put on   release
venues   viewers

1 Our acting group only plays small _____ as we can't afford to rent a large theatre.
2 My favourite singer is about to _____ a new album so I'm very excited!
3 That new TV show doesn't have many _____ , but the critics love it.
4 The _____ of the latest superhero film includes two of my favourite actors.
5 Our drama class is going to _____ a play which was written by our teacher.

2 Choose the correct option.

1 I am volunteering with a group that helps to improve *engagement* / *literacy* / *attention* rates among children who have trouble reading.
2 Listening to audiobooks can *enhance* / *review* / *encourage* the reading experience.
3 That video of a dog watching TV went *distracted* / *critical* / *viral* very fast – almost a million people viewed it in a couple of days.
4 Don't *beat* / *mess* / *turn* yourself up about forgetting your lines on stage. Everyone makes mistakes!
5 Her music video really *found* / *took* / *made* me by surprise – it was so much better than I'd expected.

3 Report the statements using the reporting verbs in brackets.

1 'Hank can win an Oscar next year,' said Kim.
   _____ (suggest)
2 'Someone uploaded the video yesterday,' Joe said.
   _____ (point out)
3 'I'm interviewing Mark O'Hara today,' said Eve.
   _____ (explain)
4 'Parkside is the best band I've ever heard,' said Andy.
   _____ (claim)
5 'We're going to practise in here,' said Joan.
   _____ (reply)

4 Report the questions and requests.

1 'Please bring me the DVDs which I left on the desk,' Frank said to his secretary.
   Frank asked _____ .
2 'Do you want to become a professional actress?' the journalist asked Helen.
   The journalist asked _____ .
3 'Where are we going to have lunch today?' Jo asked.
   Jo asked _____ .
4 'Don't move!' the photographer told everyone.
   The photographer asked _____ .

USE OF ENGLISH

5 Complete the sentences with the correct form of the words in brackets. Use up to six words in each gap and make any changes necessary.

1 When I asked Angie yesterday she _____ (explain/she/install) a camera in her garden to observe the wildlife at night.
2 I'm afraid _____ (there/not be/progress) on deciding which play to perform. It's seems no one can agree on anything!
3 Carla asked me _____ (I/can/perform) with her dance company.
4 The most important tool for a costume maker _____ (be/good/pair/scissors).
5 Jean told me that she _____ (accept/the part) if the director calls her back.
6 Your room is small. There _____ (too/furniture) so we should sell the big sofa!

6 Complete the text with the correct form of the words in the box. There are two extra words.

emotional   improve   encouragement   engage
imagine   entertain

Reality TV: A New Phenomenon?

For many people, reality television seems to be a fairly modern form of ¹_____ . For many years they have been the most ²_____ programmes with millions of people watching regularly. In fact, the very first programmes showing ordinary people in unscripted situations appeared in the 1940s and they've been with us ever since. One of the most influential programmes of this type was *An American Family*, a documentary-style programme showing the life of an ordinary family in the early 1970s. It managed to stir up the ³_____ of many people when the parents on the show decided to split up. Thousands of Americans were fascinated by the show and wanted to ⁴_____ the family to be together again by sending letters during and after the breakup. More than forty years ago, it was a groundbreaking programme, and it set such a high standard for reality TV that few others have managed to follow.

100

LISTENING

7 🔊 3.24 Listen to four people talking about the Notting Hill Carnival. Match the speakers with the statements. There is one extra sentence.

Speaker 1: ☐
Speaker 2: ☐
Speaker 3: ☐
Speaker 4: ☐

The speaker …
A has participated in the carnival as a performer.
B says people need to protect themselves from injuries.
C believes the carnival adds something to the city.
D would like to avoid the crowds and noise of the carnival.
E explains why some people don't enjoy it as much as others.

WRITING

8 Ask and answer the questions.
1 Do you ever read blogs? Why?/Why not?
2 Is it a good idea for a teenager to write a blog? Why?/Why not?
3 Would you like to write one yourself? Why?/Why not?

9 Read the writing task and write a review.

> You have recently taken part in a blogger festival in your town. Write a review of the most interesting blog written by somebody you met at the event, and describe the good and bad sides of writing a blog when you're a teenager.

SPEAKING

10 Do the task in pairs.

Student A

> You are in a band together with five other students. You want to play a concert at your school gym. You'd like to record the event, take photos and also interview the audience. The materials would later be on your band's website and social media. You'd prefer to do the gig on Saturday, but other days are possible. Start the conversation to ask Student B for permission.

Student B

> You are the school director. You can agree to the concert if Student A and his/her friends organise the equipment and clean the gym later. They can record the band and take photos of band members, but must always ask other people for permission. Some school staff always have to be present at such events, so the concert cannot take place on Saturday.

11 Look at the posters. You are taking part in a questionnaire on a new TV programme for teenagers. In pairs, follow these steps.
- Choose the programme which, in your opinion, is the most interesting for young people, and support your choice with some reasons.
- Explain why you have rejected the other options.

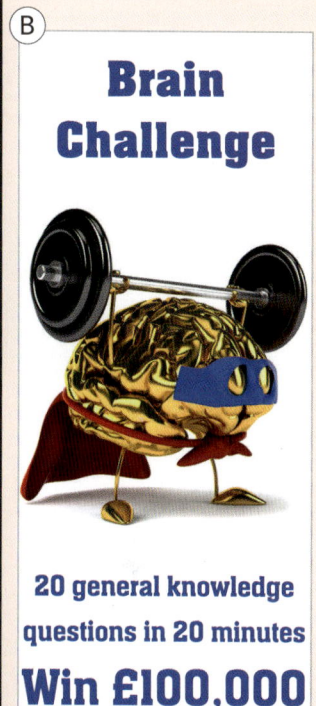

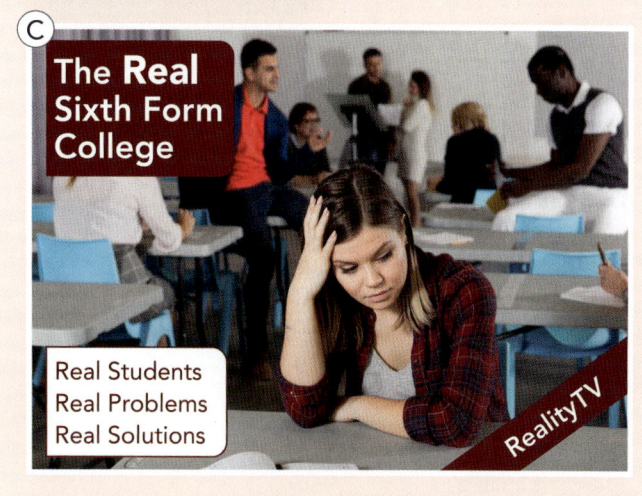

A **The Youngest UK Chef** — Looking for the best 15–18-year-old chef

B **Brain Challenge** — 20 general knowledge questions in 20 minutes. Win £100,000

C **The Real Sixth Form College** — Real Students, Real Problems, Real Solutions — Reality TV

12 Ask and answer the questions.
1 Some people say that reality TV is just a passing fashion. Do you agree? Why?/Why not?
2 In what ways can we encourage people to watch less television?
3 If you moved abroad and couldn't watch national television, which programme would you miss most? Why?
4 Watching television is often considered a waste of time. Do you agree? Why?/Why not?

8
Modern society

The greatest kindness will not bind the ungrateful.

Aesop

BBC

COFFEE STALLS

▶ 34 Watch the BBC video.
For the worksheet, go to page 130.

VOCABULARY 8.1

Crime and criminals • people involved in a crime case • the justice system

I can talk about crime and punishment.

SHOW WHAT YOU KNOW

1 Complete the UK TODAY fact file with the words in the box.

> capital   crime   elections   population   Minister
> monarchy   Head   United

UK TODAY

- The ¹<u>United</u> Kingdom: England, Wales, Scotland and Northern Ireland.
- The ² _____ : 65 million.
- The ³ _____ city: London.
- Political system: Constitutional ⁴ _____ .
- ⁵ _____ of state: The Queen (of course!).
- Head of government: The Prime ⁶ _____ .
- General ⁷ _____ : Every five years.
- Interesting fact: Nobody is further than 120 km from the sea.
- Surprising fact: It rains more in Milan than in London.
- Young people's worries: youth unemployment, the environment, ⁸ _____ .

2 Work together to prepare a similar 'fact file' for your own country.

3 Read the text and answer the questions.
  1 Which crimes are growing, falling or staying the same in number?
  2 Which crimes are a problem in your country?

4 🔊 3.25 Listen to six dialogues and name the crimes.

1 _____   4 _____
2 _____   5 _____
3 _____   6 _____

5 Imagine you are reporting a crime. Choose the correct option.

Hello, Police? I'd like to report a crime.
1 Somebody has *robbed / stolen* my phone.
2 My apartment has been *stolen / burgled*.
3 Some youths have *set fire to / mugged* a shop.
4 My sister has been *vandalised / mugged*.
5 There's a man in my store. I think he's *shoplifting / burgling*.
6 This website is *pirating / dealing* films, TV programmes and music.

UK CRIME TRENDS

In the past, burglars used to break into houses to steal TVs and DVD players. But electronic goods are so cheap now that **burglary** has become less common.

⁵Thieves are more interested in stealing small personal items like mobile phones that people carry with them. So there has been a long term fall in the number of house burglaries and **robberies** but the number of **muggings** and mobile phone ¹⁰**thefts** has grown. **Shoplifting** and **drug dealing** crimes have grown, just like Internet crimes such as hacking and online **piracy**.

Murder rates haven't changed much and although the number of car crimes fell, they are now rising ¹⁵again: one in seven reported crimes is a **car theft**. In the UK, a car is stolen every six minutes! Other crimes such as **vandalism** and **arson** have fallen.

Go to WORD STORE 8 page 17

WORD STORE 8A | Crime and criminals

6 🔊 3.26 Complete WORD STORE 8A with the base form of the words in red in Exercise 3. Then listen, check and repeat.

7 **SPEAKING** Discuss which three crimes are the most serious and why.

I think murder, arson and drug dealing are the most serious, because …

WORD STORE 8B | People involved in a crime case

8 Read two crime stories. Why are the crimes described as crazy?

CRIMINALS COMMIT CRAZY CRIMES

A <u>suspect</u> was arrested for robbing a jewellery store on Saturday afternoon. He told police that he was <u>innocent</u>. He said that he couldn't be guilty of robbing the jewellery store because on Saturday afternoon he was breaking into a school and he had a <u>witness</u> to prove it. The police immediately charged him with robbing the school. The case goes to court next month.

An eighteen-year-old man was arrested for vandalising a campsite. During the trial, the <u>judge</u> heard how the police caught the <u>accused</u>. It was the easiest case we have ever solved, the <u>detective</u> said. There was no <u>victim</u>. We didn't have to interview any witnesses or collect any evidence. The <u>criminal</u> wrote his name on a wall! He was sentenced to three months in prison.

9 🔊 3.27 Complete WORD STORE 8B with the underlined words in Exercise 8. Then listen, check and repeat.

10 Test each other. Read the seven definitions from WORD STORE 8B to your partner in a different order. Your partner writes down the word. Check how many correct answers your partner has.

WORD STORE 8C | The justice system

11 🔊 3.28 Complete WORD STORE 8C with the correct form of the highlighted words in Exercise 8. Then listen, check and repeat.

12 **SPEAKING** Imagine the sentences in Exercise 5 are the first lines in some crime stories. You are going to tell one of the stories.

- Choose an opening line 1–6.
- Imagine what happened during the case.
- Make notes based on your ideas.
- Include at least twelve words or phrases from the lesson.
- Tell your story to the class.

GRAMMAR

8.2 The Passive

I can use the Passive in a variety of tenses.

1 Read a text about Robben Island. How many different things has the island been used for?

Robben Island is situated nine kilometres from Cape Town. From the seventeenth to the twentieth century the island was used as a prison. During World War II prisoners were sent to Robben Island, but at that time it was also being used as a hospital. Later, Nelson Mandela was imprisoned there for eighteen years. After a total of twenty-seven years in prison, Mandela was elected as the first black president of South Africa.

Robben Island isn't used as a prison any more. It has been made into a museum and at the moment is being promoted as a popular tourist attraction. There is a large African penguin colony there now, but Robben Island will always be remembered as the place where Mandela was imprisoned.

Nelson Mandela

2 Read the GRAMMAR FOCUS and complete the table with the passive forms in blue in the text in Exercise 1.

GRAMMAR FOCUS

The Passive

- You use Passive forms when it isn't important or you don't know who performed the action.
- You use **by + person** (or thing) if you want to mention who (or what) performed the action.

Tense	→	Example
Present Simple	→	Robben Island ¹is situated
Present Continuous	→	² _____
Past Simple	→	³ _____
Past Continuous	→	⁴ _____
Present Perfect	→	⁵ _____
future with *will*	→	⁶ _____

3 🔊 3.29 Read about another famous 'island prison'. Complete the text with passive forms of the verbs in brackets. Then listen and check.

Alcatraz ¹*is located* (locate – Present Simple) in San Francisco Bay. It was a prison from 1933 to 1963 and during that time there were just fourteen escape attempts. The attempted escape in 1962 ² _____ (probably remember – *will*) as the most famous one. Frank Morris and the Anglin brothers dug a tunnel out of their cells and then disappeared. The three men may have drowned but their bodies ³ _____ (never discover – Present Perfect). Over the years, several postcards in the men's handwriting ⁴ _____ (send – Present Perfect) to their families. After the escape, a stolen car ⁵ _____ (find – Past Simple) and police believe it could have been used by the three men to escape. The case ⁶ _____ (keep – *will*) open until the 100th birthday of the three men. Today, Alcatraz island ⁷ _____ (use – Present Continuous) as a recreation park.

4 Complete the sentences with an appropriate passive form of the verbs in brackets.

1 The prisoners *are locked* (lock) in their cells at 9 p.m. every night.
2 John looked back. He thought he _____ (follow).
3 Last time Tina went clubbing, her phone _____ (steal).
4 Police are investigating the robbery but nobody _____ (arrest) yet.
5 As I'm writing this, three suspects _____ (question).
6 A press conference _____ (hold) tomorrow.

5 Read these facts about crime. Cross out *by* + person or thing if it is not necessary.

UK and USA CRIME FACTS

1 500,000 crimes in the UK are committed by ex-prisoners.
2 Each year in the USA, around 100 prisoners are sentenced to death by judges.
3 In the UK, the death penalty was abolished by the government in 1998.
4 Around 10 percent of murders in the USA are committed by women.
5 On average, murderers are released from UK prisons by the authorities after sixteen years.

6 Rewrite the sentences below in the passive. Start each sentence with *I* and use *by* + agent if necessary.

1 The head teacher has never told me off.
   I've never been told off by the head teacher.
2 People often invite me to parties.
3 An old childhood friend has contacted me on Facebook today.
4 People gave me money for my last birthday.
5 My father taught me how to ride a bicycle.
6 My mother is picking me up from school today.

7 Which sentences in Exercise 6 are true for you? Compare with a partner.

Grammar page 153

8.3 LISTENING

Multiple choice

I can follow an informal interview on a common topic.

1 **SPEAKING** Read UK TODAY and discuss which facts you find most surprising. Do you think the situation is similar or different in your country?

UK TODAY

- A 'young offender' can be anybody from the age of ten to seventeen (twelve to seventeen in Scotland) who commits a crime.
- Each year, almost 1,600 young offenders are sent to young offenders' prisons.
- The most common crimes are theft, violence and criminal damage.
- The average sentence is sixteen months.
- It costs over £140,000 a year to keep a young offender in prison.
- 54 percent of young offenders are aged seventeen.
- 97 percent of young offenders are boys.
- 88 percent of young offenders have been excluded from school.
- 68.1 percent of young offenders commit another crime within twelve months of leaving prison.

2 🔊 3.30 Listen to an interview with Daniel, an ex-offender, and answer the questions.
1 Why is the government worried about young offenders' prisons?
2 What happens to young offenders at night?
3 How do young offenders earn money to buy sweets and phone calls?
4 Why do some offenders want to stay in prison?
5 Who thinks young offenders should be punished more?

EXAM FOCUS Multiple choice

3 🔊 3.30 Listen to the interview again. For questions 1–5, choose the correct answer, A, B, C or D.
1 The government are planning to
  A write a special report about prisons for young offenders.
  B make an example of teenagers who break the law.
  C educate young offenders more effectively.
  D make young offenders' prisons harder.
2 When they behave badly, young offenders
  A are not allowed to watch television.
  B are locked in their cells all evening.
  C have to attend lessons.
  D cannot make phone calls.
3 One of Daniel's friends damaged a few cars
  A a few days after he was released.
  B because he wanted to steal them.
  C in a supermarket car park.
  D in order to go back to prison.
4 Daniel believes that the best way to make young offenders into better citizens is to
  A lock them in cells and punish them.
  B give them hope for the future.
  C show them that life is simple.
  D make prison like a holiday camp.
5 Based on Daniel's interview, the government's plans
  A will make prisons more enjoyable.
  B will probably help some young offenders.
  C are a complete waste of time.
  D are likely to be very popular.

WORD STORE 8D | Prison

4 🔊 3.31 Complete WORD STORE 8D with the verbs in the box. Then listen and repeat.

5 Complete the questions with the correct form of a word in WORD STORE 8D.

Should young offenders …
1 always go to prison if they _____ the law?
2 serve their whole _____ in prison?
3 be _____ in their cells at night?
4 be _____ from prison if they don't have a home to go back to?

6 **SPEAKING** Discuss the questions in Exercise 5.

PRONUNCIATION FOCUS

7 🔊 3.32 Listen and put the words into groups A, B, or C depending on the stress.

~~appreciation~~   determined   investigation   offender
sympathetic   unexpected

A ▪■▪	B ▪▪■▪	C ▪▪▪■▪
_____	_____	_appreciation_
_____	_____	_____

8 🔊 3.33 Listen, check and repeat the words.

8.4 READING

Multiple choice

I can distinguish supporting details from the main points in a text.

1 **SPEAKING** Look at some acts of kindness. Discuss whether you have done them, might do them or would never do them. Give reasons for your answers.
  - Pay for someone's cup of coffee.
  - Give someone an umbrella on a rainy day.
  - Buy a homeless person a hot drink or lunch.
  - Stop and talk to a homeless person.
  - Offer to help someone carry their bags.
  - Give someone your seat on the train or bus.
  - Give someone a compliment.

2 **SPEAKING** Text 1 is entitled 'Paying it forward'. Discuss the questions. Then read Text 1 and check your ideas.
  1 What does 'paying it forward' actually mean?
  2 What are some of the benefits of 'paying it forward'?
  3 What is the main difficulty of 'paying it forward'?

3 Read Text 2. How did the restaurant owner 'pay it forward'?

EXAM FOCUS Multiple choice

4 Read Text 1 and Text 2 again and choose the correct answer, A, B, C or D.

Text 1

1 A woman who lost her phone on the train
  A accepted money the boy offered her.
  B asked the boy to do an act of kindness.
  C wanted to send the boy some money.
  D gave back the phone to the twelve-year-old boy.
2 Michael Norton believes that
  A people spend more on others than themselves.
  B a large proportion of people are happy.
  C long-term happiness depends on your income.
  D kindness is a natural human characteristic.
3 The journalist was surprised
  A when people refused her offer of a free coffee.
  B that people were delighted with her offer.
  C that someone finally accepted the free coffee.
  D by the generosity of strangers.

Text 2

4 The restaurant owner invited the homeless person into the restaurant because
  A she wanted to give the person some leftover sandwiches.
  B she wanted to give the person some human dignity.
  C she was upset that the person had knocked over her bins.
  D she wanted to ask the person some questions.

Texts 1 and 2

5 The texts include examples of acts of kindness committed by people who
  A expect something in return.
  B wish to remain anonymous.
  C want to help homeless people.
  D want to make other people feel better.

Text 1

PAYING IT FORWARD

🔊 3.34

This week's lead article comes from journalist Amy Randall who tells us why she would like to live in a kinder society and explains the benefits of 'paying it forward'.

In today's cynical world, it's often difficult to give and accept kindness. The smallest acts of kindness are often met with suspicion, and yet there is plenty of evidence to suggest that being kind can make you healthier and happier.

5 So what sort of acts of kindness am I talking about? They can be big gestures, or just small everyday things that will make people smile. At one end of the scale, an anonymous person might pay for someone's expensive operation without expecting a thank-you. At the other,
10 there are the small gestures which might seem trivial, but are often extremely welcome.

One example of this is the story of a twelve-year-old boy who found a stranger's phone on a train. When he contacted the owner, she was so impressed by his honesty, that she
15 offered a small reward. He didn't accept the money, but he wrote a note and sent it with the returned phone. In the note he said that he didn't want the money, he just wanted the woman to do something nice for someone else.

This kind of gesture is known as 'paying it forward'. The
20 idea is that if you do a good deed for someone but ask for nothing in return, they will then do a good deed for someone else, and kindness will multiply and create a huge wave of good feeling across the globe.

There are many benefits to being kind. Giving to others
25 can make you feel more connected to other people

Text 2

No questions asked

and increase your **sense of purpose** in life. You feel you've **made a difference** and there's a reason to get out of bed in the morning. **Taking time to help others** may even protect you from disease. A thirty-year study has shown that women who
30 volunteered for a charity were sixteen percent less likely to suffer a **major** illness during that period – perhaps because it lowers stress levels.

I believe that people are naturally kind. This was also the conclusion of a study by Michael Norton at Harvard Business
35 School: he did research in more than 130 countries and found that people who spend a bigger proportion of their income on others were more fulfilled than those who spend it on themselves. He thinks the desire to give and share could be a basic human trait.

That's the theory anyway. But when I've tried out acts of kindness
40 on strangers, they often seem unsure how to react to me. In my local coffee shop, I tried to give away a cup of coffee. I thought people would be delighted, but instead I was met with **suspicious** stares. Then I realised why this was happening: we don't expect kindness from strangers – on the contrary, we expect them to trick
45 us or **take advantage of us**.

But don't let that put you off. I did find someone to take my coffee and when I saw how pleased she was, it **made my day**. We need to fight against the 'me-first' society we live in and start a kindness movement. It sounds cheesy, but I think we need it.

A woman who runs a sandwich bar selling peanut butter and jam sandwiches noticed that somebody had removed some food from her rubbish bins. When she realised that a homeless person was taking leftover food from her bins, she
5 was upset. She was sad to think that someone was so poor that they had to eat other people's leftovers. She typed a note and pinned it to her restaurant window.

The note was addressed to the person going through the rubbish for their next meal. She told this person that they were a human
10 being and worth more than a meal from a dustbin. She offered them a free peanut butter and jam sandwich, fresh vegetables and a cup of water and promised not to ask any questions.

The restaurant owner said she understands that everyone needs help at one time or another, and in this case, she was
15 happy to **offer the homeless person a helping hand**.

---

5 **SPEAKING** Discuss how much you agree or disagree with the three highlighted statements in Text 1. Change the statements so that they represent your own views.

6 🔊 **3.35** Complete the verb phrases with an appropriate noun in blue in the texts. Then listen, check and repeat.
   1 ask (for) nothing in _return_
   2 be met with _____
   3 offer a _____
   4 do a good _____
   5 give sb a sense of _____
   6 make a _____
   7 take _____ to do sth
   8 take _____ of sb
   9 make sb's _____
   10 offer (sb) a helping _____

7 Translate the phrases in Exercise 6. Which ones are positive and which are negative?

8 **SPEAKING** Complete the questions with the correct verb in Exercise 6. Then ask and answer.
   1 What could you buy that would _____ a real difference to your life?
   2 How often do you _____ your mum a helping hand?
   3 What good deed could you _____ on the way home today?
   4 In what circumstances might you _____ somebody a reward?
   5 Is it always wrong to _____ advantage of people?
   6 Can you think of one thing that would _____ your day today?

WORD STORE 8E Synonyms

9 🔊 **3.36** Complete WORD STORE 8E with the underlined adjectives in Text 1. Then listen, check and repeat.

10 Complete the common collocations with the adjectives in WORD STORE 8E to describe these comments.
   1 'Thank you so much for helping me with my shopping.' = A _____ gesture.
   2 'Nobody does anything unless they want something in return.' = A _____ remark.
   3 'Why are these people looking at me like this?' = _____ stares.
   4 'I hope you're coming to my graduation ceremony.' = A _____ event.
   5 'Hey, this is my seat!' = A _____ matter.
   6 'I'd rather not give my name.' = An _____ donation.

11 **SPEAKING** Talk about the last time you helped somebody or somebody helped you.

Last weekend, my friend helped me to tidy my room. It made my day!

GRAMMAR 8.5

Have something done

I can use have *to refer to having things done by other people.*

1 Read *Burglary: The Facts* and guess the correct answers.

BURGLARY: THE FACTS

According to statistics, the highest number of burglaries happen to ¹*terraced / detached / semi-detached* houses, ²*halfway down a street / at the end of a street / in the countryside* with a ³*purple / brown / green* door and the number ⁴*eighty-eight / sixty-six / thirteen*.

2 🔊 3.37 Listen to Judy and Mike's story and check your answers in Exercise 1. Are Judy and Mike going to move house?

3 🔊 3.37 Listen again and number the changes made to Judy and Mike's house in the correct order.

A ☐ Judy and Mike had a wall built.

B ☐ They've had the door painted green.

C ☐ They're going to have the house number changed.

D ☐ They had the locks changed.

E ☐ They had a sign about their dog put on the gate.

4 Read the GRAMMAR FOCUS. Did Judy and Mike make the changes to their house or did they arrange for somebody else to do it?

GRAMMAR FOCUS

Have something done

You use the structure **have something done** when you arrange for somebody to do something for you. (You don't do it yourself.)

Compare:
They **had** the locks **changed**. (somebody did it for them)
They changed the locks. (they did it themselves)

have + object + past participle

+	They**'ve had** the door **painted** green.
–	They **didn't have** a garage **built**.
?	**Are** they **going to have** the house number **changed**? Yes, they **are**./No, they **aren't**.

Note: You can usually use **get** instead of *have* with no change in meaning.
He's **getting** the door **painted**. = He's **having** the door **painted**.

5 Judy is explaining some of the changes to a new neighbour. Rewrite the sentences using *we* and the structure *have something done*. Use the same tenses.
   1 A carpenter changed all the locks.
      We had all the locks changed.
   2 A carpenter fitted a new door.
   3 A builder has been building a bigger wall.
   4 A decorator has just painted the front door.
   5 An electrician is putting in new security lights.
   6 A security firm is going to install a new burglar alarm.

6 Write sentences from the prompts using the structure *have something done*. Which sentences are true for you?
   1 We / redecorate / house / last year
      We had our house redecorated last year.
   2 I / never / pierce / ears
   3 My mother / service / her car / every year
   4 I'd like / colour / my hair
   5 I / take out / a tooth / the next time I go to the dentist

7 Have it done or do it yourself? Write true sentences about you from the prompts.
   1 tidy / bedroom
      I tidy my bedroom.
   2 repair / laptop or phone
   3 charge / phone
   4 test / eyes
   5 check / teeth
   6 cut / hair
   7 take / passport photo
   8 update / Facebook profile

8 **SPEAKING** Write questions based on the prompts in Exercise 7. Begin the questions with *How often do you …?* Then ask your partner the questions.
   A: *How often do you tidy your bedroom?*
   B: *Not very often … about once a week …*

Grammar page 154

8.6 USE OF ENGLISH

Reflexive pronouns

I can correctly use each other and reflexive pronouns.

1 🔊 3.38 **SPEAKING** The words and phrases in the box are from a podcast. Discuss what you think the podcast is about. Then listen and check your ideas.

> anti-virus software   digital footprint
> identity thieves   passwords   a weak password
> a password manager   videos and photos   viruses

2 🔊 3.38 Replace the underlined pronouns with appropriate words and phrases in Exercise 1. Then listen again and check.

1 If you use <u>one of these</u>, you can only blame yourself if a hacker gets into your account.
2 You can use <u>one of these</u> to save yourself some trouble.
3 Keep <u>them</u> to yourself. Even with your friends, don't tell one another.
4 Use <u>this</u> to protect yourself from viruses.
5 <u>They</u> update themselves all the time, so you need to update your software too.
6 If you send each other <u>these</u>, they're likely to stay online for a long time.

3 **SPEAKING** Discuss how safe you think you are online. What could you do to protect yourself more?

4 Read the LANGUAGE FOCUS and underline all the examples of reflexive pronouns and *each other/one another* in Exercise 2.

LANGUAGE FOCUS

Reflexive pronouns, *each other* and *one another*

- You use reflexive pronouns *myself, yourself, himself, herself, itself, ourselves, yourselves, themselves* when the subject and the direct or indirect object of a sentence are the same person or thing.
  You can only blame **yourself**.
  Viruses update **themselves** all the time.
  Verbs commonly used with reflexive pronouns: *behave, blame, cut, enjoy, express, hurt, injure, introduce, prepare, protect, teach*
  Note: *By yourself/myself*, etc. means *alone/on your own/without help*.
- **Each other** and **one another** have the same meaning. You use them when the subject and object are different. Compare the following sentences:
  *Tim and Tina are looking at **each other/one another**.* = *Tim is looking at Tina and Tina is looking at Tim.*
  *Tim and Tina are looking at **themselves**.* = *Tim is looking at himself and Tina is looking at herself.*

5 Complete the sentences with a reflexive pronoun. Which sentences are true for you?
1 My phone switches *itself* off if I don't use it for a while.
2 My father bought _____ a new laptop recently.
3 When I go out with my friends, we always enjoy _____ .
4 I hate it when people don't introduce _____ .
5 My mum is teaching _____ how to play the guitar.
6 I prefer revising for exams by _____ .

6 **SPEAKING** Complete the questions with *each other/ one another* or *themselves*. Then ask and answer the questions with a partner.
1 How often do you and your friends message *each other*?
2 How well can your parents express _____ in English?
3 What do you and your friends normally talk to _____ about?
4 How do your friends protect _____ from spam?
5 How long have you and your best friend known _____ ?
6 What do your classmates do to prepare _____ for exams?

7 **USE OF ENGLISH** Complete the second sentence so that it has a similar meaning to the first.
1 I'm afraid Matt is injured and won't be playing today.
   I'm afraid Matt has _____ .
2 Did you have fun at the party last night, Tom?
   Did you _____ ?
3 I spent the weekend completely alone.
   I spent the weekend all _____ .
4 Mary took the blame for the mistake.
   Mary blamed _____ .
5 Tom learnt how to program computers on his own.
   Tom taught _____ .
6 I got a cut while I was chopping onions.
   I cut _____ .

FOCUS VLOG | About social media

▶ 37 Watch the Focus Vlog. For the worksheet, go to page 131.

Use of English page 155

WRITING

8.7 An opinion essay

I can write an essay to express my opinion and support it with relevant examples.

1 **SPEAKING** Read the news report and discuss the questions.

1 What is your opinion of the politician's comments?
2 How frequently do you usually check your phone?
3 What do you think it means to be addicted to your phone?

Are young people enjoying life?

A politician has upset young people with the comments he made during a television interview this week. He said, 'Today's teenagers have forgotten the simple pleasures of life such as conversation with friends and family, and time spent outdoors in our beautiful country. If something isn't available in a three-minute YouTube video, or can't be 'liked' on Facebook, then it is of no interest to anyone under the age of eighteen. We live in a nation of lazy, phone-addicted young people who have no idea how to really enjoy life.'

2 After a class discussion on this news item, Oliver wrote an opinion essay. What do you think about the points he makes?

Oliver Gleeson, class 6C

It is not unusual for older generations to criticise younger people's lifestyles. For instance, a politician said recently that the young people in this country were lazy and did not know how to enjoy life. In my view, these comments are incorrect and unfair.

To begin with, I would like to point out that not all young people are addicted to their phones. Many communicate and share interests online, but most of us do not spend all our free time there. For example, my friends and I regularly meet and spend time doing and talking about the things we enjoy. In other words, we have real lives.

Next, as far as I am concerned, most young people are not lazy. For instance, like many of my friends, I am studying for my final exams and learning to drive at the moment. In addition, I play the guitar and go mountain biking most weekends. Put another way, we are too busy to be lazy.

Lastly, it seems to me that the majority of young people do enjoy life. Many of us have social lives which include a range of sports, hobbies and interests. Moreover, plenty of these activities involve spending time with friends and making the most of our beautiful country.

In summary, I do not think the politician who made these comments understands today's young people. I think he should visit some local schools, talk to some teenagers and find out what their lives are really like.

3 SPEAKING Discuss the questions.

1. How similar or different are you to Oliver and his friends?
2. How would you respond if somebody called you 'lazy' or 'phone addicted'?
3. What are the main differences between the way your generation, your parents' generation and your grandparents' generation 'enjoy life'?

4 Complete the WRITING FOCUS with the words in the box and the linkers in purple in the essay.

> linkers   ~~point of view~~   reader   summary   support

WRITING FOCUS

An opinion essay

- Introduction
  Introduce the topic and give a clear statement of your main ¹*point of view*.

- Main paragraphs
  Include two or three paragraphs with more detailed personal opinions and ²_____ these with reasons and examples.
  Remember to use ³_____ to help the reader follow your essay.
  Firstly = ⁴_____ /Secondly = ⁵_____ /
  Finally = ⁶_____ /In conclusion = ⁷_____

- Conclusion
  Include a ⁸_____ of your main point of view. Use different words to the statement in the introduction. Include a final comment which leaves the ⁹_____ with something to think about.

5 SPEAKING Discuss what you think about three more comments made by older people criticising teenage lifestyles. How many arguments can you think of in response?

1. Teenagers do not understand the value of things. They want all the latest fashions, the most expensive phones and laptops, and they want them all now. They don't seem to realise that these things cost money!
2. Teenagers do not respect the opinions of adults. They think they know best and don't value our experience. They seem to forget that we were once teenagers too.
3. Teenagers don't read anymore. They don't value the importance of books. As a result, their language skills suffer and they can't express themselves very well.

6 Choose one of the comments in Exercise 5 and prepare three detailed arguments in response.

- Decide on a logical order for your three arguments.
- Write the arguments up as three paragraphs.
- Use linkers to structure your work.

7 Read the LANGUAGE FOCUS and complete each phrase with one word. Check the underlined phrases in the essay if necessary.

LANGUAGE FOCUS

Giving your opinion and emphasising a point

- Giving your opinion:
  I think … (I do not think …)/It seems to me that …/
  In ¹*my* view …/in my opinion …/
  As far ²_____ I am concerned …

- Emphasising a point by giving an example or making an additional point:
  ³_____ instance …/For example …/
  ⁴_____ addition …/Moreover …/What is more …

- Emphasising a point by repeating in another way
  In ⁵_____ words …/Put ⁶_____ way …/
  What I mean is that …

8 Complete the second sentence so that it means the same as the first, beginning with the word given.

1. I think the celebrity's comments were extremely negative and unhelpful.
   It _____
   _____

2. My parents taught me to be well-mannered. In addition, we are expected to be polite at school.
   My parents taught me to be well-mannered.
   What _____
   _____

3. In my opinion, there are many selfish people in the world and not all of them are young.
   As _____
   _____

4. For example, lots of young people do voluntary work or raise money for charity.
   For _____
   _____

5. In other words, most young people are aware of the importance of being a good citizen.
   What _____
   _____

SHOW WHAT YOU'VE LEARNT

9 Do the writing task. Use the ideas in Exercise 8, the WRITING FOCUS and the LANGUAGE FOCUS to help you.

A celebrity said in a radio interview recently, 'Today's young people are unfriendly, selfish and have no manners. It seems they have not been taught to be good citizens by their parents or their schools'. Write an essay in which you:

- present your opinion on the celebrity's comments,
- give reasons and examples to support your point of view.

8.8 SPEAKING

Opinions: talking about advantages and disadvantages

I can discuss an idea and talk about its advantages and disadvantages.

1 **SPEAKING** Complete the following sentence in as many ways as you can think of. Discuss your ideas.

A good person is someone who …

2 🔊 **3.39** Read the school webpage and listen to a conversation. Which activities do Robert and Sonia decide to do?

PRINCE JAMES SCHOOL
home | teachers | students | parents

THREE EASY WAYS TO BE A GOOD CITIZEN!

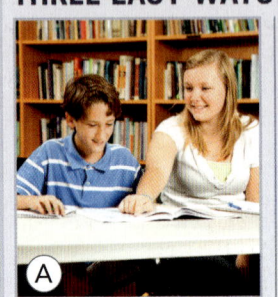

A Help younger pupils with school subjects
Are you good at a particular subject? Are you patient? Younger pupils need your help.

B Help the elderly in your community
Elderly people are often lonely. Promise to call on an elderly person two or three times a week.

C Raise money for charity
Organise a sale: second-hand clothes, cakes or books.

3 🔊 **3.39** Complete section A of the SPEAKING FOCUS with the words in the box. Then listen again and check.

(good   into   not   rather   ~~thing~~)

SPEAKING FOCUS

A Talking about your skills and interests
(Teaching) isn't my ¹*thing* at all.
You're really ² _____ at (Maths/swimming).
I'm ³ _____ (patient) enough.
I'd ⁴ _____ (visit an elderly person).
I'm really ⁵ _____ (vintage clothes).

B Giving and explaining an opinion
In my opinion …/What I mean is …/In fact …
To be honest, I think/don't think …

C Talking about advantages and disadvantages
There are a lot of advantages/disadvantages …
One/Another benefit is that …
The main advantage of voluntary work is that …
There are drawbacks too.
One of the main disadvantages of voluntary work is that …
Another disadvantage of voluntary work is that …

4 **SPEAKING** Discuss which voluntary work in Exercise 2 you would choose to do and why. Explain why you are rejecting the other activities.

5 **SPEAKING** Look at the motion for a school debate. Think of three reasons for and three reasons against doing voluntary work.

home | teachers | **students** | parents

SCHOOL DEBATE
Motion:
Everybody should do voluntary work.

6 🔊 **3.40** Listen to two people talking about reasons for and against doing voluntary work. Do they mention any of the points you thought of in Exercise 5?

7 🔊 **3.40** Read sections B and C in the SPEAKING FOCUS and complete the texts. Listen again and check your answers.

FOR
In my opinion, there are a lot of ¹_____ to doing voluntary work. ²_____ benefit is that it makes people think about other people who are less fortunate than they are. What I ³_____ is that if you do voluntary work, you will understand the problems that exist in society. Another ⁴_____ of doing voluntary work is that you become a better person – less selfish and more generous.

AGAINST
First of all, I agree that there are a lot of advantages to doing voluntary work, but I think there are ⁵_____ too. One of the ⁶_____ disadvantages of voluntary work is that it can take up a lot of time. What I mean is, voluntary work could stop you helping your own family or friends, or take time away from your studies. ⁷_____ disadvantage of voluntary work is that you don't earn money, so you are still dependent on your parents for everything. To be ⁸_____ , I think we should learn to be independent from our parents as soon as possible.

8 **SPEAKING** Choose a topic. Student A: make notes on the advantages. Student B: make notes about the disadvantages. Discuss your ideas. Use the SPEAKING FOCUS to help you.

- being an only child
- single-sex schools
- taking part in sports competitions
- wearing a school uniform
- being a man/woman
- owning a pet

ROLE-PLAY Opinions: talking about advantages and disadvantages

▶ **38** Watch the video and practise. Then role-play your dialogue.

UNIT 8   Modern society   Word list

8.1 Vocabulary 🔊 4.57

arson /ˈɑːsən/
arsonist /ˈɑːsənɪst/
be arrested /bɪ əˈrestɪd/
be charged with a crime /bɪ ˌtʃɑːdʒd wɪð ə ˈkraɪm/
be found guilty /bɪ ˌfaʊnd ˈɡɪlti/
be found not guilty /bɪ ˌfaʊnd ˌnɒt ˈɡɪlti/
be released /bɪ rɪˈliːst/
be sentenced /bɪ ˈsentənst/
burglar /ˈbɜːɡlə/
burglary /ˈbɜːɡləri/
burgle a house /ˌbɜːɡəl ə ˈhaʊs/
case /keɪs/
charge /tʃɑːdʒ/
collect evidence /kəˌlekt ˈevədəns/
commit a crime /kəˌmɪt ə ˈkraɪm/
criminal /ˈkrɪmɪnəl/
deal drugs /ˌdiːl ˈdrʌɡz/
detective /dɪˈtektɪv/
drug dealer /ˈdrʌɡ ˌdiːlə/
drug dealing /ˈdrʌɡ ˌdiːlɪŋ/
elections /iˈlekʃənz/
evidence /ˈevɪdəns/
go to court /ˌɡəʊ tə ˈkɔːt/
government /ˈɡʌvəmənt/
head of government /ˌhed əv ˈɡʌvəmənt/
innocent /ˈɪnəsənt/
interview victims/witnesses /ˌɪntəvjuː ˈvɪktɪmz/ˈwɪtnɪsɪz/
investigate /ɪnˈvestəɡeɪt/
judge /dʒʌdʒ/
kill /kɪl/
mug /mʌɡ/
mugger /ˈmʌɡə/
mugging /ˈmʌɡɪŋ/
murder /ˈmɜːdə/
murderer /ˈmɜːdərə/
piracy /ˈpaɪərəsi/
pirate /ˈpaɪərət/
pirate software /ˌpaɪərət ˈsɒftweə/
report a crime /rɪˌpɔːt ə ˈkraɪm/
rob sb/a place /ˈrɒb ˌsʌmbədi/ə ˈpleɪs/
robber /ˈrɒbə/
robbery /ˈrɒbəri/
set fire to /ˌset ˈfaɪə tə/
shoplift /ˈʃɒpˌlɪft/
shoplifter /ˈʃɒpˌlɪftə/
shoplifting /ˈʃɒpˌlɪftɪŋ/
steal /stiːl/
suspect /ˈsʌspekt/
the accused /ðɪ əˈkjuːzd/
trial /ˈtraɪəl/
theft /θeft/
thief /θiːf/
unemployment /ˌʌnɪmˈplɔɪmənt/
vandal /ˈvændl/
vandalise /ˈvændəlaɪz/
vandalism /ˈvændəlɪzəm/
victim /ˈvɪktɪm/
witness /ˈwɪtnɪs/

8.2 Grammar 🔊 4.58

abolish /əˈbɒlɪʃ/
attempted escape /əˌtemptɪd ɪˈskeɪp/
authorities /ɔːˈθɒrətɪz/
cell /sel/
death penalty /ˈdeθ ˌpenlti/
dig a tunnel /ˌdɪɡ ə ˈtʌnl/
drown /draʊn/
elect /ɪˈlekt/
escape /ɪˈskeɪp/
escape attempt /ɪˈskeɪp əˌtempt/
imprison /ɪmˈprɪzən/
on average /ɒn ˈævərɪdʒ/
prisoner /ˈprɪzənə/
promote /prəˈməʊt/
question /ˈkwestʃən/
tell sb off /ˌtel ˌsʌmbədi ˈɒf/

8.3 Listening 🔊 4.59

average /ˈævərɪdʒ/
behave badly /bɪˌheɪv ˈbædli/
break the law /ˌbreɪk ðə ˈlɔː/
citizen /ˈsɪtəzən/
criminal damage /ˌkrɪmənəl ˈdæmɪdʒ/
exclude from school /ɪkˌskluːd frəm ˈskuːl/
have a criminal record /ˌhæv ə ˌkrɪmənəl ˈrekɔːd/
lock sb (up) /ˌlɒk ˌsʌmbədi (ˈʌp)/
make an example of /ˌmeɪk ən ɪɡˈzɑːmpəl əv/
make (prisons) harder /ˌmeɪk ˌprɪzənz ˈhɑːdə/
prison guard /ˈprɪzən ɡɑːd/
punish sb severely /ˌpʌnɪʃ ˌsʌmbədi səˈvɪəli/
release from prison /rɪˌliːs frəm ˈprɪzən/
sentence /ˈsentəns/
serve a sentence /ˌsɜːv ə ˈsentəns/
violence /ˈvaɪələns/
young offender /ˌjʌŋ əˈfendə/

8.4 Reading 🔊 4.60

anonymous /əˈnɒnɪməs/
appreciated /əˈpriːʃieɪtɪd/
ask for nothing in return /ˌɑːsk fə ˈnʌθɪŋ ɪn rɪˈtɜːn/
be met with suspicion /bɪ ˌmet wɪð səˈspɪʃən/
benefit /ˈbenəfɪt/
cheesy /ˈtʃiːzi/
cynical /ˈsɪnɪkəl/
distrustful /dɪsˈtrʌstfəl/
do a good deed /ˌduː ə ˌɡʊd ˈdiːd/
donation /dəʊˈneɪʃən/
dustbin /ˈdʌstbɪn/
fulfilled /fʊlˈfɪld/
generosity /ˌdʒenəˈrɒsəti/
give a sense of purpose /ˌɡɪv ə ˌsens əv ˈpɜːpəs/
homeless /ˈhəʊmləs/
honesty /ˈɒnəsti/
human trait /ˌhjuːmən ˈtreɪt/
impressed by /ɪmˈprest baɪ/
kindness /ˈkaɪndnəs/
knock over /ˌnɒk ˈəʊvə/
major /ˈmeɪdʒə/
make a difference /ˌmeɪk ə ˈdɪfərəns/
make sb's day /ˌmeɪk ˌsʌmbədiz ˈdeɪ/
offer a helping hand /ˌɒfər ə ˌhelpɪŋ ˈhænd/
offer a reward/job /ˌɒfə ə rɪˈwɔːd/ˈdʒɒb/
peanut butter /ˌpiːnʌt ˈbʌtə/
pin /pɪn/
put off /ˌpʊt ˈɒf/
random /ˈrændəm/
sceptical /ˈskeptɪkəl/
small gestures /ˌsmɔːl ˈdʒestʃəz/
stare /steə/
suspicious /səˈspɪʃəs/
take advantage of /ˌteɪk ədˈvɑːntɪdʒ əv/
take time to /ˌteɪk ˈtaɪm tə/
trick /trɪk/
trivial /ˈtrɪviəl/
type a note /ˌtaɪp ə ˈnəʊt/
want something in return /ˌwɒnt ˌsʌmθɪŋ ɪn rɪˈtɜːn/
welcome /ˈwelkəm/

8.5 Grammar 🔊 4.61

burglar alarm /ˈbɜːɡlər əˌlɑːm/
carpenter /ˈkɑːpɪntə/
lock /lɒk/
security firm /sɪˈkjʊərəti fɜːm/
security lights /sɪˈkjʊərəti laɪts/
statistics /stəˈtɪstɪks/

8.6 Use of English 🔊 4.62

anti-virus software /ˌænti ˈvaɪərəs ˌsɒftweə/
blame yourself /ˈbleɪm jɔːˌself/
digital footprint /ˌdɪdʒətl ˈfʊtˌprɪnt/
enjoy yourself /ɪnˈdʒɔɪ jɔːˌself/
express yourself /ɪkˈspres jɔːˌself/
identity theft /aɪˈdentəti θeft/
introduce yourself /ˌɪntrəˈdjuːs jɔːˌself/
password /ˈpɑːswɜːd/
prepare yourself /prɪˈpeə jɔːˌself/
protect yourself /prəˈtekt jɔːˌself/

8.7 Writing 🔊 4.63

majority /məˈdʒɒrəti/
phone-addicted people /ˌfəʊn əˌdɪktəd ˈpiːpəl/
pleasures of life /ˌpleʒəz əv ˈlaɪf/
point of view /ˌpɔɪnt əv ˈvjuː/
polite /pəˈlaɪt/
politician /ˌpɒləˈtɪʃən/
selfish /ˈselfɪʃ/
voluntary work /ˈvɒləntəri wɜːk/
well-mannered /ˌwel ˈmænəd/

8.8 Speaking 🔊 4.64

be fortunate/less fortunate /bɪ ˈfɔːtʃənət/les ˈfɔːtʃənət/
call on /ˈkɔːl ɒn/
elderly people /ˈeldəli ˌpiːpəl/
honest /ˈɒnəst/
lonely /ˈləʊnli/
organise a sale /ˌɔːɡənaɪz ə ˈseɪl/
patient /ˈpeɪʃənt/
second-hand clothes /ˌsekəndˌhænd ˈkləʊðz/
uniform /ˈjuːnəfɔːm/

FOCUS REVIEW 8

VOCABULARY AND GRAMMAR

1 **Complete the sentences with words from the unit. The first letter of each word is given.**

  1 The bank robber will have to s_____ a s_____ of twelve years.
  2 The w_____ was afraid to show her face in court, so she was allowed to describe what she had seen in a private room.
  3 There are some criminals who t_____ a_____ of older people, getting their banking information and stealing their money.
  4 I don't think this c_____ will go to c_____ because both sides seem to be willing to forget about what happened.

2 **Complete the sentences with the correct form of the words in capitals.**

  1 It's hard to be a victim of a _____ because you never really feel safe in the streets after it happens. MUG
  2 He was accused of the _____ of a valuable painting, but he claimed he hadn't taken it. THIEF
  3 Before criminals _____ a house, they make sure no one is at home. BURGLAR
  4 It was shocking to learn that the _____ who set the school on fire was actually a fire fighter. ARSON
  5 We have reduced _____ in our area by having the offenders repair the damage. VANDAL

3 **Complete the second sentence with up to three words so that it has a similar meaning to the first.**

  1 Next month the government will release five political prisoners.
  Next month five political prisoners _____ .
  2 A prison guard took John to his new cell.
  John _____ to his new cell.
  3 The lawyer's speech has impressed the jury.
  The jury _____ by the lawyer's speech.
  4 A private detective is investigating the robbery.
  The robbery _____ by a private detective.
  5 A lot of people are installing security systems in this neighbourhood.
  A lot of security systems _____ in this neighbourhood.

4 **Complete the sentences with the correct form of the words in brackets. Use *have something done*.**

  1 I follow my dentist's advice and I _____ (check/my teeth) twice a year.
  2 We _____ (redecorate/house) for several weeks. I hope it's over soon!
  3 My sister _____ (never/cut/her hair) by a hairdresser. My mum always does it.
  4 _____ (paint/your flat) or did you do it yourself?
  5 My neighbours _____ (cut/the grass in their garden) right now – that's why it's so noisy.

USE OF ENGLISH

5 **Complete the sentences with the correct form of the words in brackets.**

  1 My uncle's _____ (shop/rob) last year so he decided to install a burglar alarm.
  2 John is going to _____ (car/service) by a mechanic.
  3 The _____ (men/introduce) as police detectives, but I don't think they really were.
  4 Yesterday, the police _____ (sketch/make) of the suspect based on witness's descriptions.
  5 _____ (John/release) from hospital yesterday?
  6 Jill was so nervous in court that she found it difficult _____ (express/clearly).

6 **Complete the text with one word in each gap.**

CHRISTMAS JUMPER DAY

Christmas is traditionally a time of giving. Apart from looking for perfect gifts for friends and family members, or buying themselves new clothes so they can look good, a lot of people also think about those who are less fortunate and need to ¹_____ helped in various ways.

At this time of the year, most charities ²_____ money collected by volunteers so that they can help the homeless or the elderly and can ³_____ a difference to these people's lives.

One of the most interesting campaigns in the UK is Christmas Jumper Day, which usually takes place on the second Friday of December.

The idea is that special Christmas jumpers should be worn on this day and that people should donate at least £1 to Save the Children, the charity which organises the event. Every year the donations ⁴_____ used to help children in 120 countries by providing them with healthcare and food which they cannot afford to purchase by themselves.

Why do people support this campaign? ⁵_____ my view, they do so because it's a fun and easy way of ⁶_____ a good deed! Almost everyone in the UK has got a Christmas jumper. Many people don't buy them – they are a popular Christmas present.

READING

7 Read the text. Choose the correct answer, A, B, C or D.

Caring for the community
How can a dog change your life?

Ever since I was quite seriously bitten by a dog when I was a young child, I had been terrified of those animals. When I saw someone walking a dog, I would immediately rush to the other side of the street. When I planned to visit friends, I always made it clear that their dogs had to be put elsewhere during my visit. I had told myself many times that my fear was silly, but I simply couldn't control myself. Every time I got close to a dog I started shaking. I didn't know how to free myself from my fear.

Then one day I read a short article in the local newspaper about a rescue shelter that needed volunteers for dog-walking and other duties, and it was as if a light came on in my mind. I suddenly realised that all I had to do was face my fear. I immediately called the shelter and made an appointment to visit the next day.

When I arrived, I introduced myself to Susan, the person who was going to train me, and then I explained my issues with dogs. She said that I wasn't the first person to come in with that problem, and she felt sure I would feel differently as soon as I had met a few of the animals. Then she led me to a kennel where a large brown dog, Buddy, was sleeping. He immediately stood up and looked at me, then walked over and put his nose close to my hand. At first, we looked at each other with suspicion, and I suddenly felt really scared. But as soon as I saw the look of hope in Buddy's eyes, I was convinced.

Susan explained that Buddy had been brought to the shelter by the police after they had arrested his owner on suspicion of drug dealing, shoplifting and other crimes. Buddy's owner was likely to spend a long time in jail, and Susan was certain that Buddy would need a new home. 'And look,' she said. 'He already likes you! You're actually the first man he's not been afraid of.'

I spent many hours with Buddy, walking and feeding him, and we became close friends. After several weeks, I announced that I was ready to take Buddy home. Some of my more cynical friends claimed that I had been pretending to be afraid of dogs all along, and others have said they were amazed to hear I was adopting a pet of any kind. But all I can say is that Buddy has introduced me to many of the small pleasures of life, and we are so close that now we are helping young offenders come back to life outside of prison by getting them to volunteer at animal shelters.

1 What was the narrator's relationship with dogs before he went to the shelter?
  A He was ashamed of the way he felt about them.
  B He did everything he could to avoid them.
  C He had learned to tolerate his friends' dogs.
  D He had made several attempts to get over his fears.

2 The narrator's first impression of Buddy was that the dog was …
  A dangerous.   **C** hopeful.
  B ill and miserable.   **D** happy to be in the shelter.

3 What does the narrator's new idea involve?
  A Adopting more pets.
  B Helping young people who have committed crimes.
  C Getting dogs away from criminals.
  D Training dogs to work with young criminals.

SPEAKING

8 Look at the diagram. It shows advice about how people can protect their homes from theft. In pairs, follow these steps.
  • Talk to each other about how useful this advice is.
  • Decide which piece of advice is the most useful.

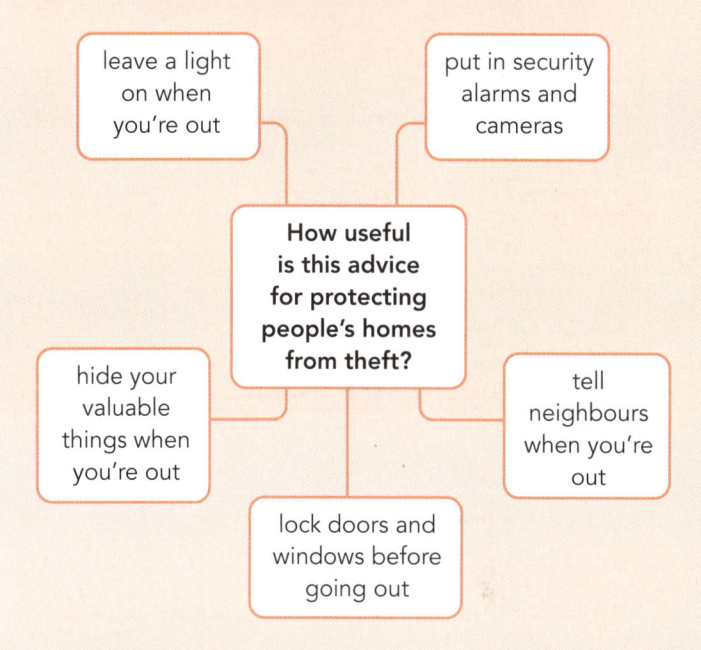

- leave a light on when you're out
- put in security alarms and cameras
- hide your valuable things when you're out
- tell neighbours when you're out
- lock doors and windows before going out

How useful is this advice for protecting people's homes from theft?

9 Ask and answer the questions.
  1 In your opinion, what is the right thing to do when you suspect your house has been burgled? Why?
  2 What can people do to make their neighbourhoods safer?
  3 Do you think that a city monitoring system would make your town or city a safer place to live? Why?/Why not?
  4 Some people say that there were fewer crimes in the past. Do you agree? Why?/Why not?

WRITING

10 In your English class you have been talking about celebrities and role models. Now your teacher has asked you to write an essay. Write your essay using all the notes and give reasons for your point of view.

Are celebrities good role models for young people today?
Notes
- positive and negative influence of celebrities
- other role models
- _____ (your own idea)

115

UNIT 1   VIDEO WORKSHEETS

BBC   Distressing jeans

BEFORE YOU WATCH

1 SPEAKING Discuss the questions.
1. How many pairs of jeans do you have?
2. Where were your jeans made?
3. Which styles and colours do you like best? Why?

2 Put the adjectives describing jeans under the appropriate heading. Use a dictionary if necessary.

~~destroyed~~   distressed   immaculate
pristine   second-hand   vintage

New/Good condition	Old/Bad condition
	destroyed

WHILE YOU WATCH

3 ▶1 Watch the video and answer the questions about distressed jeans.
1. Where are they made?
2. Why are they made?
3. How are they made?

4 ▶1 Complete four extracts from the first part of the video (up to 02:01) with the adjectives from Exercise 2. Then watch again and check your answers.
1. The worldwide market for denim jeans is enormous, and one of the most popular styles is _____ jeans.
2. We're in India, we're just heading towards a denim factory that distresses denim and makes it look _____ .
3. Do you find it slightly strange that you take something that is _____ and _____ and you totally destroy it?
4. Yes, mostly young people like garments with a more distressed look, more _____ look.

5 How does the presenter sum up the difference between young people's and old people's attitude to jeans?

6 ▶1 Watch the rest of the video (02:01–03:16) again and put the stages of the distressing process in the correct order.
a   The grinding machine ☐
b   More washing with stones and bleach ☐
c   Adjusting the crinkles by hand ☐
d   Using sand paper to produce white lines ☐
e   It's finished! ☐
f   More sanding to produce holes ☐
g   It's over to the wet processing area ☐

7 How does the presenter react to his jeans being distressed?

AFTER YOU WATCH

8 SPEAKING Discuss the questions.
1. Why do you think people pay more for distressed jeans than normal jeans?
2. Do you agree that 'destroying denim is all about pretending that you've been through something that you haven't'?

Focus Vlog About clothes

> Have you bought any new clothes recently?

1 Which of the clothes in the box do you own? Compare with a partner.

> a beanie   boots   a hoodie   fun socks   a necklace
> a perfect-fitting blazer   running shoes   sandals
> shorts   sunglasses   swimwear   a trench coat
> a waterproof jacket

2 **SPEAKING** Ask and answer the questions.
  1 Have you got a piece of clothing that you wear with everything?
  2 Have you been shopping recently? What did you get? Is there anything you've been planning to buy but haven't yet?
  3 What is your favourite place to go shopping for clothes?
  4 Do you spend a lot on clothes? Why?/Why not?

3 ▶4 Watch the beginning of the video (up to 0:48) and complete the text. What is Jason's problem?

> I ¹_____ one pair of jeans that I wear with everything. They're black, they're ²_____ and they're perfect for me. But they're so ³_____ and tatty now, I need to find some new ones. I tried to go shopping the other day, but I just couldn't ⁴_____ any that I liked.

4 ▶4 Watch the second part of the video (0:49–1:39) and write down what the people have bought recently.

Holly	
Noah	
Laura	
Kristina	
Peter	
Lauren	

5 ▶4 Watch the rest of the video (1:40–2:35) and answer the questions.
  1 Why hasn't Holly bought a bag yet?
  2 What kind of jacket does Noah need?
  3 What does Laura want to buy?
  4 Why does Kristina need new sunglasses?
  5 What kind of running shoes does Peter want to buy?
  6 How long has Lauren been looking for a blazer?

FOCUS ON LIFE SKILLS
Communication • Creativity • Teamwork

6 Work in groups of four or five and create a 30–60-second advert for a piece of clothing.

  Step 1: Think of examples of clothing adverts you like or remember. Answer the following questions:
   • Did the adverts make you laugh? Did they inspire emotions?
   • What do you particularly remember about these adverts?

  > **TIP:** Most successful adverts inspire positive emotions. Think what feelings you would like your viewers to have.

  Step 2: Select a piece of clothing or an accessory you want to sell. Choose an item from Exercise 1 or use your own ideas.
   • Give it a name.
   • Answer the following questions:
     What is most important about the product?
     What makes it different?
     Why might people want to buy it?
     Then think how you can show this in your advert.
   • Create a short story (script) for your ad. Think about the action (what happens), the location (setting) and the characters. You may take notes or draw pictures to help you.
   • Write the advert's slogan(s).

  Step 3: • Practise performing the advert.
   • Perform it to your class live OR record a video and show it to the class.

1.5 GRAMMAR

UNIT 2 VIDEO WORKSHEETS

BBC The Brujas

BEFORE YOU WATCH

1 **SPEAKING** What do you know about skateboarding? Tell a partner in 60 seconds.

2 Think about the positive and negative aspects of being a female skater. Use the words and phrases in the box and your own ideas. Compare with a partner.

> being called 'witches'   male comments
> belonging to an all-female crew   falling
> going fast   lack of female-only skate parks

Being called witches: negative.

WHILE YOU WATCH

3 ▶5 Watch the video and check your ideas in Exercise 2.

4 ▶5 Watch the video again and answer the questions.
  1 What are the Brujas?
  2 Where do they meet?
  2 Who has started the group?
  3 Why have they created the group?
  4 How many members does the group have at the moment?
  5 What do the Brujas want?

5 Match 1–8 with a–h to make phrases. Use a dictionary if necessary.

  1 settle   a belonging
  2 give you a sense of   b bond
  3 take you by   c of sth/sb
  4 be exclusive   d for sth
  5 degrading   e your comfort zone
  6 have a special   f comments
  7 be proud   g surprise
  8 out of   h to sb

6 ▶5 Complete the sentences with the phrases in Exercise 5. Then watch the second part of the video (00:45–02:46) again and check your answers.
  1 Ideally, the Brujas would like their own skatepark but in the meantime, they'd _____ one day a week when only girls were allowed.
  2 The Brujas have _____ . They're _____ their heritage and being part of an all-female skater crew gives them _____ .
  3 Street culture, it's still _____ men. Just when you're at the park, like, it can be very uncomfortable sometimes to hear, you know, _____ or even just the way that some of these men talk about the women in their lives.
  4 Falling is, in its own way, one of my favourite things about skating, because it kind of _____ and knocks you _____ , and you hit the ground, and you're like 'argh!' But then you feel invigorated by falling.

AFTER YOU WATCH

7 **SPEAKING** Discuss the questions.
  1 Which activities (if any) are better in boy-only or girl-only groups?
  2 What are the advantages of being part of a group?
  3 Do you belong to any groups or teams? What kind?
  4 What kind of activities take you out of your comfort zone? Do you enjoy it? Why?/Why not?

Focus Vlog About sport

Are you interested in sports?

1 **SPEAKING** Put the words in the correct order to make five questions. Then ask and answer with a partner.
   1 sports / you / Are / in / interested ?
   2 watching / you / Do / doing / prefer / or / sports ?
   3 do / there / any / really / can / sport / Is / you / well ?
   4 ever / sporting / won / you / Have / a / competition ?
   5 Olympics / last / watch / you / Did / the ?

2 Watch the beginning of the video (up to 0:41). Are the sentences true (T) or false (F)?
   1 Jason's neighbours' team is doing well in the match.
   2 Jason loves playing football.
   3 His cousin is worse at football than he is.
   4 Jason enjoys watching athletics.

3 Watch the second part of the video (0:42–1:37) and match the descriptions with the names in the box. There are two extra names.

   Ini Nicky Senthan Grace Ed Gillian

   1 This person prefers art to sport. _____
   2 This person finds sport quite boring. _____
   3 This person loves football and plays for a team. _____
   4 This person likes sport, especially football, rugby and basketball. _____

4 Watch the rest of the video (1:38–4:12) and complete the sentences with one word.
   1 Ed says watching sport can be hard when you want to be _____ .
   2 Ini can ride _____ really well.
   3 Gillian does Olympic style _____ .
   4 Senthan watched the _____ in the last Olympics.
   5 Gillian thinks figure skating is beautiful and _____ .

5 Watch the whole video again and write down Jason's responses to the statements. Then change the responses to make them true for you.
   1 I'm interested in football, rugby and basketball.
   2 I prefer playing sport, definitely.
   3 There's no sport I can do really well.
   4 I've never won a sporting competition.
   5 I didn't watch as much of the last Olympics as I wanted to.
   6 I watched the athletics, the running, Usain Bolt.

FOCUS ON LIFE SKILLS
Communication • Creativity • Digital skills

6 Make a timeline.
A timeline is a graphical representation of a period of time on which important events are marked. Look at the example below.

Muhammad Ali timeline

1942	1954	1960	1964	1981
first boxing lessons	date of birth (as Cassius Marcellus Clay Jr.)	world heavyweight champion	gold medal at Rome Summer Olympics	retirement from boxing

Choose a famous athlete. Research his/her biography, then prepare a timeline with the most important facts of his/her life.

TIP: It's best to use at least three different sources of information, e.g. an encyclopedia, an official website and newspaper articles.

Step 1: Research your topic.
   • While reading and collecting information about the athlete of your choice, begin making notes about important or interesting events.
   • Make a list of events to include (at least five).

Step 2: Create your project.
   • Draw your timeline and label it with the project title.
   • Put the most important dates on the timeline and write down a short description of each one.
   • Use different colours or fonts to make your timeline attractive and to draw attention to its most important elements.

Step 3: Use the timeline to make a short presentation about the athlete of your choice.

2.6 USE OF ENGLISH

UNIT 3   VIDEO WORKSHEETS

BBC   A hotel in the clouds

BEFORE YOU WATCH

1 **SPEAKING** Look at the photo. Imagine you are staying at this luxury hotel, deep in the Ecuadorian cloud forest. Discuss the questions.
   1 How do you think you would get there?
   2 How would you spend your time there?

2 Complete the information about Mashpi Lodge with the words in the box.

> 1,500   America   equator   guest   plant
> Quito   three   twenty-two   two   west

Ecuador is situated on the ¹_____ coast of South ²_____ and the ³_____ goes across the country. Mashpi Lodge is located in Mashpi Reserve in the middle of the cloud forest, ⁴_____ hours' drive from the capital, ⁵_____ . Mashpi lodge is a luxury hotel, with ⁶_____ rooms, costing up to ⁷_____ a night. There are ⁸_____ members of staff for every ⁹_____ . The hotel was opened a few years ago. It's an eco-hotel with breathtaking views from every window. It's like a giant treehouse. People travel from all over the world to experience the extraordinary animal and ¹⁰_____ life.

WHILE YOU WATCH

3 ▶10 Listen to the first part of the video (up to 01:56) without looking at the screen and check your answers to Exercise 2.

4 ▶10 **SPEAKING** Discuss what you expect to see in the video. Then watch the first part (00:00–01:56) and check your ideas.

5 ▶10 Watch the rest of the video (01:57–5:37) and answer the questions.
   1 What was Roque Sevilla's former title?
   2 Why did he build the hotel?
   3 Where does he take Giles to view the hotel and the forest?
   4 How comfortable is Giles with heights?
   5 What does Roque think people think about him?
   6 What is Roque's latest project and what is it for?
   7 How does Monica test the rescue procedure?
   8 How does she feel about testing the system?

6 ▶10 Complete the phrases with the nouns in the box. Then watch the video again and check your answers.

> forest   hotel   procedure   reserve   tower   views

   1 amazing/breathtaking/unique _____
   2 eco/luxury/sustainable _____
   3 dense/huge _____
   4 observation _____
   5 private _____
   6 rescue _____

AFTER YOU WATCH

7 Choose three phrases from Exercise 6. Write two true sentences and one false one. Read your sentences to your partner for him/her to guess which sentence is false.

8 **SPEAKING** Would you like to stay or work at Mashpi Lodge? Why?/Why not? Tell your partner.

Focus Vlog   About holidays

> Where did you use to go on holiday as a child?

1 SPEAKING Where are the places in the box located? Have you ever been to any of them? Which would you most like to visit and why?

| Arizona   California   Cape Cod   Cornwall |
| Cyprus   Dallas   the Lake District |
| Martha's Vineyard   Scotland |

2 ▶13 Watch the first part of the video (up to 0:40) and answer the questions.
1 What did Jason find?
2 Where did he use to go on holiday?
3 What did he use to do?

3 ▶13 Watch the second part of the video (0:41–1:30) and match the descriptions with the names in the box. There is one extra name.

| Alex   Lauren   Lucy   Luda   Noah   Rachel |

1 This person used to go camping, usually in the southern part of Texas. _____
2 This person's grandparents had a flat in Cyprus. _____
3 This person's family was very large and they couldn't afford holidays abroad. _____
4 Scotland and the Lake District were this person's holiday destinations as a child. _____
5 This person visited their grandparents in Arizona. _____

4 ▶13 Watch the rest of the video (1:41–3:03) and complete the sentences with one word in each gap.
1 Alex used to go camping, walking and _____.
2 Noah used to go to the pool, _____ fruit and ride bikes.
3 Lauren used to go _____ and visit National Parks.
4 Lucy used to go to the _____, sunbathe and chill.
5 Luda used to go on road trips and visit her _____.
6 Rachel used to walk around, go _____ and read.

5 SPEAKING Where did you use to go on holiday before you went to school? What did you use to do there?

FOCUS ON LIFE SKILLS
Creativity • Communication • Digital skills

6 Create a holiday photo slide show.

Holiday memories are meant to be shared. Use the photos you took during one of your holidays and create a slide show.

Step 1: Think what you want to show in your slide show, i.e. decide on your theme. Do you want to tell a specific story or just sum up the holiday from start to finish? Do you want to describe a special place or person?

Step 2: Once you know what your theme is, think about the order in which photos will be shown and any comments you want to add.

Step 3: Choose software to make your slide show and upload your own holiday photos.

Step 4: Give your slide show the look you want by using the colours, fonts and special effects that best fit the impression you want to make. You can also select background music.

Step 5: Present your slide show to the class.

3.5 GRAMMAR

UNIT 4   VIDEO WORKSHEETS

BBC   Umami

BEFORE YOU WATCH

1 **SPEAKING** Discuss the questions.

  1 How many dishes can you think of that contain tomatoes?
  2 What's your favourite savoury dish? Describe how it tastes.
  3 What's your favourite dessert? Describe how it tastes.

2 **SPEAKING** Discuss the food choices. Which would you choose? Why?

  1 courgettes or aubergines?
  2 cabbage or carrots?
  3 sausage and mash or fish and chips?
  4 beef and rice or tofu and noodles?
  5 steak and fried egg with tomato or mushrooms?
  6 pasta or bread?
  7 orange or lemon juice?
  8 stir-fry or curry?

WHILE YOU WATCH

3 ▶15 Watch the first part of the video (up to 00:44) without sound. Which of the two food choices in Exercise 2 do you see in the video?

4 ▶15 Complete the text with the words in the box. There are two extra words. Then watch the first part of the video again with sound and check your answers.

> bland   delicious   dish   range   right   smell   wrong

Flavour makes our food ^{1}_____ . Each flavour is a combination of ^{2}_____ and taste. When you get that combination ^{3}_____ , food tastes amazing. But what is taste? Thai food is particularly good at combining a wide ^{4}_____ of different tastes in one ^{5}_____ .

5 Rearrange the letters to describe the five basic tastes.

  1 yalts   = ___salty___
  2 tesew   = _____
  3 rebtit   = _____
  4 ruso   = _____
  5 imuma   = _____

6 ▶15 Watch the second part of the video (00:45–02:06) and check your answers. What three things does the presenter say about umami?

7 ▶15 Watch the rest of the video (02:07–4:20). Are the statements true or false?

  1 The presenter has come to Spain to find the umami fruit.
  2 20,000 people attend La Tomatina festival.
  3 La Tomatina is the world's biggest music festival.
  4 The festival started with a street fight.
  5 The umami extracted from tomatoes tastes 'tomatoey'.
  6 The umami taste comes from a glutamate molecule.

8 ▶15 Watch again. Check your answers and correct the false statements.

AFTER YOU WATCH

9 **SPEAKING** Would you like to go to La Tomatina festival? Why?/Why not?

Focus Vlog About food

> Where are you going to have dinner this evening?

1 **SPEAKING** Discuss the questions.
  1 Where can you get the best Italian, Chinese or Thai food in your neighbourhood?
  2 What's the national dish of your country and where would you tell a tourist to find it?
  3 What would you eat if you went to London?
  4 Have you ever cooked a meal for somebody? What was it?

2 ▶16 Watch the beginning of the video (up to 0:42) and correct four mistakes in the text. Then watch again and check your answers.

> Jason has invited his family for dinner. He is happy because he has to cook for them. He has already done it before. He would like to make some fish and chips.

3 ▶16 Watch the second part of the video (0:43–1:22) and complete the table. Who's eating out and who's eating at home?

	Eating out	Eating at home
Shannon		
Céire		
Peter		
Holly		
Luda		
Kes		
Katya		

4 ▶16 Watch the rest of the video (1:23–2:14) and write down all the dishes the speakers mention. Do you know all of the dishes? Which one would you most like to eat this evening?

5 ▶16 Watch the interviews again and answer the questions.
  1 Who is going to do some cooking tonight?
     _____ , _____
  2 Who has been out for lunch? _____
  3 Where would Jason like to go? _____
  4 Who has friends coming over for dinner?
     _____ , _____
  5 Who can't cook? _____
  6 What is Holly going to drink? _____

FOCUS ON LIFE SKILLS
Creativity • Communication

6 Prepare detailed instructions how to make your favourite dish.

  Step 1: Decide what dish you are going to talk about. It's a good idea to choose something you like and know how to make (the best would be something you have prepared before, or have seen somebody else cook it).

  Step 2: Prepare a list of the ingredients and kitchen tools (e.g. knife, pan) you need.

  Step 3: Before you prepare your instructions, look at some recipes in English in e.g. cookbooks or on the Internet.

  Step 4: Prepare step-by-step instructions for making your dish, but remember not to use its name! If possible, prepare some photos or illustrations of the ingredients. You may also have a photo of the finished dish to show the class after they make their guesses.

  Step 5: Practise saying your instructions, then present them to your class and ask them to guess the dish.

UNIT 5 VIDEO WORKSHEETS

BBC Chameleons

BEFORE YOU WATCH

1 You are going to watch a video about chameleons in the wild. Which words or phrases in the box are you likely to hear? Use a dictionary if necessary. Compare with a partner.

> hunting   high tide   targets   prey   stick insect
> weapon   tongue   matchstick   jungle   predator
> mountain range   escape   praying mantis   die out
> lightning strike   insect

WHILE YOU WATCH

2 ▶19 SPEAKING Listen to the first part of the video (up to 00:52) without looking at the screen and discuss what you expect to see.

3 ▶19 Watch the first part of the video (up to 00:52) and check your ideas in Exercise 2.

4 ▶19 Watch the whole video and answer the questions.
   1 How do the Parson's chameleon, the nasutum chameleon and the praying mantis catch their prey?
   2 What extraordinary abilities do these animals have?

5 ▶19 Watch the video again. Which three words or phrases in Exercise 1 are NOT used?

6 Match 1–6 with a–f to make expressions. Use a dictionary if necessary.

   1 see and not   a slow motion
   2 a never-ending game   b as its stomach
   3 time to unleash   c of hide and seek
   4 eyes as big   d be seen
   5 its body moves in   e still and blend in
   6 it pays to sit   f its secret weapon

7 ▶19 Complete the text with the expressions in Exercise 6. Then watch the video again and check.

Hunting is ¹_____ . Here ²_____ . Because you just never know who's watching. The Parson's chameleon is an expert in the ³_____ business. It lets its eyes do all the work while the rest of ⁴_____ so as not to scare possible targets. The problem is that he can only see prey if it moves. So, is this a stick insect or a stick? Aha. ⁵_____ : a tongue longer than its body.
The Parson's close cousin, the nasutum chameleon has the same weapon but in miniature. As small as a matchstick it needs to get much closer to its prey. But even with ⁶_____ this isn't the meal deal he was hoping for.

AFTER YOU WATCH

8 SPEAKING Discuss the questions.
   1 Has anything in the video surprised you?
   2 Do you think it is worth watching nature documentaries? Why?/Why not?
   3 If you had the chance to make a nature documentary, what topic you would focus on? Why?

124

Focus Vlog About the environment

Do you think London is an eco-friendly city?

FOCUS ON LIFE SKILLS
Critical thinking • Communication • Collaboration

5 In pairs or groups of three, write a short speech (up to eight minutes) about what every teenager can do to help protect the environment.

- **Step 1:** Develop your main idea. You should decide what you want to say and what you want the audience to learn from it.

> **TIP:** In a speech or presentation, you usually say the same thing three times, just a bit differently each time. First you introduce your idea, then you develop it, and finally you sum it up.

- **Step 2:** Decide on the details of your speech and what specific advice you want to give – this will be the main part of your presentation. You can use the solutions in the box to help you or your own ideas.

> buy less   buy local food   go vegan
> limit use of plastic packaging
> ride a bicycle or use public transport   recycle
> save energy/water

- **Step 3:** Using your notes from steps 1 and 2, prepare an outline of your speech. Your main message should be the introduction, the details from step 2 should be the main/middle part and the summary should be what you want the audience to learn.

> **TIP:** Remember to keep your ideas short and simple.

- **Step 4:** Fill in all three parts of your speech until you have a complete text.
- **Step 5:** Practise presenting your speech in groups and choose a representative to present it to the class.

Final step: Deliver your speech!

1 SPEAKING Discuss the questions.
1. How can we be eco-friendly?
2. What can be done to make a city less polluted?
3. Do you think the place where you live is eco-friendly?

2 ▶21 Watch the beginning of the video (up to 0:48) and complete the sentences.
1. My friend's just come back from Copenhagen and he keeps telling me how _____ and green and clean it is. I think it might be the _____ place in the world.
2. I've lived in London all my life and it's never seemed that _____ to me. I mean, we _____ , the air doesn't seem too dirty and we have a congestion _____ .

3 ▶21 Watch the second part of the video (0:49–2:04) and match the statements with the names in the box.

> Alex   Devesh   Kes   Noah

1. London has good access to green spaces.
2. Cycling is getting a little bit easier.
3. The use of diesel engines in taxis and buses makes the pollution very bad.
4. The Green Zone has cut down a lot of emissions.

4 ▶21 Watch the rest of the video (2:05–3:20). Are the sentences true (T) or false (F)?
1. Alex thinks the least polluted place in the UK is somewhere very rural. ☐
2. Devesh has never been to Wales. ☐
3. Kes thinks the least polluted place in the UK is a small Scottish island. ☐
4. Noah says Durham is quite polluted. ☐

5.2 GRAMMAR

UNIT 6 VIDEO WORKSHEETS

BBC Caffeine alternatives

BEFORE YOU WATCH

1 SPEAKING Discuss the questions.

1. Which caffeine-based drinks (coffee, tea, cola, energy drinks, etc.) do you drink regularly?
2. What effect does too much caffeine or not enough caffeine have on you, if any?
3. What do you eat or drink if you need to stay awake or stay alert for something?

2 Complete the table with the adjectives in the box to describe the different effects caffeine can have on people. Use a dictionary if necessary.

> active alert anxious awake
> drowsy jittery sleepy

not enough caffeine	
the right amount of caffeine	active
too much caffeine	

WHILE YOU WATCH

3 ▶24 Match natural alternatives to coffee 1–4 with descriptions a–d. Then watch the first part of the video (up to 02:02) and check your answers.

1. Sugar/fudge ☐
2. Sage ☐
3. Chewing gum ☐
4. Placebo ☐

a. A herb that contains a chemical that helps the connection between brain cells.
b. A substance used to check that people don't feel different just because they're taking a pill.
c. A sweet snack containing glucose for an energy boost.
d. A food that research suggests could make us more alert.

4 SPEAKING Discuss which alternative you think is most likely to increase alertness and which to improve performance.

5 ▶24 Watch the rest of the video (02:03–4:05) and check your ideas in Exercise 4. Which results do you find surprising?

6 ▶24 Complete the sentences from the video with the correct form of the adjectives in Exercise 2. Watch again and check.

And, of course, there's the added bad side of the fact that if I have too much of the stuff, it makes me ¹_____ and ²_____ , which is the last thing I want as a surgeon who has to hold a knife in their hands. So what are the alternatives if we want something to help us stay ³_____ and ⁴_____ ?
I would've thought that if you have sugar at that point in the day where you're feeling a bit ⁵_____ and ⁶_____ , that that really perks you up. So it seems that sage could be the alternative we've been looking for to make us more ⁷_____ in the afternoon. But are you sure you're ready to swap your cappuccino for a leaf of sage?

AFTER YOU WATCH

7 SPEAKING Do you think sage could become a popular alternative to coffee? Why?/Why not?

126

Focus Vlog About health and sleep

What do you do in order to stay fit and healthy?

FOCUS ON LIFE SKILLS
Critical thinking • Communication • Teamwork

6.6 USE OF ENGLISH

1. Order the activities in the box from your favourite to your least favourite. Which ones do you do? Compare with a partner.

   cycling   going to the gym   lifting weights
   mountain-climbing   running   swimming
   walking up stairs

2. ▶ 27 Watch the first part of the video (up to 0:59) and answer the questions.
   1. Do you think Jason is an active person? Give reasons.
   2. What ways of keeping fit and healthy does he mention?
   3. What does he say about sleep?

3. ▶ 27 Watch the second part of the video (1:00–2:03) and complete the sentences with the names in the box. Use one name twice.

   Amber   Holly   Justin   Luda
   Noah   Peter   Ruslan

   1. _____ goes to and from work by bike.
   2. Both _____ and _____ go to the gym.
   3. _____ would like to swim.
   4. _____ cycles a lot around the New Forest.
   5. _____ often goes walking.
   6. _____ takes the stairs during the day.
   7. _____ goes running and uses a bike.

4. ▶ 27 Watch the rest of the video (2:04–3:23) and answer the questions.
   1. What does Justin do to fall asleep more easily?
   2. What device helps Amber fall asleep?
   3. What does Noah do regularly?
   4. What does Holly drink before going to sleep?
   5. What does Ruslan do?
   6. What does Peter do with his phone before going to bed?

5. In small groups, prepare a 'Health and Fitness' questionnaire to research the habits of the students in your school. Then present your results to the class.

   Step 1: In groups, create a list of at least eight questions for the questionnaire. Ask about the issues in the box.

   be ill   do sport   eat regular meals
   feel tired   go to sleep at the same time
   have problems falling asleep
   spend time outdoors   study at night
   use social media before going to bed

   For each question, prepare three possible answers, e.g.

   How often do you study at night?
   a *never*
   b *only before exams*
   c *regularly*

   Step 2: Do the questionnaire in your class, then visit other classes to ask your questions. Try to visit as many classes as possible, because the more data you have, the more accurate your results will be.

   Step 3: When the questionnaire is complete, look at the results and draw conclusions. Do the students in your school have good or bad exercise/sleep habits? Why?

   Step 4: Sum up the results in graphical form (e.g. a pie chart or graph). Look at the examples below.

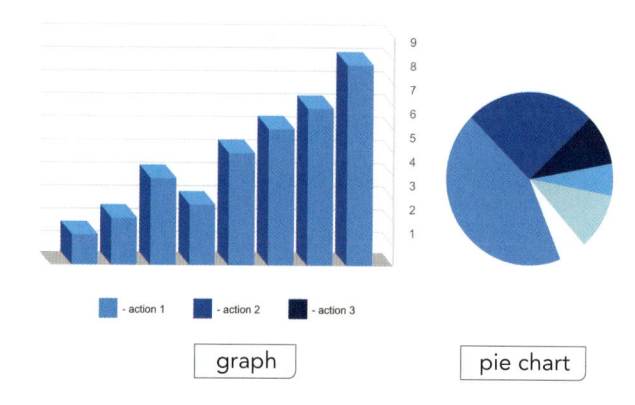

   graph   pie chart

   Create a poster or a short computer presentation, then present it to your class.

   Step 5: Inform other classes about the results of your questionnaire. For instance, you could write an article for the school magazine or a post on the school blog, or you could prepare a poster giving advice.

UNIT 7 VIDEO WORKSHEETS

BBC Shakespeare's avatars

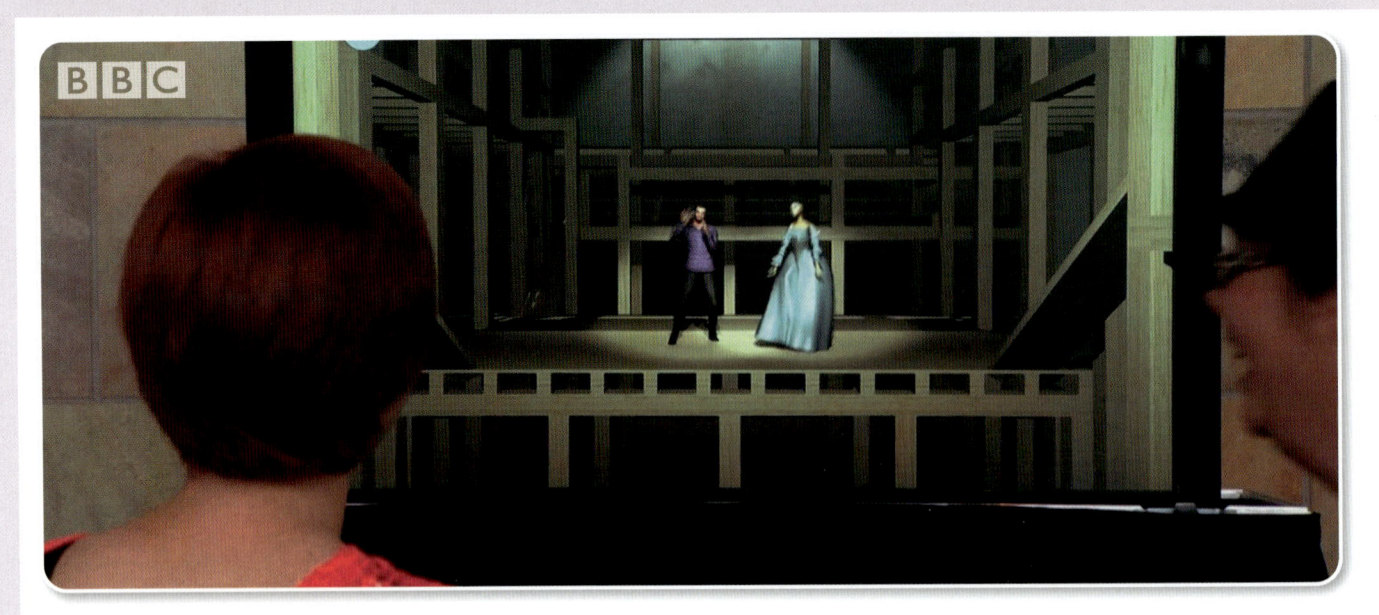

BEFORE YOU WATCH

1 **SPEAKING** Discuss the questions.
   1 How many Shakespeare's plays can you think of?
   2 How many Shakespearean characters can you name?
   3 Have you seen any Shakespeare's plays? Did you like them? Why?/Why not?

2 You're going to watch a video about a virtual reality game based on Shakespeare's plays. Match the words in the box with the headings in the table.

> 3D avatar animated film audience costume
> digital dramatic gestures language media
> perform performer scene screen stage
> technology theatre virtual reality

A virtual reality game	Shakespeare's play
3D avatar	

WHILE YOU WATCH

3 ▶ 28 Watch the first part of the video (up to 00:44) without sound and answer the questions.
   1 What are the two performers doing?
   2 What's the audience watching?
   3 What's happening on the screen?

4 ▶ 28 Watch the first part again with sound and check your ideas in Exercise 3.

5 ▶ 28 Watch the rest of the video (00:45–03:09) and answer the questions.
   1 Why was the game created?
   2 Why do people think the game is effective?
   3 Why isn't it surprising that the game is based on Shakespeare?

6 ▶ 18 Watch the whole video again. Are sentences 1–7 true (T) or false (F)?
   1 It was unusual for actors to use big gestures in Shakespeare's time. ☐
   2 Players of the virtual reality game can choose their avatar's costume. ☐
   3 The avatars on screen are Lord and Lady Macbeth. ☐
   4 The scene shows Lady Macbeth in good health. ☐
   5 The presenter finds it easy to play the game. ☐
   6 The first Elizabethan theatre in North America was built in 1932. ☐
   7 Michael Witmore is against using technology to understand Shakespeare. ☐

AFTER YOU WATCH

7 **SPEAKING** Would you like to play the game presented in the video? Why?/Why not?

8 **SPEAKING** Match 1–6 with a–f to make famous Shakespeare quotes. Then discuss what they mean.
   1 All the world's a stage, ☐
   2 To be, or not to be: ☐
   3 Good night, good night! ☐
   4 Is this a dagger ☐
   5 If music be the food of love, ☐
   6 Friends, Romans, countrymen, ☐

   a Parting is such sweet sorrow. (Romeo and Juliet)
   b which I see before me …? (Macbeth)
   c and all the men and women merely players. (As You Like It)
   d lend me your ears. (Julius Caesar)
   e that is the question. (Hamlet)
   f play on. (Twelfth Night)

Focus Vlog About television

What is your favourite TV series?

1 **SPEAKING** Do you know any of the TV series below? Which ones would you like to watch? Discuss with a partner.
  1 *The Good Place*: a fantasy-comedy about a woman who gets into heaven by mistake.
  2 *Dr Who*: a science-fiction series featuring a time machine (TARDIS) disguised as a police telephone box.
  3 *Friends*: one of the most popular sitcoms of all time.
  4 *Gilmore Girls*: a comedy drama about family and relationships.
  5 *Suits*: a legal drama.
  6 *Dear White People*: a comedy-drama about racism in America.
  7 *Still Game*: a Scottish sitcom about pensioners.

2 **30** Watch the first part of the video (up to 00:40) and complete the sentences.
  1 Jason has spent the weekend _____ .
  2 He can't remember the last time he _____ .

3 **30** Watch the second part of the video (00:41–01:34) Complete the table with the titles of TV series in Exercise 1.

	What TV series do you enjoy watching?
Céire	
Shannon	
Lauren	
Kes	
Luda	

4 **30** Watch the rest of the video (1:35–2:57) and complete the sentences.
  1 In a TV series, there are mini-story lines, which is _____ to watch than just watching one long film at once.
  2 People can see the development of _____ and then get emotionally attached.
  3 It seems like all the talent is _____ and not movies.
  4 I guess _____ is making it easier for people to choose which TV series they watch.
  5 I think TV series allow people to experience things without having to leave the _____ of their homes.

5 **SPEAKING** Do you agree with the comments in Exercise 4? Discuss with a partner.

FOCUS ON LIFE SKILLS
Communication • Creativity • Teamwork

6 In groups of four, write one or two scenes for an episode of your favourite TV series.

Step 1: Choose your favourite TV series and start exploring the main character(s), setting, genre, general plot and typical themes. Note down ideas and a few possible storylines. Decide if you want to use a continuation of an existing storyline or something new.

TIP: When writing, remember about your series genre. For example, a romantic comedy does not normally have elements of science fiction, and a crime story is not usually comic.

Step 2: Choose how many scenes (one or two) you want to write. Decide on the main plot and number of characters. Do not use the name of the TV series: your classmates will have to guess what it is.

Step 3: Write out each dialogue. You can also use visuals (drawings or photos) to help you order your ideas.

Step 4: Practise acting out your scene(s).

Step 5: Present your scene(s) to the class and have them guess the name of the series.

7.6 USE OF ENGLISH

UNIT 8   VIDEO WORKSHEETS

BBC Coffee stalls

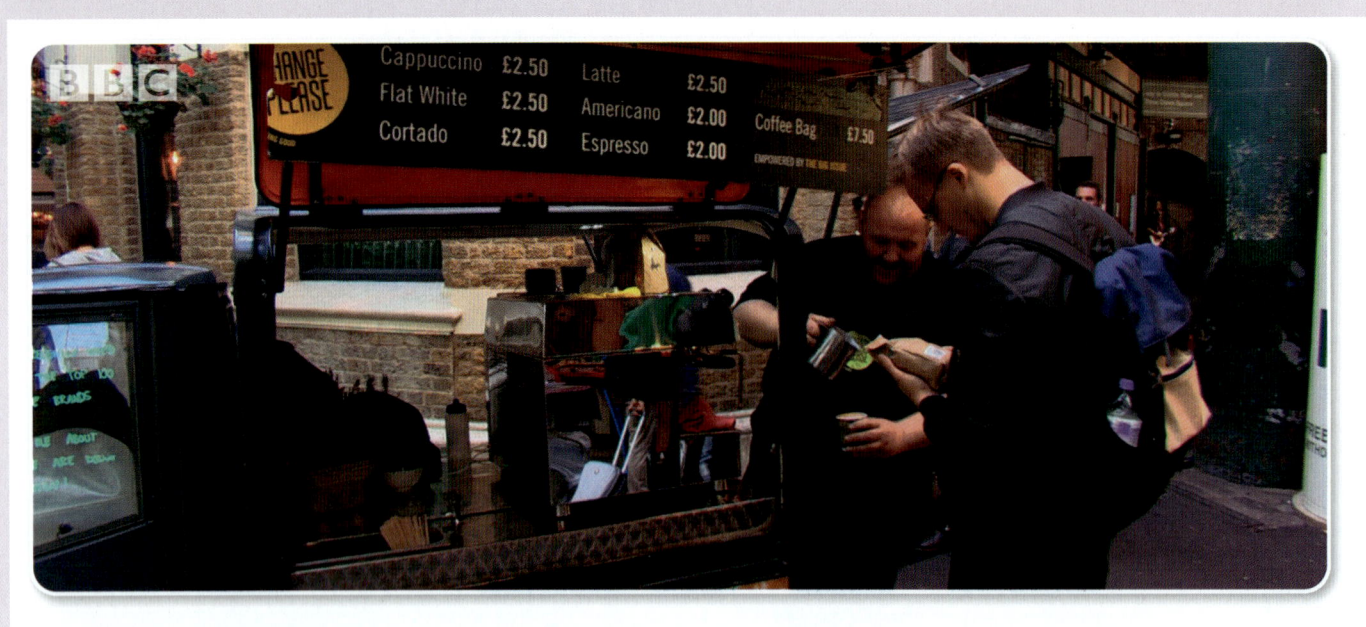

BEFORE YOU WATCH

1 **SPEAKING** Discuss how popular coffee is in your country. Where do people buy it, make it, drink it?

2 Which skills are necessary to run a coffee stall? Compare your ideas with a partner.

> foreign language skills   money-handling skills
> people management skills   IT skills
> problem-solving skills   time management skills
> leadership skills

WHILE YOU WATCH

3 ▶ 34 Watch the first part of the video (00:00–01:05). How did the organisation Change Please help Tom and Adam?

4 ▶ 34 Watch the second part of the video (01:06 – 01:26). Which of the skills in Exercise 2 do the people from Change Please mention?

5 ▶ 34 Watch the rest of the video (01:27–2:18). Has Change Please been a success? Has it solved the problem of homelessness?

6 ▶ 34 Answer the questions. Then watch the whole video and check your answers.
   1 What was Tom's situation when he arrived in the UK?
   2 What was Tom like before Change Please helped him?
   3 How is Tom helping Adam today?
   4 What does Change Please provide for its employees?
   5 Who has his face on a packet of coffee?
   6 What do recent figures on homelessness suggest?
   7 What does the speaker think the government needs to do?
   8 What are Abraham's words of encouragement?
   9 How does Abraham feel?

7 Match 1–6 with a–f to make phrases from the video.
   1 break
   2 build a
   3 gain
   4 get sb
   5 get off
   6 run

   a into work
   b the streets
   c a business
   d career
   e the cycle (of homelessness)
   f the skills

AFTER YOU WATCH

8 **SPEAKING** Read the quotes from the video and discuss the questions.

> When I got this job, it really changed everything for me.
> *Tom*

> I got a little dignity back. I've got pride back, I sleep in a bed.
> *Adam*

> I'm really proud.
> *Abraham*

   1 What does this tell us about how to help people get off the streets?
   2 Do you know of any organisations that help homeless people in your country? How do they help them?

Focus Vlog About social media

> How do you and your friends stay in touch with one another online?

1 SPEAKING Discuss the questions.
1 Do you use social media?
2 What do you generally use it for? Which apps do you use?
3 What are some of the pros and cons of using social media?
4 How do things on social media impact your life offline?

2 ▶37 In the first part of the video (up to 0:48), Jason uses the term 'cyber detox'. Complete the definition of cyber detox with the words in the box. There is one extra word.

> digital devices   interactions   state   social   media

A cyber detox refers to a ¹_____ when an individual gives up or suspends their use of ²_____ to spend that time on social ³_____ and activities.

3 SPEAKING What is Jason's opinion on cyber detoxes? Do you agree with him?

4 ▶37 Watch the second part of the video (0:49–2:14) and match the speakers with the activities.
1 Holly ☐   a uses Facebook groups and Snapchat.
2 Ruslan ☐   b no longer sends texts.
3 Alex ☐   c contacts friends through WhatsApp.
4 Shannon ☐ d uses Snapchat and Instagram.
5 Céire ☐   e uses video calls.
6 Peter ☐   f says people can follow their friends' lives through social media.

5 ▶37 Watch the rest of the video (2:15–3:44). Are the sentences true (T) or false (F)?
1 Holly doesn't find social media addictive. ☐
2 Ruslan found it easy not to use social media for a full year. ☐
3 Alex used Facebook too much and deleted it. ☐
4 Shannon never turns her phone off, even in a library. ☐
5 Céire is bored by social media. ☐
6 Peter is now more responsible after going on a cyber detox. ☐

FOCUS ON LIFE SKILLS
Creativity • Critical thinking • Collaboration

6 Technology has made it easier for people to work together to solve real problems or to support a cause. In pairs, prepare a social media campaign for a cause that you care about. Choose one of the following topics or use your own ideas:

> raising money for a local animal shelter
> donating clothes for the area's poorest families
> petitioning the town hall to keep the local bus service

Step 1: Choose the problem you want to solve or the cause you want to support.
Step 2: Set the goal(s) of your campaign: decide what goal you want to achieve and what kind of people you need to address.
Step 3: Decide how you could use social media to support your cause.
Step 4: Create a social media plan. Answer the questions:
• How will you use social media? Alone or will your campaign combine social media and other strategies?
• Which platform or social media apps will work best for your cause or project?
• What specific message or strategy will you use in each social media site or platform?
Step 5: Think of a slogan for your campaign.
Step 6: Create a visual display to present your social media plan to your classmates.

GRAMMAR AND USE OF ENGLISH

1.2 Dynamic and state verbs

Dynamic verbs like *do*, *work* and *play* describe actions and can be used in both types of tenses – simple (e.g. the **Present Simple**) and continuous (e.g. the **Present Continuous**):

*I often **listen** to classical music.*
*I'**m listening** to Mozart now.*

State (or stative) verbs include:
- attitude verbs (describing feelings, emotions, preferences, etc.), e.g. *hate, like, love, prefer*
- mental/thinking verbs, e.g. *believe, know, need, remember, think, understand, want*
- sense/perception verbs, e.g. *feel, hear, see.*

State verbs are mostly used in simple tenses, even if they refer to something happening at the moment of speaking:

***Do** you **understand** me?*
***Does** she **want** to go to a music festival?*

Some state verbs can be used in the continuous form, but with a change in meaning (e.g. *think, have, look*):

***Do** I **look** good in this dress?* (state)
*What **are** you **looking** at?* (action)

1 Choose the correct option.

1 I *think / 'm thinking* about going to a fashion show tomorrow.
2 I *don't think / 'm not thinking* the show was a success.
3 *Do you have / Are you having* a favourite fashion designer?
4 *Does Tim have / Is Tim having* breakfast right now?
5 What *does Sally look / is Sally looking* like? Is she tall?
6 I *need / 'm needing* to go to the shop. Can I get you anything?
7 Can you talk to Luisa? She is in the canteen and she *is asking / asks* everybody weird questions.
8 Every time I watch this film, *I'm feeling / I feel* really sad.

2 Complete the dialogues with the correct form of the words in brackets. Use the Present Simple or the Present Continuous.

1 **A:** _____ (George/talk) to that fashion journalist in French?
   B: No way! He _____ (not speak) any foreign languages.
2 **A:** _____ (you/like) reading fashion magazines?
   B: Of course. I _____ (buy) a few every month.
3 **A:** Why _____ (he/want) to buy that expensive suit?
   B: Because he _____ (believe) it will make him look smarter.
4 **A:** You _____ (look) miserable. What's wrong?
   B: I _____ (not usually/wear) high heels and the ones I _____ (wear) today are very uncomfortable.
5 **A:** Oh, look! There's Kimberly. What _____ (she/buy)?
   B: Something awful again. I don't know why she _____ (prefer) pink to all other colours.

3 Complete the sentences with the correct form of the words in brackets. Use the Present Simple or the Present Continuous.

1 My brother _____ (love) faded jeans.
2 I _____ (see) what you mean.
3 She _____ (think) of buying a new denim jacket.
4 Today, I _____ (need) to buy a silk tie for my dad.
5 At the moment he _____ (have) two cars and a motorbike.
6 _____ (Ben/have) a bath now?
7 I _____ (not/think) I'll buy those boots.
8 Our boss _____ (want) to know why we haven't sent him the documents yet.

4 Choose the correct option.

1 Unfortunately, they *don't remember / are not remembering* anything now.
2 Pete *plays / is playing* video games again.
3 Why *does Meg hate / is Meg hating* wearing leggings?
4 Now I *don't understand / 'm not understanding* anything he's saying.
5 Kate *smells / is smelling* her new perfume, again. She must like it a lot.
6 What *do you think / are you thinking* about this fleece? Is the colour OK?
7 Sue *looks / is looking* gorgeous in this new silk blouse. Everybody *looks / is looking* at her.
8 Did you hear Mark's story about those Spanish people he met? *I don't believe / I'm not believing* him. He doesn't even speak Spanish.

5 Write sentences from the prompts. Use the Present Simple or Present Continuous. Add extra words where necessary.

1 we / have / great time / here, in Barcelona.
   _____
2 why / it / feel / so cold / in this building?
   _____
3 I / not / remember / anything / right now.
   _____
4 you / recognise / this place?
   _____
5 my mum / not drive / today.
   _____
6 you / hear / that sound?
   _____
7 we / think / of / buy / new laptop.
   _____
8 Mika / not / drink / tea, he / hate / it.
   _____
9 he / work / on a new project / right now?
   _____
10 I usually / have / fun / at Megan's parties.
   _____

REFERENCE AND PRACTICE

1.5 Present Perfect Continuous

We use the **Present Perfect Continuous** to talk about:
- actions which started in the past and continue into the present:
  *I **have been waiting** for her since 8 o'clock.*
- events which lasted for some time (and may continue into the present) and whose results can be seen now:
  *I'm tired because I**'ve been painting** all day.*

Like the Present Perfect Simple, common time expressions used with the Present Perfect Continuous include **for** and *since*.

Affirmative			Negative		
I/You/We/They	've (have)	been crying.	I/You/We/They	haven't (have not)	been crying.
He/She/It	's (has)		He/She/It	hasn't (has not)	

Yes/No questions			Short answers
Have	I/you/we/they	been crying?	Yes, I/you/we/they have. No, I/you/we/they haven't.
Has	he/she/it		Yes, he/she/it has. No, he/she/it hasn't.

Wh- questions				Subject questions		
How long	have	I/you/we/they	been crying?	Who	has	been crying?
	has	he/she/it				

Present Perfect Continuous or Present Perfect Simple?

- We use the **Present Perfect Continuous** to focus on an action or process (which may or may not be complete). Questions in the Present Perfect Continuous often begin with **how long**:
  How long has she been writing books?
- We use the **Present Perfect Simple** to focus on an achievement or the result of an action. Questions in the Present Perfect Simple often begin with **how many**:
  How many books has he written?
- We don't use *when* in questions in either of the two tenses.
- State verbs are generally used in the **Present Perfect Simple** only.

1 Write sentences from the prompts. Use the Present Perfect Continuous. Add *since* or *for* where necessary.

1 I / study / art / 2018.
2 How long / you / wear / your glasses?
3 you / swim / all afternoon?
4 It / rain / two hours now.
5 We / not / watch / the match.
6 My parents / study English / five years.
7 How long / Joanna / work in that café?
8 Amy / surf the Internet / all day?
9 My sister / work as a photographer / three years.
10 Hannah and Eve / revise for their exam / all evening?

2 Choose the correct option.

1 I've *looked / been looking* for you for an hour!
2 How many paintings have you *sold / been selling*?
3 We have *travelled / been travelling* for a couple of weeks now.
4 The professor has *answered / been answering* more than 100 questions about the Louvre.
5 John has *known / been knowing* Cynthia since primary school.
6 I've *seen / been seeing* most of his paintings.
7 How long have you *waited / been waiting*?
8 Have you *written / been writing* your essay all morning?
9 How many art galleries has Dan *been visiting / visited* today?
10 How long have you *had / been having* this painting by van Gogh?

3 Complete the sentences with information about yourself. Use the Present Perfect Simple or Continuous.

1 _____ since last weekend.
2 _____ for at least a month.
3 _____ since my last birthday party.
4 _____ since yesterday.
5 _____ for more than a year.
6 _____ since I was ten.
7 _____ for two days.
8 _____ since I was a small child.
9 _____ for many years.
10 _____ since this morning.

4 Complete the dialogues with the correct form of the verbs in brackets. Use the Present Perfect Simple or Continuous.

1 **A:** _____ (you/finish) your essay?
  B: Well, not really. I _____ (write) it all day and hope to finish it tomorrow.
2 **A:** You look tired. _____ (you/run)?
  B: Oh, yes. I _____ (run) fifteen km.
3 **A:** I _____ (try) to call you since this morning. What's up?
  B: Oh sorry, I _____ (lose) my mobile.
4 **A:** How long _____ (he/have) that suit? It doesn't look too good.
  B: Not long, I think but he _____ (wear) it all week.
5 **A:** What _____ (you/do)? You're covered in mud!
  B: I _____ (dig) in the garden. I _____ (plant) three rose bushes, but I've still got two more to go.
6 **A:** I need a break, I _____ (study) since 8 o'clock! How about some lunch?
  B: Sorry, I can't. I _____ (not finish) this essay yet.

133

GRAMMAR AND USE OF ENGLISH

1.6 Common suffixes

Many different words are formed by adding suffixes to nouns, verbs and adjectives.

Most common suffixes used to form nouns:
-ance/-ence, used to make nouns from adjectives by changing the **-ant/-ent** ending:
import**ant** – import**ance**, viol**ent** – viol**ence**
-ion, used to form nouns from verbs: decide – decis**ion**
-ity: stupid – stupid**ity**
-ment: develop – develop**ment**
-ship: relation – relation**ship**

Most common suffixes used to form verbs:
-ate: local – loc**ate**
-en, usually added to adjectives and nouns related to measurement: deep – deep**en**, length – length**en**
-ify: simple – simpl**ify**
-ise: legal – legal**ise**

Most common suffixes used to form adjectives:

-able: comfort – comfort**able**	**-ive**: support – support**ive**
-ed: amaze – amaz**ed**	**-ous**: courage – courage**ous**
-ing: amaze – amaz**ing**	**-ic**: energy – energet**ic**
-ful: colour – colour**ful**	**-al**: economy – economic**al**
-less: colour – colour**less**	

Most common suffixes used to form adverbs:
-ly: strange – strange**ly**
-y, when the adjective ends with **-le**: possible – possib**ly**
-ily, when the adjective ends with **-y**: heavy – heav**ily**

You can add prefixes un-, in-, im-, il-, ir-, dis- to some adjectives to get the opposite meaning:
-un: familiar – **un**familiar
-im, most often added to adjectives beginning with p, b and m: balanced – **im**balanced, mature – **im**mature, polite – **im**polite
-ir, most often added to adjectives beginning with r: responsible – **ir**responsible
-il, most often added to adjectives beginning with l: legal – **il**legal
-dis: respectful – **dis**respectful
-in: sensitive – **in**sensitive

1 Choose the correct option.
1 You need to understand the *important / importance* of looking stylish.
2 My parents have always been *supported / supportive* of my ambition to become a designer.
3 The silly comments he made online showed his *immaturity / immature*.
4 The clothes she buys are all made *locally / locate* by British companies.
5 We had to make a difficult *decisive / decision* about the future of our fashion brand.
6 Although the sales were on, the shopping centre was *stranger / strangely* quiet.
7 A good suit is a *necessary / necessity* if you are working in banking.
8 It's more *economical / economic* to buy a few well-made clothes than lots of cheap items.

2 Choose the correct option, A, B or C.
1 What is the ___ of this fabric?
  A long   B length   C lengthen
2 She puts on some make-up every day to make herself ___ .
  A beauty   B beautify   C beautiful
3 What I like best about Mark's clothes is their ___ .
  A simplify   B simplicity   C simple
4 Some young people are really ___ when it comes to their hairstyles.
  A courageous   B encouraging   C discouraged
5 Although Tina studies fashion, her ___ with the history of design is rather limited.
  A unfamiliar   B familiarise   C familiarity
6 What appeals to me about the company is how they ___ their offer.
  A diversity   B diverse   C diversify
7 Ana's parents were very helpful and ___ when she decided to move abroad.
  A support   B supported   C supportive

3 Complete the sentences with the correct form of the words in the box.

(colour   energy   familiar   legal   respectful
  responsible   sensitive)

1 Going to an exam in a beanie will definitely make you look _____ .
2 You shouldn't have spent so much on this blouse. It was quite _____ of you.
3 Sue doesn't want to be the centre of attention so she wears _____ sweatshirts, mainly beige.
4 My sister's style is completely _____ to me, but she feels comfortable in her own skin.
5 It was rather _____ of Kate to criticise her friend's new fleece.
6 Producing cheap copies of designer clothes is _____ .
7 Sami's little brother is so _____ . He's never tired.

4 UNIT REVIEW Complete the sentences with the correct form of the words in brackets. Sometimes more than one answer is possible.
1 It was rather _____ (polite) of Pete to attend his friend's wedding reception in faded jeans.
2 To me, _____ (energy) people tend to go for a casual look.
3 Buying vintage clothes is not always _____ (economy) as they can be pretty expensive.
4 They _____ (behave) strangely today.
5 Don't you think Claire _____ (look) amazing in this turquoise dress?
6 Karen _____ (always/be) sensitive about her appearance.

REFERENCE AND PRACTICE

2.2 Narrative tenses

We use the **Past Continuous**:
- to describe a background scene in a story or in a description of a main event:
  *On the day of the match, it **was raining** and the fans **were getting** wet.*
- to talk about an action that was in progress when another action took place (for the shorter action, which happened while the longer one was in progress, we use the Past Simple):
  *I **was riding** my bike when a policeman **stopped** me.*
- to talk about actions in progress at the same time:
  *While Ann **was doing** some experiments, Terry **was taking** some measurements.*

We use the **Past Simple** for a series of actions that happened one after the other:
*Julia **got up** and **put on** her trainers.*

We use the **Past Perfect** to talk about an action that happened before another action in the past (for the action that came second, we use the Past Simple):
*In the taxi I realised that I **had left** the ticket at home.*

1 Complete the sentences with the correct form of the words in brackets. Use the Past Simple or the Past Continuous.

1. John _____ (walk) towards the stadium when he _____ (hear) some supporters singing.
2. The play _____ (end) and everyone _____ (leave) the theatre.
3. _____ (Sue/work) at the restaurant when she _____ (meet) Frank?
4. We _____ (cross) Green Street when we _____ (see) a bank robbery.
5. While I _____ (watch) tennis on TV, my sisters _____ (play) a video game.
6. What _____ (you/do) when I _____ (call) you last night?

2 Complete the second sentence so that it has a similar meaning to the first. Use the words in capitals and the Past Simple or the Past Perfect.

1. I saw Lionel Messi in the street. Nobody believed it. **THAT**
   Nobody believed _____ .
2. The match started. Then I got back home. **WHEN**
   The match _____ .
3. Jack's team didn't train enough. They lost the match. **BECAUSE**
   Jack's team _____ .
4. Ann looked at her watch. She realised she was late for the meeting. **AND**
   Ann _____ .
5. Andrew didn't lock his car. Somebody stole it. **BECAUSE**
   Somebody _____ .
6. The film finished. Then Mark switched the TV on. **ALREADY**
   When Mark _____ .

3 Choose the correct option, A, B or C.

1. Sarah ___ in the park when she met her neighbour.
   A jogged B had jogged C was jogging
2. Tim ___ at 7:30, had breakfast and went to the pool.
   A got up B had got up C was getting up
3. We were cycling in the forest while Tom ___ in the lake.
   A swam B was swimming C had swum
4. Adam didn't go horse-riding because he ___ his riding boots.
   A was forgetting B had forgotten C forgot
5. She didn't believe that I ___ volleyball before.
   A had never played B was never playing C never played
6. When we ___ at the court, the match had already finished.
   A arrived B had arrived C were arriving
7. Kim ___ her skating boots and stepped onto the ice rink.
   A was putting on B put on C had put on
8. Mark ___ injured while he was overtaking his rivals.
   A was getting B had got C got
9. Nina realised she ___ her mobile at home when she was already on the bus.
   A left B had left C has left
10. We ___ in a restaurant when we heard about the accident.
    A were eating B ate C had eaten

4 Complete the conversations with the correct form of the verbs in brackets. Use the Past Simple, the Past Continuous or the Past Perfect.

1. A: What _____ (you/do) when they _____ (announce) the results?
   B: I _____ (just/take) a shower and I _____ (relax) in my room.
2. A: When _____ (you/realise) you _____ (leave) your goggles at home?
   B: Well, just as _____ (I/stand) at the top of the slope, with my skis on.
3. A: Why _____ (Nick/not work out) yesterday?
   B: He _____ (promise) his daughter he would play with her, I think.
4. A: What _____ (you/do) at the sports camp?
   B: Every day we _____ (get up) early, then we _____ (go) to the gym and then we _____ (play) basketball.
5. A: So, how _____ (be) your holiday?
   B: OK. A bit boring really. We just _____ (go) to the beach every day. Earlier, I _____ (hope) we would do something exciting, but my family only _____ (want) to sunbathe.
6. A: Can you tell me what you _____ (do) in your last job?
   B: Of course. I _____ (work) as an assistant in marketing, which _____ (be) a big difference for me. Before that I _____ (work) in the call centre.

135

GRAMMAR AND USE OF ENGLISH

2.5 Verb patterns

Verbs which follow other verbs follow different patterns:

- after: *aim, arrange, attempt, can't afford, decide, expect, hope, intend, manage, offer, plan, refuse, remember, seem, tend, try, want:* **(not) to + infinitive**:
  They **decided not to work** with a sports psychologist.
- after: *advise, allow, encourage, force, remind, teach, urge, warn*: **object + (not) to + infinitive**:
  She **taught me to believe** in myself.
- after: *avoid, can't help, can't stand, don't mind, enjoy, fancy, finish, imagine, keep, miss, stop, waste time*: **-ing**:
  Just **imagine winning** the competition!
- after modal verbs: *can, could, might, should, would*: **infinitive**:
  You **should answer** his question right now.
- after *make* and *let*: **object + infinitive**:
  They **let me visit** the stadium.

1 Complete the sentences with the correct form of the verbs in brackets. Add *me* or *you* where necessary.

1 I can _____ (ski) really well, but I've never tried snowboarding.
2 Did your parents make _____ (play) the piano when you were a child?
3 I can't afford _____ (buy) a new tennis racket. It's too expensive.
4 This pool is OK, but I miss _____ (swim) in the ocean.
5 My PE teacher at school encouraged _____ (pursue) my passion for swimming.
6 The footballer refused _____ (join) the national team.
7 You shouldn't waste so much time _____ (watch) TV.
8 The doctor has warned _____ (not go) running for a month.

2 Complete the sentences with the correct form of the words in brackets.

1 I _____ (can't stand/wait) for exam results.
2 Has he _____ (decide/finish) his sports career yet?
3 My mother _____ (not let/me/do) motor-racing.
4 The coach _____ (remind/us/not eat) anything just before the match.
5 _____ (try/not worry) about the future.
6 Our team should _____ (aim/win) all the matches this season.
7 She'll always _____ (remember/meet) her favourite tennis player last year.
8 We were training hard, so we _____ (stop/take) a break.

3 Complete the sentences with the correct form of the verbs in the box.

climb   do   go   improve   play
show   take up   watch

1 They arranged _____ for a swim on Saturday.
2 Paul offered _____ me how to play tennis.
3 Do you fancy _____ badminton this afternoon?
4 I cannot imagine _____ in winter. It's too dangerous.
5 Kate has never avoided _____ sport. That's why she's so fit.
6 Last year my dad attempted _____ his skiing. He's slightly better now.
7 I don't mind _____ boxing on TV from time to time.
8 Kim should _____ yoga. It will help her relax.

4 Choose the correct option.

1 I can't help *to watch / watching* sport on TV every day.
2 Please remind them *not to leave / to not leave* before 6 p.m.
3 Last week my brother managed *to swim / swimming* the whole distance.
4 Does your coach ever let you *eat / to eat* junk food?
5 Unfortunately, she cannot afford *buying / to buy* a new tennis racket.
6 Mark expects her *to win / winning* a medal during the next competition.
7 My mum intends *taking up / to take up* cycling this summer.
8 We can't *go / going* horse-riding today.

5 Choose the correct option, A, B or C.

1 We might ___ a tennis club to improve our fitness.
  A join   B to join   C joining
2 She hopes ___ the marathon next week.
  A win   B to win   C winning
3 Have you finished ___ the replay of the football final yet?
  A watch   B to watch   C watching
4 The football players don't seem ___ too upset by the score.
  A be   B to be   C being
5 You could easily ___ me at chess if you really tried.
  A beat   B to beat   C beating
6 Just keep ___ hard and you could be a champion one day.
  A train   B to train   C training
7 My doctor advised the athlete ___ more protein in his diet.
  A have   B to have   C having
8 Alice enjoys ___ in the sea, even in winter.
  A swim   B to swim   C swimming

136

REFERENCE AND PRACTICE

2.6 so, too, neither/nor, either

We use expressions **so/too** and **neither/nor/either** in short statements meaning *(me) too* or *(me) neither*. We use these constructions in reaction to somebody's statements to let the other person know that we are in the same situation.

We use **so** and **too** in positive statements. The form of an auxiliary or modal verb in short statements must be the same as the form of the main verb and the subject in the sentence to which it refers.

The structure of the short statement is the following:

- **so** + auxiliary/modal verb + subject (noun/pronoun):
  Our football team has let us down recently. **So** *has ours.*
  I should go jogging every day. **So** *should I.*

- subject (noun/pronoun) + auxiliary/modal verb + **too**:
  Michael broke his personal record yesterday. You did **too**.

We use **neither/nor** and **either** to say something is the same or agree with a negative statement.

The structure of the short statement is the following:

- **neither/nor** + auxiliary/modal verb in a positive form + subject (noun/pronoun):
  My coach isn't going to be pleased with my score.
  Neither/Nor *is mine.*
  Jerry will never give up running marathons.
  Neither/Nor *will I.*

- subject (noun/pronoun) + auxiliary/modal verb in a negative form + **either**:
  She didn't play for the school team last year. I didn't **either**.

In the **Present Simple** the auxiliary verb is *do/does*:
Rob takes part in tennis competitions twice a year.
So does *Joan.*

In the **Past Simple** the auxiliary verb is *did*:
Last week we qualified for the finals. **So did** *we.*

Using **Really?** and **Oh**, we react to other person's statement to say something is different, or to disagree with a statement.

The structure of the short comment is the following:

Really?/Oh + subject (noun/pronoun) + auxiliary/modal verb in a form opposite to the one used in the statement to which we are reacting:
I believe that some children should start training at a very early age. **Really?** *I don't.*
Most of our fans couldn't get tickets to watch the match.
Oh. *Ours could.*

1 Choose the correct option.

1 Alex is a great tennis player. *So / Too* is Stefanos.
2 My cricket bat isn't new. *So / Nor* is Tom's.
3 We watched the Olympic Games. So we *did / did* we.
4 He won't go to practice tomorrow. *Neither / So* will I.
5 Emma didn't go cycling. David didn't *either / neither*.
6 We've got our tickets for the match. So *do / have* we.

2 Complete the sentences with so/too or neither/either and the correct auxiliary.

1 To keep fit, Dan goes for a swim every Friday.
  _____ Pam.
2 Martin has never played squash.
  _____ they.
3 Sam is going to try out the new gym.
  _____ I.
4 They shouldn't give up chess.
  _____ we.
5 As a child, Olga wasn't very competitive.
  Her sister _____ .
6 Hopefully, Pete will talk his parents into doing Nordic walking.
  Tina _____ .

3 Complete the conversations with the words in brackets. Add verb forms where necessary.

1 A: They have never let their coach down.
  B: _____ . (neither/we)
2 A: Their teammates are really ambitious.
  B: _____ . (ours/too)
3 A: Unfortunately, Pat lost a match yesterday.
  B: _____ . (I/too)
4 A: We aren't going to go in for that competition.
  B: _____ . (really/we)
5 A: My sister doesn't watch any sport on TV.
  B: _____ . (nor/mine)
6 A: My dad will never take up yoga.
  B: _____ . (really/mine)

4 UNIT REVIEW Choose the correct sentence, A, B, or C to complete the conversations.

1 X: Can you imagine? They have never lost a match.
  Y: ___
  A Neither have we.   B We too.
  C So have we.
2 X: I think they should be more decisive.
  Y: ___
  A Really? I shouldn't.   B Really? I don't.
  C Oh. So should I.
3 X: She is going to watch a rugby match tonight.
  Y: ___
  A Neither am I.   B I am too.
  C I'm not either.
4 X: You look sad. What's the matter?
  Y: My friend ___
  A can't help helping me.   B can't afford to help me.
  C doesn't mind helping me.
5 X: What did you do when you saw that accident?
  Y: ___
  A I called an ambulance.
  B I was calling an ambulance.
  C I had called an ambulance.
6 X: Are you going to enter this competition?
  Y: Definitely. I love ___ new challenges.
  A taking on   B giving up
  C burning off

GRAMMAR AND USE OF ENGLISH

3.2 Present and past speculation

Speculating about the present

When speculating about a present situation, we use a **modal verb + infinitive**. We use:

- **must**, to express a strong belief that something is true:
  John **must** be very happy working at the zoo.
- **might, may** and **could** when we think that it's possible that something is true:
  The lions **might/may/could** be very hungry now.
- **can't**, to express a strong belief that something isn't true:
  It **can't** be a domestic cat. It's too big.

Speculating about the past

When speculating about a past situation or event, we use a **modal verb + have + the Past Participle form of the main verb**.

We use:

- **must have**, to express a strong belief that something happened:
  You **must have lost** your mobile at the zoo.
- **might have, may have** and **could have**, when we think that it's possible that something happened:
  Lucy **might/may/could have missed** the train.
- **can't have** and **couldn't have**, to express a strong belief that something didn't happen:
  Peter **can't/couldn't have gone** home.

---

1 Choose the correct option.

1 The key *can't / must* be somewhere here but I can't find it right now.
2 You *can't / may* remember me – we met on a trip to China last year.
3 What, you forgot your ticket and passport? You *might / can't* be serious!
4 You failed the exam, so your answers *must / can't* have been wrong.
5 I'm not sure if you are right. You *could / can't* have made a mistake.

2 Complete the sentences with the correct form of the verbs in brackets.

1 I might _____ (leave) my mobile at the hotel but I don't remember.
2 Susan has been travelling for the last two weeks – she must _____ (be) very tired by now.
3 Wendy's accent is a bit strange. She could _____ (be) Northern Irish, but I'm not sure.
4 You can't _____ (see) Joe in town at noon – he was at home with me.
5 Thomas was really upset last week. He must _____ (have) problems at home.

3 Choose the correct option, A, B or C.

1 We ___ go to Greece this summer, but we haven't decided yet.
  A must   B might   C can't
2 They ___ have visited that museum. It's closed.
  A might not   B couldn't   C mustn't
3 They ___ know this place. They've been here many times.
  A may   B can't   C must
4 I don't know why Pat hasn't arrived yet. She ___ have missed the bus.
  A must   B could   C can't
5 It ___ be Diana's tent. She never goes camping.
  A must   B may   C can't
6 Greg ___ have reached his destination yet. It's only 7 p.m.
  A could   B can't   C mustn't
7 Ben knew everything about Gothic painting. Definitely, he ___ have studied art history.
  A couldn't   B might   C must
8 It's impossible to keep a puma as a pet. She ___ have lied.
  A must   B can't   C might

4 Complete the second sentence so that it has a similar meaning to the first. Use modal verbs.

1 I am sure a cruise down the Nile is very expensive.
  A cruise down the Nile _____ very expensive.
2 I am sure Kate hasn't eaten that local speciality. She's allergic to seafood.
  Kate _____ that local speciality. She's allergic to seafood.
3 I am sure they are not at the office. Pam called me from the airport an hour ago.
  They _____ at the office. Pam called me from the airport an hour ago.
4 Maybe we will spend a few days near the sea, I'm not sure.
  We _____ a few days near the sea.
5 I am sure they have brought a lot of souvenirs from their trip. They always do.
  They _____ a lot of souvenirs from their trip.
6 Let's ask Ian. Maybe he has been to Japan.
  Let's ask Ian. He _____ to Japan.
7 We'd better take a map. Maybe it is not the right way.
  We'd better take a map. It _____ the right way.
8 I don't know why Janet is still not here. Maybe she got stuck in traffic.
  I don't know why Janet is still not here. She _____ in traffic.

138

REFERENCE AND PRACTICE

3.5 Used to and would

We use **used to/would** (+ infinitive) to talk about past states or actions that happened regularly in the past:

- We use **used to** for states (e.g. *be, have, believe, like, love, live*) or actions:
  I **didn't use to like** travelling by plane. (But I do now.)
  She **used to write** travel guides. (But she doesn't any more.)
- We use **would** for actions (but not states), usually in affirmative sentences:
  When I was a teenager, I **would visit** my grandma every Sunday.

Affirmative	I *used to go* backpacking every summer. I *would go* backpacking every summer.
Negative	I *didn't use to buy* flight tickets online.
Yes/No questions	*Did* he *use to* go on holiday in August?
Wh- questions	What *did* he *use to* eat?
Subject questions	Who *used to go* to the seaside on holiday?

When we talk about a single past action or when we don't want to emphasise the difference between the past and the present, we use the Past Simple instead of *used to/would*:
Two years ago they **went** on holiday to France.
I often **travelled** to China.

1 Write sentences from the prompts. Use *would* if possible. If not, use *used to*.

1 Jill / get home / at 7 p.m. every day
  _____
2 We / not have / a lot of money / in those days
  _____
3 My family / live / next to a luxury hotel
  _____
4 Damien / not drink / coffee / in the past
  _____
5 As a child / I / like / reading adventure novels
  _____
6 My grandparents / not travel / by car
  _____
7 When I was a child / I / be / very shy
  _____
8 They / go on / summer camps / at primary school
  _____
9 My aunt / not have / a computer / as a teenager
  _____
10 Every morning / he / make / breakfast for the whole family.
  _____

2 Choose the correct option, A, B or C. Sometimes more than one answer is possible.

1 Just like many boys, I ___ to be a pilot when I grew up.
  A wanted   B used to want   C would want
2 I ___ smoke when I was at school.
  A didn't   B didn't use to   C wouldn't
3 Last Sunday Jack ___ too late to catch the train.
  A turned up   B used to turn up
  C would turn up
4 How ___ feel when your parents sent you to summer camps every summer?
  A did you   B did you use to   C would you
5 My parents ___ me to the seaside every summer.
  A took   B used to take   C would take
6 Dad, ___ a happy child?
  A were you   B did you use to be   C would you be
7 Yesterday we ___ our flight back to Australia.
  A used to miss   B would miss   C missed
8 What do you mean you don't like apples? You ___ them as a child!
  A didn't use to love   B would love   C used to love

3 Choose the correct option.

1 Last year we *went / used to go* on a trip with a travel agency.
2 As a student, my mum *would love travelling / used to love travelling*.
3 My grandpa *would read / read* me stories about the Aztecs that day.
4 They *didn't use to be / wouldn't be* keen on flying.
5 Our uncle *had / would have* about 100 guidebooks.
6 As a child, *did you use to sleep / would you sleep* in a tent during summer?
7 My dad *didn't use to like / wouldn't like* going to the seaside.
8 Yesterday, he *closed / would close* the door and went to bed, like every other evening.

4 Complete the sentences with the correct form of the verbs in brackets. Sometimes more than one answer is possible.

1 Kim _____ (travel) to Asia twice a year but now she cannot afford this.
2 When we lived in London, we _____ (go) jogging in Hyde Park every day.
3 _____ (Mark/visit) his family in Scotland last year?
4 We _____ (not/enjoy) spending time in the countryside. Now we love it!
5 When Ben was a child, he _____ (play) in the forest.
6 _____ (Luke/like) sightseeing when he was a child?
7 Back in kindergarten, they _____ (play) hide and seek every day.
8 I _____ (love) swimming in the river as a child. The water never felt too cold.

GRAMMAR AND USE OF ENGLISH

3.6 Phrasal verbs

Phrasal verbs are expressions that consist of a verb or a particle (particles), thanks to which the verb gains a new meaning:
look – look up (=check)

Most phrasal verbs have their equivalents in formal language:
put up a tent = construct/erect a tent

The meaning of phrasal verbs may be:
- literal: *Why don't you **take off** your coat?*
- idiomatic: *The plane **takes off** at 10 a.m.*

We can divide phrasal verbs into two groups:

1) inseparable:
- **verb + particle + object**

  There is always an object after the phrasal verb.
  *When I was running, I **bumped into** my form teacher.*
  *We dropped our bags and **made for** the passport control.*

- **verb + particle**

  There is no object after the phrasal verb:
  *Fortunately, a lot of people **turned up** to the exhibition.*
  *It was a long journey so we **set off** early in the morning.*

- **verb + particle + particle + object**

  There is alway an object after the phrasal verb.
  *I **look forward to** travelling around America next summer.*
  *It was very hot and we **ran out of** water very quickly.*

2) separable:
There is always an object. If the object is a noun, it can come before or after the particle.

- **verb + particle + object**

  *Can you please **pick up** Laura from the airport?*
  ~~*Can you please pick up her from the airport?*~~
  *We can't **put off** booking tickets forever.*
  ~~*We can't put off it forever.*~~

- **verb + object + particle**

  *Can you please **pick** Laura **up** from the airport?*
  *Can you please **pick** her **up** from the airport?*
  *We can't **put** booking tickets **off** forever.*
  *We can't **put** it **off** forever.*

1 Match the sentence halves.

1 Guess who I bumped ☐
2 I think the bus is at 7, but it's easy to look ☐
3 Due to heavy rain, the plane took ☐
4 Let's buy our tickets and make ☐
5 Driving to work, Jim ran ☐

a up the timetable online.
b off an hour later than scheduled.
c out of petrol.
d into on the train.
e for the platform.

2 Complete the sentences with the correct form of the phrasal verbs in the box.

> bump into   look up   pick up   put off   turn up

1 Are you going to _____ Pen from the station?
2 We got lost so we _____ the address in our mobiles.
3 We have so much work that we have to _____ our weekend trip.
4 I _____ my old friend while I was boarding the plane.
5 Only a few people _____ at the station to say goodbye to her yesterday.

3 Complete the second sentence so that it has a similar meaning to the first. Use the words in capitals.

1 We had no food left, nevertheless we continued to walk. **RUN/CARRY**
   We _____, nevertheless we _____ .
2 Kate has quit her career as a manager and she can't wait to go to India. **WALK/LOOK**
   Kate _____ her career as a manager and she _____ to India.
3 Dan took us to the station in his car. He went to work and we went towards the platform. **DROP/MADE**
   Dan _____ at the station. He went to work and we _____ the platform.
4 Pat stopped by the side of the road and tried to find the hotel's address in her guidebook. **PULL/LOOK**
   Pat _____ and _____ the hotel's address in her guidebook.
5 I met my old friend unexpectedly when we were delayed at the airport. **BUMP/HOLD**
   I _____ my old friend when we were _____ at the airport.

4 UNIT REVIEW Choose one word, A, B or C to complete both sentences.

1 Is Dan going to pick us ___ from the station?
   Mark is a great cyclist and it's really hard to keep ___ with him.
   A on   **B** off   **C** up

2 The taxi driver dropped us ___ at the wrong terminal.
   Pat had a long way to go so she set ___ at dawn.
   A down   **B** off   **C** out

3 They're going to ___ this old building into a hostel.
   What time did they finally ___ up?
   A turn   **B** make   **C** put

4 We were held ___ in a traffic jam and we missed the last train home.
   The hotel was full but, fortunately, Sue put them ___ .
   A up   **B** off   **C** down

5 Paul gave ___ his job to travel the world.
   Have you ever put ___ a tent in the rain?
   A over   **B** off   **C** up

6 Let's not put this trip ___ any more.
   The plane didn't take ___ due to the fog.
   A off   **B** away   **C** down

REFERENCE AND PRACTICE

4.2 Future forms

You can use a variety of forms to talk about the future: **Present Simple, Present Continuous, Future Simple** (*will/won't*) and *be going to* + infinitive.

You use the **Present Simple** to talk about a fixed future event – on a timetable, a schedule or a programme:
*Lunch break **starts** at 12:30 and **finishes** at 13:30.*

You use the **Present Continuous** to talk about a future arrangement – you often mention a time, a date or a place:
*They**'re giving** prizes to the winners of the cookery competition tomorrow in the Town Hall.*

You use the **Future Simple** (*will/won't*):
- to talk about a spontaneous decision made at the moment of speaking – you react to circumstances:
  *Wait for me. **I'll help** you peel the carrots.*
- in questions with *I* and *we*, for offers and suggestions, you use **shall** (NOT *will*):
  *These bags look heavy. **Shall I carry** them for you?*
  ***Shall we have** a barbecue this evening?*
- to talk about a future prediction – based on your opinion, prediction or experience:
  *I can lend you this cookery book but **I'll probably need** it next week.*

You use *be going to* + infinitive to talk about:
- a future intention – something you have already decided to do:
  *What **are you going to prepare** for dinner?*
- a future prediction – based on what you can see or what you know:
  *This cake looks really sweet. Sue **isn't going to have** any of it.*

When you are talking about the future, in complex sentences you use the **Present Simple** after the conjunctions *if, when, as soon as, unless, before* and *after*:
***If you drink** coffee in the evening, you won't be able to sleep.*
*Be careful. The biscuits will get dry **unless you put** them in a tin.*

1 Choose the correct option, A, B or C. Sometimes more than one answer is possible.

1 This recipe looks complicated. ___ help you prepare the ingredients?
   A Am I going to   B Shall I   C Will I
2 I'll let you know when the dinner ___ ready.
   A is   B will be   C is going to be
3 Don't worry! I ___ the tins for you.
   A am opening   B will open   C open
4 I've checked their offer. The cookery course ___ next Monday.
   A starts   B is going to start   C shall start
5 Tomorrow I ___ to the fruit market outside the town. I can't wait!
   A go   B will go   C am going
6 We will not manage to prepare the food for the party unless you ___.
   A won't hurry up   B hurry up   C don't hurry up
7 I think the curry ___ ready in five minutes.
   A is   B is going to be   C will be

2 Write sentences from the prompts.

1 What time / the party / start?
   _____
2 You / feel better / as soon as / you / start drinking / more mineral water.
   _____
3 I / hope / the soup / not be / too bland for Pete.
   _____
4 Kate / eat / all those cherries? They are still unripe!
   _____
5 This dessert isn't sweet enough. I / add / some sugar?
   _____
6 Those apricots look fresh. They / be / tasty.
   _____

3 Complete the sentences with the correct form of the verbs in brackets. Use future forms.

1 They _____ (meet) for lunch on Monday. Mary has told me.
2 Ben will not get fit unless he _____ (start) eating healthy food.
3 This bread is stale. I _____ (not/buy) it.
4 The cookery show _____ (start) at 9 p.m.
5 Meg _____ (probably make) some crunchy biscuits tonight.
6 If I have time in the morning I _____ (prepare) some snacks at home.
7 How _____ (you/decorate) this birthday cake?

4 Match the sentence halves.

1 Are you going to ☐
2 Shall we bake ☐
3 Our local open-air market ☐
4 How much black pepper ☐
5 Well, I think I ☐

a are you going to add?
b a carrot cake for Joan?
c will start eating more fish.
d the supermarket in the afternoon?
e opens at 7 a.m.

5 Choose the correct option, A, B or C.

Tim has decided to improve his health, so he's enrolled in a short course for healthy cooking. He [1]_____ to his first class on Monday evening. According to the programme, the classes [2]_____ at 6 o'clock. He [3]_____ notes in the class, so he [4]_____ a notebook later today. He hopes the dishes that he learns to cook [5]_____ boring or tasteless!

1 A goes   B is going   C is going to go
2 A start   B is starting   C will start
3 A probably takes   B is probably taking
  C will probably take
4 A is going to buy   B is buying   C buys
5 A aren't going to be B won't be   C aren't being

141

GRAMMAR AND USE OF ENGLISH

4.5 Future Continuous and Future Perfect

Future Continuous

You use the **Future Continuous** to talk about longer unfinished actions in progress at a time in the future:

*We **will be making** a cake **at** 5 p.m.*

Affirmative			Negative		
I/You/He/She/It/We/They	'll (will)	be working at 10 a.m.	I/You/He/She/It/We/They	won't (will not)	be working at 10 a.m.
Yes/No questions			**Short answers**		
Will	I/you/he/she/it/we/they	be working at 10 a.m.?	Yes, I/you/he/she/it/we/they will. No, I/you/he/she/it/we/they won't.		
Wh- questions			**Subject questions**		
What	will	I/you/he/she/it/we/they	be doing at 10 a.m.?	Who	will	be working at 10 a.m.?

Future Perfect

You use the **Future Perfect** to talk about an action that will be completed before a certain time in the future:

*I **will have cooked** all the dishes **by** 3 o'clock.*

Affirmative			Negative		
I/You/He/She/It/We/They	'll (will)	have finished lunch by 2 p.m.	I/You/He/She/It/We/They	won't (will not)	have finished lunch by 2 p.m.
Yes/No questions			**Short answers**		
Will	I/you/he/she/it/we/they	have finished lunch by 2 p.m.?	Yes, I/you/he/she/it/we/they will. No, I/you/he/she/it/we/they won't.		
Wh- questions			**Subject questions**		
What	will	I/you/he/she/it/we/they	have finished doing by 2 p.m.?	Who	will	have finished lunch by 2 p.m.?

1 Match the questions and answers.

1 Can you meet me for lunch tomorrow? ☐
2 When will dinner be ready? ☐
3 Are you looking forward to your holiday? ☐
4 Should I book a table for five o'clock tonight? ☐
5 What did you think of the new café? ☐

a I'll have prepared everything by six.
b It was great! We'll be going back again soon.
c No, six or later; the restaurant won't have opened by then.
d Sorry, tomorrow I'll be shopping with my friend. Maybe Friday?
e Yes! This time next week, I'll be eating pizza in Italy!

2 Choose the correct option.

1 A: Can we meet at 1 p.m. on Saturday?
   B: Sorry, I *'ll be having / 'll have had* lunch with my family.
2 A: Do you need a lot of time to finish this birthday cake?
   B: I *'ll be decorating / 'll have decorated* it by 12 o'clock.
3 A: What is John so worried about?
   B: Getting a new job. If he doesn't find one, he *'ll be spending / 'll have spent* all his money by the end of the year.
4 A: Tom, I really need to return that library book tomorrow.
   B: No problem. I *'ll be finishing / 'll have finished* it by then.
5 A: *Will you be seeing / Will you have seen* your boyfriend tonight?
   B: Yes, he's taking me out to a restaurant.
6 A: What *will you be doing / will you have done* at 7 p.m. tomorrow?
   B: I don't have any plans. Shall we go to the cinema?

3 Complete the sentences with the correct form of the verbs in brackets. Use the Future Continuous or the Future Perfect.

1 Don't phone me before 9 a.m. I _____ (sleep)!
2 By the end of the month she _____ (finish) her training as a waitress.
3 Peter, _____ (you/use) the oven this evening? I'd like to make pizza.
4 I'm going to do a cookery course in September. So now I'm helping at my mum's restaurant. I hope I _____ (learn) something useful by the end of the summer.
5 How many exams _____ (you/take) by the end of the academic year?
6 What _____ (Sam/do) this time tomorrow?
7 Call Simone at seven. She _____ (leave) the office by then.

4 Answer the following questions. Use the Future Continuous or the Future Perfect.

1 What will you have learnt by the end of the year?
_____
2 What will you be doing this time on Sunday?
_____
3 How many meals will you have eaten by 10 p.m.?
_____
4 What will you be doing tomorrow at 9 a.m.?
_____
5 How many books will you have read by next autumn?
_____
6 Where will you be living in five years' time?
_____

REFERENCE AND PRACTICE

4.6 Question Tags

Question tags are short questions added at the end of the sentence. They appear almost only in spoken English. We use them for confirmation or to ask a question.

Question tags used for confirmation have a falling intonation:
You know how to cook scrambled eggs, **don't you**? (↓ We are almost certain the person we are talking to knows how to do it.).

Question tags used to ask a question have a rising intonation:
Your sister is a vegan, **isn't she**? (↑ We aren't certain the person we are talking about is a vegan.).

You form question tags with an **auxiliary verb** (*be, have, do*) or **modal verb** (e.g. *can, will, should*) + **pronoun** (e.g. *I, you, she*). After a positive statement, you use a negative tag, after a negative statement – a positive tag.

Positive statement + negative tag
You're going to use stale bread, **aren't you**?

Negative statement + positive tag
You haven't eaten unripe bananas, **have you**?

Special cases
In sentences with *I'm*, the question tag is **aren't I?**:
I'm a good cook, **aren't I?**

In imperatives, the question tag is **will you?**:
Grate some Parmesan cheese, **will you?**
Don't order too much food, **will you?**

In sentences with *let's*, the question tag is **shall we?**:
Let's have a quick snack, **shall we?**

In sentences with the pronoun *that* used as a subject, we use the pronoun *it* in a question tag:
That's pumpkin soup, **isn't it?**

1 Choose the correct option.

1 You have never liked grapefruit juice, *have you / haven't you*?
2 In kindergarten we had a lot of fresh fruit and vegetables every day, *hadn't we / didn't we*?
3 That's the best dessert she has ever prepared, *isn't that / isn't it*?
4 Organic products should cost a bit less, *shouldn't they / don't they*?
5 Let's try out that new restaurant round the corner, *shall we / will we*?
6 Don't add too many chilli peppers, *will you / do you*?
7 You don't have any orange juice, *have you / do you*?
8 Moussaka is a Greek dish, *isn't it / doesn't it*?
9 They could deliver our pizzas, *can't they / couldn't they*?
10 He'd eaten Japanese food before, *hadn't he / wouldn't he*?

2 Complete the sentences with the correct question tag.

1 You can't be fit without eating healthy food, _____?
2 This curry isn't very spicy, _____?
3 Small children shouldn't eat fattening food, _____?
4 You're not on a diet, _____?
5 I'm quite good at making Thai dishes, _____?
6 Buy some fresh fruit on your way back, _____?
7 He's going to go on a cooking show, _____?
8 She'd give you the recipe, _____?
9 You haven't burnt the cake, _____?
10 This soup can be served cold, _____?

3 UNIT REVIEW Choose the correct option, A, B or C to complete the conversations.

1 X: Let's have a burger, ___?
   Y: Well, I'd rather have pasta if you don't mind.
   A will we   B shall we   C don't we
2 X: This soup is absolutely delicious, ___?
   Y: My mum is a great cook. Would you like the recipe?
   A isn't it?   B isn't that?   C isn't this?
3 X: OK, so what shall I get you?
   Y: Maybe some apples. But don't buy the green ones, ___? They are sour.
   A shall you   B will you   C do you
4 X: So guys, what shall we order? Steak for everyone?
   Y: No, a salad for me, please. I'm not the only vegan, here, ___?
   A aren't I   B are you   C am I
5 X: Kate is taking part in this new cooking show, ___?
   Y: Yeah, she's a fantastic cook.
   A isn't she   B is she   C isn't it
6 X: We had a fantastic dinner last night, ___?
   Y: Yes, it was really great.
   A hadn't we   B had we   C didn't we
7 X: That was the best chocolate cake I've ever had.
   Y: You bought it at the new bakery, ___?
   A hadn't you   B haven't you   C didn't you
8 X: Sorry I'm late. You haven't ordered yet, ___?
   Y: No, we only got here a few minutes ago.
   A have you   B do you   C will you
9 X: They will have finished dinner by now, ___?
   Y: Yes, let's call them.
   A haven't they   B won't they   C don't they
10 X: He can cook an omelette, ___?
   Y: Of course. It isn't difficult!
   A couldn't he   B doesn't he   C can't he

GRAMMAR AND USE OF ENGLISH

5.2 Articles: no article, *a/an* or *the*

We do NOT use an article:
- when we are talking about something in general, before uncountable nouns or before plural countable nouns:
  Primary education is compulsory in this country.
  Farmers in poor countries earn very little.
- before the names of continents and most countries and towns:
  in Europe, in Ireland, in Dublin
  Exceptions: *in the United States, in the United Kingdom, in the Netherlands, in The Hague*

We use *a/an*:
- when we mention something for the first time or to refer to any one of a kind or group:
  *London is **a** big city.* (one of many big cities in the world)
- when talking about someone's job:
  *Lucy is **a** doctor.*

We use *the*:
- before singular and plural countable nouns, to refer to something that we have mentioned before:
  *He lived in **a** big city. **The** city was polluted.*
- to refer to something specific or unique:
  *I like **the** colour of that shirt.*
  *Who is **the** Prime Minister of your country?*
- to refer to a period in history:
  ***the** Renaissance*
- with the superlative forms of adjectives:
  ***the** worst*
- with ordinal numbers:
  ***the** third*

1 Complete the sentences with *a/an* or *the*.
1 My mum's _____ secondary school teacher. She works in _____ school just around _____ corner.
2 I was born in _____ last week of January. All _____ children in our family are born in winter.
3 Are you hungry? I can make you _____ chicken sandwich or _____ salad. We can also have _____ soup from yesterday.
4 Canberra is _____ capital of Australia, but is it also Australia's biggest city?
5 It's _____ first time I've been to _____ USA. I've never crossed _____ Atlantic before.
6 Leonardo da Vinci, one of _____ most famous artists and inventors of all time, lived during _____ Renaissance.
7 _____ Middle Ages was a period of history that lasted from _____ 5th to 15th centuries AD.
8 Sam works as _____ environmental engineer with _____ group that protects the oceans.
9 Climate change is _____ worst thing for _____ future of our planet.
10 Shanghai, which has a population of over 24 million, is _____ city in _____ east of China.

2 Choose the correct option, A, B or C.
1 Jake is ___ captain of our junior football team.
  A –   B a   C the
2 ___ information about global warming can be found online.
  A –   B An   C The
3 There's ___ article in the paper today about endangered species.
  A –   B an   C the
4 It's terrible that ___ Great Barrier Reef is under threat.
  A –   B a   C the
5 Are you excited about your trip to ___ South America?
  A –   B a   C the
6 This is ___ great beach – we should come here again.
  A –   B a   C the

3 Complete the sentences with *a/an*, *the* or Ø (no article).
1 Wendy is _____ famous artist. You can see her paintings in _____ best museums in _____ world.
2 I think that _____ private health care is going to become more popular soon.
3 _____ capital of _____ Netherlands isn't _____ Hague. It's _____ Amsterdam.
4 _____ scientist has said recently that _____ cities haven't changed much since _____ 19th century.
5 Yesterday my brother asked me _____ question about natural disasters. I didn't know _____ answer.
6 Do you think _____ secondary school students should wear _____ uniforms?

4 Complete the texts with *a/an*, *the* or Ø (no article).
DHAKA
40 percent of people in ¹_____ Dhaka, ²_____ capital of Bangladesh, live in ³_____ slums where many people are without ⁴_____ water and ⁵_____ electricity. ⁶_____ government are trying to improve the living standards of slum-dwellers. ⁷_____ organisations are working with slum-dwellers and offer them ⁸_____ medicine and ⁹_____ education.

MUMBAI
In ¹⁰_____ Mumbai, ¹¹_____ capital of India, 62 percent of inhabitants live in ¹²_____ slums. ¹³_____ Mayor is trying out ¹⁴_____ different solution: she wants to move these people from ¹⁵_____ slums into new homes.

MEXICO CITY
In the 1990s ¹⁶_____ Mexico city was ¹⁷_____ most polluted place in the world. Traffic congestion was ¹⁸_____ biggest cause of pollution. ¹⁹_____ government has invested in ²⁰_____ new bus network and ²¹_____ bike-sharing programme. Instead of using ²²_____ cars, people are now using ²³_____ bus network to get to work. The next step is to replace ²⁴_____ petrol cars with ²⁵_____ electric cars.

REFERENCE AND PRACTICE

5.5 Non-defining relative clauses

Non-defining relative clauses:
- give additional information about the person, thing, place, etc. we are talking about. The sentence still makes sense without this information:
  *Giant pandas, **which** are an endangered species, live in the mountains in central China.* → *Giant pandas live in the mountains in central China.*
- are always separated from the rest of the sentence using commas,
- start with relative pronouns **who**, **which**, **where** or **whose** (but NOT *that*):
  *Last year we visited our friends on Aran Islands, **where** you can see lots of bird species.*

We can't leave out the relative pronouns in non-defining relative clauses.

1 Complete the sentences with *who*, *which*, *where* or *whose*.

1 That young man over there, _____ name I can't remember at the moment, is a famous ecologist.
2 We went on an expedition to the Amazon, _____ none of us had ever been before.
3 The doctor, _____ can't have been older than thirty, examined Lisa's leg carefully.
4 Mrs Janet McGregor's favourite holiday destination is London, _____ people don't recognise her.
5 One of my friends, _____ wife runs a big business, has made a big donation to an environmental charity.
6 The elephants, _____ were drinking water from the river, suddenly became very anxious.

2 Rewrite the sentences with non-defining relative clauses. Use the information in brackets.

1 The company plans to build a skyscraper here. (The company's owner is Tania Hillman.)
  _____
2 This T-shirt is a prize in the competition. (This T-shirt is made of organic cotton.)
  _____
3 Sandra saw giant pandas last year in China. (Sandra studies zoology.)
  _____
4 I'm moving to Belfast. (I'll work at a travel agency there.)
  _____
5 Padua attracts many tourists in the summer. (Padua is very close to Venice.)
  _____
6 Frank studies science. (His brother is a biologist.)
  _____
7 Pompeii was destroyed in 79 AD. (Pompeii was a Roman city.)
  _____
8 Simon loves working with animals. (Simon's parents have a farm.)
  _____

3 Choose the correct option.

1 My friend, *whose / which* project about environmental protection won the competition, goes to an eco-school.
2 Car exhaust fumes, *who / which* cause a lot of pollution, are dangerous to human health.
3 Diving in a turquoise ocean, *where / which* is inhabited by numerous species, is an extraordinary experience.
4 The WWF, *which / whose* mission is to conserve nature, is known worldwide.
5 Last week I interviewed Mark, *who / which* is in charge of our school's eco team.
6 The Amazon, *which / where* you can see amazing fauna and flora, has become a popular travel destination.
7 The panda, *which / who* is an endangered species, has been WWF's logo since 1961.
8 The animal rescuers finally caught an injured dolphin *which / who* was seen near the coast.
9 The leader of the expedition, *who / which* was a well-known scientist, discovered a new species.
10 The Mediterranean, *which / where* many dolphins live, is becoming increasingly polluted.

4 Complete the sentences with the correct form of the words in brackets. Add articles or prepositions if necessary.

1 Egypt, _____ (be/great/holiday destination), attracts loads of divers.
2 Tom, _____ (sister/be/vet), doesn't care about nature.
3 My friends, _____ (be/very much/ecology), are obsessed with recycling.
4 The Sahara desert, _____ (temperatures/be/really high) during the day, can be rather cold at night.
5 Last year we spent a few days in a jungle, _____ (inhabitants/be/quite dangerous).
6 Environmentalists, _____ (aim/help/our planet), have a real mission.
7 The Amazon river, _____ (flow through/six countries), is the longest river in South America.
8 My friend Vetha, _____ (come from/India), doesn't eat meat.
9 Antarctica, _____ (rain/rarely/fall), is actually the largest desert in the world.
10 Machu Picchu, _____ (be/high/the Andes), was built by the Incas in the 15th century.

GRAMMAR AND USE OF ENGLISH

5.6 Prepositions at the end of clauses

We put a preposition at the end of clauses:
- in **relative clauses**:
  *This is the scientist I have been waiting **for**.*
  *Camping by a lake is something we're enthusiastic **about**.*
  *There are several environmental issues you have to prepare a presentation **about**.*
- in **wh- questions**:
  When creating a detailed question in which a verb or an adjective is followed by a preposition and a noun, such as *listen to music, afraid of spiders*, etc., we leave the preposition after the verb or adjective.
  ***What** kind of animals are you afraid **of**?*
  ***What** are you good **at**?*
- in **infinitive structures**:
  *Cape Horn is probably the most hazardous place **to sail around**.*
  *Here are the safety procedures you need **to be aware of**.*

1 Write sentences from the prompts.

1 are / people / for / those / waiting / what ?
_____

2 rely / energy / are / renewable / on / a / sources / good / to / alternative
_____

3 people / jams / about / many / complain / something / traffic / are / that
_____

4 solution / on / light bulbs / might / low-energy / be / spend / good / a / to / money
_____

5 care / is / you / that / ecology / about / something ?
_____

6 issues / you / particularly / about / what / are / ecological / worried ?
_____

7 forward / lecture / looking / are / to / which / you ?
_____

8 something / global / is / to / need / we / on / warming / work
_____

9 famous / achievement / for / he / what / is ?
_____

10 that / provided / we / she / pleased / a / were / with / solution
_____

2 Complete the second sentence so that it has a similar meaning to the first.

1 My dad is really proud of climbing Mont Blanc.
  Climbing Mont Blanc _____ .
2 It's rather difficult to deal with pollution in big cities.
  Pollution in big cities _____ .
3 It's really interesting to listen to his lectures on the Amazon rainforests.
  His lectures about the Amazon rainforests
  _____ .
4 The government should spend more money on eco-friendly solutions.
  Eco-friendly solutions _____ .
5 It's dangerous to swim in a fast-flowing mountain river.
  A fast-flowing mountain river _____ .
6 Schools must focus on educating children about the environment.
  Educating children about the environment
  _____ .
7 What he's anxious about is climate change.
  Climate change _____ .
8 Can you comment on the issue?
  Is the issue _____ ?
9 She's capable of dealing with the problem.
  Dealing with the problem _____ .
10 What I want to ask about is volunteering for the animal charity.
  Volunteering for the animal charity _____ .

3 **UNIT REVIEW** Complete the sentences with the correct form of the words in brackets. Add articles or prepositions if necessary.

1 Which part of the project
  _____ (you/interested)?
2 The new ecological policy
  _____ (something/everybody/talk) now.
3 Recycling bins might be difficult
  _____ (get used).
4 My older sister is _____
  (somebody/you/always/rely).
5 I don't think he _____ (be/aware) these problems.
6 My uncle, _____ (whose/story/we/listen), is a keen traveller.
7 One of _____ (big) problems in developing countries is poverty.
  Poor access to education and healthcare is
  _____ (grow/problem) too.
8 Which members of staff
  _____ (be/responsible) the animals?
9 Canada, _____ (Ann/come), is particularly cold in the winter.
10 In my opinion, _____ (impress) city in the world is Paris.

REFERENCE AND PRACTICE

6.2 Second Conditional • wish/if only

Second Conditional sentences

We use **Second Conditional** sentences to talk about present situations or states which are impossible or very unlikely or about something that could happen in the future but is rather improbable:

If you **had** an accident, who **would** you **call** first?

Either of the two clauses can come first in the sentence. When the *if*-clause comes first, we use a comma after it.

If + Past Simple (condition),	would/wouldn't + infinitive (effect)
If he **cycled** to work every day,	he **would feel** healthier.
would/wouldn't + infinitive (effect)	if + Past Simple (condition)
He **would feel** healthier	if he **cycled** to work every day.

wish/if only

We use **wish/if only + Past Simple** to express dissatisfaction with a present situation:

I **wish/If only** people **cared** about their own health.

We use **wish/if only + would + infinitive** to talk about a present situation that we would like to be different, usually when we find it annoying. It usually refers to things we can't change or control:

I **wish/If only** my sister **would hurry up**!

If only expresses a stronger feeling of regret than the verb **wish**.

1 Complete the sentences with the correct form of the verbs in brackets. Use the Second Conditional.

1 I _____ (not take up) jogging if I _____ (have) breathing problems.
2 People in my city _____ (do) sport more often if there _____ (be) more sports centres.
3 What _____ (you/do) if your teacher _____ (ask) you to play in the school basketball team?
4 If my grandfather _____ (have) a dog, he _____ (go) for walks more often.
5 If you _____ (see) an accident, _____ (you/be) able to give someone first aid?
6 I _____ (not apply) for this job as a nurse in France if I _____ (not know) the language.
7 If Tiago _____ (have) a pet, I'm sure he _____ (look) after it well.
8 I think I _____ (speak) English much better if I _____ (spend) some time in the UK.
9 You _____ (not feel) tired if you _____ (go) to bed earlier instead of playing video games.
10 If I _____ (win) the lottery, I _____ (travel) around the world.

2 Choose the correct option.

1 My neighbours are very annoying. If only they *stop / 'd stop* their dog chasing after my cat!
2 My sister usually makes wrong decisions. If only she *follows / would follow* my advice!
3 I wish this pain *goes / would go* away.
4 I want to go to school today. I wish I *didn't have / wouldn't have* a temperature.
5 If only I *can / could* go to school by motorcycle!
6 I wish my leg *didn't / doesn't* hurt so much.

3 Choose the correct option, A, B or C.

1 If he ___ allergic to pollen, he would spend more time outdoors.
   A wouldn't be   B wasn't   C isn't
2 I wish my brother ___ get over his laziness.
   A would   B should   C will
3 If only I ___ more time, I would take up yoga.
   A have   B will have   C had
4 I wish my grandma ___ infections so often.
   A doesn't catch   B wouldn't catch   C won't catch
5 They would feel better if they ___ a bit more.
   A exercise   B would exercise   C exercised
6 Martha ___ a professional swimmer if she didn't suffer from asthma.
   A will be   B would be   C was

4 Rewrite the second sentence so that it has a similar meaning to the first. Use the words in capitals.

1 I often feel dizzy and that is why I cannot do much jogging. **IF ONLY**
   _____.
2 Unfortunately, Kate often has headaches. I feel sorry for her. **WISH**
   I _____.
3 I'm not you. But my suggestion is: take up a sport. **IF**
   _____.
4 Paul doesn't practise enough. That is why he has poor results. **WOULD**
   If Paul _____.
5 My brother doesn't want to see a doctor. It makes me sad. **ONLY**
   If _____.
6 Unfortunately, I don't have many friends. **WISH**
   I _____.
7 Stop complaining and get down to work! **WISH**
   I _____.

GRAMMAR AND USE OF ENGLISH

6.5 Third Conditional

We use **Third Conditional** sentences to talk about possible events in the past that did not happen. We often use them to express regret or criticism.

*If I **had worn** a helmet, I **wouldn't have got** hurt so badly during the fall.*

***Would** you **have reached** the top earlier if you **had chosen** a different route?*

We use the **Past Perfect** in the *if*-clause (describing the condition). In the main clause (describing the effect), we use **would/wouldn't + have + the Past Participle** of the main verb.

Either of the two clauses can come first in the sentence. When the *if*-clause comes first, we use a comma after it.

If + Past Perfect (condition),	would/wouldn't have + Past Participle (effect).
*If I **had cycled** more carefully,*	*I **wouldn't have broken** my arm.*
would/wouldn't have + Past Participle (effect)	if + Past Perfect (condition).
*I **wouldn't have broken** my arm*	*if I **had cycled** more carefully.*

1 Match the sentence halves.

1. We would have lost our way in the wood ☐
2. Susie wouldn't have cycled to school ☐
3. If you had left earlier, ☐
4. If my mum hadn't packed any food, ☐
5. The climbers would have been in serious danger ☐
6. If she had known his true nature, ☐
7. If I had known this activity was illegal, ☐
8. If Tom had prepared for the trip better, ☐

a she wouldn't have married him.
b I would have been very hungry.
c if the rescue team hadn't arrived so quickly.
d you would have caught the train.
e if she had known it was going to rain.
f if we hadn't had our GPS with us.
g I would never have signed the contract.
h he would have enjoyed it much more.

2 Complete the sentences. Use the Third Conditional.

1. _____ (the explorers/survive) if they _____ (take) better equipment?
2. If Liu _____ (not warn) me, I _____ (make) a serious mistake.
3. If you _____ (leave) an hour earlier, _____ (you/miss) the plane?
4. If I _____ (not take) a torch with me, I _____ (not find) my way out.
5. What _____ (you/do) if your parents _____ (not let) you take a gap year?
6. I'm convinced that Rory _____ (pass) his exams if he _____ (study) all year.

3 Rewrite the sentences in the Third Conditional.

1. They didn't reach the North Pole because they ran out of food.
   _____
2. I was tired yesterday, so I didn't go out with my friends.
   _____
3. It took us ages to get to the airport because there was a lot of traffic.
   _____
4. Ann didn't phone me, so I didn't know about her problems with the equipment.
   _____
5. He had an accident in the mountains and had to go to hospital.
   _____
6. Gina didn't use a mosquito net, so a mosquito bit her and she became ill with malaria.
   _____
7. Joe didn't wear warm clothes last weekend, so he caught a cold.
   _____
8. We didn't reach our destination because the weather conditions were very bad.
   _____
9. Rami left the party early because it was boring.
   _____
10. Betty didn't take part in the marathon because she didn't have time to train.
    _____

4 Choose the correct option.

1. If we *would have / hadn't* eaten that food, we *wouldn't have had / wouldn't have* indigestion yesterday.
2. If I *wouldn't have / hadn't* felt ill last week, I *would have / had* gone to school.
3. They *would have been / had been* late if they *wouldn't have / hadn't* taken a taxi.
4. If Sue *would have / had* known about the meeting sooner, *would she have / she had* agreed to go there?
5. Rob *wouldn't have had / hadn't had* a temperature yesterday if he *would have / had* put on a coat and a hat.
6. *Would you have / Had you* told them the truth if they *would have / had* asked you then?
7. If Mia *would have been / had been* there before, she *wouldn't have / had* got lost.
8. I *wouldn't have / hadn't* called Mike if I *would have / had* known he was busy.
9. If I *had gone / would go* to Italy instead of Bea, I'm sure I *would have done / would do* more sightseeing than shopping.
10. He *wouldn't / would* have had so many problems if he *had talked / talked* to somebody at the time.

REFERENCE AND PRACTICE

6.6 Clauses of purpose

You can use clauses of purpose to say why somebody does something.

Clauses of purpose are formed using a **to + infinitive** or **not to + infinitive**.

In a more formal style, you can also use **in order (not) to + infinitive** / **so as (not) to + infinitive**.

Mia worked at a local surgery as a receptionist **to earn** some money for her medical studies.

The doctor told me **not to chew** the tablets.

The paramedic gave Philip an injection **in order to ease** the pain.

We slept under a mosquito net **in order not to be bitten** by insects.

The children's ward was painted in bright colours **so as to cheer up** the little patients.

You should stop eating sweets **so as not to gain** weight.

You can also form clauses of purpose using **so that** + sentence containing a **modal verb**.

- **can** to talk about the present:
  I go jogging every day **so that I can run** a marathon one day.
- **could/would** to talk about the past:
  The hospital was closed for visitors **so that the patients wouldn't catch** the flu.

1 Choose the correct option.

1 My doctor told me *to not / not to* drink coffee.
2 When you go trekking, put on good boots *in order / so that* not to sprain your ankle.
3 Paul took up swimming *so as / so that* to stay in good shape.
4 They're organising a concert so that they *can / could* raise money for charity.
5 Kate attends yoga classes *so as / so that* she can feel better.
6 They trained every day so that they *can / could* belong to an emergency team.
7 My trainer told me *not to / don't* lift anything heavy.
8 They went on a diet *in order / so that* they could lose weight.

2 Choose the correct option, A, B or C.

1 You should go to bed early ___ get enough sleep.
   A so that   B in order   C so as to
2 They've run into the burning house so that they ___ rescue the people.
   A can   B could   C would
3 Her dentist advised her ___ too many sugary foods.
   A not to eat   B to not eat   C not eat
4 He became a vet ___ care for animals.
   A so that   B in order to   C could
5 I've bought some workout clothes ___ I can join a gym.
   A in order   B so as to   C so that
6 Be careful when you use this equipment ___ injure yourself.
   A so that not   B so as not to   C in order to not

3 Complete the second sentence so that it has a similar meaning to the first. Use the words in capitals.

1 If you want to get better, take more vitamins. **ORDER**
   Take more vitamins _____ better.
2 Dan put on protective gloves because he didn't want to burn his hands. **SO AS**
   Dan put on protective gloves _____ his hands.
3 They didn't want to get bitten by mosquitoes so they stayed in in the evening. **SO THAT**
   They stayed in in the evening _____ by mosquitoes.
4 She put on a warm coat because she didn't want to catch a cold. **ORDER**
   She put on a warm coat _____ a cold.
5 Meg gets up at six because she wants to do some stretching. **SO THAT**
   Meg gets up at six _____ some stretching.
6 His finger was bleeding so Mark put a plaster on it. **WOULD**
   Mark put a plaster on his finger _____ bleeding.
7 To see the specialist, she made an appointment. **SO AS**
   She made an appointment _____ the specialist.
8 He said to me that I shouldn't go jogging in extreme weather. **TO**
   He told me _____ in extreme weather.

4 UNIT REVIEW Complete the text with one word in each gap.

Our busy lifestyles can put pressure on both adults' and teenagers' well-being. Experts claim that if teenagers [1]_____ five portions of fruit and vegetables a day, they wouldn't feel tired so often. They should also choose water as a drink rather than soft drinks so [2]_____ to avoid extra sugar. If teenagers [3]_____ been shown how to choose healthy foods, they would [4]_____ developed good eating habits in childhood.

Another vital thing is getting enough sleep so that their bodies [5]_____ rest properly. Young people should do physical activity on a regular basis in [6]_____ to stay the right weight.

149

GRAMMAR AND USE OF ENGLISH

7.2 Reported Speech – statements

When we want to report what someone said, we can use **Direct** or **Reported Speech**.

In Direct Speech the speaker's words are not changed in any way:

'Your son draws well.' → They said, 'Your son draws well.'

In Reported Speech we often report the speaker's words using verbs like *add, claim, explain, point out, reply, say, suggest, tell* and the pronoun *that* (which can be omitted). The verb *tell* takes an object (*me, us, John, my friend,* etc.).

'I **sell** paintings.' → She **told me/said (that)** she **sold** paintings.

We make the following changes in Reported Speech:

- tenses:

Direct Speech	→	Reported Speech
Present Simple Ann: 'I paint pictures.'	→	**Past Simple** Ann said (that) she painted pictures.
Present Continuous Ann: 'I am painting a picture.'	→	**Past Continuous** Ann said (that) she was painting a picture.
Present Perfect Ann: 'I have painted two pictures.'	→	**Past Perfect** Ann said (that) she had painted two pictures.
Past Simple Ann: 'I didn't paint it.'	→	**Past Perfect** Ann said (that) she hadn't painted it.
Past Perfect Ann: 'I hadn't painted before.'	→	**Past Perfect** Ann said (that) she hadn't painted before.
can/can't Ann: 'I can paint.'	→	**could/couldn't** Ann said (that) she could paint.
will/won't Ann: 'I won't paint anymore.'	→	**would/wouldn't** Ann said (that) she wouldn't paint anymore.
am/is/are going to Ann: 'I'm going to paint.'	→	**was/were going to** Ann said (that) she was going to paint.

- time expressions and words referring to places (depending on the context):

now → at that time/then
today → that day
yesterday → the day before
two hours ago → two hours earlier/before
tomorrow → the following day
next → the following
last → the previous
here → there

- time expressions and words referring to places (depending on the context):

this/these → that/those
I/we → he/she/they
me/us → him/her/them
my → his/her
our → their

1 Complete the second sentence so that it has a similar meaning to the first.

1 'I've never heard of this artist,' said Susan.
  Susan said _____.
2 'Dad, I'm meeting Ann tomorrow,' said Helen.
  Helen told _____.
3 'Yesterday someone painted some graffiti in my street,' said Olga.
  Olga said _____.
4 'I can sell you some of my pictures,' Paul said to me.
  Paul told _____.
5 'My wife doesn't collect paintings,' said George.
  George said _____.
6 'You cannot take photos here,' the guard told me.
  The guard said _____.
7 'I'm not going to point out anybody,' said Alice.
  Alice said _____.
8 'My sister signed a recording contract last week,' Rob said to me.
  Rob told me _____.
9 'We can't stay here much longer', said Lara.
  Lara said _____.
10 'I'll come over at 10 o'clock tomorrow and help you pack', said Nadia to me.
  Nadia told me _____.

2 Report what John and Amanda said. Choose the correct verb and complete the sentences.

1 **Journalist:** In your opinion, who is the most talented British painter?
  John: Of course, I'm the most talented painter in the UK.
  John *claimed / added* _____.
2 **Teacher:** Are you interested in arts?
  Amanda: I like opera. And I like modern art too.
  Amanda said _____
  and she *added / replied* _____.
3 **Nancy:** You've lived here for about a year now, haven't you?
  John: No, we moved here in 2010.
  John *suggested / explained* _____.
4 **Wendy:** Will your parents let you go to the club?
  Amanda: No, my parents will never let me go to the club.
  Amanda *replied / suggested* _____.
5 **John:** Someone has made a mistake.
  Tina: Let me check it.
  John *pointed out / replied* _____.
6 **Wendy:** Have you seen the new Bond film yet?
  Amanda: No, but I'm going to see it this weekend.
  Amanda said _____ but she
  pointed out / added _____.

150

REFERENCE AND PRACTICE

7.5 Reported Speech – questions and imperatives

Questions

To report questions, we use the verb **ask** and make the same changes as in reported statements (tenses, pronouns, time expressions, words referring to places, etc.)

- When we report yes/no questions, we use **if** or **whether**:
  'Has Darina answered all the questions?' → Jan asked me **if/whether** Darina had answered all the questions.
  'Do you often watch TV?' → I asked her **if/whether** she often watched TV.

- When we report wh- questions, we keep the question word (e.g. what, who, how, where, when):
  'How old are you?' → The policeman asked the boy how old he was.
  'When did John and Mary split up?' → Sam asked us when John and Mary had split up.

Imperatives

To report imperatives, we use the verbs **ask** or **tell**, an **object** (noun or pronoun) and **(not) to + infinitive**:
'Please stop talking!' → The director **asked us to stop talking**.
'Don't take any photos of me!' → Darina **told the reporter not to take** any photos of her.

1 Complete the sentences with the correct pronouns.

1 'Has your cousin directed a film before?' Sue asked Tom.
   _____ asked _____ whether _____ cousin had directed a film.
2 'Switch on your tablets,' Miss Smith asked her students.
   _____ asked _____ to switch on _____ tablets.
3 'What are you doing with my DVDs?' Jake asked Mary.
   _____ asked _____ what _____ was doing with _____ DVDs.
4 'Don't use your mobile phones in class!' the teacher told us.
   The teacher asked _____ not to use _____ mobile phones.
5 'Where did you first meet your best friend?' Ann asked me.
   _____ asked _____ where _____ had first met _____ best friend.
6 'Join us!' Jake and Ron told us.
   _____ told _____ to join _____.
7 'Did you enjoy the horror film?' Nick asked Sally.
   _____ asked _____ if _____ had enjoyed the horror film.
8 'Will you come with me to the concert?' Angela asked her friends.
   _____ asked _____ if _____ would go to the concert with her.
9 'Film your dog chasing the ball!' Tim and Tom told us.
   _____ told _____ to film _____ dog chasing the ball.
10 'Don't give our tickets to Peter!' Gill and Luke said to me.
   _____ told _____ not to give _____ tickets to Peter.

2 Complete the second sentence so that it has a similar meaning to the first. Use reported speech.

1 'Please, close the window,' the teacher said to Sara.
   The teacher asked _____ .
2 'Don't interrupt me!' she told John.
   She told _____ .
3 'Don't be late for lunch again, Helen' said Dad.
   Dad asked _____ .
4 'Stop watching TV and do you homework!' my mum said to me.
   My mum told _____ .
5 'Please, come in and wait for me in the living room,' Gary told us.
   Gary asked _____ .
6 'Don't ask me about my ex-husband again,' the film star told the journalist.
   The film star told _____ .
7 'Please give me your phone' my brother said to me.
   My brother asked _____ .
8 'Be quiet while I watch the movie,' she said to us.
   She told _____ .
9 'Ask her for a selfie,' Joe said to Bob.
   Joe told _____ .
10 'Don't play your music loudly,' my dad said to me.
   My dad told _____ .

3 Complete the second sentence so that it has a similar meaning to the first. Use reported speech.

1 'Are you interested in art?' the teacher asked Jack.
   The teacher asked _____ in art.
2 'How often does your boss update his Facebook profile?' Jen asked me.
   Jen asked _____ Facebook profile.
3 'Are you going to see this film again?' Jim asked Ann.
   Jim asked _____ again.
4 'Will you give us an autograph?' the boys asked the actress.
   The boys asked _____ an autograph.
5 'When did you lose your mobile phone?' Nick asked Eve.
   Nick asked _____ her mobile phone.
6 'Has Paula painted all these pictures herself?' I asked Olga.
   I asked _____ herself.
7 'Can I borrow your tablet?' Jim asked him.
   Jim asked _____ .
8 'Is this the best film you've ever seen?' he asked me.
   He asked _____ .
9 'Have you finished writing your novel?' I asked Jane.
   I asked _____ .
10 'Will they let us take photos?' they asked us.
   They asked _____ .

GRAMMAR AND USE OF ENGLISH

7.6 Nouns

Countable nouns have a singular and a plural form:
a review – reviews

The plural of nouns:
- is formed by adding the following endings:
  -s
  a play – plays, a vocalist – vocalists
  -ies, when the noun ends with a consonant + *-y*:
  a story – stories, a comedy – comedies
  -es, when the noun ends with *-s, -ss, -x, -ch, -sh*:
  a watch – watches, a sketch – sketches
  -ves, when the noun ends with *-fe, -f*:
  a shelf – shelves, life – lives
- may be the same as the singular form:
  a species – species, a series – series, a fish – fish
- may differ from the singular form:
  a man – men, a tooth – teeth

Uncountable nouns
- only have a singular form:
  ***Knowledge is** the key to the door of happiness.*
  *Don't you think that your **hair is** a bit too short?*
- in sentences, you only use a singular verb form:
  *The lead guitarist's **luggage hasn't arrived** yet so we can't start the rehearsals.*
- are used with such expressions of quantity as: **some**, **much**, **a piece of**:
  *Last night **there was much traffic** in the city centre because of a light show.*
- end with *-s* and although they look like plural nouns, they are uncountable and singular: *news, physics, politics, statistics*.

You can't put *a/an* or a number in front of uncountable nouns:
Tom gave me two pieces of contradictory information about the concert. (NOT Tom gave me two contradictory informations.)

Plural nouns
- only have a plural form and you can't put *a/an* or a number in front of them:
  *Where exactly **are the police headquarters**?*
- some of them consist of two parts (e.g. clothes) and are used with *a pair of*:
  *I bought **a pair of trousers** and a jacket yesterday.*

1 Choose the correct option.

1 The police *is / are* looking for the stolen painting.
2 Statistics *is / are* quite a difficult subject.
3 The fish in the Red Sea *is / are* absolutely amazing.
4 My new furniture *hasn't / haven't* been delivered yet.
5 The latest news *was / were* really shocking.
6 My new pair of jeans *is / are* really trendy.

2 Complete the sentences with the correct form of the words in the box.

> fish hand luggage information jewellery
> person politics sheep shelf skin species

1 **A:** How much _____ are you allowed on a plane?
  B: Just one piece, I think.
2 There were quite a few famous _____ at that gig.
3 We need a few more pieces of _____ about the venue before we book it.
4 Apparently, more than 5,000 _____ are endangered worldwide.
5 There were not many _____ grazing on the meadow. Just a few.
6 How many _____ do we still need for our books? Will three be enough?
7 The movie star wore an expensive piece of _____ to the film premiere.
8 That actor is interested in _____ and social issues.
9 After spending the summer on a tropical island, their _____ was quite dark.
10 You need three or four _____ to make this soup.

3 Complete the sentences with the words in the box.

> are is (x2) many much one

1 **A:** Where can we stay in this town?
  B: I'm afraid there aren't _____ accommodation options.
2 **A:** *Stranger Things* _____ the best series ever!
  B: It's OK, but I prefer *Dark*. The plot's more complex.
3 **A:** Do you read _____ in your free time?
  B: Yes, I do. I love reading good books.
4 **A:** What _____ the police doing here?
  B: I think there's been an accident.
5 **A:** Oh look, Amy's brought some cakes. Would you like _____?
  B: Yes, please!
6 **A:** Tell me about your new job. It must be exciting!
  B: Well, I like it, but politics _____ more stressful than I'd expected.

4 UNIT REVIEW Choose the correct option.

1 I need *a new pair of glasses / new glasses*.
2 My friend gave me *some / a few* advice, which helped me a lot.
3 They *said / told* us not to go to that exhibition.
4 There is *a lot of / many* research into different aspects of pop culture.
5 The journalist wanted to know when she *was / is* going to sign a recording contract.
6 After the show, Harry asked Anna if she *had enjoyed / enjoyed* it.
7 I like your new shorts. Where did you get *it / them*?
8 She asked me whether I *can / could* visit her.
9 The information I have for you *is / are* very important.
10 He *told / said* to me that he was happy with my work.

REFERENCE AND PRACTICE

8.2 The Passive

We use the **Passive** when we are more interested in the action itself than the 'doer' (the agent) of the action:
*This bank **has been robbed** three times.*
However, if we want to mention the agent, we need to use the word **by**:
*The bank **was robbed by** three men.*
We form the passive with an appropriate form of the verb **to be** and the Past Participle form of the main verb:
*The robbers **will be arrested** soon.*
*The robbers **have been arrested**.*
*The robbers **were arrested** last night.*

Present Simple	Too many crimes **are committed** every year.
Present Continuous	Tony **is being questioned** by the police.
Past Simple	When **was** the money **stolen**?
Past Continuous	The police station **was** still **being built** in 2005.
Present Perfect	A homeless shelter **has** just **been opened** in my town.
Past Perfect	Someone told me I **had been seen** at the crime scene.
will	He **will be sentenced** to at least ten years in prison.

1 Rewrite the sentences from active to passive forms. Use *by* where necessary.

1 Somebody has stolen my bicycle.
   _____ .
2 Somebody will clean the office later.
   _____ .
3 The police are using a new computer system to investigate crimes.
   _____ .
4 People destroyed twenty books at the city library last month.
   _____ .
5 Journalists were asking a lot of questions.
   _____ .
6 We have sold ten silver rings today.
   _____ .
7 Somebody found a wallet full of money yesterday.
   _____ .
8 Students at our school will remember Miss Jenkins, the head teacher.
   _____ .

2 Complete the sentences with the correct form of the verbs in brackets. Use the active or the passive forms.

1 a We didn't know anything about the results of the new project because we _____ (not inform) about it.
  b Our boss didn't know anything about the results of the new project because we _____ (not inform) him.
2 a I _____ (follow) him. I'm right behind him.
  b I _____ (follow). They're right behind me.
3 a I regularly _____ (donate) money to this charity.
  b How much money _____ (donate) to this charity every year?
4 a I'm sure scientists _____ (find) a solution in the future.
  b I'm sure a solution _____ (find) scientists in the future.
5 a He _____ (drive) to work in his car when I saw him yesterday.
  b He _____ (drive) to work in a taxi when I saw him yesterday
6 a They _____ (just/discover) a new animal species in Australia.
  b A new species of spider _____ (just/discover) in Australia.
7 a They _____ (not film) the episodes a few months ago.
  b The episodes _____ (not film) a few months ago.
8 a No one _____ (see) the eccentric actor in months.
  b The eccentric actor _____ (not see) by anybody in months.

3 Complete the sentences with the correct form of the verbs in the box. Use the passive forms.

| build   elect   employ   exclude   find   investigate |
| offer   organise   raise |

1 A new president _____ at the moment.
2 _____ the case still _____ by the police officers two days ago?
3 Amy _____ just _____ as the manager of the local animal shelter.
4 How often _____ the charity bake sale _____ at your school?
5 Tim told us he _____ a job as a prison psychologist two days before.
6 When _____ Peter _____ from school? Was it last week?
7 I don't think the stolen painting _____ very soon.
8 How much money _____ for charity since last month?
9 Politicians have promised that the new prison _____ next year.

153

GRAMMAR AND USE OF ENGLISH

8.5 Have something done

We use **have + object + Past Participle** to talk about things that we don't do ourselves but arrange for someone else (usually a professional) to do for us.

Present Simple	I **have my house cleaned** every Friday. (by a professional cleaner)
Present Continuous	**Are** you **having the locks changed**? (by a locksmith)
Past Simple	We **had the kitchen painted**. (by a professional painter)
Past Continuous	Last week Jack **was having his bathroom remodelled**. (by a specialist)
Present Perfect	They **have** just **had a pool installed** in the garden. (by a professional)
will	When **will** Helen **have the paintings hung** in her flat? (by a specialist)
be going to	When **are** you **going to have a garage built**? (by professionals)

We **will redecorate** our flat next year. (we will do it ourselves)
We will **have our flat redecorated** next year. (by specialists)
We can use **get** instead of **have**:
We **had** new windows fitted. = We **got** new windows fitted.

---

1 Complete the sentences with the correct form of *have*.

1 Last weekend I _____ my bike repaired, so I couldn't go for a bike ride.
2 A: _____ you _____ your wedding organised?
   B: Yes, we are. We're too busy to do it on our own.
3 Aunt Sophie is eighty years old and she doesn't cook any more. She _____ her meals delivered every day.
4 The windows look really shiny! _____ you _____ them cleaned recently?
5 A: Where did you buy your new wooden furniture?
   B: I _____ it designed and made by a carpenter.
6 Hi Sandra. Sorry, can I call you back later? I _____ my portrait painted at the moment.
7 I think it's best if we meet at your place. We _____ the bathroom redecorated and there's dust everywhere.
8 Of course Samantha's dress was expensive! She _____ it made specially for the party.

2 Will and Bill are neighbours. Rewrite the sentences for Will with *have something done*.

1 Bill cuts his grass twice a week.
   Will _____ twice a week.
2 After the storm last week Bill repaired his roof.
   After the storm last week Will _____ .
3 Bill is going to change his locks because of burglaries in the area.
   Will _____ because of burglaries in the area.
4 At 10 a.m. Bill was painting his garden wall.
   At 10 a.m. Will _____ .
5 Bill has just planted some apple trees.
   Will _____ .
6 Bill is building a tree house for his children.
   Will _____ for his children.
7 Bill will walk his dog in the afternoon.
   Will _____ in the afternoon.
8 At 4 p.m. Bill was washing his windows.
   At 4 p.m. Will _____ .
9 Bill cleans his carpets once a month.
   Will _____ once a month.

3 Complete the sentences with the correct form of the words in brackets. Use *have something done* where necessary.

1 a Susan is a hairdresser. She _____ (cut/people's hair) for money.
   b I'm afraid you can't see Joan yet. She's in her room with her hairdresser – she _____ (style/her hair).
   c When I was a little kid, I once _____ (cut/my hair) myself.
2 a Excuse me, could you _____ (take/a photo) of us, please?
   b I need to _____ (take/a photo) for my new passport.
   c You have to pay ten euros if you want to _____ (take/photos) inside the museum.
3 a I'm using public transport this week because my car is at the mechanic's. I _____ (it/repair).
   b Tom's a mechanic. He _____ (repair/cars).
   c We can _____ (repair/your car) at our garage. Here are our prices.
4 a Tom is a travel agent. He _____ (book/holidays) for other people.
   b Last year, we _____ (book/our holiday) by a travel agent.
   c I'm online right now and I _____ (book/my holiday).
5 a These wooden floors look old. Mum _____ (all of them/clean) by a professional at the moment.
   b I was exhausted because I _____ (clean/all the floors) on my own.
   c If you use this product, you _____ (clean/all your floors) really well.

REFERENCE AND PRACTICE

8.6 Reflexive pronouns

You use reflexive pronouns *myself, yourself, himself, herself, itself, ourselves, yourselves, themselves* when the subject and the direct or indirect object of a sentence are the same person or thing.
*Angela **injured herself** when she was trying to help an elderly woman.*

Personal pronouns	Reflexive pronouns
I	myself
you	yourself
he	himself
she	herself
it	itself
we	ourselves
you	yourselves
they	themselves

Verbs commonly used with reflexive pronouns: *behave, blame, cut, enjoy, express, hurt, injure, introduce, prepare, protect, teach*:
***Behave yourself** otherwise I'll call your parents.*

- You use reflexive pronouns to talk about the action related to the person who performs it:
  *Kate **looked at herself** in the mirror to see if she had removed all her make-up.*
- You use *by* + reflexive pronoun to underline that the action was done alone/without any help:
  *The boys **repaired** the park benches **by themselves** – nobody helped them.*

To describe a relation or an activity performed by two or more persons, you use *each other* and one *another*. You use them when the subject and object are different.
*The neighbours **accused each other/one another** of who had set fire to the garden shed.*

1 Choose the correct option.

1 They were friends but they blamed *themselves / each other* for what had happened.
2 Paula, stop talking about *yourself / yourselves*. Let the others say something about *them / themselves*.
3 The policeman collected all the evidence by *him / himself*.
4 They were all involved in that robbery but in court they thought only about *themselves / each other*.
5 The police found a new witness of that crime and interviewed *herself / her*.
6 Fortunately, they didn't punish *us / ourselves*.
7 I hurt *me / myself* when I was opening a tin of beans.
8 You're under a lot of stress. You should allow *yourself / you* to relax a bit.

2 Complete the sentences with the correct reflexive pronoun or Ø (no pronoun). Add the preposition *by* where necessary.

1 After a hard day, I made _____ a cup of tea, just to relax _____ .
2 The door opened _____ , the woman entered and introduced _____ .
3 When he was released from prison, Paul decided to learn _____ new skills and taught _____ some basic English.
4 They had known _____ for many years and never offered _____ a helping hand.
5 The suspect put the whole blame on _____ and said he had committed the crime all _____ .
6 We went to see the new James Bond and really enjoyed _____ .
7 The two strangers looked at _____ and realised they had been neighbours years ago.
8 My mum often talks to _____ when she's doing the housework.
9 Alex burnt _____ when he was lighting the barbecue.
10 Be careful, boys! You could fall _____ and injure _____ !

3 UNIT REVIEW Complete the second sentence so that it has a similar meaning to the first.

1 When the burglary took place, she was at home completely alone.
When the burglary took place, she was at home all _____.
2 A good alarm system can give you protection against robbery.
You can protect _____.
3 She entered the courtroom and said what her name was.
She entered the courtroom and _____.
4 Yesterday at 9 a.m. the police were transporting the suspect to the court.
Yesterday at 9 a.m. the suspect _____.
5 Tomorrow, a man is coming to change all the locks in our house.
Tomorrow, we _____.
6 They have just installed an alarm in our flat.
We _____.
7 She was jogging when she fell. Now her foot hurts.
She _____ when she was jogging.
8 Someone is going to install a dishwasher for us tomorrow.
We _____ tomorrow.

PREPOSITIONS

PREPOSITIONS IN PHRASES

AT
at a (house) party/wedding (3.7): *I met him at a party a couple of months ago.*
at the beach/a ski resort (3.3): *We stayed at a well-known Swiss ski resort.*
at work/home/school/university (1.1): *Dad's at work.*

FOR
for charity (1.1): *The children collected over fifty toys for charity.*
for instance (4.4): *We can cut down on food waste, for instance by sharing food with other people.*

IN
in a boat (3.1): *He's crossing the river in a boat.*
in a crisis (1.3): *It's important to have employees you can rely on in a crisis.*
in a queue (1.5): *We stood in a queue for half an hour.*
in addition (5.7): *The school has twelve classrooms. In addition, there is a large office that could be used for meetings.*
in bagage reclaim (3.2): *The plane landed over an hour ago. Bill must still be in baggage reclaim.*
in common (2.3): *I found I had a lot in common with Jo.*
in conclusion (5.7): *In conclusion, I would like to say how much I have enjoyed myself today.*
in fact (1.2): *I know the mayor really well. In fact, I had dinner with her last week.*
in love with (2.7): *I fell in love with bungee jumping.*
in other words (7.4): *So he is a fraud, a common thief in other words.*
in prison (8.1): *He was sentenced to five years in prison.*
in shape (2.1): *She's bought an exercise bike to keep in shape.*
in spite of (3.4): *We went out in spite of the rain.*
in the background/middle/foreground (1.8): *In the background you can see my college friends.*
in the centre (5.2): *The capital city is located in the centre of the country.*
in the middle (of) (1.8): *Alan was standing in the middle of the room.*
in the mind (2.5): *He's one of those doctors who say you're not really sick and it's all in the mind.*
in the photo/picture/poster (1.1): *In the photo you can see a group of teenagers.*
(just) in time (6.5): *They weren't late, they arrived just in time for dinner.*
in your early/mid/late twenties (1.7): *She was in her early twenties when I met her.*
in your teens (1.7): *He was in his teens when he started playing the violin.*

OF
of course (2.5): *Of course, there are exceptions to every rule.*
of all time (7.1): *What's your favourite hit single of all time?*

ON
on a plane (3.1): *You can't talk to him now. He's on a plane over the Atlantic.*
on a campsite (5.4): *We'll stay on a campsite outside the village.*
on a night out (1.1): *I met him on a night out.*
on average (8.2): *On average, men still earn more than women.*
on land (3.1): *The crocodile lays its eggs on land.*
on stage (7.1): *If you mess up on stage, don't worry about it.*
on the loose (3.2): *The police have issued a warning about a dangerous criminal on the loose.*
on the one hand (5.7): *On the one hand, there are several arguments for making contact.*
on the other hand (5.7): *On the other hand, there are also many arguments against making contact.*
on the road (=travelling) (3.1): *We were on the road just one hour after landing.*
on the way (to) (8.4): *She should be on the way to Brighton by now.*
on time (7.1): *Always turn up on time. Being late doesn't make a good impression.*
on top (4.1): *The cake was a bit burnt on top.*
on your own (8.6): *I've been living on my own for two years.*

PREPOSITIONS AFTER NOUNS
a couple of (3.1): *There are a couple of girls waiting for you.*
advantages/disadvantages of (3.4): *One of the many advantages of living in New York is that you can eat out at almost any time of day.*
amount of (4.4): *They spend equal amounts of time in California and New York.*
combination of (4.7): *The menu you suggested represents an ideal combination of healthy and exciting food.*
contact with (5.7): *Animals become stressed because of contact with zoo visitors.*
flight from (3.1): *There are two non-stop flights from London to Tehran daily.*
break from (2.4): *I wanted a break from university life.*
leader of (5.5): *He is the leader of the local community.*
means of transport (3.1): *For most people, the car is still their main means of transport.*
member of (1.4): *He is a member of the local tennis club.*
number of (2.1): *The number of people using this technology is increasing daily.*
pain in (6.8): *I had a nasty pain in my leg.*
parts of the body (6.1): *More heat is lost through the head than any other part of the body.*
plenty of (2.5): *No need to hurry – you've got plenty of time.*
prize for (2.1): *The prize for best original screenplay has been won by a young British writer.*
programme about (1.3): *There's a programme about killer whales in ten minutes.*
relationship with (1.3): *I have a good relationship with my parents.*
sense of humour (1.7): *It's vital to have a sense of humour in this job.*
slice of (7.4): *Can you pass me a slice of bread?*
variety of (4.3): *The girls come from a variety of different backgrounds.*
way of life (5.7): *The British way of life is not much different from ours.*

PREPOSITIONS AFTER VERBS
be into sth (1.7): *I'm really into folk music.*
be made of/from (1.4): *Paper is made from wood. This shirt is made of silk.*
be there for sb (1.3): *That's what I loved about my father – he was always there for me.*
blame sb for (8.6): *Marie still blames herself for Patrick's accident.*
charge sb with sth (8.1): *Gibbons has been charged with murder.*
come first/last in (2.1): *The choir came first in all sections of the competition.*
compete in (2.1): *He'd like to compete in the 1,000 metres.*
cover sth in (4.1): *I'm making a pizza and I want to cover it in cheese.*
die from (5.4): *The drug will not help patients who are dying from cancer.*
donate money to (6.3): *Last year he donated $1,000 to cancer research.*
escape from (3.2): *He escaped from prison in October.*
feel about (4.7): *How would you feel about working with Nicole for a while?*
get rid of (2.1): *You should get rid of all these old toys.*
learn from (7.1): *We learn from our mistakes.*
lose touch with (1.3): *I'm moving abroad, but I don't want to lose touch with you.*
make contact with (5.7): *We'd like to make contact with other schools in the area.*
nominate sb for sth (7.5): *Ferraro was nominated for the job of vice president.*
pay for (3.3): *Mum paid for my driving lessons.*
play for (2.1): *Moxon played for England in ten matches.*
raise money for (6.3): *We're organising a concert to raise money for charity.*
recover from (6.4): *He's in hospital, recovering from a heart attack.*
release from (8.3): *Mike was released from hospital yesterday.*
report on (1.2): *The Times sent her to Bangladesh to report on the floods.*
sentence to (8.1): *Sanchez was sentenced to three years in prison.*
share with (6.3): *I have an office that I share with some other teachers.*
take part in (2.1): *About 400 students took part in the protest.*
train for (6.3): *Brenda spends two hours a day training for the marathon.*
travel by air/car/train (3.5): *Emma and Jo travelled by train across Eastern Europe.*
vote for (7.5): *I voted for the Labour candidate in the last election.*
work for (1.2): *He works for a law firm.*
worry about (1.6): *I worry about my brother.*

PREPOSITIONS AFTER ADJECTIVES
addicted to (8.7): *Fifty million Americans are addicted to nicotine.*
allergic to (4.8): *I'm allergic to onions.*
aware of (8.7): *Most smokers are aware of the dangers of smoking.*
dependent on (8.8): *You don't earn money, so you are still dependent on your parents for everything.*
famous for (5.2): *Italy is famous for its olive oil.*
good/bad for (2.4): *Watching so much TV isn't good for you.*
guilty of (8.1): *They were found guilty of murder.*
important for (2.8): *It was important for the president to continue his visit.*
independent from (8.8): *I think we should learn to be independent from our parents.*
interested in (1.1): *He's interested in computer games.*
involved in (8.1): *How many politicians are involved in the scandal?*
open to new ideas (1.7): *Here at PLX, we listen to our employees. We're always open to new ideas.*
passionate about (4.4): *I'm passionate about football.*
proud of (1.1): *Her parents are very proud of her.*
responsible for (5.8): *He's the man responsible for the Oklahoma bombing.*
sure about (2.8): *Are you quite sure about this?*
unusual for (8.7): *It's unusual for Dave to be late.*

OTHER
because of (1.4): *He had to retire because of health problems.*
by the end of (2.7): *Costs will double by the end of 2025.*
thanks to (3.4): *She learnt new things about the world thanks to her smartphone.*

PHRASAL VERBS

Use a dictionary to translate the phrasal verbs into your language.

base sth on sth (1.2) – _____ : He has based his theory on scientific facts and figures.
beat yourself up (7.1) – _____ : When you make a mistake, don't beat yourself up – we learn from our mistakes.
break down (3.6) – _____ : What happened when the car broke down?
break into (8.1) – _____ : In the past, burglars used to break into houses to steal TVs and DVD players.
burn off sth (2.1) – _____ : If you work out at the gym, you burn off calories.
call on sb (8.8) – _____ : Why don't you call on Mary and see how she's feeling?
carry on (3.6) – _____ : You'll make yourself seriously ill if you carry on working so much.
cheer sb on (2.1) – _____ : There were thousands of fans in the stadium, all cheering their team on.
come across as (1.1) – _____ : Be careful you don't come across as shallow or vain.
come across sb/sth (5.1) – _____ : I came across this photograph among some old newspapers.
come from (1.1) – _____ : His father came from France.
come in (of tide) (5.1) – The tide comes in.
come out (7.1) – _____ : When does his new book come out?
concentrate on sth (2.5) – _____ : I want to concentrate on my career for a while.
cut sth off (4.1) – _____ : I only like lean meat so I cut off the fat and leave it on the side of my plate.
cut sb off from sth (3.4) – _____ : It's common to complain that computers cut us off from reality.
deal with sth (5.6) – _____ : These kinds of fires are very difficult to deal with.
die out (5.1) – _____ : The wild population of koalas is in danger of dying out.
dress up (1.1) – _____ : It's only a small party. You don't need to dress up.
drop sb off (3.6) – _____ : I'll drop you off on my way home.
drop out (of sth) (2.1) – _____ : Bill dropped out of college after his first year.
fall into sth (5.5) – _____ : I slipped and fell into the hole.
fall off sth (2.2) – _____ : He fell off his bike and broke his wrist.
fall out (with sb) (1.3) – _____ : Nina's fallen out with her brother.
fall over (2.4) – _____ : My hair keeps falling over my eyes.
find sth out (1.3) – _____ : We never found out who sent the letter.
get along/on (well) with sb (1.3) – _____ : They get along really well together.
get into sth (2.1) – _____ : You'll have to work harder if you want to get into university.
get off (3.6) – _____ : Let's get off at the next stop.
get out of sth (8.4) – _____ : There's a reason to get out of bed in the morning.
give sth away (8.4) – _____ : In my local coffee shop, I tried to give away a cup of coffee.
give (sth) up (2.3) – _____ : Mark has given up trying to teach me to ski.

go ahead (7.8) – _____ : 'Do you mind if I open the window?' 'No, go ahead.'
go away (3.3) – _____ : We're going away for the weekend.
go in for sth (2.1) – _____ : I go in for competitions.
go off – _____ : 1. (5.4) The cheese and bread had to be eaten before they went off. 2. (5.4) I continue sleeping in spite of my alarm going off in the morning.
go out – _____ : 1. (4.4) Are we going out tomorrow? 2. (of tide) (5.1) Where does the water depth only change by ten centimetres when the tide comes in and goes out?
go over to sb/sth (5.5) – _____ : The gorilla went over to the boy.
go through sth (8.4) – _____ : Dave went through his pockets looking for the keys.
hand sth over (2.4) – _____ : I handed over my bag but took out one racket.
hang out with sb (1.3) – _____ : They hang out with their friends a lot.
heat sth up (5.1) – _____ : I heated up the remains of last night's supper.
hold sb up (3.6) – _____ : I don't want to hold you up – I know you're in a hurry.
hurry up (4.2) – _____ : Hurry up! We'll miss the bus.
keep up with sb (3.6) – _____ : Dave isn't keeping up with the rest of the class in reading.
let sb down (2.1) – _____ : Sometimes it's difficult when you let your team down.
lock sb (up) (8.3) – _____ : The guards locked the prisoner up in the cell.
look after sb/sth (1.5) – _____ : We look after his children in the evening.
look at sb/sth (1.1) – _____ : 'It's time to go,' said Patrick, looking at his watch.
look into sth (7.4) – _____ : We're looking into the cause of the fire.
look up to sb (2.3) – _____ : He looks up to his older brother.
make sth into sth (8.2) – _____ : It has been made into a museum.
make sth out (1.8) – _____ : I can't make the sign out.
mess up (7.1) – _____ : If you mess up on stage, don't worry about it. Just carry on.
pick sth up (2.3) – _____ : She picked up how to windsurf as soon as she could swim.
pick sb up (3.6) – _____ : Mum's picking me up at midday.
point out (7.2) – _____ : Art critics pointed out that a child could not produce those paintings.
pull over (3.6) – _____ : He pulled the car over.
put sth in (8.5) – _____ : They're having a new bathroom put in.
put sb off sth (2.3) – _____ : Don't be put off by the title – it's a really good book!
put sth on (2.4) – _____ : Put your hat on – it's cold outside.
put on (7.1) – _____ : One summer the children put on a play.
put on (weight) (7.5) – _____ : Mary put on weight when she quit smoking.
put sb up (3.6) – _____ : I was hoping Kenny could put me up for a few days.

put sth up (3.6) – _____ : The kids were putting a tent up in the garden.
rely on sb/sth (5.6) – _____ : We're relying on him to help.
run out of sth (3.6) – _____ : I've run out of milk.
sell out (4.2) – _____ : I'm sorry, but the tickets are all sold out.
set off (on a journey) (3.6) – _____ : We'd better set off now, before it gets dark.
set sth up (4.4) – _____ : In 2000, he set up his own company.
sign up for (7.1) – _____ : I'm thinking of signing up for a yoga course.
sit around (5.4) – _____ : We sat around for a bit, chatting.
sleep through sth (5.4) – _____ : How did you manage to sleep through that thunderstorm?
speed up (2.2) – _____ : The truck speeded up going down the hill.
split up with (7.5) – _____ : Eve's parents split up when she was three.
start out (7.1) – _____ : When the band first started out, they played at small clubs.
stay out (2.5) – _____ : She lets her children stay out until midnight.
stir sth up – _____ : 1. (5.1) The wind had stirred up a powdery red dust. 2. (7.3) These clips stirred up our emotions.
switch sth off (8.6) – _____ : My phone switches itself off if I don't use it for a while.
take after sb (2.3) – _____ : Sue takes after her Dad.
take sth away (8.8) – _____ : Voluntary work could take time away from your studies.
take sth off (2.4) – _____ : He took off his shoes.
take on (a challenge) (2.1) – _____ : I like taking on new challenges.
take sth up (2.5) – _____ : My best friend is going to take up running.
take up sth (8.8) – _____ : Voluntary work can take up a lot of time.
talk sb into sth (2.3) – _____ : Has anybody ever talked you into taking up a sport or joining a team?
throw sth away (4.4) – _____ : Do you need these newspapers, or can I throw them away?
try sth on (1.8) – _____ : Would you like to try these jeans on?
try sth out (2.3) – _____ : Can I try out your new motorbike?
turn into (3.6) – _____ : The company has turned into a global corporation.
turn up (3.6) – _____ : Danny turned up late as usual.
wake up (5.4) – _____ : I woke up at 7 a.m. today.
walk away from sth (3.6) – _____ : You can't just walk away from fifteen years of marriage!
wear off (7.1) – _____ : When you feel you are stuck, keep practising and eventually the feeling will wear off.
write back (4.7) – _____ : I sent them a card once, but they never wrote back.
work out – _____ : 1. (2.1) She works out at the gym twice a week. 2. (3.7) Don't worry. I'm sure everything will work out fine.

157

PRONOUNS & NUMERALS

SUBJECT, OBJECT AND POSSESSIVE PRONOUNS, POSSESSIVE ADJECTIVES

Subject pronouns	Object pronouns	Possessive pronouns (+ noun)	Possessive pronouns (no noun)
I'm a student.	Come with **me**.	It's **my** house.	It's **mine**.
Have **you** got a cat?	I like **you**.	It's **your** bike.	It's **yours**.
He works at home.	Can you help **him**?	It's **his** book.	It's **his**.
She's been to Prague.	Listen to **her**.	It's **her** room.	It's **hers**.
Is **it** a famous city?	I can't find **it**.	Oxford (= it) is famous for **its** university.	—
We live in Peru.	Wait for **us**.	It's **our** tablet.	It's **ours**.
You can't sit here.	Can I talk to **you**?	It's **your** car.	It's **yours**.
Are **they** working?	Do you know **them**?	It's **their** money.	It's **theirs**.

DEMONSTRATIVE, QUESTION AND RELATIVE PRONOUNS

Demonstrative pronouns		Question pronouns	Relative pronouns
Singular	Plural		
this that	these those	What? Who? Whose? Which? Where? When? Why? How? (How often? How long? How far? How much? How many?)	who which that whose when where

NUMBERS

Numbers: 1 – 100

Cardinal numbers	Ordinal numbers	Cardinal numbers	Ordinal numbers
1 – one	first (1st)	20 – twenty	twentieth (20th)
2 – two	second (2nd)	21 – twenty-one	twenty-first (21st)
3 – three	third (3rd)	22 – twenty-two	twenty-second (22nd)
4 – four	fourth (4th)	23 – twenty-three	twenty-third (23rd)
5 – five	fifth (5th)	24 – twenty-four	twenty-fourth (24th)
6 – six	sixth (6th)	25 – twenty-five	twenty-fifth (25th)
7 – seven	seventh (7th)	26 – twenty-six	twenty-sixth (26th)
8 – eight	eighth (8th)	27 – twenty-seven	twenty-seventh (27th)
9 – nine	ninth (9th)	28 – twenty-eight	twenty-eighth (28th)
10 – ten	tenth (10th)	29 – twenty-nine	twenty-ninth (29th)
11 – eleven	eleventh (11th)	30 – thirty	thirtieth (30th)
12 – twelve	twelfth (12th)	40 – forty	fortieth (40th)
13 – thirteen	thirteenth (13th)	50 – fifty	fiftieth (50th)
14 – fourteen	fourteenth (14th)	60 – sixty	sixtieth (60th)
15 – fifteen	fifteenth (15th)	70 – seventy	seventieth (70th)
16 – sixteen	sixteenth (16th)	80 – eighty	eightieth (80th)
17 – seventeen	seventeenth (17th)	90 – ninety	ninetieth (90th)
18 – eighteen	eighteenth (18th)	100 – one/a hundred	hundredth (100th)
19 – nineteen	nineteenth (19th)	101 – one/a hundred and one	hundred and first (101st)

Examples of numbers over 100

1,000 – one/a thousand
3,555 – three thousand, five hundred **and** fifty-five
56,223 – fifty-six thousand, two hundred **and** twenty-three
725,000 – seven hundred **and** twenty-five thousand
1,000,000 – one/a million
1,000,000,000 – one/a billion

IRREGULAR VERBS

Infinitive	Past Simple	Past Participle
be [biː]	was/were [wɒz/wɜː]	been [biːn]
beat [biːt]	beat [biːt]	beaten ['biːtn]
become [bɪ'kʌm]	became [bɪ'keɪm]	become [bɪ'kʌm]
begin [bɪ'gɪn]	began [bɪ'gæn]	begun [bɪ'gʌn]
bite [baɪt]	bit [bɪt]	bitten ['bɪtn]
bleed [bliːd]	bled [bled]	bled [bled]
blow [bləʊ]	blew [bluː]	blown [bləʊn]
break [breɪk]	broke [brəʊk]	broken ['brəʊkən]
bring [brɪŋ]	brought [brɔːt]	brought [brɔːt]
broadcast ['brɔːdkɑːst]	broadcast ['brɔːdkɑːst]	broadcast ['brɔːdkɑːst]
build [bɪld]	built [bɪlt]	built [bɪlt]
burn [bɜːn]	burned [bɜːnd]/burnt [bɜːnt]	burned [bɜːnd]/burnt [bɜːnt]
burst [bɜːst]	burst [bɜːst]	burst [bɜːst]
buy [baɪ]	bought [bɔːt]	bought [bɔːt]
can [kæn]	could [kʊd]	been able to [biːn 'eɪbl tə]
catch [kætʃ]	caught [kɔːt]	caught [kɔːt]
choose [tʃuːz]	chose [tʃəʊz]	chosen ['tʃəʊzn]
come [kʌm]	came [keɪm]	come [kʌm]
cost [kɒst]	cost [kɒst]	cost [kɒst]
cut [kʌt]	cut [kʌt]	cut [kʌt]
deal [diːl]	dealt [delt]	dealt [delt]
dig [dɪg]	dug [dʌg]	dug [dʌg]
do [duː]	did [dɪd]	done [dʌn]
draw [drɔː]	drew [druː]	drawn [drɔːn]
dream [driːm]	dreamed [driːmd]/dreamt [dremt]	dreamed [driːmd]/dreamt [dremt]
drink [drɪŋk]	drank [dræŋk]	drunk [drʌŋk]
drive [draɪv]	drove [drəʊv]	driven ['drɪvn]
eat [iːt]	ate [et]	eaten ['iːtn]
fall [fɔːl]	fell [fel]	fallen ['fɔːlən]
feed [fiːd]	fed [fed]	fed [fed]
feel [fiːl]	felt [felt]	felt [felt]
fight [faɪt]	fought [fɔːt]	fought [fɔːt]
find [faɪnd]	found [faʊnd]	found [faʊnd]
fit [fɪt]	fit [fɪt]	fit [fɪt]
fly [flaɪ]	flew [fluː]	flown [fləʊn]
forget [fə'get]	forgot [fə'gɒt]	forgotten [fə'gɒtn]
forgive [fə'gɪv]	forgave [fə'geɪv]	forgiven [fə'gɪvən]
freeze [friːz]	froze [frəʊz]	frozen ['frəʊzən]
get [get]	got [gɒt]	got [gɒt]
give [gɪv]	gave [geɪv]	given ['gɪvən]
go [gəʊ]	went [went]	gone [gɒn]/been [biːn]
grow [grəʊ]	grew [gruː]	grown [grəʊn]
hang [hæŋ]	hung [hʌŋ]	hung [hʌŋ]
have [hæv]	had [hæd]	had [hæd]
hear [hɪə]	heard [hɜːd]	heard [hɜːd]
hide [haɪd]	hid [hɪd]	hidden ['hɪdn]
hit [hɪt]	hit [hɪt]	hit [hɪt]
hold [həʊld]	held [held]	held [held]
hurt [hɜːt]	hurt [hɜːt]	hurt [hɜːt]
keep [kiːp]	kept [kept]	kept [kept]
know [nəʊ]	knew [njuː]	known [nəʊn]
lead [liːd]	led [led]	led [led]
learn [lɜːn]	learned [lɜːnd]/learnt [lɜːnt]	learned [lɜːnd]/learnt [lɜːnt]
leave [liːv]	left [left]	left [left]
lend [lend]	lent [lent]	lent [lent]
let [let]	let [let]	let [let]
lie [laɪ]	lay [leɪ]	lain [leɪn]
light [laɪt]	lit [lɪt]	lit [lɪt]
lose [luːz]	lost [lɒst]	lost [lɒst]
make [meɪk]	made [meɪd]	made [meɪd]
mean [miːn]	meant [ment]	meant [ment]
meet [miːt]	met [met]	met [met]
overtake [ˌəʊvə'teɪk]	overtook [ˌəʊvə'tʊk]	overtaken [ˌəʊvə'teɪkən]
pay [peɪ]	paid [peɪd]	paid [peɪd]
put [pʊt]	put [pʊt]	put [pʊt]
read [riːd]	read [red]	read [red]
ride [raɪd]	rode [rəʊd]	ridden ['rɪdn]
ring [rɪŋ]	rang [ræŋ]	rung [rʌŋ]
rise [raɪz]	rose [rəʊz]	risen [rɪzən]
run [rʌn]	ran [ræn]	run [rʌn]
say [seɪ]	said [sed]	said [sed]
see [siː]	saw [sɔː]	seen [siːn]
seek [siːk]	sought [sɔːt]	sought [sɔːt]
sell [sel]	sold [səʊld]	sold [səʊld]
send [send]	sent [sent]	sent [sent]
set [set]	set [set]	set [set]
shake [ʃeɪk]	shook [ʃʊk]	shaken [ʃeɪkən]
shine [ʃaɪn]	shone [ʃɒn]	shone [ʃɒn]
show [ʃəʊ]	showed [ʃəʊd]	shown [ʃəʊn]
shut [ʃʌt]	shut [ʃʌt]	shut [ʃʌt]
sing [sɪŋ]	sang [sæŋ]	sung [sʌŋ]
sit [sɪt]	sat [sæt]	sat [sæt]
sleep [sliːp]	slept [slept]	slept [slept]
slide [slaɪd]	slid [slɪd]	slid [slɪd]
smell [smel]	smelled [smeld]/smelt [smelt]	smelled [smeld]/smelt [smelt]
speak [spiːk]	spoke [spəʊk]	spoken ['spəʊkən]
spend [spend]	spent [spent]	spent [spent]
spill [spɪl]	spilled [spɪld]/spilt [spɪlt]	spilled [spɪld]/spilt [spɪlt]
split [splɪt]	split [splɪt]	split [splɪt]
spread [spred]	spread [spred]	spread [spred]
stand [stænd]	stood [stʊd]	stood [stʊd]
steal [stiːl]	stole [stəʊl]	stolen ['stəʊlən]
stick [stɪk]	stuck [stʌk]	stuck [stʌk]
sting [stɪŋ]	stung [stʌŋ]	stung [stʌŋ]
strike [straɪk]	struck [strʌk]	struck [strʌk]
swell [swel]	swelled [sweld]	swollen ['swəʊlən]
swim [swɪm]	swam [swæm]	swum [swʌm]
take [teɪk]	took [tʊk]	taken ['teɪkən]
teach [tiːtʃ]	taught [tɔːt]	taught [tɔːt]
tear [teə]	tore [tɔː]	torn [tɔːn]
tell [tel]	told [təʊld]	told [təʊld]
think [θɪŋk]	thought [θɔːt]	thought [θɔːt]
throw [θrəʊ]	threw [θruː]	thrown [θrəʊn]
understand [ˌʌndə'stænd]	understood [ˌʌndə'stʊd]	understood [ˌʌndə'stʊd]
upset [ʌp'set]	upset [ʌp'set]	upset [ʌp'set]
wake [weɪk]	woke [wəʊk]	woken ['wəʊkən]
wear [weə]	wore [wɔː]	worn [wɔːn]
win [wɪn]	won [wʌn]	won [wʌn]
write [raɪt]	wrote [rəʊt]	written ['rɪtn]

Pearson Education Limited
KAO Two
KAO Park
Hockham Way,
Harlow, Essex,
CM17 9SR England
and Associated Companies throughout the world.

english.com/focus

© Pearson Education Limited 2020

Focus 3 Second Edition Student's Book

The right of Sue Kay, Vaughan Jones, Daniel Brayshaw, Izabela Michalak, Bartosz Michałowski and Beata Trapnell to be identified as authors of this Work has been asserted by them in accordance with the Copyright, Designs and Patents Act 1988.

All rights reserved; no part of this publication may be reproduced, stored in a retrieval system, or transmitted in any form or by any means, electronic, mechanical, photocopying, recording, or otherwise without the prior written permission of the Publishers.

First published 2020

ISBN: 978-1-292-39060-4

Set in Avenir LT Pro
Printed and bound by Mexico

Acknowledgements

The publishers and authors would like to thank the following people and institutions for their feedback and comments during the development of the material:

Humberto Santos Duran
Anna Maria Grochowska
Beata Gruszczyńska
Inga Lande
Magdalena Loska
Barbara Madej
Rosa Maria Maldonado
Juliana Queiroz Pereira
Tomasz Siuta
Elżbieta Śliwa
Katarzyna Ślusarczyk
Katarzyna Tobolska
Renata Tomaka-Pasternak
Beata Trapnell
Aleksandra Zakrzewska
Beata Zygadlewicz-Kocuś

Sue Kay and Vaughan Jones's acknowledgements

We would like to thank all the students and teachers we have met and observed during the development of Focus Second Edition. We are also especially grateful to our wonderful editorial team for their expertise, encouragement and dedication.
Finally, a big thank you to our families without whose support and understanding none of this would have been possible.

Texts

Andrew Grant: 4; **Elbert Hubbard:** 7; **George Herbert:** 7; **Jarod Kintz:** 88; **Linda Grayson:** 7; **Little, Brown Book Group:** from Rafa: *My Story* by Rafael Nadal and John Carlin 23; **Penguin Random House:** Excerpt(s) from *A Walk in the Woods: Rediscovering America on the Appalachian Trail* by Bill Bryson, copyright © 1997 by Bill Bryson. Used by permission of Broadway Books, an imprint of the Crown Publishing Group, a division of Penguin Random House LLC. All rights reserved 65, 74; **St Augustine:** 32; **Telegraph Media Group:** © Telegraph Media Group Limited 2017 37; **The Guardian:** copyright Guardian News & Media Ltd 2018 93; **William Wordsworth:** 60

Images

123RF.com: Asimjp 34, Christopher Heil 73, enkaparmur WS9, Iakov Filimonov 101, Ian Allenden 101, Julien Tromeur 101, Luisa Puccini 45, moodboard 114, Nebojsa78 34, okssi68 73, Olena Kachmar 59, Pongphan Ruengchai WS9, smileus WS9, Stanislav Popov 73, torsak WS3, utima WS9, Wang Tom WS13; **Alamy Stock Photo:** A. T. Willett 67, Age fotostock 21, Agencja Fotograficzna Caro 27, Blend Images 27, Bruno D'Andrea 11, Classic Image 10, Cristina Fumi 32, Cultura Creative 13, Cultura RM 35, Danita Delimont 65, Della Huff 104, Gari Wyn Williams 10, 77, Giannis Katsaros 5, Goodluz 52, Herman Zapp / dpa 39, Hero Images Inc. 11, Image Source 11, 18, ImageBROKER 35, Images of Africa Photobank 104, incamerastock 55, Jason Smalley Photography 11, JGI/Jamie Grill 17, Juice Images 93, 94, Krzysztof Zablocki 5, Life on white 35, Lisa F. Young 112, Luciano de polo Stokkete 107, Lumi Images 13, Mark Harvey 105, Martyn Evans 32, Mike Hill 67, Miles Davies 89, MS Creative Photography – Maarten Jozef Billen 66, Nektarios Androutsos / Stockimo 10, OJO Images Ltd 14, PCN Photography 21, Radius Images 56, Rami Aapasuo 66, Realimage 111, redbrickstock.com 67, Simon Turner 82, Ted Foxx 11, Ton Koene 78, Trebor 35, Vadym Drobot 40, Yummy_pic 17, Zoonar GmbH 76, 95; **BBC Worldwide Learning:** 4, 18, 32, 46, 60, 74, 88, 102, 116, 118, 120, 122, 124, 126, 128, 130; **Fotolia.com:** pico 63; **Getty Images:** Barcroft Media 33, Bloomberg 48, Caiaimage 82, Caiaimage / Paul Viant 91, Caiaimage/Chris Ryan 25, Caiaimage/Sam Edwards 25, Clive Rose 21, Commercial Eye 98, Dangubic 96–97, Digital Vision 14, Easyturn 102–103, Epicurean 32, Eric Audras 28, Filipefrazao 68–69, Fred Froese 62, Glyn Kirk 51, Hero Images 6, Jan Kruger/Stringer 21, John Kobal Foundation 9, kali9 7, Kasipat 78, Laurence Griffiths 25, Louise Gubb 104, Lumi Images/Dario Secen 37, Luxy Images 6, Popperfoto 20, Tataks 106, Twomeows 46–47, Visionhaus 23, VM 79, Westend61 13; **Pearson Education Ltd:** Silversun Media Group 117, 119, 121, 123, 125, 127, 129, 131; **Shutterstock.com:** Africa Studio 112, Africa Studio. WS9, AlexandrBognat WS3, Alones 6, Andrea Danti 70, auremar 8, Axis / Kobal 90, Beretta / Sims 77, Bikeworldtravel 77, Borislav Bajkic WS3, Brent Hofacker 49, Chiyacat WS3, Corepics VOF 25, creo77 12, Da-ga WS9, Dan Breckwoldt 45, David Steele 66, design56 WS3, DGLimages 112, Dionisvera WS9, WS9, Dmytro Kolesnikov 11, Dmytro Vietrov 27, dotshock 10, DronG 49, Egor Rodynchenko WS9, elenovsky WS3, WS3, Elnur WS3, ESB Professional 76, Fizkes 54, foodiepics 123, Frantic00 42, GeorgeVieiraSilva WS3, Gustavo Frazao 72, Guy Shapira WS9, Heijo 11, Hekla WS3, IM_photo 45, Ints Vikmanis 62, iryna1 70, Jeremy Sutton-Hibbert / Film Four / Pathe / Kobal 80, Joyfuli 35, Karkas WS3, WS3, Kondor83 49, lush WS9, Matej Kastelic 45, matin WS9, Monkey Business Images 100, 110, Mpi09 / Mediapunch 9, Nattika WS9, nexus WS9, Nick Starichenko 5, NYS WS3, Patrick Lewis/Starpix 88, Paul S. Wolf 61, Photobac WS3, PT Images 24, Quirky China News 33, Rawpixel.com 81, Rohappy 9, Romaset 49, SCOTTCHAN 70, Sipa Press 33, Snap Stills 88, sniegirova mariia WS3, Strahil Dimitrov 27, 27, Studio 1One 45, Svetlana Foote WS9, Tarzhanova WS3, Timmary WS9, topseller WS9, Vadim Zakharishchev 26, Vitalii Nesterchuk 27, Volosina WS9, Wavebreakmedia, 5, 25, 5 Yes Man 127, Yuriy Golub 53; **Superstock.com:** Frank Bienewald / imageBROKER 34; **Tim Marrs:** 5

Cover images: Back: **Shutterstock.com**

Illustrations

Joanna Balicka 63, 70, 108
Stephen Collins 74–75
Nicolas Gremaud (GREMS) 38
Joanna Kerr 84, 109
Tim Mars 5
Ewa Olejnik 45, WS5, WS15
Kate Walker 20, 38

Videos

BBC video footage supplied by BBC Studios Distribution Limited
FOCUS VLOGS and Interactive Speaking Videos supplied by
A Silversun Media Group production for Pearson

Every effort has been made to trace the copyright holders and we apologise in advance for any unintentional omissions. We would be pleased to insert the appropriate acknowledgement in any subsequent edition of this publication.

Esta obra se terminó de imprimir en enero de 2023
en los talleres de Litográfica Ingramex, S.A. de C.V.
Centeno 162-1, Granjas Esmeralda, Iztapalapa,
C.P. 09810, México, Ciudad de México.

#	Unit	Use of English	Word Store
1	A new look	USE OF ENGLISH 1 p. 2	WORD STORE 1 p. 3 Clothes and accessories Fashion and style Personality Relationship phrases Compound adjectives WORD IN FOCUS | look
2	It's just a game	USE OF ENGLISH 2 p. 4	WORD STORE 2 p. 5 Phrasal verbs (x 2) Collocations People in sport Word families WORD IN FOCUS | just
3	On the go	USE OF ENGLISH 3 p. 6	WORD STORE 3 p. 7 Noun phrases Collocations Synonyms for trip Compound nouns Negative adjectives WORD IN FOCUS | go
4	Eat, drink and be healthy	USE OF ENGLISH 4 p. 8	WORD STORE 4 p. 9 Fruit and vegetables Describing food Collocations (x 3) WORD IN FOCUS | up
5	Planet Earth	USE OF ENGLISH 5 p. 10	WORD STORE 5 p. 11 Phrasal verbs Collocations Word families Compound nouns Verb phrases WORD IN FOCUS | one
6	Good health	USE OF ENGLISH 6 p. 12	WORD STORE 6 p. 13 Parts of the body Injuries Body idioms Charity fund-raising Health issues WORD IN FOCUS | get
7	Entertain me	USE OF ENGLISH 7 p. 14	WORD STORE 7 p. 15 Entertainment People in entertainment Phrasal verbs Collocations Word building WORD IN FOCUS | in
8	Modern society	USE OF ENGLISH 8 p. 16	WORD STORE 8 p. 17 Crime and criminals People involved in a crime case The justice system Prison Synonyms WORD IN FOCUS | good

USE OF ENGLISH 1

Multiple-choice cloze

1 Read the text and and choose the correct answer A, B, C or D.

Exchange programmes

When did you start to ^{0}_____ interested in clothes? When you were at school, ^{1}_____ your teens or much younger? It's not unusual for children to become fashion-conscious at a(n) ^{2}_____ age. Most under-fives have a fairly clear idea of what they like to ^{3}_____ and what colours they want. Most often this is because of what their friends have or what they see in films or on TV. However, it looks ^{4}_____though one little girl in the USA has gone a step further. Four-year-old Mayhem has started to design her own clothes.

According to her mother, Angie, Mayhem decided that she didn't like the princess dresses in the stores and started to make her own from cotton ^{5}_____ and sheets of paper. Angie gave her pictures of celebrities wearing ^{6}_____ dresses at award shows and Mayhem copied them. Now she has her own ideas and an important fashion chain likes them a lot.

Is Mayhem ^{7}_____ all thanks to her Mum? Not at all! Angie says that she herself is completely unfashionable and nowhere near as ^{8}_____ as her daughter. Watch out for Mayhem's new fashion line next spring!

0	A go	(B get)	C find	D take
1	A on	B at	C in	D by
2	A young	B early	C mature	D childish
3	A wear	B carry	C dress	D resemble
4	A like	B as	C for	D so
5	A scarves	B trainers	C bangles	D beanies
6	A fashion	B good-looking	C trendy	D well-dressed
7	A success	B successful	C succeed	D successfully
8	A disobedient	B caring	C creative	D shallow

Sentence transformation

2 Complete the second sentence using the word in capitals so that it has a similar meaning to the first. Do not change the word in capitals.

0 Anna is the most sensible and practical person I've ever known. **EARTH**
Anna is the most <u>down-to-earth person</u> I've ever known.

1 This is my big brother's suitcase – he bought it last summer. **BELONGS**
This suitcase _____ – he bought it last summer.

2 Susie's new top has got short sleeves and it's black. **SHORT-SLEEVED**
Susie's got a _____ top.

3 Simon joined the company in 2010. **WORKING**
Simon _____ here since 2010.

4 You should make it clear what you want. **CLARIFY**
You should _____ .

5 Yumi is twenty-two years old, but she looks younger. **EARLY**
Yumi is _____ , but she looks younger.

6 This is a great film. **ENJOYING**
I'm _____ .

WORD STORE 1 — A new look

WORD STORE 1A | Clothes and accessories

1 a waistcoat
2 _____
3 _____ 
4 _____ 
5 _____ 
6 _____ 
7 _____ 
8 _____
9 _____ 
10 _____
11 _____ 
12 _____ 
13 _____ 
14 _____ 
15 _____ 
16 _____ 

WORD STORE 1B | Fashion and style

He/she …
1 knows what's ___in___ fashion or out of fashion.
2 likes to be the _____ of attention.
3 goes _____ a casual look.
4 comes _____ as kind and friendly.
5 cares a lot _____ his/her appearance.
6 feels comfortable in his/her own _____.
7 likes to go _____ the flow.
8 is _____.

WORD STORE 1C | Personality

1 _carefree_ = happy and without worries
2 _____ = sensible and practical
3 _____ = difficult or disobedient
4 _____ = not interested in serious things
5 _____ = not easily upset or annoyed
6 _____ = too proud of the way you look

WORD STORE 1D | Relationship phrases

1 hang out with = _socialise with_
2 lose touch with = _____
3 get to know = _____
4 be always there for = _____
5 fall out with = _____
6 get along with = _____

WORD STORE 1E | Compound adjectives

1 fast-_drying_
2 short-_____
3 hard-_____
4 brightly-_____
5 cutting-_____
6 multi-_____

WORD IN FOCUS | look

look + at/for = focus your attention to see or find sth
Look at the painting.
I'm looking for a festival programme.

look as a noun
the 'festival look' = the 'festival style'

look + like + noun = have a similar appearance to sb/sth
It looks like a word in my language.

look + as if/as though + clause = suggest an appearance or situation is because of sth
It looks as though they're near the changing rooms.
He looks as if he's thinking about trying it on.

look + adjective = have a particular appearance
I just want to look good. It looks great. She looks bored.

look in phrasal verbs
look after sb/sth = take care of sb/sth

USE OF ENGLISH 2

Open cloze

1 Complete the text with one word in each gap.

A boxing success

Women have always had a more difficult time in sport ⁰ _than_ men. However, female boxers ¹_____ found following their sport particularly hard. The 2012 Olympics in London were the first games that allowed women boxers ²_____ compete and that was when Nicola Adams became the first female gold medal winner.

Nicola started ³_____ when she was just thirteen. She went to classes at a gym ⁴_____ her mother was doing aerobics classes and discovered that she loved the sport. Success, however, wasn't easy for Nicola as ⁵_____ were very few competitions for women. In fact, women's boxing was banned by the Amateur Boxing Association ⁶_____ 1996.

Then, ⁷_____ lots of discussions, women's boxing became an Olympic sport. Nicola qualified for the British team although she wasn't on top form. She ⁸_____ fallen down the stairs a year before and her back was still giving her a lot of pain. But Nicola is a real fighter and the rest is history!

Sentence transformation

2 Complete the second sentence using the word in capitals so that it has a similar meaning to the first. Do not change the word in capitals.

0 I started playing tennis when I was five. **BEEN**

   I've been playing tennis since I was five.

1 Sophie doesn't like swimming. Mark doesn't like it either. **NEITHER**

   _____ like swimming.

2 I'm happy to help you practise for the game. **MIND**

   I _____ practise for the game.

3 Don't worry about the competition. **STOP**

   You _____ about the game.

4 Mike broke his ankle during the football match. **WHILE**

   Mike broke his ankle _____ football in the match.

5 I forgot my racket and I couldn't play tennis. **BECAUSE**

   I couldn't play tennis _____ my racket.

6 Peter said, 'Tim, you need to spend more time at the gym.' **ADVISED**

   Peter _____ more time at the gym.

WORD STORE 2

It's just a game

WORD STORE 2A | Phrasal verbs

1. _cheer sb on_ = shout loudly to encourage sb
2. _____ = get rid of (fat or calories)
3. _____ = quit being part of sth
4. _____ = be chosen for (a team)
5. _____ = take part in sth
6. _____ = make sb disappointed
7. _____ = accept sth (a challenge)

WORD STORE 2B | Collocations

1. **beat** or **defeat** _an opponent_ /the champion
2. **break** a world record
3. **come** _____ /second/last
4. **keep** fit/_____
5. **lose** a match/a game/a point
6. **miss** a goal
7. **score** a goal/_____
8. **win** a prize/_____ /a game/a point

WORD STORE 2C | People in sport

> coach/trainer   ~~fan/supporter~~   opponent
> referee   spectator   teammate

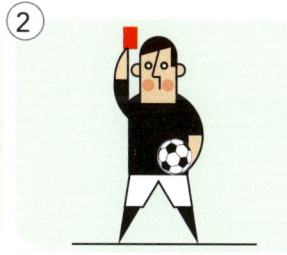

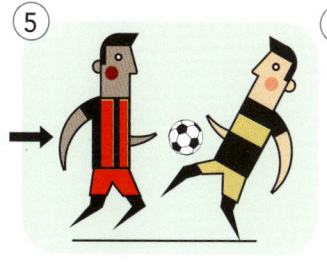

1. fan/supporter
2. _____
3. _____
4. _____
5. _____
6. _____

WORD STORE 2D | Phrasal verbs

> ~~give up~~   look up to   pick sth up   put sb off
> take after   talk sb into   try sth out

1. _give up_ = stop trying sth
2. _____ = be like sb
3. _____ = learn sth
4. _____ = do sth for the first time
5. _____ = admire and respect sb
6. _____ = encourage sb
7. _____ = discourage sb

WORD STORE 2E | Word families

NOUN	VERB	ADJECTIVE
1 action	_activate_	active
2 decision	decide	_____
3 _____	–	powerful
4 repetition	_____	repetitive
5 _____	–	resilient
6 _____	–	superstitious

WORD IN FOCUS | just

just = only
It's just me against my opponent.

just = very recently
Messi's just scored a fantastic goal.

just to add emphasis
I just don't think they are good role models.
Your head just gets in the way.

USE OF ENGLISH 3

Word building

1 Complete the text with the correct form of the words in brackets.

I think that travelling to ⁰<u>unfamiliar</u> (FAMILIARISE) places and staying in completely different surroundings can be very ¹_____ (REWARD). When we do things we earlier saw as ²_____ (THINK), this can help us deal with our fears and worries. For example, when I was on a ³_____ (TREK) trip in Vietnam last year, my friends and I stayed in a small guesthouse far away from any town or village. To get there, you had to walk down a long ⁴_____ (WIND) path to a river. Then, you had to go across to the other side on an old suspension bridge. The ⁵_____ (CROSS) was a big problem for me. I was sure the bridge would collapse, but it was easier every day. I was also surprised I didn't have a problem with being ⁶_____ (CONNECT) from all my friends and family (there was no Wi-Fi) and in fact it was a very ⁷_____ (PLEASE) break. This winter we're going on a ⁸_____ (SKI) holiday and staying in a hut high up in the mountains. I can't wait!

Sentence transformation

2 Complete the second sentence using the word in capitals so that it has a similar meaning to the first. Do not change the word in capitals.

0 This is our fourth day here. **FOR**
  We _'ve been here for_ four days.
1 When I was younger, I didn't like long car journeys. **USE**
  When I was younger, I _____ long car journeys.
2 The pilot arrived late, so the flight was delayed! **TURNED**
  The pilot _____ late, so the flight was delayed!
3 Dad's been driving for three hours and he's hungry! **STARTED**
  Dad _____ and he's hungry!
4 I'm sure that Micky was very tired because he went straight to bed. **BEEN**
  Micky _____ because he went straight to bed.
5 I reminded my sister to collect me at the airport. **PICK**
  I reminded my sister to _____ at the airport.
6 When we went somewhere by car, my mum always took far too many sandwiches. **WOULD**
  When we went somewhere by car, my mum _____ far too many sandwiches.

WORD STORE 3 — On the go

WORD STORE 3A | Noun phrases
1 cable __car__
2 dirt _____
3 public _____
4 rush _____
5 short _____
6 suspension _____
7 traffic _____
8 winding _____

WORD STORE 3B | Collocations
1 catch — __a bus__ / a train
2 cross — a continent / _____ / _____
3 cycle — _____ / downhill
4 walk — _____
5 get — a lift / _____ (in traffic)
6 fasten — _____
7 miss — _____ / a train

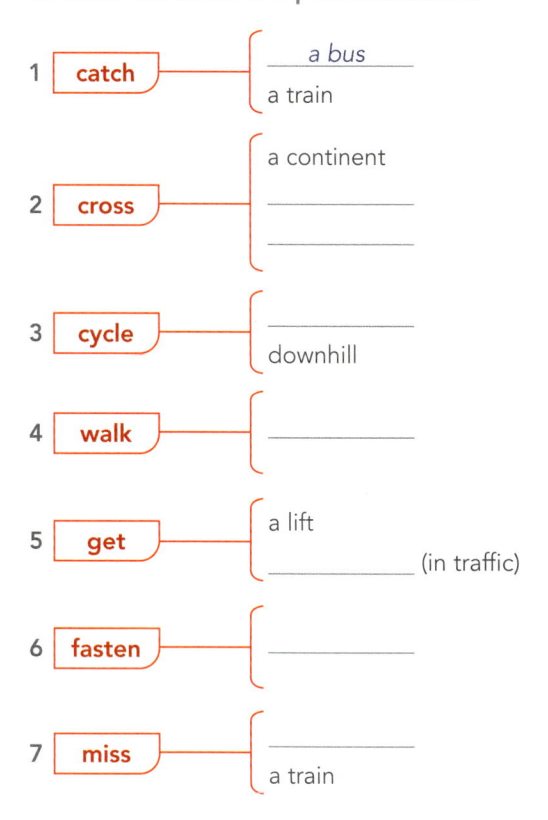

WORD STORE 3C | Synonyms for trip

a crossing a cruise a drive a flight
a̶ j̶o̶u̶r̶n̶e̶y̶ a ride a tour a voyage

1 __a journey__ = a long trip overland
2 _____ = a trip in a car
3 _____ = a trip by boat from one piece of land to another
4 _____ = a short trip on a bus, a bike, a motorbike, a horse, etc.
5 _____ = a long trip by sea (or in space)
6 _____ = a trip on a plane
7 _____ = a trip to see specific things of interest
8 _____ = a trip by ship to visit various places for pleasure

WORD STORE 3D | Compound nouns

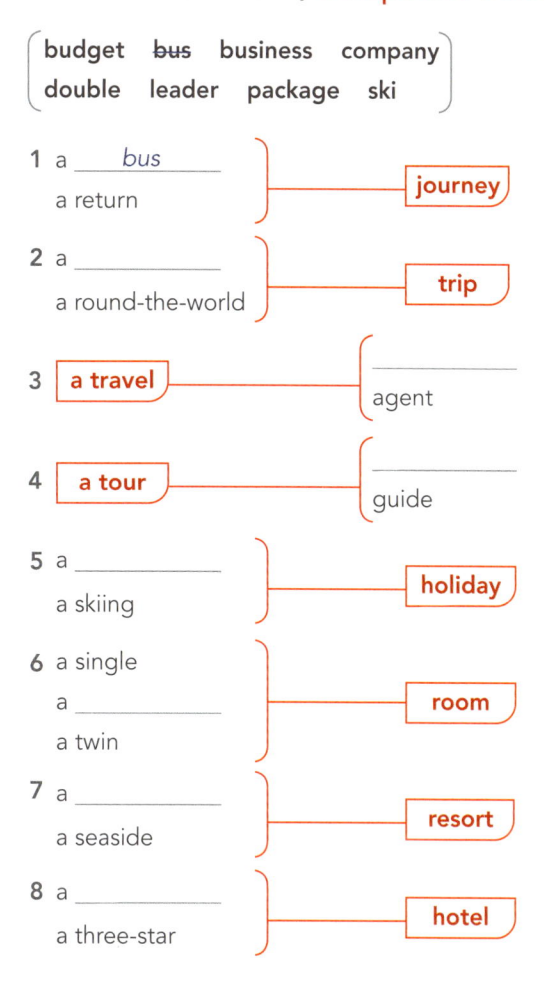

budget b̶u̶s̶ business company
double leader package ski

1 a __bus__ / a return — journey
2 a _____ / a round-the-world — trip
3 a travel / _____ — agent
4 a tour / _____ — guide
5 a _____ / a skiing — holiday
6 a single / a _____ / a twin — room
7 a _____ / a seaside — resort
8 a _____ / a three-star — hotel

WORD STORE 3E | Negative adjectives
1 __un__avoidable
2 ___connected
3 ___familiar
4 ___informed
5 ___pleasant
6 ___rewarding
7 ___thinkable

WORD IN FOCUS | go

go + -ing = go somewhere to do an activity
You're too young to go backpacking.

go + a place
She must have gone home.
Harry used to go to school by bus.

gone to or been to?
Ron has gone swimming.
(= He's there now.)
Have you ever been to Paris?
(= gone and come back)

go in phrases
When did you last go on a bike ride?
On the go.

go in phrasal verbs
You have to go through security.

7

USE OF ENGLISH 4

Multiple-choice cloze

1 Read the text and choose the correct answer A, B, C or D.

Food diary – Friday

Today has been a hard day! I started well and just had a ⁰_____ meal for breakfast. I didn't spend a lot of time preparing it. I just squeezed a couple of fresh oranges and then toasted a ¹_____ of brown bread – very healthy. Last week I tried to ²_____ breakfast completely, but it didn't work. I was so hungry by lunch that I ate loads of fattening things!

It all went wrong this afternoon. Sophie phoned to say that she'd booked a table at Mario's restaurant for this evening. It's a pizzeria, and that's basically ³_____ food! She's naughty, really. She knows I'm trying to lose weight. I've been on a diet for two months now! I've ⁴_____ chocolate, biscuits, potatoes and everything else that's ⁵_____ . I really need to get back in ⁶_____ for my summer holiday. So, a ⁷_____ meal at Mario's and NOTHING healthy on the menu? Sophie and I get on really well and I wanted to celebrate her birthday – but she could have chosen a restaurant with some healthy options, ⁸_____ she?

0 **A** light	**B** slim	**C** balanced	**D** short
1 **A** loaf	**B** starter	**C** slice	**D** side
2 **A** jump	**B** leave	**C** throw	**D** skip
3 **A** fast	**B** balanced	**C** hot	**D** healthy
4 **A** cut off	**B** cut down on	**C** put off	**D** turned down
5 **A** fresh	**B** delicious	**C** disgusting	**D** crunchy
6 **A** form	**B** figure	**C** shape	**D** outline
7 **A** three-part	**B** three-section	**C** three-plate	**D** three-course
8 **A** could	**B** couldn't	**C** can't	**D** can

Sentence transformation

2 Complete the second sentence using the word in capitals so that it has a similar meaning to the first. Do not change the word in capitals.

0 I'm sure Nina didn't see Tom yesterday, he was at work all morning. **CAN'T**
Nina _can't have seen_ Tom yesterday, he was at work all morning.

1 You should eat this yoghurt by 10 May. **EXPIRY**
The _____ is 10 May.

2 The coach told Marco it was a good idea to get some rest. **ENCOURAGED**
The coach _____ get some rest.

3 Have some soup! We made it ourselves and it's delicious. **HOME-MADE**
Have some _____ soup!

4 How much meat do you eat? **CONSUMPTION**
How big is your _____ ?

5 The final test starts at 1 p.m. and lasts an hour. **TAKING**
At 1:15 p.m., they _____ the final test.

6 Sally takes the 8 a.m. bus and she's at work at 8:30. **ARRIVED**
Sally takes the 8 a.m. bus, so by 9 a.m. _____ at work.

8

WORD STORE 4 — Eat, drink and be healthy

WORD STORE 4A | Fruit and vegetables

1 Red   
- cherries
- _____
- _____

2 Orange
- _____
- _____
- _____

3 Green
- _____
- _____
- _____

4 Yellow
- _____
- _____
- _____

5 White
- _____
- _____
- _____

6 Purple
- _____
- _____
- _____

WORD STORE 4B | Describing food

1 bitter or ___sour___ ≠ sweet
2 cooked ≠ _____
3 fresh ≠ _____, rotten or sour
4 hot or spicy ≠ mild or _____
5 unripe ≠ _____
6 _____ ≠ fatty

REMEMBER THIS
When they are not fresh, bread, biscuits and cakes are *stale*, but vegetables and meat are *rotten* and milk is *sour*.

WORD STORE 4C | Collocations

1 crunchy/stale/___dry___ _____
2 wholemeal/sliced/_____ _____
3 black/ground/_____ _____
4 brown/long-grain/_____ _____
5 mixed/side/_____ _____
6 home-made/tinned/_____ _____
7 sugar/chocolate/_____ _____
8 sparkling/still/_____ _____

WORD STORE 4D | Collocations

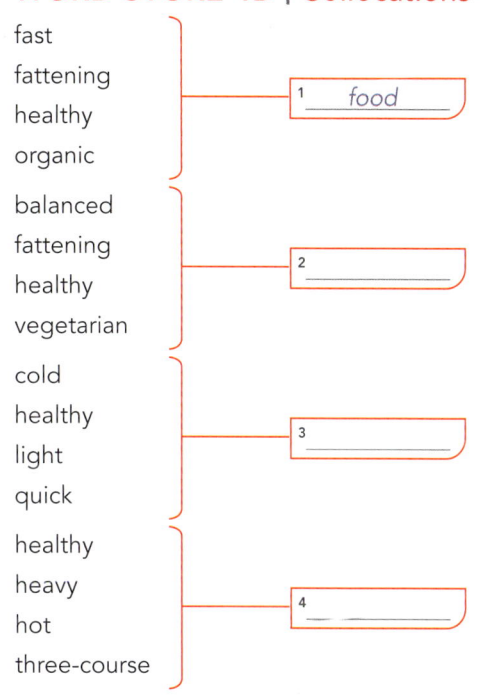

fast / fattening / healthy / organic → 1 ___food___

balanced / fattening / healthy / vegetarian → 2 _____

cold / healthy / light / quick → 3 _____

healthy / heavy / hot / three-course → 4 _____

WORD STORE 4E | Collocations

1 industrial/household/___food___ waste
2 financial/voluntary/_____ sector
3 tourist/manufacturing/_____ industry
4 energy/meat/_____ consumption
5 expiry/due/_____ date
6 safety/international/_____ standard(s)
7 minimum/record/_____ level
8 alarming/official/_____ statistics

WORD IN FOCUS | up

up in phrasal verbs that don't take an object = move to a higher position or increase
Hurry up.
At 6 a.m. they'll be getting up.

up in phrasal verbs that take an object
He chopped the carrots up.
(or *chopped up the carrots*)
How did he get the idea to set up the project?
(or *set the project up*)

up in phrases
It's up to you.

USE OF ENGLISH 5

Open cloze

1 Complete the text with one word in each gap.

Time to make changes

We all know that environmental problems are getting worse and we need to solve them or ⁰ _the_ planet will be in big trouble in the future. But what can we do? Can individual people really make a difference? Or ¹_____ we leave it to governments and politicians?

There are ²_____ lot of ways we can help. ³_____ instance, we can recycle things and save water and electricity. However, one of ⁴_____ most important things to do is to find different ways of getting power. Scientists have developed clever ways to do this. We can get power ⁵_____ the sun and the sea as well as the wind. The trouble is that local people, ⁶_____ don't want to look at ugly wind farms or solar panels, often object to the plans. Because of this, we don't have enough alternative sources of power.

Perhaps soon people ⁷_____ learn that our way of life needs to change. After all, ⁸_____ we do something now, we won't have any lights or power in a few decades' time, will we?

Sentence transformation

2 Complete the second sentence using the word in capitals so that it has a similar meaning to the first. Do not change the word in capitals.

0 In the past people had coal fires in their homes. **USED**
 In the past _people used to have_ coal fires in their homes.
1 I have a few more pages to read, so I think I will finish the book next week. **FINISHED**
 By the end of next week _____ reading the book.
2 The man's land was near the wind farm and he complained about it. **WHOSE**
 The man, _____ the wind farm, complained about it.
3 Jack wants to teach science one day. **BECOME**
 Jack wants _____ one day.
4 I'm sure pollution levels haven't dropped recently because scientists still talk about them all the time. **HAVE**
 Pollution levels _____ because scientists still talk about them all the time.
5 Wildlife protection is something important to her. **ABOUT**
 Wildlife protection is something _____ .
6 Oslo is in Norway and that's where politicians had an international meeting about climate change. **WHICH**
 Oslo, _____ , is where politicians had an international meeting about climate change.

WORD STORE 5

Planet Earth

WORD STORE 5A | Phrasal verbs

1. be made up of = _be formed from_
2. come across = _____
3. come in = _____
4. die out = _____
5. go out = _____
6. heat sth up = _____
7. stir sth up = _____

WORD STORE 5B | Collocations

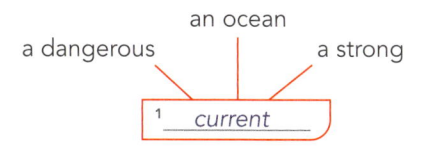

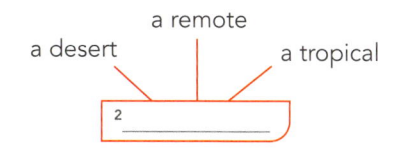

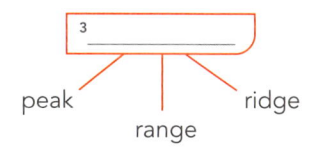

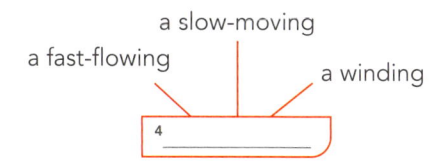

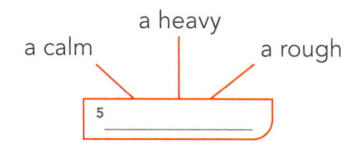

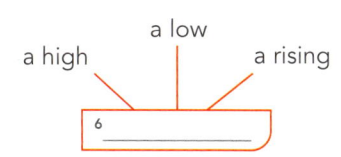

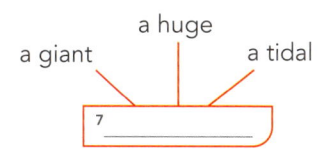

1. a dangerous / an ocean / a strong **current**
2. a desert / a remote / a tropical _____
3. peak / _____ / ridge / range
4. a fast-flowing / a slow-moving / a winding _____
5. a calm / a heavy / a rough _____
6. a high / a low / a rising _____
7. a giant / a huge / a tidal _____

WORD STORE 5C | Word families

NOUN	VERB	ADJECTIVE
1 breadth	broaden	_broad_
2 depth	deepen	_____
3 height	heighten	_____
4 length	lengthen	_____
5 strength	strengthen	_____
6 width	widen	_____

REMEMBER THIS

Wide is used to measure the space between two points – it's more concrete than *broad*, e.g. *How wide is it? a wide road, wide open …*

Broad is used more to describe the thing that fills the space – it's more abstract, e.g. *broad-minded, broad shoulders …* NOT *How broad is it?*

WORD STORE 5D | Compound nouns

1. _recycling_ bins
2. _____ light bulbs
3. _____ change
4. _____ energy
5. _____ issues
6. _____ panels
7. _____ warming

WORD STORE 5E | Verb phrases

1. _come_ face to face with = meet
2. _____ from = lose your life because of sth
3. _____ off = become rotten
4. _____ for = try to pick up
5. _____ through = look for
6. _____ around = relax and do nothing
7. _____ through = not wake up

WORD IN FOCUS | one

one (a number)
move to a higher position or increase
Hurry up.
At 6 a.m. they'll be getting up.

one of + plural noun = refers to one member of a group of people or things
Choose one of the options.

one/ones (a pronoun) = refers to a countable noun that has already been mentioned
The best way to survive a bear encounter is to never have one.
There are so many fires that the firefighters don't know which ones to focus on.

one in phrases
one day, one morning, etc.: *We saw trees that may one day disappear from our planet.*
On the one hand: On the one hand, there are several arguments for making contact.

USE OF ENGLISH 6

Word building

1 Complete the text with the correct form of the words in brackets.

Help for the youngest

Staying in hospital is hard for anyone, but it's ⁰ *particularly* (PARTICULAR) hard for children. They are in a strange place and surrounded by strange ¹_____ (FRIGHTEN) equipment. Some children need to go to hospital for an ²_____ (OPERATE) or for a blood test. Others may have a long-term ³_____ (DISABLED) and need to stay in hospital quite ⁴_____ (REGULAR). Now, in our hospital, groups of ⁵_____ (VOLUNTARY) are helping to make those hospital stays less scary. These people spend time entertaining and helping young patients, ⁶_____ (HOPE) letting them forget about their health problems for a while. When children feel they are in a safe and friendly place, their condition becomes more stable and they often ⁷_____ (RECOVERY) more quickly. To sum up, they are happier patients and ⁸_____ (NATURE) this is something we all support.

Sentence transformation

2 Complete the second sentence using the word in capitals so that it has a similar meaning to the first. Do not change the word in capitals.

0 You should go to the doctor about your headaches. **WERE**
  If __I were you, I'd__ go to the doctor about your headaches.
1 I didn't take the doctor's advice and I was ill last weekend. **HAVE**
  If I'd taken the doctor's advice, I _____ last weekend.
2 Did you eat healthy food when you were a child? **USE**
  _____ healthy food when you were a child?
3 It's possible that Max hasn't left the hospital yet. **MIGHT**
  Max _____ the hospital yet.
4 It's a shame that I'm not with my friend right now. **WISH**
  I _____ my friend right now.
5 I'm certain he'll recover completely between now and his birthday! **BY**
  I'm certain he _____ his birthday!
6 I never look at my phone in the evening because I want to sleep better. **ORDER**
  I never look at my phone in the evening _____ sleep better.

WORD STORE 6 — Good health

WORD STORE 6A | Parts of the body

~~ankle~~   cheek   chin   elbow   rib   spine   thigh   thumb   waist   wrist

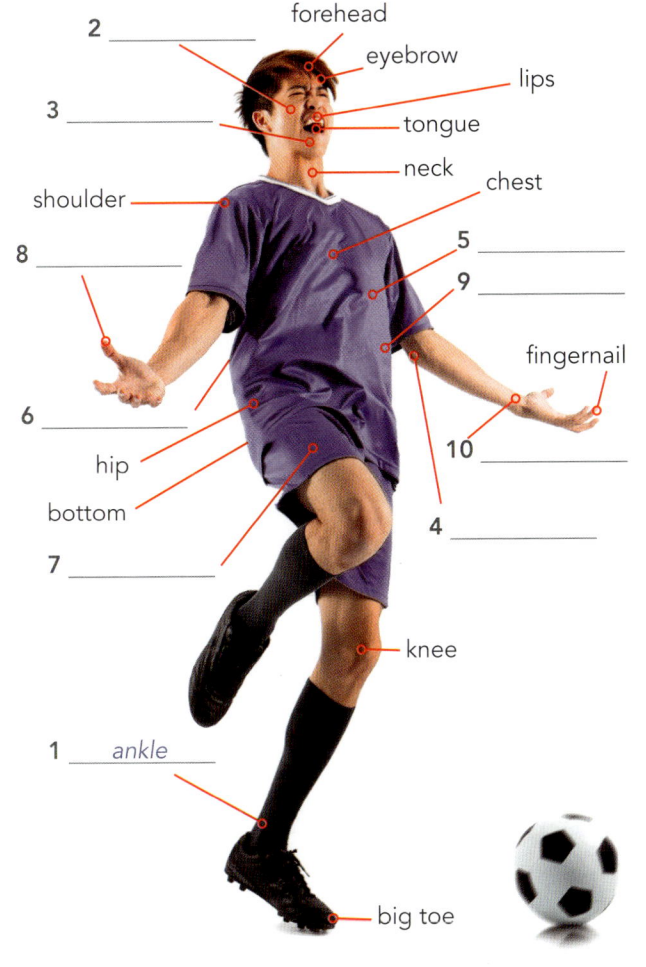

Labels on image:
- forehead
- eyebrow
- lips
- tongue
- neck
- chest
- shoulder
- fingernail
- hip
- bottom
- knee
- big toe
- 1 ankle
- 2 _____
- 3 _____
- 4 _____
- 5 _____
- 6 _____
- 7 _____
- 8 _____
- 9 _____
- 10 _____

WORD STORE 6B | Injuries

1 be bitten by a dog/a rat/a snake/_an insect_
2 break your leg/thumb/_____ /toe
3 burn your fingers/hair/tongue/_____
4 dislocate your _____ /hip/thumb/knee
5 have a black eye/a bruise/a sore _____ /a cut
6 sprain your foot/_____ /wrist/knee

WORD STORE 6C | Body idioms

1 _I laughed my head off_ = I laughed very loudly.
2 _____ = I know it but can't remember it now.
3 _____ = Can you help me?
4 _____ = I'm joking.
5 _____ = She really upset him.
6 _____ = I was extremely surprised.

WORD STORE 6D | Charity fund-raising

for (x2)   in   ~~to~~   up

1 donate money _to_ sb/sth
2 raise money _____ sb/sth
3 set _____ /share a webpage
4 sponsor sb
5 take part _____ sth
6 train _____ sth

WORD STORE 6E | Health issues

1 _treat_ patients
2 _____ a prescription
3 _____ first aid
4 _____ a panic attack
5 _____ lives
6 _____ a disease
7 _____ weight
8 _____ a baby

WORD IN FOCUS | get

get = buy or obtain
I wish my sister would get her own laptop.
If I had hay fever, I would get some antihistamine tablets.

get = receive
Young people get enough sport at school.
We get a lot of non-emergency calls.

get + adjective = become
What do you do to get better when you have a cold?
If I panic, everybody else gets anxious too.

get + illness/injury
I got dizzy from reading too much.

get in phrasal verbs
When you get out of the bath or shower your body temperature will drop.

13

USE OF ENGLISH 7

Multiple-choice cloze

1 Read the text and choose the correct answer A, B, C or D.

I was on holiday with my parents in the west of England and we came ⁰_____ a wonderful little theatre. It's an outdoor theatre on the coast and the ¹_____ has a brilliant view of the sea behind the actors. The local people ²_____ that it's one of the most beautiful theatres in the world! And I can see why!

A lady at our hotel ³_____ us about the theatre and how fantastic it was. We decided to go to see a(n) ⁴_____ there last night. The weather was good and we were looking forward to it. Quite a lot of people turned ⁵_____ . The show was certainly deeply ⁶_____ . I couldn't believe my eyes when I saw the sun setting across the water during the performance. I call that an ⁷_____ of surprise!

It seems that there are some ⁸_____ gardens near the theatre, so we're going back to explore the area tomorrow. I really recommend this place!

0	A over	B by	C up	**D across**
1	A vocalist	B audience	C performer	D cast
2	A report	B expect	C claim	D explain
3	A said	B asked	C told	D replied
4	A entertainment	B programme	C TV series	D play
5	A in	B on	C up	D at
6	A distracting	B improving	C enhancing	D engaging
7	A element	B emotion	C experience	D attention
8	A encouraging	B ecstatic	C hilarious	D amazing

Open cloze

2 Complete the text with one word in each gap.

Are you missing *The Missing*?

The popular thriller series *The Missing* finished last night ⁰ _after_ eight weeks. The story is about a young boy who disappears ¹_____ he's in a park with his dad in France. The eight episodes show the parents' search for Olly when he disappears and also over the ²_____ six years. His dad keeps going back to France to ³_____ for his son.

The series has been very successful ⁴_____ of the excellent script and the very good acting of ⁵_____ main characters. The story is about normal people ⁶_____ suddenly experience a terrible tragedy. The awful thing is that it could happen to anyone.

After the first episode, critics predicted that it ⁷_____ become a popular series and they were right. Now everyone is saying that ⁸_____ will win a lot of TV awards later in the year.

WORD STORE 7 — Entertain me

WORD STORE 7A | Entertainment

1. a*ppear* in a TV series
2. b_____ in the charts
3. d_____ a live gig
4. h_____ a hit single
5. h_____ great reviews
6. p_____ the part of …
7. p_____ a venue
8. b_____ streamed
9. r_____ an album
10. s_____ a recording contract

WORD STORE 7B | People in entertainment

the audience   the cast   ~~a drummer~~
a lead guitarist   a musician   a singer-songwriter
a viewer   a vocalist

1. *a drummer*
2. _____ 
3. _____ 
4. _____ 
5. _____ 
6. _____ 
7. _____
8. _____ 

WORD STORE 7C | Phrasal verbs

1. *beat yourself up* = blame yourself
2. _____ = continue
3. _____ = be released or published
4. _____ = do sth badly
5. _____ = organise a show
6. _____ = begin organised lessons or join a course
7. _____ = begin your career
8. _____ = start learning or doing sth new
9. _____ = arrive
10. _____ = gradually disappear

WORD STORE 7D | Collocations

attention   ~~element~~   emotions   laugh
surprise   video (x2)   viral

1. contain an *element* of surprise
2. go _____
3. have a short _____ span
4. make sb _____
5. stir up _____
6. take sb by _____
7. upload a _____
8. view a _____

WORD STORE 7E | Word building

VERB	NOUN
1 accompany	*accompaniment*
2 create	_____
3 distract	_____
4 encourage	_____
5 engage	_____
6 enhance	_____
7 entertain	_____
8 improve	_____
9 memorise	_____

WORD IN FOCUS | in

in + a place
in public, in the UK, in my office

in + a period of time
in the 1940s, in a couple of days

in + a profession
She's been in the movie business for ten years.

in in phrases
In other words, can an audio soundtrack help people to understand a book?
In comparison with this traditional way of reading, the downloaded text can seem dull.

USE OF ENGLISH 8

Word building

1 Complete the text with the correct form of the words in brackets.

Can you help fight crime?

Everyone who lives in Moorston knows that crime is rising ⁰ _quickly_ (QUICK) in the area. People have reported more ¹_____ (BURGLE) in the last year than ever before and there has also been an increase in fights using knives. So, the police have had an interesting idea. They would like to bring crime ²_____ (PROFESSION) and students together to talk about the problem. In particular, they want students' ³_____ (ADVISE) about how to stop young people from becoming ⁴_____ (CRIME). The ⁵_____ (SAFE) of the Moorston people is the most important thing for the police. Crime ⁶_____ (PREVENT) is a big priority for them. So, if anyone would like to give a ⁷_____ (HELP) hand and come to the series of ⁸_____ (DISCUSS), please go online and sign up!

Sentence transformation

2 Complete the second sentence using the word in capitals so that it has a similar meaning to the first. Do not change the word in capitals.

0 'Yes, I'll help with the police search,' said Dave. **AGREED**
  Dave _agreed to help with_ the police search.

1 A neighbour reported a fight in James Road at 10:15. **WAS**
  At 10:15 a fight in James Road _____ a neighbour.

2 'Tim, when did you last see your brother?' the policeman asked. **HAD**
  The policeman asked Tim when _____ brother.

3 My friends and I always have fun at parties. **OURSELVES**
  My friends and I always _____ at parties.

4 The police haven't arrested the burglar yet. **BEEN**
  The burglar hasn't _____ .

5 I'm sure the old lady is lonely because no one ever visits her. **BE**
  The old lady _____ because no one ever visits her.

6 The school paid electricians to put up new security cameras in the corridors. **HAD**
  The school _____ put up in the corridors.